Y0-BZV-246

VISUAL
DEVELOPER

Web
Commerce
Programming
with VISUAL C++

Don Gaspar

CORIOLIS GROUP BOOKS

an International Thomson Publishing company I(T)P®

Albany, NY • Belmont, CA • Bonn • Boston • Cincinnati • Detroit • Johannesburg • London
Madrid • Melbourne • Mexico City • New York • Paris • Singapore • Tokyo • Toronto • Washington

PUBLISHER	KEITH WEISKAMP
PROJECT EDITOR	MICHELLE STROUP
PRODUCTION COORDINATOR	DENISE CONSTANTINE
COVER DESIGN	SQUARE ONE DESIGN
LAYOUT DESIGN	NICOLE COLÓN
CD-ROM DEVELOPMENT	ROBERT CLARFIELD

Visual Developer Web Commerce Programming with Visual C++
Copyright © 1998 by The Coriolis Group, Inc.

Limits of Liability and Disclaimer of Warranty
The author and publisher of this book have used their best efforts in preparing the book and the programs contained in it. These efforts include the development, research, and testing of the theories and programs to determine their effectiveness. The author and publisher make no warranty of any kind, expressed or implied, with regard to these programs or the documentation contained in this book.

The author and publisher shall not be liable in the event of incidental or consequential damages in connection with, or arising out of, the furnishing, performance, or use of the programs, associated instructions, and/or claims of productivity gains.

Trademarks
Trademarked names appear throughout this book. Rather than list the names and entities that own the trademarks or insert a trademark symbol with each mention of the trademarked name, the publisher states that it is using the names for editorial purposes only and to the benefit of the trademark owner, with no intention of infringing upon that trademark.

The Coriolis Group, Inc.
An International Thomson Publishing Company
14455 N. Hayden Road, Suite 220
Scottsdale, Arizona 85260

602/483-0192
FAX 602/483-0193
http://www.coriolis.com

Printed in the United States of America

ISBN 1-57610-199-1

10 9 8 7 6 5 4 3 2 1

To Madoka with eternal love
To Don Thor and Charles Tyr, my sons, with love

Acknowledgments

A book of this depth and magnitude is never an individual effort. Several people with a variety of backgrounds were placed together to produce what you are reading right now. This book is an ensemble of ideas and the work of lots of various individuals. I would like to thank them all here:

Michelle Stroup, my editor from Coriolis Group Books. Michelle worked with me from the beginning and was very encouraging, motivating, and did substantial edits with me.

Bo Rinaldi of the Trattner Network (www.trattner.com), my consulting agent. Bo thought this would be a great idea and encouraged me to write this book; he also found a consulting contract for me that was flexible enough to let me write a book while doing coding and architectural designs in telephony.

David Fugate, my literary agent from Waterside Productions (www.waterside.com). David helped me with my original outline, title, and finding a great publisher, Coriolis.

Ric Parks of the Learning Company. Ric and I met a few years ago when I was assisting him with the Interactive Math Journey as a consultant. Ric provided substantial code reviews, and content evaluations for the entire book.

BMB for helpful engineering design reviews, code reviews, etc. Your fluff really made this happen.

Peter Brown and Roger Wiens of IBM's Lotus Division. Both Peter and Roger reviewed the content, the accuracy, and provided invaluable feedback.

Peter Reeves of NetObjects, Inc. who actually wrote the original Foosball HTML that we used for our Foosball store. Peter provided substantial HTML review and corrections. Good luck with the STL, Peter.

Chris Fitch of Forte for phenomenal evaluation of content and chapter ordering.

Dick Gemoets of Telepost for being flexible with my consulting times as I completed this book. I worked with Dick at Apple Computer many years ago, and some of his ideas are in this book!

Clifford Brooks from Verisign, special thanks for the extra help with the SSL and the encryption keys for Netscape and IIS servers.

Microsoft for providing IIS and ISAPI, and excellent developer tools that enabled me to implement solutions faster than ever. Microsoft has been leading the industry as businesses transition to the Internet, so be sure to keep up to date with them and their technology.

Thank you everyone. It was a tough time putting this all together, but we made it happen.

CONTENTS

INTRODUCTION   XVII

CHAPTER 1   INTRODUCTION TO INTERNET COMMERCE   1

The Internet, Online Stores, And Malls   2
The Market Now And In The Year 2000   3
Overhead Of Operating A Virtual Store   3

The 24×7 Store   6
From Conventional To Virtual Business   7
How Internet Commerce Works   8

Some Real Examples   9
Amazon.com   9
Southwest Airlines   9
The Foosball Store   12

Ordering Merchandise On The Internet   13
Types Of Payment   14
Secure Ordering   16

Summary   17

CHAPTER 2   TAKING ORDERS WITH HTML FORMS   19

What Are HTML Forms?   20
HTML Form Examples   21
HTML Source   23

How The Server Handles The Data   33
HTML Variables   34
Corresponding C++ Structures   34
Various Controls   36

More Examples   38
The Guest Book HTML   39
Example Survey   42
Taking Orders   45

How The Server Sees Things   48
HTML For Calling CGI And ISAPI   51
Submit And Reset   52
Returning Feedback To The Client   52

Summary   53

CHAPTER 3   THE CGI CRASH COURSE   55

What Is CGI?   56
How CGI Extends The Server   57
Examples Of Other CGI Tasks   60
Server Variables   64
POST And GET   71

How To Use POST And GET   73
Intercepting And Processing HTML Variables   73
Processing HTML Controls   84

CGI Code Examples   88
Hello World Revisited   89
Guest Book Revisited   95

CGI Architecture   106
Overhead   107
Advantages Of CGI   109

Summary   109

CHAPTER 4   THE ISAPI CRASH COURSE   111

What Is ISAPI?   112
A Comparison Of ISAPI And CGI   114

Creating ISAPI Code Fragments   115
Extending CHttpServer   123
Server Variables   129
Parsemaps And NewHelloISAPIWorld   131

Some More ISAPI Examples   138
Debugging   138
Guest Book Revisited With ISAPI   139
Order Taking   146

Disadvantages Of ISAPI   150

Summary   151

CHAPTER 5   USING THE DATASTORE FOR ORDERS   153

Tables   155
How To Use Tables   157

Table Examples   157
Inventory Storage   157
Orders   160
Handling Dynamic Order Forms   162
Generating Dynamic HTML Forms   166

Back To The Guest Book   166

The Foosball Datastore   168
The Shopping Cart Table   168
The Product Table   169
The Customer Table   170
The Payment Table   171
The Order Table   172
Linking The Tables Together   172

Using MS SQL Server   173
ODBC And Sharing Tables   175

Summary   176

CHAPTER 6   ODBC AND LINKING THE DATASTORE   177

ODBC And CRecordset   179
Using ODBC   181
Using CRecordset   199
Using The CDatabase Class   213

Summary   214

CHAPTER 7   FINISH THAT GUEST BOOK   215

The Guest Book HTML   216
The Guest Book Database Table   218
The CGI Guest Book   218
The ISAPI Guest Book   229

Summary   240

CHAPTER 8   COOKIES   241

Storing Information   242

Search Engine Pages   243
The Foosball Shop   244

CCookieMonster   245
Retrieving Cookies   246
Making Cookies   255
Sending Cookies   258
Making Cookies Stale   258

Summary   262

CHAPTER 9   THE SHOPPING CART   263

Forms And Orders   264
Virtual Shopping Carts   264
Shopping Cart Examples   269

Design And Implementation   270
Shopping Cart Cookies   273
Adding Items To The Cart   278
Removing Items From The Cart   280
Reviewing Orders   281
Using CShoppingCart   283

Summary   308

CHAPTER 10   SECURE ORDERING   309

Secure Sockets   309

Redirection   310

The Luhn Algorithm   319

Summary   324

CHAPTER 11   REALTIME CREDIT CARD PROCESSING   325

Credit Card Servers   326
Our Server   330
Our Client   343
Storing Credit Tables   363

CyberCash   364

Emailing Status   365

Summary   366

Chapter 12   Queued Order Processing   369

Queues   370

Batch Processing A Code Fragment   374

Summary   384

Chapter 13   The Foosball Store   387

The Merchandise   387

Custom Options   431

Summary   463

Chapter 14   Software Distribution Ideas   465

Distribution Costs   467

Overhead   468

Concepts   469

Online Software Stores   471
Commercial Solutions   471

Summary   472

Chapter 15   Internet Software Distribution   473

Design   474

U.S. Export Regulations   476
Encryption   477
Payment Collection   480

Summary   495

Appendix A   More HTML   497

Appendix B   TCP/IP Clients And Servers   503

APPENDIX C   THREADS   511

APPENDIX D   HTML EDITORS   515

APPENDIX E   CPONYEXPRESS   519

APPENDIX F   CREDIT CARD PROCESSING COMPANIES   529

APPENDIX G   CREDIT CARD SOFTWARE SERVERS   531

APPENDIX H   DIGITAL CERTIFICATES   533

APPENDIX I   WEBSTAR AND THE MAC   535

INDEX   553

INTRODUCTION

In this country you have to run as fast as you can to stay in the same place.

The red Queen to Alice

Lewis Carrol's **Alice in Wonderland**

The World Wide Web accelerated to a pace that no one had anticipated in 1996. Businesses evolved and adapted, or lost market share. While this was occurring, we witnessed a major shift in the engineering skills required by employers. Instead of using PowerPlant or other frameworks, programming for the Internet became paramount. New languages like Java appeared, and topics like CGI and ISAPI came from apparently out of the blue. As an engineer, if you didn't adapt, your salary didn't either.

On my main book shelf are more than 50 new technical books—all purchased in the last 12 to 18 months. The topics? STL, Java, HTML, CGI, ISAPI, MFC, ActiveX, and various mixtures of all of these. Gone are volumes of *Inside Mac* volumes. Back are Unix programming volumes. Few of these topics existed in 1995 or earlier! This change in the demand of skills has forced all of us to evolve with the Information Revolution. As engineers, we have to learn these new technolgies and how to deploy them.

As this change was occurring, I was reading about tons of new topics in various books, and I decided to open an online store, much like Amazon.com did with their bookstore. However, I couldn't find any technical books available to help with this task! There was nothing on shopping carts, cookies, or credit card processing. There was some mediocre code showing poor implementations of parsing HTML forms, and various CGI volumes of PERL scripts. PERL scripts! I'd rather stick needles in my eyes than use PERL! C++ is the answer, not some slow, bulky scripting language that requires an interpreter. In my quest for an engineering book covering these topics, I found none.

I implemented an online store, and later a credit card server for realtime transaction processing. Because I realized that there was nothing that covered Internet commerce in C++, I decided to write my own book—having implemented both ends, client and server, my experience was perfect for the task. You are holding the results of this effort.

I have implemented several online stores, and even provided online Telephony Conferencing for a major telephone company. The fruits of my experience are included in this book. I mention problems that I encountered, and provide powerful C++ classes that simplify every task involved in Internet commerce. The entire source code is included on the CD-ROM enclosed with this book, and we even have a support site that contains updates and the latest information on Internet commerce for C++ programmers.

Who Is This Book For?

If you're a C++ programmer or engineer with an interest in Web commerce, this book was written just for you. If you are interested in HTML form parsing, understanding how Web servers work and how to extend their functionality with CGI and ISAPI, this is a great reference and tutorial. If you want to process high-performance financial transactions securely and inexpensively, this book is for you. Finally, if you want to implement Internet shopping carts and the like, this is your book.

I am not a professional journalist, but rather one of the leading engineers in my field—this book is written by an engineer, for an engineer. This book was written from the trenches of programming, so there are lots of technical details, design and coding throughout. If you're a Visual Basic programmer, this book is not for you. If you're a consulting engineer, professional engineer or developer, you're in the right place.

What's In Here?

Chapter 1 introduces the concepts of online stores and discuss commerce on the global Internet.

Chapter 2 dives into HTML and start by writing HTML forms. We show how the data is handled by the Web server and received from a client's browser. We write several pages of HTML forms.

Chapter 3 covers CGI and write a powerful form handling class called **CFormParser**. This class handles variable parsing automatically, and you can use it immediately. A few lines of code are all that's required to process the most complicated HTML forms ever written. We also write several HTML forms and provide code to handle them on the Web server, and even discuss server variables and how to get and use them.

Chapter 4 covers the Internet Information Server's ISAPI. This server extension resembles CGI somewhat, and has quite a few advantages, including speed. We include several examples, and show how to override the few limitations ISAPI has.

Chapter 5 covers the datastore, and shows how to make tables in a database that correspond to data on HTML forms. We show how to build dynamic HTML forms based on content provided from a database.

Chapter 6 uses ODBC and an MFC class, **CRecordset**, to store and retrieve information to and from the database. We show how to perform SQL queries and other functions form CGI/ISAPI code fragments.

Chapter 7 covers the guest book example, and implements an ISAPI and CGI guest book that uses SQL server for storing data. You can use this guest book for your Web site within minutes.

Chapter 8 discusses HTTP cookies, what they are, how to make them, how to use them, and so on. We write a cookie handling/creator class called **CCookieMonster** that simplifies the tasks of using cookies to just a few lines of code.

Chapter 9 looks at Internet shopping carts and discusses them in detail. We then implement our own shopping cart class, **CShoppingCart**. This class handles orders for us and maintains a customer's merchandise automatically.

Chapter 10 discusses secure commerce, SSL, HTTP redirection, and the Luhn Mod 10 algorithm for validating the numbers on a credit card. If you're going to perform secure commerce on the Web, this chapter is a must read.

Chapter 11 writes a class called **CCreditCard**, which you can use with your CGI and ISAPI code fragments to process credit card orders on the Web in realtime. This class validates the credit card numbers and card types, and then connects to a credit card server for order verification, and the transfer of funds to your bank account. Using **CCreditCard** requires only a few lines of code. We also write a Credit Card Bridge that allows you to use low-cost credit card servers for transaction processing.

Chapter 12 mentions batch order processing, and provides a code example to process batches using an STL queue adapter and deque container. This chapter is for order processing that doesn't require realtime validation.

Chapter 13 presents a full-blown online store. We cover the store implementation, logic, and code. All code is included.

Chapter 14 presents a new idea in software distribution—give it away on the Internet. If you want a large audience, begin by enabling payment collection in your programs. Here we get you started.

Chapter 15 touches encryption and keys that you can use in your software programs for Internet distribution. You can use these keys to unlock a product on the Internet, and we offer several new ideas and code examples. Distributing your programs then becomes an easy task, as is payment collection.

Finally, there are several appendices for reference, one that provides a TCP/IP client/server example and another that provides an SMTP mailing class, **CPonyExpress**, so you can email clients who visit your Web site.

How To Reach The Author

I would like to hear from you and also have you visit our support site at **www.gigantor.com/coriolis**. If you have an email program handy, my address is don@gigantor.com—I will respond to every email that I can. Questions, comments, suggestions are all welcome. Because I travel frequently, I cannot offer phone support. You can also contact me via the Web, so if you're visiting our site, feel free to send me a note.

1

Introduction To Internet Commerce

May you live in interesting times.

Ancient Chinese curse

Twenty miles from the Mexican border in the middle of the Arizona desert: a T1 line and a business conducting commerce on the Internet. In the middle of the California Redwood Forest: another T1 line connecting yet another online store to the global Internet. Both stores are open and taking orders 24 hours a day, 7 days a week; the stores or gas stations closest to their physical locations are several miles away. The pattern is obvious: Internet commerce is for real.

Virtual stores are cropping up all over—stores whose physical locations don't matter. These stores, thanks to the Internet, can go anywhere in the world that Internet access goes. Shopping at far-off locations is limited only by the speed of your Web browser. Now that we have AT&T, IBM, Hewlett Packard, and Microsoft all jumping into the arena, you can bet this is going to be the biggest financial opportunity for businesses that has appeared in the last 100 years. What we're witnessing is a consequence of the Information Revolution that began in the '60s. Like those who experienced the Industrial Revolution, we're going to witness major changes in how we run our personal lives and conduct business—all business. We're also going to witness many businesses in denial—and when the train passes them by, these businesses will be no more. Do you think AT&T or IBM would enter this arena if they didn't believe it represented a phenomenal business opportunity?

In this chapter, we're going to visit a few virtual stores and look at how they conduct business on the Internet before we set up shop with our own virtual store. If you're already familiar with virtual stores and commerce on the Internet, you might want to skip this chapter and look at Chapter 2, which dives right into HTML forms and order-taking.

The Internet, Online Stores, And Malls

Stores and malls are now all over the Internet. True, we're seeing the same old merchandise we're used to—only now, we're able to purchase things more easily than ever before. We can even search for things ourselves—without waiting on a salesperson. The Internet is fast and immediate.

On the Internet, our entrances to virtual stores are the company Web pages. Our salesperson now becomes a search engine, or a Web page. Our shopping cart is now virtual; we can add and remove items, and don't have to run back and put them on a shelf somewhere. What about waiting in line to pay for your purchases? Not anymore. Now you click on a Pay or Order button, and your payment is electronically and securely transmitted. Merchandise is usually shipped by Airborne Express or Fed Ex, and you receive your order within one to three days.

Five years ago, malls were just acres and acres of concrete and buildings with thousands of employees. These days, they may be just a server or two, located in a room. Replacing the thousands of employees are a few software engineers and others who write software, process orders and handle errors. And location, as I've mentioned, doesn't matter: If you want to be located in a castle in the Czech Republic (and you have a palette for "different" cuisine), drag your server there and turn it on!

So, a virtual store is a commercial Web page, and a virtual mall is a central Web page that lists the stores and hypertext links to them—tons of them. Consumers can sort them by name, merchandise, anything. You'll find stores within the same mall with physical locations in vastly different parts of the globe. Things sure have changed.

The Market Now And In The Year 2000

Commerce on the Web totaled $600 million last year alone, while a few years ago it was nonexistent. Are these huge sales due to new products? Perhaps some are, but most online buying is of merchandise that shoppers used to buy offline, and can now obtain more quickly and more efficiently with the Internet. No more lines to wait in, no more rude sales people to see. While this volume of business sounds tremendous, think of the Internet sales expected by the year 2000: $66 billion! And it's expected to continue growing for several more years, well into the next millennium.

Not only is it convenient to have virtual shopping carts and virtual cash registers, but people can now shop whenever they want. These virtual stores are open all day, so you can as easily shop at midnight or 3 a.m. as during "normal" business hours at the local mall. Talk about convenience.

We're also now witnessing global commerce. Because location is unimportant for some businesses, you can expect heavily taxed businesses to relocate to places with lower taxation rates, or places with no taxation. Why not? The burden of excessive taxation will make a business on the Internet even less competitive than ever before. How will this impact the immigration or emigration in your country? Your state?

Consider the possibilities: Countries with high taxation rates could either radically change or dissolve. Because of the Information Revolution, we're witnessing a global Darwinism of business in which there is no turning back. The competition is global, and places with high taxation rates aren't going to be able to compete economically.

Overhead Of Operating A Virtual Store

Have you ever opened a store or retail front in a mall? It's absolutely horrendous when you calculate the rent, not to mention electric signs and remodeling work.

Years ago I looked at opening a comic book shop, and the rent for a small store was in excess of $5,000 per month. It was so outrageous I couldn't afford to do it.

Let's look at hiring employees. I can't count all the "inside" thefts that occurred when I ran my other businesses, but they were substantial. Then there are benefits and wages, employees who don't show up for work, and the list goes on and on. Well, that's a convincing list of reasons not to open a conventional business, but what about opening an Internet-based business? It has its own set of problems, albeit different problems.

For starters, you really don't need your own T1 line running to your place of business; you can have an ISP house your Web pages. Fees for housing your pages usually range from $250 through $500 per month—a substantial difference when you compare it to the rent mentioned above. For a frame relay, your costs will run around $250 through $1,000 a month. Also, before deciding in favor of a T1 line or not, plan out how many simultaneous connections you will be handling—because a faster line and a faster server can obviously handle more connections.

Table 1.1 shows the startup costs of a Bay-area ISP associated with getting various connections, as well as the monthly fees. Note that the fees can be deceivingly inexpensive: You generally get one fee from the ISP and another from the phone company for leasing a line to your business.

TABLE 1.1

STARTUP COSTS OF A SAN FRANCISCO BAY-AREA ISP.

Connectivity Type	Startup	Monthly
28.8K Full-Time IP Access (Single IP number only)	$200	$125
28.8K Dedicated LAN Dial	$450	$145
Include Livingston OfficeRouter and USR 28.8K Modem	$1,795	$145
56K Dedicated Frame Relay Include 56K DSU Only (at customer location)	$350 $650	$250 $250
Include Proteon GlobeTrotter Router and 56K DSU	$1,295	$250
Include Livingston IRX Router and 56K DSU	$1,945	$250

(continued)

TABLE 1.1

STARTUP COSTS OF A SAN FRANCISCO BAY-AREA ISP (*CONTINUED*).

Connectivity Type	Startup	Monthly
Include Livingston Firewall Router and 56K DSU	$2,595	$250
Include Cisco 2501 Router and 56K DSU $2,595	$250	
Include Cisco 2514 Firewall Router and 56K DSU	$2,995	$250
128K Dedicated Frame Relay	$350	$425
Include T1 DSU Only (at customer location)	$995	$425
Include Proteon GlobeTrotter Router and T1 DSU	$1,995	$425
Include Livingston IRX Router and T1 DSU	$2,595	$425
Include Livingston Firewall Router and T1 DSU	$3,195	$425
Include Cisco 2501 and T1 DSU	$3,195	$425
Include Cisco 2514 Firewall Router and T1 DSU	$3,595	$425
Virtual T1	$350	$650
Include T1 DSU only (at customer location)	$995	$650
Include Proteon GlobeTrotter Router and T1 DSU	$1,995	$650
Include Livingston IRX Router and T1 DSU	$2,595	$650
Include Livingston Firewall Router and T1 DSU	$3,195	$650
Include Cisco 2501 and T1 DSU	$3,195	$650
Include Cisco 2514 Firewall Router and T1 DSU	$3,595	$650
T1 (1.544Mbps)	$2,400	$1,000
Include T1 DSU only (at customer location)	$3,395	$1,000
Include Proteon GlobeTrotter Router and T1 DSU	$4,395	$1,000
Include Livingston IRX Router and T1 DSU	$4,995	$1,000
Include Livingston Firewall Router and T1 DSU	$5,595	$1,000
Include Cisco 2501 and T1 DSU	$5,595	$1,000
Include Cisco 2514 Firewall Router and T1 DSU	$5,995	$1,000

If you do get your own T1 line, you'll have to get your own machines from which to run your servers. If you're selling lots of merchandise, you'll need another machine for your datastore. Now, for your major expenses: software and engineering services.

As a reader of this book, you're most likely a professional engineer or consultant, so the service portion is probably an area you can cover with the aid of this book. In fact, you probably bought this book to implement someone else's software. This expense for your own stores could then become minimal—and this part could be fun.

For my stores, I used Windows NT Server 4.0, IIS, and Microsoft SQL Server, for which I paid about $800, $0, and $1,000, respectively. While sizable when added to the hardware costs of $3,000, it's still less than the fixtures I would have to purchase in a regular store, and it's also less than the cost of an electric sign. Opening a typical store in a shopping center would cost a minimum of $2,500 a month, a mall location would be from $5,000 to $10,000 a month, and either one would call for another $50,000 for signs, inventory, equipment, and so on. A virtual store is less risky, has more potential for profit because it has a larger potential customer base, and it costs a ton less.

Consulting fees for implementing graphics, Web pages, and CGI/ISAPI code for a live transaction site can run as high as $1,000,000; in fact, that alone could go to CGI/ISAPI consultants. Good thing you have this book—we'll show you how to implement sophisticated store fronts in about two weeks, after you get used to all the components used on the server end. You'll still need to buy some artwork (or even hire a top-notch Web page designer), but with all the rest of the stuff under control, choosing a "face" for your online store can be fun.

The 24×7 Store

The term 24×7 first appeared when mail servers were touted as running " 24×7," that is, 24 hours a day, and 7 days a week. When a virtual store is implemented, you're going to be open 24×7, something that would be nearly impossible to imagine if you were running a conventional store with employees. Imagine the schedules and salaries that would come into play when operating a 24-hour store with just two or three employees!

One night, I was working on a bug fix for one of my clients' sites—a commerce server. At 2 a.m., while I was fixing the bug, the server was being hit by people from Japan, Taiwan, Korea, and Russia. Users from literally all over the world were connecting to the site and conducting business. While everyone else in town was sleeping, my client's server performed three or four new transactions between 2 and 3 a.m.

From Conventional To Virtual Business

How else do virtual and physical stores differ? While security is an issue with both types of stores, in virtual stores, it's usually done in your router or with your network configuration rather than with a staff of security guards. Believe me, you can expect security issues anytime money is involved.

Instead of training workers to use the cash register and record inventory, now you'll have an engineer (probably you) who will write programs that handle the tasks that you used to train your employees to do.

Some virtual stores also have no inventory; they work out deals with the distributor so that when an order is placed, they fax it to the distributor, who then ships it directly to the customer. Some businesses even have their server CGI/ISAPI modules fax the order to a distributor—talk about automation! In this case, the virtual store is merely a front to display different products from an entire spectrum of distributors. Without inventory, you no longer worry about shelf space, rent for a physical space, inventory control, and so on. Some virtual stores will still have inventories, but it's definitely not a requirement.

You might be thinking that with no inventory, you probably wouldn't get the best discount. After all, isn't the profit margin increased by buying in bulk? This is true in some cases, but if your store buys significant volume from your distributor, you can get as good a deal as you would with a regular warehouse full of stocked shelves. The other major difference between virtual and physical stores is price for the customer: You generally can offer a better bargain when you sell a product on the Internet. Why? The overhead for the business is less, and if the distributor gives you a decent price break, you can pass it on to the consumer. Now I'm sure you've seen virtual businesses that don't offer better prices, but as a general rule, if an Internet business doesn't offer a better price, something is awry.

The other reason prices for consumers are better is the serious competition on the virtual store front. Now consumers have more choices—they're no longer limited to the options at their local hardware, department, and music stores. More competition always lowers prices. Take a look at book prices on the Internet: Because of recent competition, hardback books have dropped 30 percent. Why would a consumer buy a book at a store down the street when they could get a 30 percent discount online? Again, some virtual store owners will feel some regional disadvantages here—for example, when competing with other businesses, those in California have the handicap of needing to pay their silent business partner, the state, 8.25 percent sales tax. How many Internet stores do you think will stay in California? While California offers conventional businesses an excellent location and lots of other advantages, it offers a virtual store nothing but a hefty tax. You'll be seeing more businesses migrating to states where it makes more tax sense and ISP sense.

How Internet Commerce Works

Internet commerce works by having a server that is running all the time, 24×7. You'll implement your Web pages, write your CGI/ISAPI code (debug it first, hopefully), and leave the machine running! Virtual business is like fishing—you bait your hook, throw the line out, and wait until the pole moves. However, in this case, the pole reels itself in, filets the fish, then cooks it while you're doing something else—maybe baiting more hooks, maybe working on next month's products. It then notifies you when your meal is complete.

Your server will display merchandise or services using *HTML forms* (we'll cover these in detail in Chapter 2). Essentially, a user's Web browser uses forms to send information to the server. How do you get this information from the server and do something with it? That's where CGI and ISAPI come in, and we'll cover both of these in great detail in Chapters 3 and 4, respectively. For now, suffice it to say that CGI/ISAPI are small programs (code fragments) that you will write, and the Web server will interface with them and pass the data to you from the user's Web browser. While all of this sounds fairly complicated, and can get quite tough to debug, we'll show you how all the pieces fit together.

Some Real Examples

We've discussed Internet commerce and provided details, but no specific examples. Here we'll take a look at a few clever stores that have been put on the Net. We'll start with the world's largest online bookstore, Amazon.com, then look at ticket reservations and advance purchases with Southwest Airlines. Finally, we'll have a look at shopping on the Internet and the options available for the consumer at a Foosball store.

Amazon.com

Want a book but can't get to a bookstore? Or can't find it? A perfect place to look is at an online bookstore. There are general Internet bookstores, such as Barnes & Noble, but Amazon.com was the first one out there, and its success story warrants a quick look.

When you first connect to Amazon.com, you get several pages of top-selling books—which are great marketing materials—and you can order them right there. You can also search with various options using the store's search page, shown in Figure 1.1.

You can search Amazon.com "by author," "by publisher," or "by title"—all standard. You can search for various subtitles, and when the search engine builds a page with new hits for you, it asks you if you want to view some related items. Talk about an electronic salesperson! If you accept this option, the engine displays related books with similar topics for you to inspect, and even purchase. Figure 1.2 shows some titles related to our original searched-for title.

At Amazon.com, you can view and purchase the books as you would on most sites; however, it does have one very cool option: You can get your books gift-wrapped and sent to the address you specify. Got a last-minute gift to send out? This is a great place to look.

Southwest Airlines

Recently I needed to fly out of state, so I browsed the Web sites of various airlines to find the best price and least amount of transfers from plane to plane. Some of the sites looked really good, but I kept getting errors like "site busy, try again later." Sure—who in their right mind is going to "try again later" when

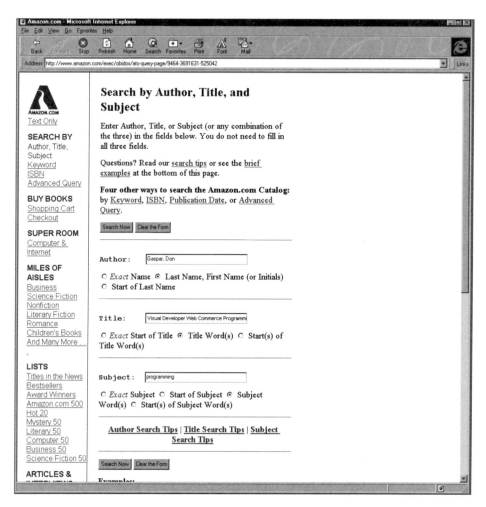

Figure 1.1
The search page at Amazon.com.

there are dozens of other airlines to choose from? This is a key issue when conducting business on the Internet—people are not going to wait for your server problems when there are several other businesses they can immediately choose from.

I've picked the Southwest site because it was responsive, fast, and allowed flexibility of dynamic flight times and locations with just a few mouse clicks. Because it was simple and fast, it was convenient, and it got my business. Note the attitude most Internet consumers have: If it's not immediate, they will go elsewhere.

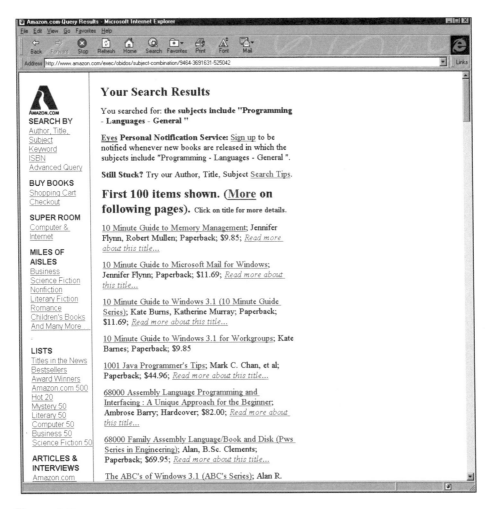

Figure 1.2
Topics related to the title we searched for.

The interface is quite simple (see Figure 1.3): You select your approximate departure time, departure location, and destination. These are just drop-down list items, which we'll learn about in depth in Chapter 2. Next, you choose your return options, and hopefully—if your destination has flights to it—an entire selection of different flight options appears. Select what you want, and pay for it electronically by filling out the online form.

What's really neat about this is that you don't even need a ticket. You get an authorization number that you present at the flight gate—no long line. With your ID card you walk right onto your flight with a minimal wait, if any.

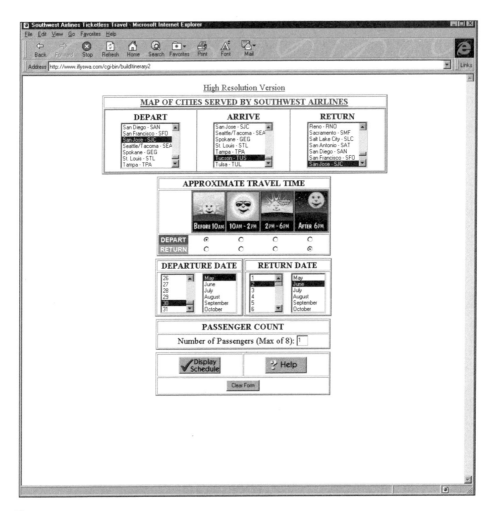

Figure 1.3
The Southwest Airlines flight scheduling page.

The Foosball Store

This is a simple store that I helped implement because I like Foosball, and so do most of my friends. Someone said, "What a great idea to sell Foosball tables," so over a weekend we implemented an online store that handles realtime order processing automatically. This store shows the typical virtual shopping carts and virtual cash registers that are common on Internet sites where you can purchase goods. We'll use the setup and implementation of the Foosball example throughout this book.

For those of you who want to check it out, the URL is **www.gigantor.com/ games**. Keep in mind that this is a real site—don't order anything unless you're in the market for a Foosball table! (If you're in the market for a Foosball table, however, go wild and buy one here!)

Each page shows pictures of the merchandise, with a vivid description of what it is—even how much it weighs. Potential customers can compare all the features, with more information at their disposal than most salespeople would offer at a conventional store. To reserve an item for purchase, users click on the Add to Shopping Cart button and enter the quantity of the item they want to purchase. Users are then brought to a dynamic HTML page that shows the contents of their virtual shopping cart—this virtual shopping cart is merely a link to items in our database. Figure 1.4 shows a typical merchandise-ordering page.

Users can look through the site, add and remove merchandise, and change the quantity of items. They can even disconnect, reconnect later in the day, and their shopping cart will still be there. We'll cover how to remember states of a browser using cookies in Chapter 8.

To order an item, users merely click on the Order Now button, which takes them to a page that requests their shipping address and other necessary information. The order is then recalculated with shipping costs and tax, if applicable; users enter their credit card information, and we securely verify the transaction in realtime. The realtime verification can take between 3 and 15 seconds, which is faster than a checkout at any conventional store. The purchased Foosball table is then shipped out directly from the factory.

Ordering Merchandise On The Internet

The Foosball store is a classic example of a virtual shopping cart. Customers place items into a cart, and can review the cart at any time and change the order; finally, when ready to purchase, the user usually clicks on an Order or Checkout button. This prompts a page that requests user and payment information. We'll briefly cover how to implement such pages, and then cover them in complete detail using Visual C++ in Chapter 11.

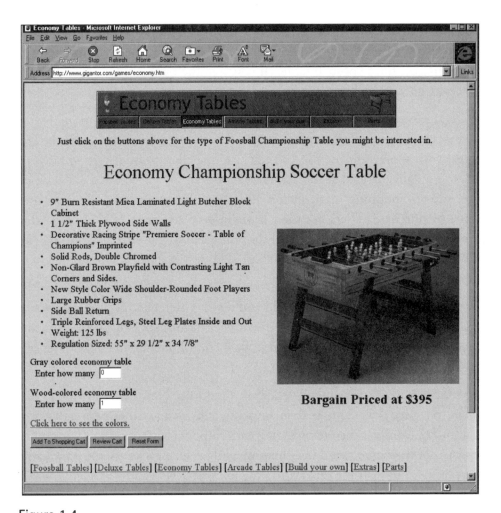

Figure 1.4
To reserve an item for purchase, users just enter the quantity of an item, then click on Add to Shopping Cart.

Types Of Payment

Internet users generally use credit cards for buying goods. This is a great idea, especially because if you get bad merchandise and have trouble dealing with a merchant in a remote place, your credit card company will deal with them for you. My MasterCard even gives me price protection when I purchase something, so if I don't find the lowest price or someone beats the price in 30 days, I get the difference credited back to me. What kinds of credit cards are the most common and easiest to process on a virtual store?

The big two are MasterCard and Visa, welcomed all over the world. Figure 1.5 shows a credit card processing form. A few other popular cards in North America are American Express, Diner's Club, and Carte Blanche. I don't see Discover being used very much with Internet businesses, probably because Discover has very stringent guidelines for Internet-based businesses: Too bad, they're going to lose out big time as that $66 billion pie leaves no slice for them.

A popular card in Japan is the Japanese Bank Card, which is taken all over the world at major establishments. If you're going to have clients in Asia, you need to find a way to accept this card (the site I mentioned earlier that was getting all those hits from Asia at 2 a.m. gets 14 percent of its total business from Japan alone). We'll cover how to accept this card in Chapter 11, so don't worry about losing customers from Asia.

Standard debit or ATM cards are not yet used on the Internet. For people who don't want to use a credit card, an option is C.O.D. orders, but it can be difficult for a merchant doing a large volume of transactions. C.O.D. orders typically require more overhead, and because of this extra cost most merchants frown upon selling merchandise this way. Another choice is the new CyberCoin system, in which buyers will have CyberWallets that link directly into their bank accounts, much like the ATM card does at the bank terminal. These systems are in development, and our Web page at **www.gigantor.com/coriolis** will detail

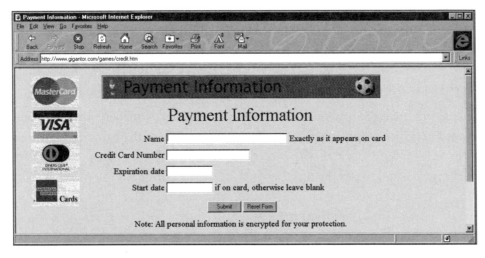

Figure 1.5
Typical credit card processing form.

any new developments and changes as these advance. An authentication scheme is being developed to verify the cyber-pay systems, and to verify the person using the system. There's even a Microsoft Wallet in development that uses the same scheme.

Any type of payment that is taken must also be transfer secure, meaning that the probability of someone getting your credit card number and using it to order merchandise is small or nonexistent. In Chapter 11, we'll cover how to do this for the sites you implement. *Never, ever* send your credit card over email or to a non-secure site. There are literally thousands of people listening on the Net, reading packets of data and just looking for credit card numbers or bank account information. Be careful.

Secure Ordering

We advise using only secure ordering, but how do we know it's secure? There are companies, like Verisign, that issue digital certificates, which validate the authenticity of the merchant and guarantee the server is encrypting the credit card information. Here's how it works.

You, the developer, contact Verisign and ask for a digital certificate. Verisign verifies you are a business, verifies who you are, and then looks your company up with Dunn and Bradstreet for authentication. You have your server generate an encryption key, and Verisign sends you some information to add to your server to encrypt things. Verisign has information for most servers on how to generate encryption keys. If Verisign doesn't support your server, you might want to try the author of your software. Verisign can be reached at **www.verisign.com**.

Now when the user's browser connects to a secure page, your server will provide his or her browser with a key to encrypt the data. When the browser sends the form information back to the server, it's completely encrypted. The server unencrypts it and passes the data to your CGI/ISAPI program to process. When the client sends over further information from an HTML form to the server, the server provides a new, unique key that changes every time this data interchange occurs.

Companies like Verisign require their digital certificates be renewed annually. Having such a certificate is a prerequisite for anyone serious about doing business on the Internet. Appendix H will show you how to get yours.

Summary

Business is evolving into a true global market—location no longer matters. Virtual malls and stores are appearing by the dozens every day, and their commerce is being done completely and securely on the Internet. The virtual market, given its world-wide scope, has a great potential to make online businesses significantly more profit than location-specific businesses. Additionally, the cost of entering into an Internet business and maintaining it is substantially lower than for conventional businesses.

As a software engineer, you have a unique opportunity to get in at the ground floor and be a part of this Information Revolution. You'll learn to put virtual stores on the Internet, take orders for merchandise, and collect credit card payments in realtime. Learning commerce on the Net will complement your existing programming abilities by helping you understand how clients (Web browsers) and servers (Web) work together, how to extend both of them for your use, and how to satisfy your clients' Internet engineering needs. Now then, where's that chapter on HTML forms and how to use them?

TAKING ORDERS WITH HTML FORMS

Things should be made as simple as possible, but not any simpler.

Albert Einstein

Why has the Web's growth been so explosive? Because for both users and developers, it's so intuitive and easy to use. HTML (Hypertext Markup Language) is very simple to understand, and that simplicity is taken a step further when we apply HTML to forms. Forms are just a standardized method of allowing a browser (client) to pass information to the server.

Forms allow a user to input data onto a Web page, and then send that data to the server for further processing via CGI/ISAPI (like the server saving the information into a database, for example). This data can also be secured via encryption in a Secure Socket Layer (SSL). On the server, you can have either some kind of script like PERL running with an interpreter that can process the data from a form, or you can have a CGI/ISAPI-compiled code fragment to process the data.

PERL stands for Practical Extraction and Reporting Language, and is a fine scripting language that was originally made for generating reports on older Unix machines, not for processing HTML forms or performing any complex tasks. PERL has been successful for Web server use because it's simple to use, much like HTML. PERL was also readily available for non-programmers who used to put up Web sites but didn't know C or C++—hence its popularity. However, PERL has some serious drawbacks, which may keep you from using it for your professional sites.

Imagine you're using PERL. When your Web server receives form data for processing, it launches a language interpreter, loads the PERL script, and then executes it. When it's done, the Web server sends any results back to the user and then unloads the interpreter from memory. Several problems arise. First, this loading and unloading is an expensive operation in terms of computer time cycles. Second, the interpreter needs to be fairly large, as it's parsing a language script on the fly and must handle a variety of special cases with variables and keywords. Also, because it's an interpreted language, the overhead is going to cause this form processing to be substantially slower than an executable code fragment would be. Now imagine using these PERL scripts and having 50 people connected to your site simultaneously—that means lots of overhead and possibly long delays for customers. If a delay is long enough, your potential customer will go to another site.

You can see why a compiled code fragment is the way to go for high-performance sites. Even if your site isn't designed for high performance, executing code is always going to be faster than loading an interpreter and running a script—it will respond better to the user. In this chapter, we're going to look at HTML forms and how to write them, relate HTML form elements to C++ data structures, and write several useful examples using various form tags.

If you're already familiar with HTML forms and processing data from them, you may want to skip to Chapter 3 and get started on the CGI crash course, which is where we start doing things based on the data from a form.

What Are HTML Forms?

We've succinctly mentioned what forms do, but now it's time to explore how they do it. How does the form data get sent to the server, and how does the server receive it for parsing and instantiating our CGI/ISAPI code fragment?

Let's explore the different form tags and what we can do with them. If you're completely unfamiliar with HTML, you might want to review some of the basic HTML tags (see Appendix A), as we're covering only forms in detail here. What if you're using an HTML generator, such as NetObject's Fusion or Microsoft's FrontPage? Well, you still need to understand forms and how their variables are passed to the server so that you can tell your generator program how to set things up. Also, your site will most likely need to send a variety of responses to the user, and you'll need to write the HTML on the fly, dynamically, from your CGI/ISAPI code fragment. Therefore, you'll definitely find this section useful.

HTML Form Examples

Anyone who has used a Web browser can name several different types of form fields. Every form field is an element from the Graphical User Interfaces (GUI) that became common in the mid-to-late '80s. You've seen radio buttons, check boxes, drop-down list boxes (pop-up menus for you Macintosh folks), and buttons. We'll cover how to implement these in a few more pages, but right now let's look at a few forms in detail.

Figure 2.1 shows us a form that allows the consumer to customize a product. In this case, it's a Foosball table, but it could be anything. Clicking on the various drop-down list boxes and moving the mouse through the items allow the customer to choose from many possible configurations. When the customer is ready, the results are submitted to the server.

When the consumer wants the price of the selected configuration, he or she clicks on the Calculate Price button. The information for each drop-down list, and the associated values, is sent to the server, which then calls a CGI/ISAPI code fragment specified in the form (we'll cover this shortly) with all the selected data. The code fragment then processes this data, generates a custom HTML page, and passes it back to the server (see Figure 2.2). If the customer wants to purchase this merchandise, he or she can add it to the virtual shopping cart, or even order it right now if he or she is through shopping.

The consumer can repeat this configuration process an indefinite number of times. From a business perspective, the beauty is that no employees are working on this! Well, that's not entirely true; you'll code and update it periodically, but no employees need to work on it continuously, as in a physical store situation. The CGI or ISAPI code fragment you write handles all of these varying

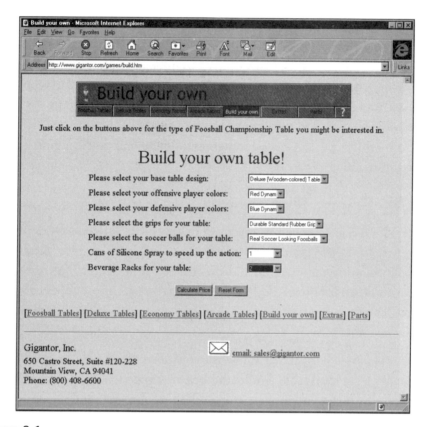

Figure 2.1
Typical form allowing multiple selections to create a customized product.

options, so the customer has a lot of latitude when selecting merchandise. Because you're writing a compiled code fragment, the dynamic response in HTML is sent back without delay. The customer can try every option until he or she finds exactly the right configuration and price range.

A great application of forms for configurable merchandise is a computer hardware retailer. If you haven't already, check out the Dell Computer site at **www.dell.com**. Here, you can configure any type of computer, and immediately get a response with a price quotation. The overhead for Dell is minimal when compared to having a staff handle phone orders and questions. Dell literally gets thousands of orders per week directly from it's Web site, as shown in Figure 2.3. It's the perfect example of a successful application of using HTML forms.

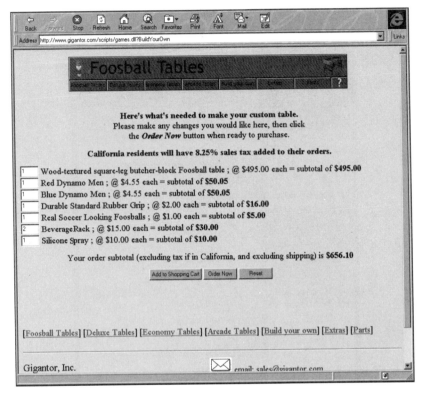

Figure 2.2
Sample dynamic HTML form generated as a response to the consumer's selection.

In Chapter 1, we saw some other examples, but you might want to do some Web surfing to find more helpful ones. Forms are everywhere, but robust sites that respond with dynamic HTML in a timely manner are difficult to find.

HTML Source

Now it's time to look at some HTML source code and how these forms look from the programmer's vantage. What's exciting here is you'll be writing HTML code that will work on all browsers. It doesn't matter if the client uses a Macintosh, Windows NT, Motif, or another system—it will work properly. In Chapters 3 and 4, we'll cover the server side, and we'll write CGI and/or ISAPI code in Visual C++ that the browsers never need to understand—only the server does. Part of the fun here is working on both ends simultaneously: client and server.

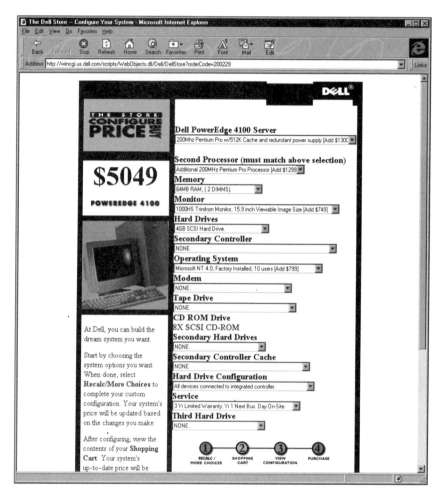

Figure 2.3
Dell Computer page for configuring a computer to purchase.

 Use An Editor That Knows HTML

When you write your HTML source code, be sure to use an editor that understands the HTML tags. Programs like Developer Studio, Metrowerks CodeWarrior and others will allow you to see your tags in a different style and color. This helps you match delimiter tags correctly, and your pages will have the expected result.

The HTML for the "Build your own" Foosball page is shown in Listing 2.1. We have included the entire HTML here with a succinct review for either those who don't write it every day, or those who are new to it. For convenience, we've shaded the form elements.

HTML consists of starting and delimiting tags. For example, to center some text, you would place something like <CENTER> before the text, and delimit it after the text with </CENTER>. If the tag is not delimited, all items until the </CENTER> delimiter would be centered as well. Let's take a look at how the forms are handled.

All forms contain a beginning <FORM> tag, and an **ACTION** attribute. The **ACTION** attribute tells the browser what command to send to the server when the user is ready to **submit** the form:

```
<FORM ACTION="/scripts/games.dll?BuildYourOwn" METHOD=POST >
```

All items after the **<FORM>** tag until the **</FORM>** delimiter tag are considered part of the form. Note that only certain items will be part of the form, and that these items allow the user to perform input with the GUI elements we mentioned earlier. Here, the **ACTION** attribute tells the browser to call a DLL named "games.dll" in the "/scripts" directory, and the function **BuildYourOwn** is the code to be instantiated. If this were a CGI application, the .dll would probably be missing and you would have a different suffix or none at all. If you want your forms to do anything, you must have the tags correctly coded, and you must specify an action type for the form to tell the server to instantiate. If you're missing anything, you'll have a form that looks great, but won't do anything at all.

You're probably curious about the **POST** item: This tells the browser how to send its form data back to the server. The other approach is to send the data via the **GET** method. Both methods will work, but your CGI modules will need to know which one you're using so that they can properly parse the variables. ISAPI has a Parsemap, which we'll cover in Chapter 4, that will handle both cases for you automatically. We'll cover both the **GET** and **POST** methods in detail in Chapter 3, along with benefits and downsides of each. Here, I have opted to use the **POST** for convenience and personal preference. Listing 2.1 shows the HTML for the "Build your own" Foosball page (at **www.gigantor.com/games/build.htm**).

LISTING 2.1   HTML SOURCE CODE FOR THE FOOSBALL PAGE.

```
<HTML>
<HEAD>
<TITLE>Build your own</TITLE>
</HEAD>
```

```
<BODY BGCOLOR="#DDDDDD" LINK="#0000EE" VLINK="#EE0000" TEXT="#000000">
<FORM ACTION="/scripts/games.dll?BuildYourOwn" METHOD=POST>

<CENTER>
<TABLE BORDER=0 CELLSPACING=0 CELLPADDING=0>
<TR>
<TD COLSPAN=8>
<IMG HEIGHT=48 WIDTH=595 SRC="Header5.gif" BORDER=0
    ALT="Build your own">
</TD>
</TR>

<TR>
<TD WIDTH=80>
<A HREF="default.htm">
<IMG HEIGHT=24 WIDTH=80 SRC="OneOff.gif" BORDER=0
    ALT="Foosball Tables">
</A>
</TD>

<TD WIDTH=80>
<A HREF="deluxe.htm">
<IMG HEIGHT=24 WIDTH=80 SRC="TwoOff.gif" BORDER=0
    ALT="Deluxe Tables">
</A>
</TD>

<TD WIDTH=80>
<A HREF="economy.htm">
<IMG HEIGHT=24 WIDTH=80 SRC="ThreeOff.gif" BORDER=0
    ALT="Economy Tables">
</A>
</TD>

<TD WIDTH=80>
<A HREF="arcade.htm">
<IMG HEIGHT=24 WIDTH=80 SRC="FourOff.gif" BORDER=0
    ALT="Arcade Tables">
</A>
</TD>

<TD WIDTH=80>
<A HREF="build.htm">
<IMG HEIGHT=24 WIDTH=80 SRC="FiveOn.gif" BORDER=0
    ALT="Build your own">
</A>
</TD>
```

```
<TD WIDTH=80>
<A HREF="extras.htm">
<IMG HEIGHT=24 WIDTH=80 SRC="SixOff.gif" BORDER=0 ALT="Extras">
</A>
</TD>

<TD WIDTH=80>
<A HREF="parts.htm">
<IMG HEIGHT=24 WIDTH=80 SRC="SevenOff.gif" BORDER=0 ALT="Parts">
</A>
</TD>

<TD WIDTH=35>
<A HREF="fooshelp.htm">
<IMG HEIGHT=24 WIDTH=35 SRC="HelpOff.gif" BORDER=0 ALT="Help!">
</A>
</TD>
</TR>
</TABLE>
</CENTER>

<CENTER>
<P>Just click on the buttons above for the type of Foosball
Championship Table you might be interested in.<br><br><br>
<FONT SIZE="+3">Build your own table!</FONT><br>
</CENTER>

<CENTER>
<TABLE CELLPADDING=0 CELLSPACING=0 BORDER=0 WIDTH=535>

<TR>
<TD HEIGHT=10></TD>
</TR>

<TR>
<TD><P>Please select your base table design:</TD>
<TD>
    <SELECT NAME="foosball">
    <OPTION VALUE="grayDeluxe">Deluxe (Gray) Table</OPTION>
    <OPTION VALUE="woodDeluxe"
        SELECTED>Deluxe (Wooden-colored) Table</OPTION>
<OPTION VALUE="grayEcono">Economy (Gray) Table</OPTION>
    <OPTION VALUE="woodEcono">Economy (Wooden-colored) Table</OPTION>
    <OPTION VALUE="grayArcade">Arcade Premier Table</OPTION>
    </SELECT>
</TD>
</TR>
```

```
<TR>
<TD HEIGHT=10></TD>
</TR>

<TR>
<TD><P>Please select your offensive player colors:</TD>
<TD>
    <SELECT NAME="offense">
    <OPTION VALUE="redDynamos">Red Dynamo</OPTION>
    <OPTION VALUE="blueDynamos">Blue Dynamo</OPTION>
    <OPTION VALUE="yellowBobs" SELECTED>Yellow</OPTION>
    <OPTION VALUE="tanBobs">Tan</OPTION>
    <OPTION VALUE="ltGrayBobs">Light Gray</OPTION>
    <OPTION VALUE="dkGrayBobs">Dark Gray</OPTION>
    <OPTION VALUE="purpleBobs">Purple</OPTION>
    </SELECT>
</TD>
</TR>

<TR>
<TD HEIGHT=10></TD>
</TR>

<TR>
<TD><P>Please select your defensive player colors:</TD>
<TD>
    <SELECT NAME="defense">
    <OPTION VALUE="redDynamos">Red Dynamo</OPTION>
    <OPTION VALUE="blueDynamos">Blue Dynamo</OPTION>
    <OPTION VALUE="yellowBobs">Yellow</OPTION>
    <OPTION VALUE="tanBobs" SELECTED>Tan</OPTION>
    <OPTION VALUE="ltGrayBobs">Light Gray</OPTION>
    <OPTION VALUE="dkGrayBobs">Dark Gray</OPTION>
    <OPTION VALUE="purpleBobs">Purple</OPTION>
    </SELECT>
</TD>
</TR>

<TR>
<TD HEIGHT=10></TD>
</TR>

<TR>
<TD><P>Please select the grips for your table:</TD>
```

```
<TD>
    <SELECT NAME="handles">
    <OPTION VALUE="rubberGrips" SELECTED>
        Durable Standard Rubber Grip</OPTION>
    <OPTION VALUE="woodenGrips">Quality Wooden Grip </OPTION>
    <OPTION VALUE="brownGrips">Brown Grips</OPTION>
    <OPTION VALUE="qualityRubberGrips">Soft Quality Rubber Grips
        </OPTION>
    </SELECT>
</TD>
</TR>

<TR>
<TD HEIGHT=10></TD>
</TR>

<TR>
<TD><P>Please select the soccer balls for your table:</TD>
<TD>
    <SELECT NAME="hits">
    <OPTION VALUE="realSoccerBalls">Real Soccer Looking Foosballs
        </OPTION>
    <OPTION VALUE="soccerBalls" SELECTED>Normal Soccer Balls</OPTION>
    <OPTION VALUE="compositionBalls">Composition Soccer Ball</OPTION>
    <OPTION VALUE="engravedBalls">Soccer Balls Engraved Surfaces
        </OPTION>
    <OPTION VALUE="smoothBalls">Soccer Balls Smooth Surface</OPTION>
    </SELECT>
</TD>
</TR>

<TR>
<TD HEIGHT=10></TD>
</TR>

<TR>
<TD><P>Cans of Silicone Spray to speed up the action:</TD>
<TD>
    <SELECT NAME="cans">
    <OPTION VALUE="one" SELECTED>1</OPTION>
    <OPTION VALUE="two">2</OPTION>
    <OPTION VALUE="three">3</OPTION>
    <OPTION VALUE="four">4</OPTION>
    <OPTION VALUE="five">5</OPTION>
```

```
        <OPTION VALUE="none">None</OPTION>
        </SELECT>
</TD>
</TR>


<TR>
<TD HEIGHT=10></TD>
</TR>


<TR>
<TD><P>Beverage Racks for your table:</TD>
<TD>
        <SELECT NAME="num_racks">
        <OPTION VALUE="one" SELECTED>1</OPTION>
        <OPTION VALUE="two">2</OPTION>
        <OPTION VALUE="none">None</OPTION>
        </SELECT>
</TD>
</TR>


<TR>
<TD HEIGHT=10></TD>
</TR>


</TABLE>
<br>
<INPUT TYPE="submit" NAME="task" VALUE="Calculate Price" >
<INPUT TYPE="reset" NAME="" VALUE="Reset Form">
</CENTER>
</TR><br><br>


[<A HREF="default.htm">Foosball Tables</A>]
[<A HREF="deluxe.htm">Deluxe Tables</A>]
[<A HREF="economy.htm">Economy Tables</A>]
[<A HREF="arcade.htm">Arcade Tables</A>]
[<A HREF="build.htm">Build your own</A>]
[<A HREF="extras.htm">Extras</A>]
[<A HREF="parts.htm">Parts</A>]
<p>
<HR>


<TABLE CELLPADDING=0 CELLSPACING=0 BORDER=0 WIDTH=100%>


<TR VALIGN="middle" ALIGN="left">
        <TD WIDTH=50%>
```

```
        <FONT SIZE="+1">Gigantor, Inc.</FONT>
    </TD>

    <TD WIDTH=50%><IMG HEIGHT=31 WIDTH=47 SRC="Envelope.gif" BORDER=0
    ALT="Envelope Picture">
    <A HREF="mailto:sales@gigantor.com">email: sales@gigantor.com</A></TD>
    </TR>

    <TR>
    <TD>650 Castro Street, Suite #120-228</TD>
    </TR>

    <TR>
    <TD>Mountain View, CA 94041</TD>
    </TR>

    <TR>
    <TD>Phone: (800) 408-6600</TD>
    </TR>
</TABLE>

</FORM>
</BODY>
</HTML>
```

All of the form items have variable names that you can see by looking at the HTML for keywords like **NAME="variableName."** The variable names are set to the values specified by the **VALUE** keyword. These are important items to understand in order to use forms, because the variables and their values are sent to the server for your CGI/ISAPI code fragments to process.

Each list box begins with a **<SELECT>** tag and ends with a **</SELECT>** delimiter tag. This tells the browser that everything within these blocks is part of the drop-down list box item, and hence an option for the user to select. There is also one name associated with each one (each **<SELECT>...</SELECT>** block), our HTML variable name —just like a variable in any other language. The **VALUE** attribute identifies possible values this variable can be set to, and exists between the **<OPTION>** tag and **</OPTION>** delimiter. The text displayed between the **<OPTION>** tag and the **</OPTION>** delimiter are the words in the pop-up menu that the user sees. Figure 2.4 shows what the user would see with this source.

Watch Variable Names

Your variable names in your HTML source will have the identical name in your CGI/ISAPI sources. Have a copy of your HTML present in text form while writing the code to handle your form. Names are case-sensitive unless you write code for them to be otherwise.

There is also a **SELECTED** attribute within the various drop-down list box items: This tells the browser that this is the default item and should be selected on a refresh or a reset action. If the user selected nothing, this default value specified by the **SELECTED** attribute would set the variable **NAME** to that **VALUE** (shown in Figure 2.4) and send it to the server upon a submit action (which we'll discuss later in this chapter). In the drop-down list shown in Figure 2.4, the variable **foosball** would equal the string **woodDeluxe**.

In Table 2.1, all the items on the left are the values that the variable **foosball** can be set to. The **foosball** variable is set to the value when the user selects the item on the right from the drop-down list element. The items on the right side before the </OPTION> delimiter are the text appearing in the drop-down list box that the user sees.

How are the variables selected? For example, when the customer selects the item "Arcade Premier Table" from the drop-down list (Figure 2.4) and if he or she submitted that data to the server, the variable **foosball** would be equal to the string **grayArcade** when the server received the form data. But how is the data transmitted to the server? These values are transmitted to the server as strings, and it's up to us to convert them to numerical values (floating-point values or integers, for example) if that's what our server CGI/ISAPI code fragments are expecting.

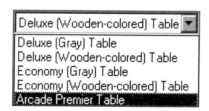

Figure 2.4

A drop-down list box control. The items displayed to the user are after the <OPTION> tag, and before the </OPTION> delimiter.

TABLE 2.1

THIS HTML CODE SNIPPET SHOWS HOW THE FORM ELEMENT IS HANDLED.

Values That foosball Can Be Set To	Text Visible
<OPTION VALUE=""grayDeluxe">	Deluxe (Gray) Table</OPTION>
<OPTION VALUE=""woodDeluxe">	Deluxe (Wood) Table</OPTION>
<OPTION VALUE=""grayEcono">	Economy (Gray) Table</OPTION>
<OPTION VALUE=""woodEcono">	Economy (Wood) Table</OPTION>
<OPTION VALUE=""grayArcade">	Arcade Premier Table</OPTION>

The **submit** tag identifies to the browser when the data is to be sent to the server:

```
<INPUT TYPE="submit" NAME="task" VALUE="Calculate Price">
```

In this case, the Calculate Price button will cause the server to send the form data to the browser. We'll explain **submit** with the **reset** tag later in this chapter in the section *How the Server Sees Things*.

When the customer selects this **submit** button, all the variable **NAME**s from the drop-down list boxes are sent back to the server, with their **VALUE** equal to that of the selected items. In addition, the button has a variable **NAME** that is also sent to the server. You can probably see how we can now process the customer's selections and later on we'll show you how to dynamically make a custom HTML form to send back.

From this example, we've seen how a form is coded in HTML, how options in drop-down list boxes are selected, and how the variables with their associated values are submitted back to the server. Now we need to investigate how this form data is sent from the server to our CGI/ISAPI code fragments.

How The Server Handles The Data

The server receives the form data from the browser and determines what code fragment to instantiate. The server is responsible for passing this information correctly to the designated code fragment, and even tells the fragment what function to call. How do these variables look to our code fragment? Surely we're not sharing global address space between the server and the code fragments, so let's see how the data is passed through.

HTML Variables

The variables come over in a contiguous string of data, and are separated by an ampersand (&). Each variable has an equals sign (=) following it that tells us what its value should be. All the variables are passed over as strings, and if you want a numerical value you'll have to convert it yourself, as mentioned earlier. The last variable will have no ampersand following it, but rather a carriage return.

Using HTML form in Listing 2.1, we would receive something like the following string upon a typical submit action from the user:

```
BuildYourOwn&task=Calculate%20Order&foosball=grayArcade&offense=redDynamos&
    defense=blue
        Dynamos&handles=woodGrips&hits=soccerBalls&cans=two&num_racks=none<CR>
```

Note that the task variable is assigned the string **Calculate%20Order**. The %20 is the space character translated by the client's browser when it has sent it to the server for processing. For control and special characters, the browser will put a "%" in its place, followed by its hexadecimal representation on the ASCII table. To properly parse these variables, we need to translate any changes that the browser made during data transmission. We'll cover this in Chapter 3, and will write some code to handle all of these cases for us automatically.

Essentially, our code fragment will receive a contiguous block of strings that we'll need to parse—and will even translate some special characters—in order to find the variables and their associated values. The variables and their values are dependent on the HTML form, and what the user selected.

Corresponding C++ Structures

In the previous section, we looked at the custom Foosball table page; here, we're going to look at how we would view those variables in a C/C++ structure. Previously, we saw a contiguous stream of characters that contained our variables and their associated values. For now, we'll ignore the parsing of the name/value pairs from the string and look at how that data would translate into a structure we could use in C++.

As a general rule, when translating variables from an HTML form to C/C++, if the variable is descriptive, keep it as a string; if it deals with quantity or monetary values, find the appropriate numerical container, such as an integer or a floating-point number. Let's take a look at Table 2.2, which shows the HTML variable names and an appropriate C++ data type. The "string" items are part of an ANSI **string** class that are officially part of the C++ language; if you're using MFC, you might prefer to replace these with the **CString** class.

You can clearly see this is screaming "structure," which leads us to something like the following:

```
typedef struct CustomFormStruct
{
    string    functionToPerform;
    string    taskSelected;
    string    foosballTable;
    string    offensiveBobsBigBoys;
    string    defensiveBobsBigBoys;
    string    tableHandles;
    string    ballsToHit;
    short     cansOfSpray;
    short     numberOfRacks;
}
```

TABLE 2.2

THE VARIABLE NAME FROM THE HTML FORM, AND AN APPROPRIATE DATA TYPE TO USE IN OUR C++ STRUCTURE.

Variable	C++ Data Type
function to call	string
task	string
foosball	string
offense	string
defense	string
handles	string
hits	string
cans	short int
num_racks	short int

Use The String Class Rather Than A Character Array

Using the ANSI **string** class is much more powerful than using a static array of characters. If it needs additional memory space, the **string** class handles these cases for you. It also binds string operations to the class, which makes your code more object-oriented.

Note that the **cans** and **num_racks** variables that are passed over send us text representations of numbers. To complicate things further, we used string representations of numerical values like "one," "two," and so on. This string representation of numerical values is easily remedied with a translation table. The variable should still be translated over as an integer, as we're only interested in the quantity of that particular item, not the item description. For numbers that are represented as strings such as "1" and "2," Standard C Library functions like **atoi()** and **atof()** will really come in handy.

Structures Are Not Always Best

There are cases in which you will build dynamic HTML forms and you will not know all of the form items on the page. In such cases, you cannot realistically make a structure to contain what you don't know. The best solution is to use an associative container, like the map template that's part of STL (which we use in Chapter 3).

HTML forms translate directly into C/C++ structures quite easily, which makes writing CGI/ISAPI code fragments a breeze. When translating numerical values from a string to a number-representative type, make sure your structure item has enough storage for the value. For example, don't convert a string that's over 32,767 to a short integer when you should use a long integer. Likewise, don't convert a decimal number string representation to a long integer rather than a float or double type. Also be sure to know your storage sizes for all possible variables, and keep this in mind when implementing your HTML form.

Various Controls

We've seen how to write HTML for the drop-down list box, but what about the other form elements in HTML? Here, we'll look at each one, learn how to implement them with HTML, and find out when to use them. In the next section of this chapter, we'll write some HTML forms that use the various elements, as well as briefly go through each one.

The most important things to remember when looking at form elements is that all are formatted **INPUT=type**, the variables are always **NAME=variable**, and the variable value is always **VALUE=something**. Once you understand this, all of the basic form elements are relatively easy to master.

We know the form elements come from our GUI operating systems like the Macintosh and Windows, and we'll use the same terminology here. The various types are drop-down list boxes, radio buttons, check boxes, text input, and multi-select list boxes. In addition to those common elements, there are also hidden items, image items, password input boxes, and **reset** and **submit** controls.

A user can choose radio buttons from many options. Radio buttons are functionally nearly identical to drop-down list boxes, and are used in the same interface situations. When a user selects an item, radio buttons allow all the other items in the same radio button group to become unselected. The radio button group is a collection of radio buttons that together affect the state of an item. Here's how you would write HTML to display radio buttons that give the user three options:

```
<INPUT TYPE="radio" NAME="group1"
    VALUE="Pepperoni"CHECKED>Pepperoni
<INPUT TYPE="radio" NAME="group1" VALUE="Anchovies"> Wonderful Fish
<INPUT TYPE="radio" NAME="group1" VALUE="Garlic">Garlic
```

Upon a **submit** action that sends the form to the server, we would have one variable, **group1**, equal to the text of the selected item. For example, in the string that the server receives, we would have something like:

```
"group1=Pepperoni&nextvariable=something
```

Radio buttons take up more real estate in the users' browser than drop-down list boxes. However, with radio buttons, users can see all the items without having to click on something. To implement a group of radio buttons, be sure to set the **NAME** field identically in each radio button item; the client's browser will then handle this as one group.

To implement multiple groups of radio buttons, be sure to use a different **NAME** for each group.

Check boxes represent a toggle state, generally turning something on or off. There are no group-type options as with radio buttons or drop-down list boxes. If a check box is not selected, no variable name is passed to the server, as in the following:

```
<INPUT TYPE="checkbox" NAME="country1" VALUE="Czech"
    CHECKED>Czech Republic
<INPUT TYPE="checkbox" NAME="chexMix" VALUE="ChexPartyMix">
    Check this if you like Chex Party Mix
```

The first check box has variable **country1** and the value, when selected, will be **Czech**; this check box is by default checked by using the **CHECKED** directive. The user would see the string "Czech Republic."

Text input items are trivial; all you need to note is that you can limit the size of the text by using the MAXLENGTH directive and the width of the text box using the SIZE directive. Here's an example:

```
<INPUT TYPE="text" NAME="textField1" SIZE="4"MAXLENGTH="8">
    Number of Foosball Tables
```

Here, we have a variable named **textField1**, with no initial value set; the text is then blank. We could have set some default text using **VALUE**="some text," but we opted not to in this case so that the field will be initially blank for user input. We've limited the width of the input text to four characters and the size to 8 characters; the client's browser will then restrict input to this many characters. A beep or alert will sound if a user tries to enter more. Text input items are great for gathering user information, such as phone number and email address, and for user feedback, such as a message or comment about your site.

Other form elements that we'll be using later on are hidden variables, images, and password text; they're set up in nearly the same way as the items we've just covered.

More Examples

In this section, we're going to create several new forms that use the various types of input form element tags. If you're new to HTML, this section will help you understand forms in even greater detail than we've already discussed.

The Guest Book HTML

There's nothing more classic than the guest book page. Surprisingly, some people act like it's rocket science to implement one—nothing could be further from the truth. Here, we'll implement the HTML for our guest book; in Chapter 7, we'll implement the CGI and ISAPI code, and the datastore for this same HTML page. This example is not only very simple, but it also demonstrates the fundamentals of HTML form handling that you'll use on other forms you implement.

For a guest book page, we normally want some type of banner at the top that tells us what this page does. We might also want some navigational buttons. Here, however, we're only going to look at the guest book, so the navigational buttons would go to nowhere and would therefore be overkill.

A typical guest book will want user information, such as name, address, city, state, zip, phone number, and email address. That's all. They're relatively simple strings and look something like:

```
Your Name<INPUT TYPE="text" NAME="name" SIZE=48 MAXLENGTH=48>
Your Street<INPUT TYPE="text" NAME="address1" SIZE=48 MAXLENGTH=48>
```

You can see how we're formatting the input text items with their variables. We've also included a size limitation that the user's browser will enforce—this prevents 3 percent of the population from writing their entire life's story within the confines of your name field. Believe me, if you do not restrict the amount of text a user can input, someone will test these limits. Add size restrictions where possible to prevent potential problems down the road. When the server receives the size limitation and passes it on to your code fragment, you'll typically store it in a file, or some database that you can interface with using ODBC; we'll do just that in more detail in Chapter 6. Listing 2.2 shows the guest book HTML, Figure 2.5 shows the result. For your convenience, the text input items are shaded. Also, the text input items and the text that the user sees are aligned with HTML tags.

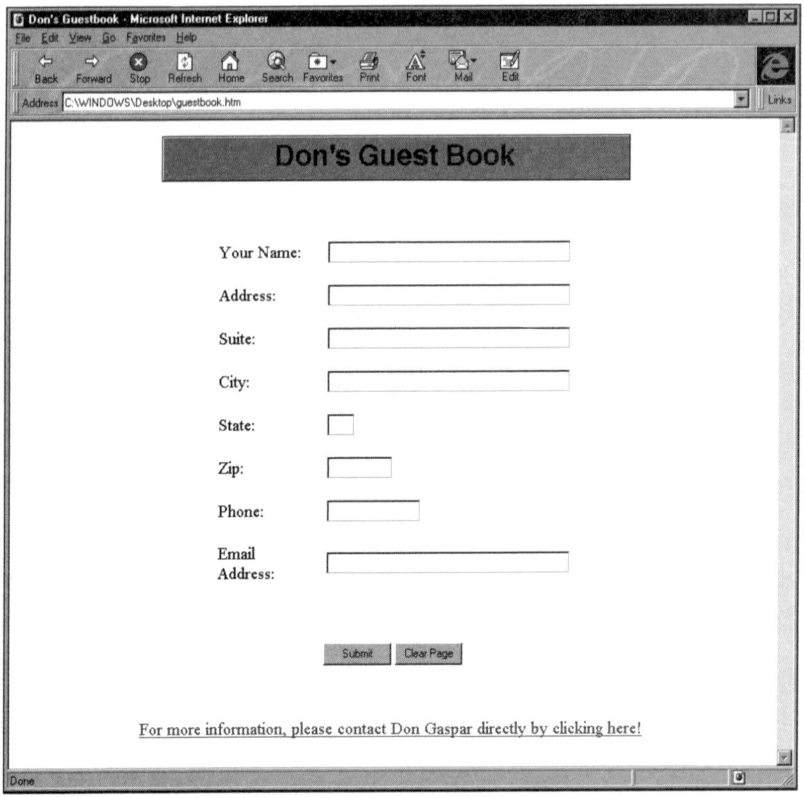

Figure 2.5
The guest book as the user views it with the browser.

LISTING 2.2   THE GUEST BOOK HTML.

```
<!Chapter 2 Guestbook HTML by Don Gaspar>
<HTML>

<HEAD>
<!Here's the title of our page. Note the beginning and ending tags.>
<TITLE>Don's Guestbook</TITLE>
</HEAD>

<BODY BGCOLOR="#FFFFFF" LINK="#FF0000" VLINK="#800080"
    TEXT="#000000">

<!This is just our fancy border at the top of the page>
<CENTER>
<IMG HEIGHT=48 WIDTH=504 SRC=
```

```
   "http://www.gigantor.com/articles/assets/auto_generated_images/
   img_10b1c001.gif"
   BORDER=0 >
</CENTER>

<!These place spaces vertically between items>
<BR><BR><BR>

<!Everything from the FORM tag until the /FORM tag is encapsulated within
    the form>
<FORM ACTION="/scripts/GuestBook.dll?AddUser" METHOD="POST">

<!Here, we've placed our items in a table to line them up>
<CENTER>
<TABLE BORDER=0 CELLSPACING=20 WIDTH=400 HEIGHT=18>
<TR><TD><P>Your Name:</TD><TD><INPUT TYPE="text" NAME= "name"
    SIZE=48></TD></TR>
<TR><TD><P>Address:</TD><TD><INPUT TYPE="text" NAME= "address1"
    SIZE=48></TD></TR>
<TR><TD><P>Suite:</TD><TD><INPUT TYPE="text" NAME= "address2"
    SIZE=48></TD></TR>
<TR><TD><P>City:</TD><TD><INPUT TYPE="text" NAME= "city"
    SIZE=48></TD></TR>
<TR><TD><P>State:</TD><TD><INPUT TYPE="text" NAME= "state"
    SIZE=2></TD></TR>
<TR><TD><P>Zip:</TD><TD><INPUT TYPE="text" NAME= "zip"
    SIZE=10></TD></TR>
<TR><TD><P>Phone:</TD><TD><INPUT TYPE="text" NAME= "phone"
    SIZE=16></TD></TR>
<TR><TD><P>Email Address:</TD><TD><INPUT TYPE="text" NAME= "emailAddress"
    SIZE=48></TD></TR>
</TABLE>
</CENTER>

<BR><BR><BR>
<CENTER>
<INPUT TYPE="submit" VALUE="Submit">
<INPUT TYPE="reset" VALUE="Clear Page">
</CENTER>
</FORM>

<BR><BR><BR>
<CENTER>
<P><A HREF="http://www.gigantor.com">
```

```
    For more information, please contact Don Gaspar directly by clicking
        here!</A>
</CENTER>

</BODY>
</HTML>
```

Example Survey

Ever need to ask some questions and pool the results? The form in Figure 2.6 presents a few different form elements all on one convenient page to demonstrate

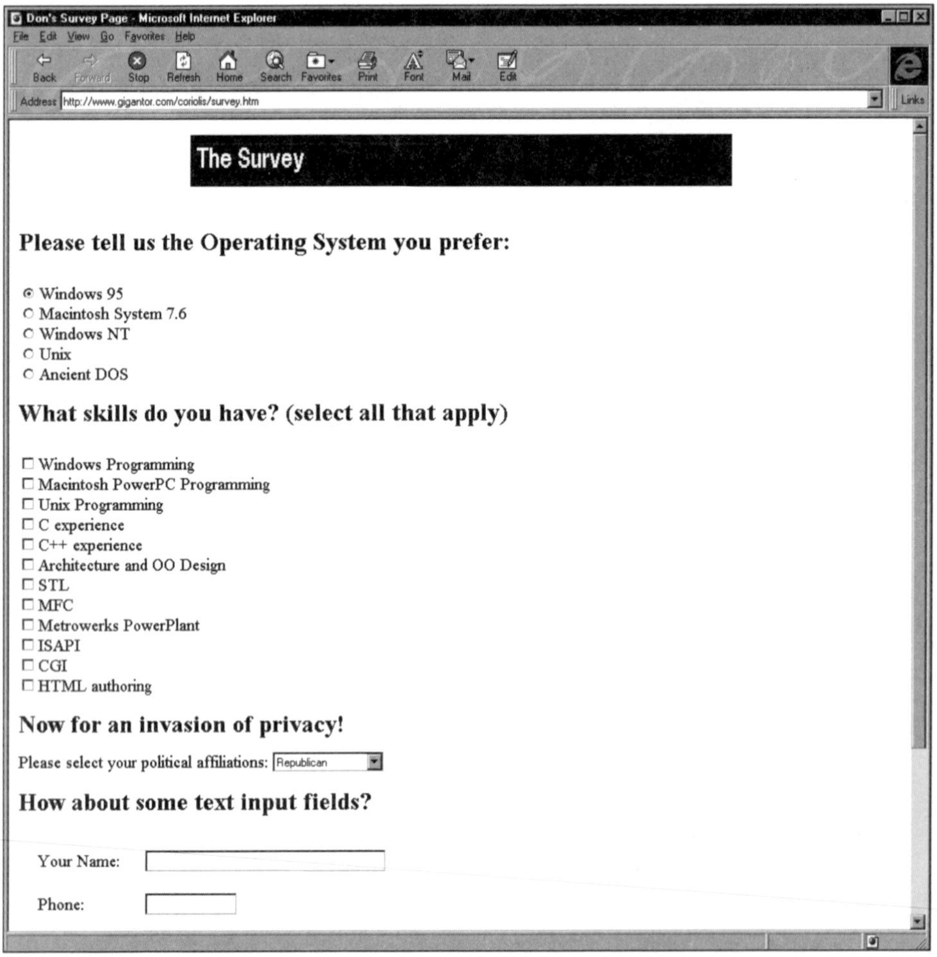

Figure 2.6
Example survey form.

how to use the various form elements with HTML. It's mostly provided as a test of the various control elements of HTML. Listing 2.3 shows the survey page HTML sources (the control form items are shaded). If you have any questions about how any of these form items works, this is the example to read through.

LISTING 2.3   THE SURVEY PAGE HTML SOURCES.

```
<!Chapter 2 Sample Survey HTML by Don Gaspar>
<HTML>

<HEAD>
<!Here's the title of our page. Note the beginning and ending tags>
<TITLE>Don's Survey Page</TITLE>
</HEAD>

<BODY BGCOLOR="#FFFFFF" LINK="#FF0000" VLINK="#800080"
    TEXT="#000000">

<!This is just our fancy border at the top of the page>
<CENTER>
<IMG HEIGHT=48 WIDTH=504 SRC=
    "http://www.gigantor.com/articles/assets/auto_generated_images/
    img_10b1c001.gif"
    BORDER=0 >
</CENTER>

<!These place spaces vertically between items>
<BR><BR><BR>

<!Everything from the FORM tag until the /FORM tag is encapsulated
    within the form>
<FORM ACTION="/scripts/GuestBook.dll?DoSurvey" METHOD="POST">

<!Here, we'll do one radio button group>
<H2>Please tell us the Operating System you prefer:</H2><BR>
<INPUT TYPE="radio" NAME="group1" VALUE="Windows"
    CHECKED>Windows 95<BR>
<INPUT TYPE="radio" NAME="group1" VALUE="Mac">
    Macintosh System 7.6<BR>
<INPUT TYPE="radio" NAME="group1" VALUE="WinNT">Windows NT<BR>
<INPUT TYPE="radio" NAME="group1" VALUE="Unix">Unix<BR>
<INPUT TYPE="radio" NAME="group1" VALUE="DOS">Ancient DOS<BR>
```

```
<!Now for some check boxes>
<H2>What skills do you have? (select all that apply)</H2><BR>
<INPUT TYPE="checkbox" NAME="windersProg" VALUE="yes">
    Windows Programming<BR>
<INPUT TYPE="checkbox" NAME="macProg" VALUE="yes">
    Macintosh PowerPC Programming<BR>
<INPUT TYPE="checkbox" NAME="unixProg" VALUE="yes">
    Unix Programming<BR>
<INPUT TYPE="checkbox" NAME="cProg" VALUE="yes">
    C experience<BR>
<INPUT TYPE="checkbox" NAME="cppProg" VALUE="yes">
    C++ experience<BR>
<INPUT TYPE="checkbox" NAME="ooaProg" VALUE="yes">
    Architecture and OO Design<BR>
<INPUT TYPE="checkbox" NAME="stlProg" VALUE="yes">STL<BR>
<INPUT TYPE="checkbox" NAME="mfcProg" VALUE="yes">MFC<BR>
<INPUT TYPE="checkbox" NAME="powerplantProg" VALUE="yes">
    Metrowerks PowerPlant<BR>
<INPUT TYPE="checkbox" NAME="isapiProg" VALUE="yes">ISAPI<BR>
<INPUT TYPE="checkbox" NAME="cgiProg" VALUE="yes">CGI<BR>
<INPUT TYPE="checkbox" NAME="htmlProg" VALUE="yes">
    HTML authoring<BR>

<!Here, we will use a drop-down list>
<H2>Now for an invasion of privacy!</H2>
Please select your political affiliations:
<SELECT NAME="dropListVariable">
<OPTION VALUE="fascist">Republican</OPTION>
<OPTION VALUE="weakling">Democrat</OPTION>
<OPTION VALUE="radical">Green Party</OPTION>
<OPTION VALUE="marxist">Communist/Socialist</OPTION>
</SELECT>

<!Now some text input items aligned in a table>
<H2>How about some text input fields?</H2>
<TABLE BORDER=0 CELLSPACING=20 WIDTH=400 HEIGHT=18>
<TR><TD><P>Your Name:</TD><TD><INPUT TYPE="text"
    NAME= "name" SIZE=48></TD></TR>
<TR><TD><P>Phone:</TD><TD><INPUT TYPE="text"
    NAME= "phone" SIZE=16></TD></TR>
<TR><TD><P>Email Address:</TD><TD><INPUT TYPE="text"
    NAME= "emailAddress" SIZE=48></TD></TR>
</TABLE>
```

```
<BR><BR><BR>
<CENTER>

<INPUT TYPE="submit" VALUE="Submit">
<INPUT TYPE="reset" VALUE="Clear Page">
</CENTER>
</FORM>

<BR><BR><BR>
<CENTER>
<P><A HREF="http://www.gigantor.com">
    For more information, please contact Don Gaspar directly by clicking
      here!</A>
</CENTER>

</BODY>
</HTML>
```

Taking Orders

Let's say we've opened up an online pizza shop, and we're taking orders from our Web server. To do this, we need to implement a process to automatically print our orders when they arrive to our store's Web server. Right now, however, we're only going to concern ourselves with the HTML to implement the correct form for our store. Why would we print out the orders rather than have them emailed to us? For food, unlike other merchandise, delivery time is not in hours or days, but rather in minutes. With email systems, long delays are common, which would be rather perturbing to your customer if his or her order was not ready upon pickup. Figure 2.7 shows the home page for our online pizza shop. Here, the customer creates a pizza and gets a price quotation. When the customer is ready to order, he or she selects the Order Now button. You could require online customers to pre-pay for their pizza with a charge card; we'll be doing this later on.

A really great use of this concept would be to implement your code fragment to check what time it is when the customer orders. This way you could tell the consumer you were closed if it was after hours. You could also verify the customer's area code to make sure he or she is local, so someone from the Czech Republic isn't ordering a pizza from your shop in California! Listing 2.4 shows the online pizza order form.

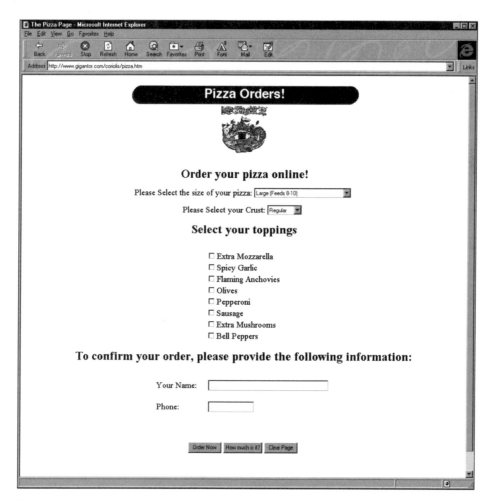

Figure 2.7
The online pizza shop home page.

LISTING 2.4   THE ONLINE PIZZA ORDER FORM.

```
<!Chapter 2 Pizza Order HTML by Don Gaspar>
<HTML>

<HEAD>
<!Here's the title of our page. Note the beginning and ending tags>
<TITLE>The Pizza Page</TITLE>
</HEAD>

<BODY BGCOLOR="#FFFFFF" LINK="#FF0000" VLINK="#800080"
    TEXT="#000000">
```

```
<!This is just our fancy border at the top of the page>
<CENTER>
<IMG HEIGHT=48 WIDTH=504
    SRC="http://www.gigantor.com/articles/assets/pizzabanner.gif"  BORDER=0 >
<BR><IMG HEIGHT=100 WIDTH=100
    SRC="http://www.gigantor.com/articles/assets/pizzafest.gif">

<!These place spaces vertically between items>
<BR><BR><BR>

<!Everything from the FORM tag until the /FORM tag is encapsulated within
the form>
<FORM ACTION="/scripts/Pizza.dll?OrderPizza" METHOD="POST">

<!Here we will use a drop-down list>
<H2>Order your Pizza online!</H2>
Please select the size of your pizza:
<SELECT NAME="pizzaSize">
<OPTION VALUE="personal">Personal Pan Pizza</OPTION>
<OPTION VALUE="medium">Medium (Feeds 4-5)</OPTION>
<OPTION VALUE="large">Large (Feeds 8-10)</OPTION>
<OPTION VALUE="godzilla">The King Kong Monster Pizza (Feeds 20)
    </OPTION>
</SELECT>
<BR><BR>

Please select your Crust:
<SELECT NAME="crust">
<OPTION VALUE="regular">Regular</OPTION>
<OPTION VALUE="thick">Thick</OPTION>
<OPTION VALUE="thin">Thin</OPTION>
<OPTION VALUE="pan">Square Pan</OPTION>
</SELECT>

<! Now for some check boxes>
<H2>Select your toppings</H2><BR>
<TABLE>
<TR><TD><INPUT TYPE="checkbox" NAME="extraCheese" VALUE="yes">
    </TD><TD>Extra Mozzarella</TD></TR>
<TR><TD><INPUT TYPE="checkbox" NAME="garlic" VALUE="yes">
    </TD><TD>Spicy Garlic</TD></TR>
<TR><TD><INPUT TYPE="checkbox" NAME="anchovies" VALUE="yes">
    </TD><TD>Flaming Anchovies</TD></TR>
<TR><TD><INPUT TYPE="checkbox" NAME="olives" VALUE="yes">
```

```
    </TD><TD>Olives</TD></TR>
<TR><TD><INPUT TYPE="checkbox" NAME="pepperoni" VALUE="yes">
    </TD><TD>Pepperoni</TD></TR>
<TR><TD><INPUT TYPE="checkbox" NAME="sausage" VALUE="yes">
    </TD><TD>Sausage</TD></TR>
<TR><TD><INPUT TYPE="checkbox" NAME="footFungus" VALUE="yes">
    </TD><TD>Extra Mushrooms</TD></TR>
<TR><TD><INPUT TYPE="checkbox" NAME="peppers" VALUE="yes">
    </TD><TD>Bell Peppers</TD></TR>
</TABLE>

<!Now some text input items aligned in a table>
<H2>To confirm your order, please provide the following information:</H2>
<TABLE BORDER=0 CELLSPACING=20 WIDTH=400 HEIGHT=18>
<TR><TD><P>Your Name:</TD><TD><INPUT TYPE="text"
    NAME= "name" SIZE=48></TD></TR>
<TR><TD><P>Phone:</TD><TD><INPUT TYPE="text"
    NAME= "phone" SIZE=16></TD></TR>
</TABLE>

<BR><BR><BR>
<INPUT TYPE="submit" VALUE="Order Now">
<INPUT TYPE="submit" VALUE="How much is it?">
<INPUT TYPE="reset" VALUE="Clear Page">
</FORM>

<BR><BR><BR>
<CENTER>
<P><A HREF="mailto:don@gigantor.com">Click here to email us!</A>
</CENTER>

</BODY>
</HTML>
```

How The Server Sees Things

We've briefly seen how variables are passed to the server from the user's browser, then from the server to your code fragment. Your code fragment (CGI/ISAPI) passes information back to the user's browser through the server. Here, we're going to briefly see how the server figures out what code fragment to call, and what triggers the actual submission of data from the client to the server.

HANDLING DATA BEFORE THE SERVER

There are a number of scripting languages that can embed themselves within an HTML document. Since the scripts are embedded as HTML comments, browsers without the capability to interpret them do nothing. Two notable scripting languages are Microsoft's VBScript, and Netscape's JavaScript. JavaScript has nothing to do with Java, but is based on LiveScript (the Java name was licensed from Sun). You can then use a script to parse your data before it gets passed to the server.

For example, why use a busy server to check for the presence of a name field on a form, and then send an error message back to the user? This not only keeps your server busy performing mundane tasks, but prevents it from handling serious CPU-intensive chores as well as it should.

Listing 2.5 shows how to use VBScript for the Guest Book HTML page. Here we check for the presence of necessary form field data, and if it's not present, we display an alert to the user.

This keeps the server free from checking for the presence of this data, and also from responding to the user. The script runs on the clients' processor within their Web browser as a plug-in (or is build in) , so it costs the server nothing. The only expense here is the few minutes it takes to write the script.

Because some browsers won't have scripting language interpreters installed, you'll still have to check for data being properly submitted on the server. However, adding a script ensures that some of your clients will have preprocessing of their data before submitting it to your already-busy server.

Coriolis Group Books offers a VBScript book, *VBScript and ActiveX Wizardry*, which is a fine introductory-level text.

LISTING 2.5   SOURCE FOR VBSGUESTBOOK.HTM.

```
<!Chapter 2 Guestbook HTML by Don Gaspar>
<HTML>

<HEAD>
<!Here's the title of our page. Note the beginning and ending tags>
<TITLE>Don's Guestbook</TITLE>
</HEAD>

<BODY BGCOLOR="#FFFFFF" LINK="#FF0000" VLINK="#800080" TEXT="#000000">
```

```
<!This is just our fancy border at the top of the page>
<CENTER>
<IMG HEIGHT=48 WIDTH=504 SRC=
    "http://www.gigantor.com/articles/assets/auto_generated_images/
      img_10b1c001.gif"
        BORDER=0 >
</CENTER>

<!These place spaces vertically between items>
<BR><BR><BR>

<!Everything from the FORM tag until the /FORM tag is encapsulated withing
the form>
<FORM NAME="VBForm" ACTION="/scripts/FormHandler.exe" METHOD="POST">

<!Here we've placed our items in a table to line them up>
<!This sample uses VBScript to check the input form items>
<!By Don Gaspar>
<CENTER>
<TABLE BORDER=0 CELLSPACING=20 WIDTH=400 HEIGHT=18>
<TR><TD><P>Your Name:</TD><TD><INPUT TYPE="text" NAME= "name"
    SIZE=48></TD></TR>
<TR><TD><P>Address:</TD><TD><INPUT TYPE="text" NAME= "address1"
    SIZE=48></TD></TR>
<TR><TD><P>Suite:</TD><TD><INPUT TYPE="text" NAME= "address2"
    SIZE=48></TD></TR>
<TR><TD><P>City:</TD><TD><INPUT TYPE="text" NAME= "city"
    SIZE=48></TD></TR>
<TR><TD><P>State:</TD><TD><INPUT TYPE="text" NAME= "state"
     SIZE=2></TD></TR>
<TR><TD><P>Zip:</TD><TD><INPUT TYPE="text" NAME= "zip"
    SIZE=10></TD></TR>
<TR><TD><P>Phone:</TD><TD><INPUT TYPE="text" NAME= "phone"
    SIZE=16></TD></TR>
<TR><TD><P>Email Address:</TD><TD><INPUT TYPE="text" NAME= "emailAddress"
    SIZE=48></TD></TR>
</TABLE>
</CENTER>

<BR><BR><BR>
<CENTER>
<INPUT NAME="VBParseControl" TYPE="button" VALUE="Send">
<INPUT TYPE="reset" VALUE="Clear Page">
</CENTER>
</FORM>
```

```
<script language="VBS">
<!--
SUB VBParseControl_OnClick()
IF ((LEN(VBForm.name.value) > 2) AND (LEN(VBForm.address1.value) > 4) AND _
    (LEN(VBForm.city.value) >= 2) AND (LEN(VBForm.state.value) >= 2) AND _
    (LEN(VBForm.zip.value) >= 5) AND (LEN(VBForm.phone.value) >= 7) AND _
    (LEN(VBForm.emailAddress.value) > 5)) THEN
    VBForm.Submit' here's our submit to server action
ELSE
  MsgBox "Please fill in all items on this form before submitting.",0,
        "Missing Form Data"
END IF
END SUB
-->
</script>

<BR><BR><BR>
<CENTER>
<P><A HREF="http://www.gigantor.com">For more information,
    please contact Don Gaspar directly by clicking here!</A>
</CENTER>

</BODY>
</HTML>
```

HTML For Calling CGI And ISAPI

We've seen how the module name was called from HTML using the **<FORM>** tag. Now, let's briefly go over that item. The tag

```
<FORM ACTION="/scripts/games.dll?BuildYourOwn" METHOD="POST">
```

encapsulates all form items from the tag, until the **</FORM>** delimiter tag is reached. All the form elements in between these tags will be sent to the server in a stream of text.

Another way to do the same thing is to use hidden variables. In HTML, you could hide a variable on your page within a form, and this variable would always be sent to the server upon receiving a **submit** directive. Something like

```
<INPUT TYPE="MfcISAPICommand" NAME="BuildYourOwn">
<FORM ACTION="/scripts/games.dll">
```

would have the same action as the **FORM** tags above.

The key to remember is that all your **INPUT** items will reside within your **FORM** tags, or the customer's data will not be sent over to the server. The **ACTION** the server takes will depend on what you specify as an option in the beginning **FORM** tag. If this tag is incorrect, your data will be invalid. In the case of an ISAPI MFC DLL, it won't locate the correct member function and will return an error to the user. It's important to be very careful when writing your tags so that proper code is instantiated on the server.

Submit And Reset

To understand **submit** and **reset** better, let's review the code from Listing 2.1 and see the form from Figure 2.1.

When the user selects the Calculate Price button, this **INPUT** tag tells the browser that it should submit all the form data between the <**FORM**> tag and the <**/FORM**> delimiter to the Web server. In addition, this button has a variable associated with it called **task**, whose value will be the same as the name of the button. It doesn't need a variable, unless you're planning on doing something with it. If there is no variable associated with a **submit**, all the form data is still sent over. If there is a variable, it's among the data sent to the server.

A variable name for a **submit** button is required with a page you've implemented that contains multiple **submits**, each with different actions; here, the variable name will then identify to your CGI/ISAPI code fragment what action you are to take when receiving the form data.

One other button that needs some explaining: the **reset** button. This will change all the items back to their default values. For example, if the user changed some of the list box items, the original settings will return. In this case, this information is not sent to the server; rather, the browser refreshes the page and clears everything out without troubling the server.

Returning Feedback To The Client

After your CGI/ISAPI code fragment has received some data, you're going to want to return some kind of feedback to the user: either an acknowledgement that the data was received properly, or an error message. An example might be a credit card processing form (which we'll implement in Chapters 10 and 11) where a bad card number or incorrect expiration date was sent over. In such a case, you must then inform the customer, and possibly redirect him or her back to the page where there was a problem.

Feedback is necessary when writing HTML forms, so it's essential to understand a couple things: how forms work and how to write HTML in general. At one time or another, you'll be required to make dynamic HTML and send it directly to the user's browser (well, through the Web server). This dynamic HTML will make your sites robust and different for every user depending upon his or her actions. HTML is also simple to master, and after writing a few pages of your own, you'll see why.

Summary

We've covered a lot of material in this chapter. We looked at HTML, and how to implement forms in general. Next, we saw all the various form elements, and how their variables and values are set. Finally, we learned how the data is sent in a contiguous stream to the server. In the next chapter, we'll start to actually process this data and perform actions based on the form items a user selects.

While we're going to be working predominantly in C++, you' ll still have to write forms in HTML to interact with your C++ code fragments. Chapter 3 will link together the server-end processing of the forms we've written in HTML in this chapter.

THE CGI CRASH
COURSE

3

But what is it good for?

*Engineer at the Advanced Computing Systems Division of IBM,
1968, commenting on the microchip*

What is this CGI—and what can we do with it? CGI stands for Common Gateway Interface, which supplies a way to extend the capabilities of a Web server programmatically. Think of CGI code fragments as plug-ins that add new commands and capabilities to the Web server, giving it near-unlimited flexibility.

With CGI, we can use **stdin** and **stdout** to receive and send data through the Web server to the client's Web browser. We can also do the same through arguments passed in **main**(); we'll cover both approaches in this chapter. You can use your knowledge of programming with streams as well as these standard methods to extend your server's capabilities.

An HTML form is, after all, just some variables and their associated values. With CGI, we'll use streams and other familiar concepts to parse these variables, perform tasks on the server side, and send the results back to the client's browser.

With CGI, we can:

- Verify a credit card

- Store information in a database

- Retrieve a catalog of items from a database

- Build a graphic dynamically

- Build HTML dynamically

- Display images from a video camera

- Do anything else you can do with **stdio** from an application

We'll do all of these things (except use a video camera) in this book.

In this chapter, we'll discuss CGI in detail and then implement several code fragments. We'll learn to generate HTML dynamically, and isolate and parse the variable stream sent over from the browser with a C++ class that we'll write ourselves.

What Is CGI?

CGI is not a programming language, but a specification: CGI code fragments can be written in PERL, Visual Basic, AppleScript, VBScript, Delphi, Pascal, C, C++, and probably several other languages. In this book, we'll focus on using Visual C++, and emphasize performance.

CGI consists of small programs—code fragments—that the server instantiates after receiving the go-ahead from a client's browser. These code fragments are loaded into memory and executed. When they finish their task, they exit and clean up after themselves (theoretically). Every time the server runs a copy of the code fragment, it's independent of the previous state—a new copy loads each time.

Loading a new copy of a code fragment and unloading it after every use is expensive in terms of an operating system's time. However, your CGI code fragments are (hopefully) efficient miniature applications that perform specific small tasks. As a result, overhead will be as minimal as the CGI architecture will permit.

In Chapter 4, we'll revisit this loading and unloading of code fragments when we cover ISAPI, which takes care of this problem and enormously improves performance.

How CGI Extends The Server

CGI extends the server by offering custom actions based on client responses in their HTML pages and by allowing you to write nearly anything you want in C++. There are a few limitations, however. Let's talk about a way we can extend the server by using the classic textbook example Hello World. In this case, we'll create an HTML form. The user will click on a button, causing our CGI code fragment to generate an HTML page that is sent back to the user's browser and states, "Hello CGI World!"

As CGI uses **stdio**, a code fragment like

```
void main(int argc, char *argv[])
{
    printf("Hello world\n\n");
} // main...
```

certainly represents a simple CGI application (provided the Web server instantiates it at some point). It is, however, missing a few details and wouldn't return the expected results to the client's browser. The server and browser communicate with one another using a protocol called HTTP, using a language called—you guessed it—HTML. For the above program to work, we need to describe what type of data we're sending to the browser: A server could be sending an image or some other MIME type. If it thought the Hello World character string was the incorrect content type, it would try to display it accordingly.

For the above code fragment to work, we need to change a few things in the source code and make it appear as in Listing 3.1.

LISTING 3.1   THE HELLO WORLD CGI CODE FRAGMENT.

```
//
//    File: HelloWorld.cpp
//    By: Don Gaspar
//
//    This is the source for the CGI Hello World example from Chapter 3
//    in the book Visual Developer Web Commerce Programming With Visual
//    C++.
```

```
//      The publisher is The Coriolis Group.
//
//      You may reach the author at: don@gigantor.com
//

// Some standard headers we're going to need in here
#include <ostream.h>
#include <fstream.h>
#include <stdio.h>

//
//      Function: BeginHeader
//      Purpose: Outputs the appropriate header information to
//         stdout for a Web browser to display.
//      Arguments: inTitle, the title of the dynamic page you are
//         creating.
void
BeginHeader(const char* inTitle)
{
    cout << "Content-type:TEXT/HTML\n\n" << "<HTML><HEAD><TITLE>\n" <<
        inTitle << "\n</TITLE></HEAD><BODY>\n";
} // BeginHeader...

//
//      Function: EndHeader
//      Purpose: Outputs the delimiter tags corresponding to those set by
//         PrintHeader() for proper HTML display.
//      Arguments:  None
//
void
EndHeader()
{
    cout << "</BODY></HTML>\n";
} // EndHeader...

//
//      Well, we gotta start somewhere.
//
void
main()
{
    BeginHeader("Hello World");
    cout << "<H1> Hello CGI World!</H1>";
    EndHeader();
} // main...
```

We need to mention a few things briefly. The **BeginHeader**() function sends the content type of the page we're generating—text—to **stdout**, along with some tags that begin our HTML data. We then send the "Hello CGI World" string to **stdout**. The **EndHeader**() function sends delimiter tags to **stdout**, and ends our page. Listing 3.2 shows the HTML for instantiating the CGI code fragment.

LISTING 3.2 SOURCE FOR HELLOWORLD.HTM.

```
<!CGI Test page-By Don Gaspar>

<HTML>
<HEAD>
<TITLE>
<H1>CGI Test Page</H1><BR><BR><BR>
</TITLE>
</HEAD>

<BODY>

<FORM ACTION="/scripts/HelloWorld.exe" METHOD=POST>

<!Note:there's no form items to send over, only a submit for now>

<INPUT TYPE=submit VALUE="Hello CGI World!">
</FORM>

</BODY>
</HTML>
```

We can see from Listing 3.2 that the HelloWorld.exe code fragment instantiates when the user clicks the **submit** button; this is visible because the Form tag's attribute action is HelloWorld.EXE. The server launches the code fragment when it receives this **submit**, and then it builds HTML output so the client's browser can see what it has to say—"Hello CGI World!" Figure 3.1 displays the data that the code fragment sends back.

This useful, albeit simple, example demonstrates the basics of using **stdout** to perform input to a client's browser based on his or her clicking on the **submit** button. We sent text to the client's browser, but we could have sent another content type, such as an image, or another MIME type.

> **Note:** *HTML's content type is always text, because HTML is just a specially formatted text file.*

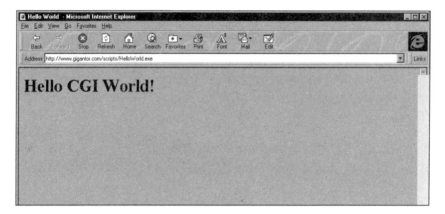

Figure 3.1
The dynamic results of the Hello World CGI code fragment.

We're now going to see more complex examples of CGI as well as some powerful tasks we can perform using CGI.

Examples Of Other CGI Tasks

Well, so what? Who wants a Hello World code fragment anyway, right? And who wants to manually send HTML strings through **stdout**? While this technique is powerful, it could get tiring rather quickly for a large CGI code fragment. For the Foosball site, instead of sending out strings through **stdout** over and over, I opted to stream headers for each page, and then add specific data to **stdout** following this header and then streams a footer. This allowed the HTML data I had to manually stream over to be minimal, as I didn't have to send the data for the same header and footer repeatedly. I then wrote a generic header and footer in HTML, and placed those files on our Web server so that my code fragment could have access to them. Combining this with sending strings via **stdout** like the Hello World example allows you to generate dynamic HTML with a minimal amount of code.

Listing 3.3 shows the code for a similar fragment that streams this header, builds a sample form dynamically, and streams the footer file. The routine **StreamFile()** is responsible for sending header and footer via **stdout**.

LISTING 3.3   SOURCE CODE FOR DYNAMICFORM.CPP.

```
//
//     File: DynamicForm.cpp
```

```
//      By: Don Gaspar
//
//      This is the source for the CGI Dynamic Form example from
//      Chapter 3 in the book Visual Developer Web Commerce Programming
//      With Visual C++. The publisher is The Coriolis Group.
//
//      You may reach the author at: don@gigantor.com
//

// Some standard headers we're going to need in here
#include <ostream.h>
#include <fstream.h>
#include <stdio.h>

// Our header and footer file names
const char *cHeaderName = "c:\\inetpub\\gigantor\\games\\head.htm";
const char *cFooterName = "c:\\inetpub\\gigantor\\games\\foot.htm";

//
//      Function: BeginHeader
//      Purpose: Outputs the appropriate header information to
//          stdout for a Web browser to display.
//      Arguments: inTitle, the title of the dynamic page you are creating.
//
void
BeginHeader(const char* inTitle)
{
    cout << "Content-type:TEXT/HTML\n\n" << "<HTML><HEAD><TITLE>\n" <<
        inTitle << "\n</TITLE></HEAD><BODY>\n";
} // BeginHeader...

//
//      Function: EndHeader
//      Purpose: Outputs the delimiter tags corresponding to those set by
//          PrintHeader() for proper HTML display.
//      Arguments: None
//
void
EndHeader()
{
    cout << "</BODY></HTML>\n";
} // EndHeader...

//
//      StreamFile
//      Input: char*, which is the name of the file to use with path.
//      Purpose:  Opens the designated file and streams it out through
//          stdout so the client's browser will get this dynamic HTML page.
```

```cpp
void
StreamFile(const char* inFile)
{
    try
    {
        ifstream file(inFile);        // file stream

        if (!file)                    // if we don't get the file, then
            throw(-1);                // throw an exception

        char buffer[80];              // just a line of characters

        // Here, we loop through the file line by line until we hit the
        // end sending all the data to cout.
        while (file.get(buffer,sizeof(buffer)))
            cout << buffer;

        file.close();
    }

    catch(...)
    {
        cout << "<center><b>Couldn't locate the header file.
            <br></center></b>";
    }
} // CGamesExtension::StreamFile...

//
//    Function: WriteFormItem
//    Purpose: Just makes an edit text item for the user to change.
//    Arguments: Quantity of the items to initially display, text to
//    display.
void
WriteFormItem(int inQty, const char *inFormText)
{
    cout << "<INPUT TYPE=TEXT SIZE=2 NAME='' VALUE=" << inQty << ">" <<
        inFormText << "<br><br>";
} // WriteFormItem...

//
//    Well, we gotta start somewhere.
//
void
main()
```

```
{
    // As we're streaming a file, we'll need to identify the
    //  content type here.
    BeginHeader("Dynamic Forms Page");
    StreamFile(cHeaderName);          // fetch, Rover

    // Now we're going to build a mock form of items to test
    // this out with.
    cout << "<H1>Everything from here...!</H1><BR><BR><BR>";
    WriteFormItem(3, "Deluxe Foosball Tables");
    WriteFormItem(2, "Economy Foosball Tables");
    WriteFormItem(25, "Sets of Bob's Big Boy Foosball guys");
    cout << "<H1>To here was made by the CGI code fragment!
        </H1><BR><BR><BR>";

    StreamFile(cFooterName);       // fetch
    EndHeader();
} // main...
```

StreamFile() takes a path to a file as input, and uses an **ifstream** class (ANSI C++) to open the file and stream the data to the client. This function assumes the HTML is written correctly, and merely opens the file and streams it out. If the file cannot be found, an exception is thrown, which causes our code to immediately jump to the **catch**() block. The **catch**() block then displays an error to the client using **stdout** (refer back to Listing 3.3).

Streaming files dynamically allows you to write your HTML separately from your code fragment, which lets you write generic headers and footers, or even entire pages, and use them for a variety of CGI code fragments you write. Figure 3.2 shows how this dynamically generated form looks.

A function called **WriteFormItem**() takes an **integer** as input, and a **const char***. This function builds an input form item just to demonstrate how to do so from your code fragment. The form items here have no input **NAME**s in use, and are hence nonfunctional; I provide them here only as a demonstration.

Streaming files allows you to select any file, and pass it to the client's browser. If you want to change the content type and send an image back, you merely pass the file name into **StreamFile**(), and change the content type to your file type (assuming the browser supports this type of file).

We've written a few useful functions thus far. Later on in this chapter, we'll design a C++ class to encapsulate handling of this dynamic data.

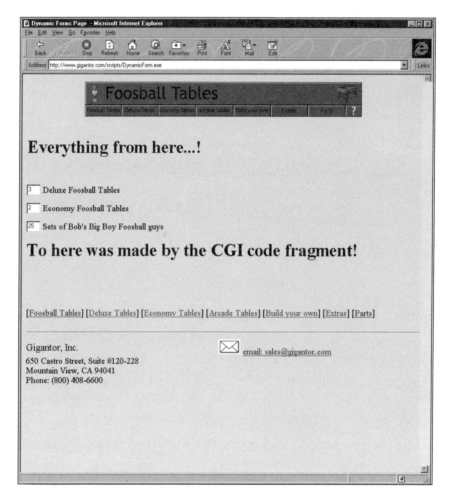

Figure 3.2
A dynamically generated form.

Server Variables

Thus far, we've only sent data back to the client using **stdout**, but there must be much more we can do here. In the next section of this chapter, we'll learn about bringing in data via **POST** and **GET**. Right now, let's visit the Web server and see what data we can gather from it for our code fragment to use.

A Web server contains a treasure trove of information that we can access via CGI: what operating system it's running on top of, who directed the client to our site, the size of the data being sent over is, and more. We can get this information from environment variables, using the **stdlib** function **getenv()**.

Note: The environmental variables in Table 3.1 detail information about the server. Very few of them contain information about the client.

Table 3.1 shows the available environmental variables. Not all of them are always valid—they will return **NULL** when you call **getenv**(). Figure 3.3 shows a sample page we've generated to display the available environmental variables for the client in HTML.

	TABLE 3.1

INTERNET INFORMATION SERVER ENVIRONMENT VARIABLES.

Variable	Meaning
ALL_HTTP	All HTTP headers that were not already parsed into one of the listed variables. These variables are of the form HTTP_<header field name>, for example.
HTTP_ACCEPT	Types of data that this server accepts. For IIS 3.0, the following types are supported: */*, q=0.300, audio/x-aiff, audio/basic, image/jpeg, image/gif, text/plain, and text/html.
HTTP_COOKIE	Any cookie set for the client that deals with your site.
HTTP_USER_AGENT	The client's browser. For example: Microsoft Internet Explorer/0.1 (Win32). Often lists "Mozilla" which is Netscape or compatible browser.
HTTP_REFERER	The URL of the page that referred us to this page. For example:webserver/samples/dbsamp/dbsamp3.htm.
HTTP_CONTENT_TYPE	Type of data sent over from the client to us, the server. For example: application/x-www-form-urlencoded.
HTTP_CONTENT_LENGTH	The size, in bytes, of the data the client sent to us.
AUTH_TYPE	The type of authorization in use. If the server has authenticated the user name, this will say "Basic." Otherwise, it will not be present.

(continued)

TABLE 3.1

INTERNET INFORMATION SERVER ENVIRONMENT VARIABLES (*CONTINUED*).

Variable	Meaning
CONTENT_LENGTH	The number of bytes that the script can expect to receive from the client.
CONTENT_TYPE	The content type of the information supplied in the body of a **POST** request.
GATEWAY_INTERFACE	The revision of the CGI (Common Gateway Interface) specification with which this server complies.
LOGON_USER	The user's Windows NT account.
PATH_INFO	Additional path information, as given by the client. This comprises the trailing part of the URL after the script name but before the query string (if any).
PATH_TRANSLATED	The value of PATH_INFO, but with any virtual path name expanded into a directory specification.
QUERY_STRING	The information that follows the question mark (?) in the URL that referenced this script.
REMOTE_ADDR	The IP address of the client.
REMOTE_HOST	The host name of the client.
REMOTE_USER	The user name that the client supplies and that the server authenticates.
REQUEST_METHOD	The HTTP request method. **POST** or **GET**, for example.
SCRIPT_NAME	The name of the script program being executed.
SERVER_NAME	The server's host name (or IP address) as it should appear in self-referencing URLs.
SERVER_PORT	The TCP/IP port on which the request was received. This is generally 80 for normal HTTP connections.
SERVER_PORT_SECURE	The value 0 or 1. The value 1 indicates the request is on the encrypted port.

(continued)

TABLE 3.1

INTERNET INFORMATION SERVER ENVIRONMENT VARIABLES (*CONTINUED*).

Variable	Meaning
SERVER_PROTOCOL	The name and version of the information-retrieval protocol relating to this request, usually HTTP/1.0.
SERVER_SOFTWARE	The name and version of the Web server under which the Internet Server Extension is running.
URL	The URL of the request.

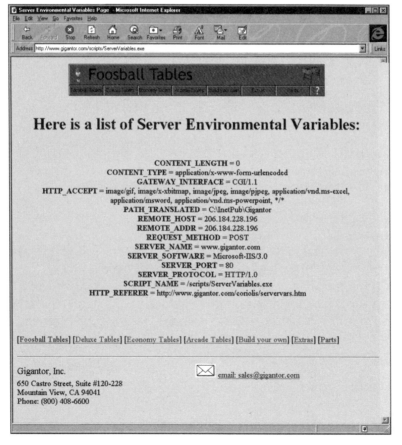

Figure 3.3
Server environmental variables displayed from the client's Web browser.

In the CGI source code, we make a string table that contains all the environment variables, and then we loop through the entire table and call **getenv**() for each one while streaming the results to **stdout** (see Listing 3.4).

LISTING 3.4 SOURCE CODE FOR RETRIEVING AND DISPLAYING WEB SERVER ENVIRONMENT VARIABLES.

```cpp
//
//      File: ServerVars.cpp
//      By: Don Gaspar
//
//      This is the source for the CGI Server Variables example from
//      Chapter 3 in the book  Visual Developer Web Commerce Programming
//      With Visual C++. The publisher is The Coriolis Group.
//
//      You may reach the author at: don@gigantor.com
//

// Some standard headers we're going to need in here
#include <ostream.h>
#include <fstream.h>
#include <stdio.h>
#include <stdlib.h>

// Our header and footer file names
const char *cHeaderName = "c:\\inetpub\\gigantor\\games\\head.htm";
const char *cFooterName = "c:\\inetpub\\gigantor\\games\\foot.htm";

// Here's a table of all the available Server
//       Environmental Variables
const char *cEnvironment[] = {"ALL_HTTP", "AUTH_TYPE", "CONTENT_LENGTH",
    "CONTENT_TYPE", "HTTP_AUTHORIZATION", "LOGON_USER", "URL",
    "GATEWAY_INTERFACE", "HTTP_ACCEPT", "USER_AGENT", "PATH_INFO",
    "PATH_TRANSLATED", "QUERY_STRING", "REMOTE_HOST", "REMOTE_ADDR",
    "REMOTE_IDENT", "REQUEST_METHOD", "REMOTE_USER", "SERVER_NAME",
    "SERVER_SOFTWARE", "SERVER_PORT", "SERVER_PROTOCOL", "SCRIPT_NAME",
    "HTTP_COOKIE", "HTTP_REFERER"};

const int cNumberOfVars = 25;

//
//      Function: BeginHeader
//      Purpose: Outputs the appropriate header information to stdout for a
//         Web browser to display.
//      Arguments: inTitle, the title of the dynamic page
//         you are creating.
```

```
void
BeginHeader(const char* inTitle)
{
    cout << "Content-type:TEXT/HTML\n\n" << "<HTML><HEAD><TITLE>\n" <<
        inTitle << "\n</TITLE></HEAD><BODY>\n";
} // BeginHeader...

//
//    Function: EndHeader
//    Purpose: Outputs the delimiter tags corresponding to those set by
//        PrintHeader() for proper HTML display.
//    Arguments:  None
//
void
EndHeader()
{
    cout << "</BODY></HTML>\n";
} // EndHeader...

//
//    StreamFile
//    Input:  char*, which is the name of the file to use with path.
//    Purpose:  Opens the designated file and streams it out through
//        stdout so the client's browser will get this dynamic HTML page.
//
void
StreamFile(const char* inFile)
{
    try
    {
        ifstream  file(inFile);  // file stream

        if (!file)                // If we don't get the file, then
            throw(-1);            // throw an exception

        char buffer[80];          // just a line of characters

        // Here, we loop through the file line by line until
        // we hit the end
        // sending all the data to cout.
        while (file.get(buffer,sizeof(buffer)))
        cout << buffer;

        file.close();
    }

    catch(...)
    {
```

```
        cout << "<center><b>Couldn't locate the header file.
            <br></center></b>";
    }
} // CGamesExtension::StreamFile...


//
//    Well, we gotta start somewhere.
//
void
main()
{
    // As we're streaming a file, we'll need to identify the
    // content type here.
    BeginHeader("Server Environmental Variables Page");
    StreamFile(cHeaderName);        // fetch, Rover

    // Now we're going to build a mock form of items to
    // test this out with
    cout << "<H1><CENTER>Here is a list of
        Server Environmental Variables:</H1><BR><BR><BR>";

    // Use the table we made above and display all the
    //    server variables
    char *var;
    for(int index = 0; index < cNumberOfVars; index++)
    {
        if ( (var = getenv(cEnvironment[index])))
        cout << "<b>" << cEnvironment[index] << " </B>= "
            << var << "<BR>";
    } // for...

    cout << "</CENTER><BR><BR><BR>";

    StreamFile(cFooterName);        // fetch
    EndHeader();
} // main...
```

HTTP_REFERER and **CONTENT_LENGTH** will be very useful. **HTTP _REFERER** tells us who directed the client to our server. For example, what URL were they at before they visited our site? **CONTENT_LENGTH** tells us how much data the client sent to us, so we can allocate sufficient storage.

You should check **CONTENT _LENGTH** before reading an input stream—quite a few CGI books do not mention this. Instead, they advocate allocating a monstrous array on the stack, and they assume it will be large enough to handle anything it receives. Never do this. First off, you might not need that much storage. Why allocate a huge 10K block of data if you don't need it? And what happens to available memory if you have several of these pig-code fragments running? (By the way, "pig-code" is a term used for code written by programmers who have no regard for memory usage.) Obviously, memory space that other processes could use is being eaten up by your reckless pig-code fragment. Next is the other extreme: It might not be large enough to contain the data! When this abomination happens, memory in the code fragment's heap is overwritten. For example, if a memory overwrite of some important data occurs, the CGI code fragment saves this garbage to your database.

Never "guestimate" the stream's size. Always check it and allocate dynamically. All it takes to improve performance and reliability is a few lines of code:

```
char *dataSize = getenv("CONTENT_LENGTH");
// cause an exception if we can't get the size
THROWIF(!dataSize);
long theSize = atol(dataSize);
// always be paranoid
THROWIF(!dataSize);
// new() throws an exception on failure, so no need to check the result
Char *inputBuffer = new char[dataSize];
...
// give a hoot, don't pollute
delete [] inputBuffer;
```

Now that we've seen how to make dynamic HTML forms with streams and how to get environmental variables from the server, we need to talk about **POST** and **GET**, which we mentioned in Chapter 2.

POST And GET

You might be wondering how **POST** and **GET**, the two ways the client (browser) sends data to the Web server, do just that, and better yet, how we get our stream on it.

Specifying **POST** as the method inside a <FORM> tag tells the browser that we'll send over the data via a stream. When we write a code fragment, we can use **stdin** to retrieve the data, which remains in a contiguous string. (Remember our discussion in Chapter 2?) In the next section of this chapter, we'll see how to isolate such strings into meaningful variables. **POST** also sends its information to the server transparently: The user doesn't see any mangled garbage in the URL edit text field of his or her Web browser (see Figure 3.4).

GET receives its information via **main()** and its arguments, **argc** and **argv[]**. However, no matter how many variables are sent over, **argc** will never contain the correct number of arguments. The contiguous string that the browser sends us comes over as one large string variable, so **argc** thinks we've got one variable in addition to **argv[0]**, which is our code fragment's name. Therefore, **argc** is always 2 and **argv[1]** is the string containing everything. Why use **argc** if its information isn't helpful? It's a matter of preference. Some heavy-duty CGI

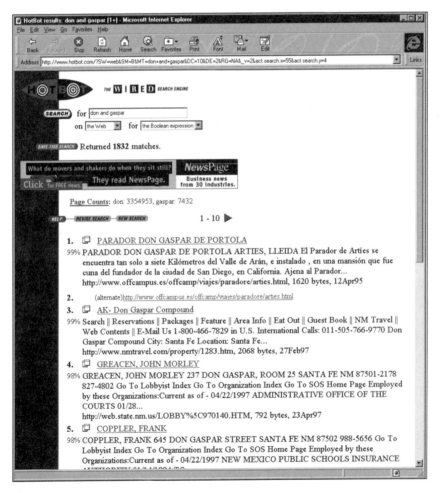

Figure 3.4
A browser's edit text (address) field when you submit data via **GET**.

programmers use **GET** because they can pass data to their code fragments from an anchor or other HTML links—something you can't do with **POST**.

When you use **GET** (refer back to Figure 3.4), the data is visible to the user and looks terrible in terms of usability aesthetics. Another strike against **GET** is that earlier browsers like Mosaic didn't support it, but used **POST** in its place. So if your code fragment expects to receive data in **argc** and **argv[]**, it will be sent over in **stdin** instead, and you'll never get the information.

How To Use POST And GET

To stream data over using **POST**, we would do something like the following snippet:

```
char * contentSize = getenv("CONTENT_LENGTH");
THROWIF(!contentSize);
long dataSize = atol(contentSize);
THROWIF(!dataSize);
// Note: new() throws an exception on failure
char *inStream = new char [dataSize];      // Get the stream
cin >> inStream;                           // That's it
DoSomethingWithIt(inStream);
```

With **GET**, the data comes in through **main**(), so getting the **strlen**() of **argv[1]** tells you the allocation size of your input buffer. Another option is to use **argv[1]** directly. Also, **CONTENT_LENGTH** is always zero when you use **GET**. Always check that **argc** is greater than one: Remember that **argc** returns how many **argv[]** arguments there are (and should be two for a CGI fragment using GET), and that **argv[0]** is always the code fragment's name.

Now that you know how to send data to the server, what do you do with it? We need to break up that contiguous string into isolated variable/value pairs that contain meaning for our code fragment.

Intercepting And Processing HTML Variables

We need to develop a class to handle isolating variables and their associated values from a single, possibly Godzilla-sized, string. This class needs to perform two functions: convert the %XX values that were sent over into meaningful

ASCII character equivalents, and translate ASCII characters like a "+" (meaning a concatenation of character strings) into a white-space character. The class corresponds to a form and its data, so we'll call this our **CFormParser** class. Because we're going to take a large string as input, why not make our constructor load that same string? We can retrieve variables through a member function in which we pass a variable name as an argument—much like **getenv**() does. The other members could be private members that convert and translate characters to their appropriate ASCII values.

This class is very simple, and does not require that you know the names of your variables from your form. When you connect to a database, it seems like overkill to get each variable by name, translate it into a field for the database, and then query the database. In such cases, the variable names should be handled automatically: The variable **NAME** on your HTML form could then be the inventory ID of an item in your database. Using this approach, we could make an *iterator* that could move through the variable list and take specified action for each variable.

In this instance, we could use one container to store the **NAME/VALUE** (variable/value) pair. We can find a value if we know its variable, or we can iterate through the entire container. The Standard Template Library (STL) provides us with such containers, which are part of ANSI, and are therefore part of the C++ language now.

A LOOK AT THE STANDARD TEMPLATE LIBRARY

STL represents a revolution in the way that you program: The C++ language now includes standard containers, iterators, and more than 80 new functions that can be used to manipulate your data. Instead of writing a new linked list class for every project, now you can look at a performance chart, and use an STL template that fits your needs. Figure 3.5 shows an overview of the components of STL.

STL was designed with a time/space complacency; it's extremely fast, efficient, and 100 percent portable between several different compilers. I've used STL with projects in MFC, GNU, Borland, and Metrowerks—the code was completely portable.

The first step in using STL is to consider what kind of container you need to store your data, and how insertions are to be done. STL offers a variety of

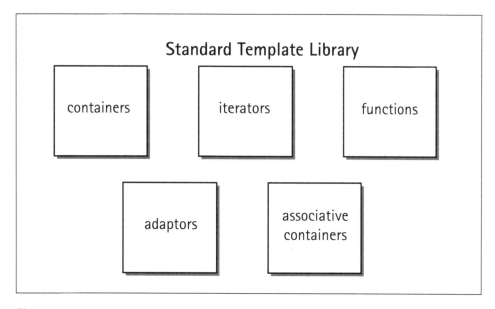

Figure 3.5
STL components.

different template containers that are tailored to meet various needs in terms
of performance and storage use. For example, you might only insert things
at the end of an array and remove them in the same order; this would be a
perfect case for a *vector* container. Table 3.2 shows some of the sequential
access containers' time cost for various operations, while Table 3.3 shows
the various operations supported by the same containers.

TABLE 3.2

STL SEQUENTIAL CONTAINER OPERATION TIME COST.

Operation	array[]	vector<>	deque<>	list<>
insert/delete front	n/a	linear	constant	constant
insert/delete middle	n/a	linear	linear	constant
insert/delete end	n/a	constant	constant	constant
access 1st element	constant	constant	constant	constant
access last element	constant	constant	constant	constant
access middle element	constant	constant	constant	linear

				TABLE 3.3

STL SEQUENTIAL CONTAINER FEATURES.

Characteristics	array[]	vector<>	deque<>	list<>
[] operator	yes	yes	yes	no
sequential access	yes	yes	yes	yes
insert/delete front	no	no	yes	yes
insert/delete back	no	yes	yes	yes
insert/delete middle	no	no	no	yes
overhead	none	minimal	low	medium

Our **CFormParser** class uses a **map** container, which is an associative container that stores things as a red-black tree for fast associative lookups via a key. Because we used STL for developing that class, it should be portable to Unix, and even Metrowerks so you could use it for Mac WebStar development.

Another powerful item provided with STL is iterators. These are pointers that move through your data items in your STL containers. Iterators provide an efficient method of moving through all of your items, or even just a range of items. STL treats these iterators as first-class entities, meaning that your iterator can do anything that the object it's iterating though can do. There are even stream iterators, which iterate over an **iostream** (which can even be a file); we'll be using these throughout this book.

A final part of STL is the 80 new functions offered. The ANSI committee saw that there were several things that are generally done in every project, and should be included as part of the language. Take a look at some of the STL functions offered and you'll see the power it really offers. Sorting, uniqueness, number generation, and more.

What's missing from STL? Bjarne Stroustrup thought that Hash tables were absent—they are. However, the proposals to add them to the language have been shot down so far. This is probably due more to the poor quality of the submissions rather than the ANSI committee not wanting additions.

> Other items missing might include some matrix operations for mathematical operations and so forth—items we seem to use frequently from project to project.
>
> Overall, STL provides a wealth of opportunity to simplify your development efforts. Pick and choose what you need, and your development time will speed up substantially.

Which container should we use? STL offers several varieties, all of which were designed with time/space complacency up front. Therefore, you can expect maximum time performance and minimum memory requirements. You might be thinking a *vector* (if you're familiar with STL) would be the easiest. True, it would work great, but it is neither the easiest nor the fastest solution. There are some associative containers that will perform our tasks even better.

The **map** container allows us to store key/value pairs in a dynamic container—perfect. The variable is the key, because it's always unique, and the pair allows value storage as well. You can use **map** by inserting pairs (key/value) of data into the container. You then look up a value by using the key. You can easily insert, search, and delete as well. We'll encapsulate a **map** container within our **CFormParser** class for convenience.

We make the **map** container a template, and when using it for our class, we declare an instance of it with the appropriate key/value pair. Something like

```
map< string, string, less<string> >   mVariableMap;
```

declares an instance of a **map** container using a **string** as both a key and the value stored, and lexicographically stores the strings in order using the **less<>** comparitor. The **map** container is ideal for us to use because it stores anything we want as key/value pairs.

The **map** container sorts items based on a comparitor that we provide. Here, we've used one (**less<>**) that is part of STL, which stores things as they are inserted automatically, and orders them with the comparitor. The ordering algorithm is a red-black tree, which allows for fast associative lookup later on. When we want to access a variable, we can now do something like:

```
string var = mVariableMap["Variable Name"];
```

This will cause the **map** container to look up the key "**Variable Name**" and give you the value that's stored there. With all of this in mind, let's glance at our class design, shown in Listing 3.5.

LISTING 3.5 CLASS DECLARATION FOR CFORMPARSER.

```
class CFormParser
{
    public:
        CFormParser(const char *inStringToParse = NULL);

        ~CFormParser();

        void OutputMap();

        string& operator[] (string& inKey) { return GetMap()[inKey]; }

        string& GetVariable(string& inKey) {return GetMap()[inKey];}

    private:
        // copy of the input string we can manipulate
        string m_InputString;         // Here's our map for storing things
        map< string, string, less<string> >  m_StorageMap;

        // some internally used member functions
        void CleanupString();
        void MakeVariables();
        int     hextoi(const char inChar);

        // convenient accessors
        string& GetInputString() {return m_InputString;}

        map< string, string, less<string> >&
            GetMap() { return m_StorageMap; }


}; // class CFormParser...
```

Let's go through our class' architecture in some detail. We've provided a constructor that accepts a **string** as input. We copy this to an internal data member, **m_InputString**, which is used internally. We use another member function called **OutputMap()** that I've provided for debugging purposes: It outputs all form data in HTML (see Figure 3.6). We use only two other member accessors that are public. One is a [] **operator** that returns the specified variable's value

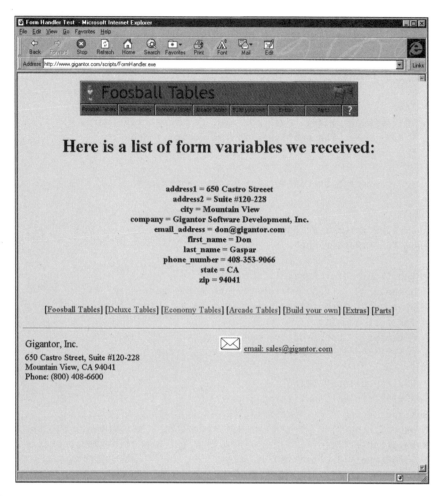

Figure 3.6
Output of a CGI code fragment using the **CFormParser** class for a guest book. Note that the variable names are in alphabetical order.

using the associative **map** container. This allows you to access variables using a [] **operator**, such as form["variable"]. The other is **GetVariable()**, which returns a **string** reference and requires a key **string** for lookup (this is modeled after the Unix **getenv()** function).

There are no other public operations, so the constructor must parse the input string. The constructor also makes the associative **map** container and inserts all key/value pairs based on the input string. Listing 3.6 shows the source for our new class.

LISTING 3.6   SOURCES FOR CFORMPARSER.CPP.

```
//
//      File: CFormParser.cpp
//      By: Don Gaspar
//
//      This is the source for the CFormParser class from Chapter 3
//      in the book  Visual Developer Web Commerce Programming With
//      Visual C++.  The publisher is The Coriolis Group.
//
//
//      You may reach the author at: don@gigantor.com
//


// Headers we've written and need
#include "CFormParser.hpp"

//      function:   CFormParser::CFormParser
//      purpose:    A constructor for our forms parsing class.
//      Breaks the form input string into an associative map container
//      for fast access
//      returns:    Constructors can't return anything
CFormParser::CFormParser(const char *inputString)
{
    THROWIFNULL(inputString);
    THROWIF(!strlen(inputString));
    GetInputString() = inputString;
    CleanupString();                // remove ctrl characters, and so on
    MakeVariables();                // fill our map with the goodies
} // CFormParser::CFormParser...

//      function:   CFormParser::~CFormParser
//      purpose:    CFormParser destructor — our own chance to clean up
//                  after ourselves.
//      returns:    destructors can't return things
//
CFormParser::~CFormParser()
{

} // CFormParser::~CFormParser...

//
//      function:   CFormParser::hextoi()
//      purpose:    Takes a character as input and if it's a hex number,
//          returns the appropriate ASCII value.
```

```
//    returns:     mentioned above.
//
int
CFormParser::hextoi(const char inChar)
{
    int    result;
    char   charToCompare = inChar;

    if (isdigit( inChar))           // check for base 10 digits
        result = inChar - '0';
     else                           // check for hex numnber a-f
    {
        // we can work with the lower case here
        charToCompare = tolower(inChar);
if (charToCompare >= 'a' && charToCompare <= 'f')
        result = charToCompare - 'a' + 10;
    }

  return result;                    // all we really wanted
} // CFormParser::hextoi...

//
//    function:     CFormParser::CleanupString
//    purpose:      Cleans up the input string by removing the browser's
//    8sp encoded
//                  %XX characters, and translates '+' to white space.
//    returns:      Nothing
//
void
CFormParser::CleanupString()
{
    try
    {
        int  index = 0;             // Start at the string's beginning
        // get outta here if it's empty
        THROWIF(!GetInputString().length());
        while (index < GetInputString().length())
        {
                // remember browsers translate a space to '+'
            if (GetInputString()[index] == '+')  GetInputString()
                [index] = ' ';
            else if (GetInputString()[index] == '%' &&
                (index + 2 < GetInputString().length()))
            {
                int value = hextoi(GetInputString()[index + 1]);
                GetInputString()[index] = static_cast<char>(value * 16 |
```

```
                    hextoi(GetInputString()[index + 2]));
                GetInputString().remove(index+1,2);
                index += 2;
            }
          index++;                    // check next character
        } // while...
    } // try...

    catch(...)
    {
        cout << "Error in CFormParser::CleanupString()<BR>";
        throw(-1);                   // propagate exception up the chain
    } // catch...
} // CFormParser::CleanupString...


//
//    function:     CFormParser::MakeVariables
//    purpose:      Converts a form input string and inserts it into a map
//        of key/value pairs. Uses internal map
//    return:       Nothing
//
void
CFormParser::MakeVariables()
{
    try
    {
        int index = 0, pos;
        string key, value;          // We'll use these for map insertion

        // go through the entire string
        while (index < GetInputString().length())
    {
            // Remember: values are after the '='
            // get up to the variable name
            pos = GetInputString().find('=', index);
            if (pos <= 0)
                break;
            key.resize(pos-index,0);
            copy(&GetInputString()[index], &GetInputString()[pos],
                &key[0]);
            index = pos + 1;

            // Remember: next variable starts with a '&'
            // get up to the variable's value
             pos = GetInputString().find('&', index);
             if (pos <= 0)
                break;
```

```
                value.resize(pos-index,0);
                copy(&GetInputString()[index], &GetInputString()[pos],
                    &value[0]);
                index = pos + 1;

                GetMap()[key] = value;   // insert into our map container!
            } // while...
        }

        catch(...)
        {
            cout << "Error in CFormParser::MakeVariables()...<BR>";
        }
    } // CFormParser::MakeVariables...

    //
    //    function:    CFormParser::OutputMap...
    //    purpose:     Takes our map container and iterates through all the
    //    items outputting them to stdout.
    //    returns:     Nothing
    //
    void
    CFormParser::OutputMap()
    {
        map< string, string, less<string> >::iterator iter;

        if (!GetMap().empty())
            for(iter = GetMap().begin(); iter != GetMap().end(); iter++)
                cout << "<B>" << (*iter).first << "</B> = <B>" <<
                    (*iter).second << "</B><BR>";
        else
            cout << "Error: map container is empty.<br>";
    } // CFormParser::OutputMap...
```

The constructor does nearly everything, so how are errors returned? (Constructors are forbidden from having return results.) Well, when there is an error condition, an exception is thrown. This allows us to design our code more tightly, and we're using a key feature of the C++ language. Error handling is always a major design portion of any project, and using exception handling simplifies your code by removing nested error condition checking all over: It allows you to place your error handler where you want, and therefore only deal with error-handling in a few specific places in your source code.

Our constructor throws an exception when it receives an error, as does STL. If we accessed a memory element outside of our **map's** allocated space, STL would throw an out-of-bounds exception. We've used exceptions in our design, and both STL and the **new**() operator use them. Therefore, when you use the **CFormParser** class, you must place your code within a *try* block, and have a **catch**() routine to handle error codes. If you do not **catch**() a thrown exception, the topmost catcher will receive the exception. If the topmost exception catcher does not exist, then **terminate**() receives the exception and your code fragment will quit for no apparent reason.

What if you don't care about the variable names, but perform an action based on all of the variables? Take a look again at **OutputMap**() in Listing 3.6. There we create a **map** iterator and move through every variable from the form that we received. What if you need to perform the same action for every variable? STL provides a **for_each**() function that takes a function pointer and the container's beginning and ending iterators, and iterates over every element, calling the function you specified for each item. We'll be doing this throughout this book.

Processing HTML Controls

Now that we've developed a class for handling all types of forms, we need to apply it to some real examples. Here, we'll write a versatile form and use the **CFormParser** class to gather all of the data in a meaningful way. Remember those examples from Chapter 2 in which we made some various forms with controls? Let's just try out our new class, **CFormParser**, and write a CGI code fragment that will intercept and display the data that you input.

Listing 3.7 displays the CGI source code for a fragment we've called FormHandler. In your HTML sources, be sure to change the **FORM ACTION** to use the FormHandler.exe code fragment. Let's also write a single HTML page that links these various test pages together for convenience.

LISTING 3.7   SOURCE FOR FORMHANDLER.CPP.

```
//
//    File: FormHandler.cpp
//    By: Don Gaspar
//
```

```
//      This is the source for the translating and displaying form
//      variables from an example from Chapter 3
//      in the book Visual Developer Web Commerce Programming
//      With Visual C++.
//      The publisher is The Coriolis Group.
//
//      You may reach the author at: don@gigantor.com
//

// Some standard headers we're going to need in here
#include <ostream.h>
#include <fstream.h>
#include <stdio.h>
#include <stdlib.h>

// Now, headers we've written
#include "CFormParser.hpp"

// our header and footer file names
const char *cHeaderName = "c:\\inetpub\\gigantor\\games\\head.htm";
const char *cFooterName = "c:\\inetpub\\gigantor\\games\\foot.htm";

//
//      Function: BeginHeader
//      Purpose: Outputs the appropriate header information to
//         stdout for a Web browser to display.
//      Arguments: inTitle, the title of the dynamic page you
//         are creating.
//
void
BeginHeader(const char* inTitle)
{
    cout << "Content-type:TEXT/HTML\n\n" << "<HTML><HEAD><TITLE>\n" <<
        inTitle << "\n</TITLE></HEAD><BODY>\n";
} // BeginHeader...

//
//      Function: EndHeader
//      Purpose: Outputs the delimiter tags corresponding to those set by
//         PrintHeader() for proper HTML display.
//      Arguments:  None
//
void
EndHeader()
{
```

```
        cout << "</BODY></HTML>\n";
} // EndHeader...

//
//      StreamFile
//      Input:       char*, which is the name of the file to use with path.
//      Purpose:     Opens the designated file and streams it out through ''
//      stdout so the client's browser will get this dynamic HTML page.
//
void
StreamFile(const char* inFile)
{
    try
    {
        ifstream file(inFile);      // file stream

        if (!file)                  // if we don't get the file, then
            throw(-1);              // throw an exception

        char buffer[80];            // just a line of characters

        // Here, we loop through the file line by line until we
        // hit the end
        // ending all the data to cout.
        while (file.getline(buffer,sizeof(buffer)))
            cout << buffer;

        file.close();
    }

    catch(...)
        {
        cout << "<center><b>Couldn't locate the header file.
            <br></center></b>";
    }
} // CGamesExtension::StreamFile...

//
//      function:    HandleForm
//      purpose:     Creates a CFormParser object and passes the data
//      received
//          from a POST in cin to CFormParser. Checks length, and so on
//          and throws an exception
//          upon detection of any error.
//      returns:     Nothing, exceptions are used for error handling.
//
```

```
void
HandleForm()
{
    try
    {
        char *streamSize = getenv("CONTENT_LENGTH");
        THROWIF(!streamSize);
        long dataSize = atol(streamSize);
        THROWIF(!dataSize);

        char *buffer = new char[dataSize];
        cin >> buffer;

        CFormParser ourParser(buffer);
        ourParser.OutputMap();

        delete [] buffer;
    }

    catch(...)
    {
        cout << "<B>An unrecoverable error occurred.<BR></B>";
    }
} // HandleForm...

//
//  Well, we gotta start somewhere.
//
void
main()
{
    // As we're streaming a file, we'll need to identify the
    // content type here
    BeginHeader("Form Handler Test");
    StreamFile(cHeaderName);       // fetch, Rover

        // Now we're going to build a mock form of items to test
        // this out with
    cout << "<H1><CENTER>Here is a list of form variables we received:
        </H1><BR><BR><BR>";

    HandleForm();
```

```
    StreamFile(cFooterName);      // fetch
    EndHeader();
} // main...
```

The amount of code here is very minimal—you always want your designs to have the fewest possible number of code (small lines) lines, as it makes tracking down errors easier, and performance better. On numerous occasions, I've heard many engineers brag about how many lines of code are in their project—well, how about bragging about how few lines you've written to perform a certain task? Or, how about judging projects by fewest bugs per line of code instead? Counting lines of code is significant only for managers who want to gauge performance, but who are completely unfamiliar with the software development process. In this book, we try to write as few lines as possible—a daunting task; however, they are high-quality lines.

We need to provide a general HTML form to link our form's test pages together. As this was becoming a large site with lots of pages, I decided to use NetObjects' Fusion (**www.netobjects.com**) and put together an entire site for all the examples we use throughout this book. The URL is **www.gigantor.com/coriolis**. In Figure 3.7, we fill out the guest book page and submit the data you see. In Figure 3.8, we display the results of calling the FormHandler.exe code fragment.

Using **CFormParser** and getting variables from the class are easy. Now that we've seen how to use **CFormParser** and know how it works, we need to build some more sophisticated examples. In these next examples, we'll do more than just sending back the data. Receiving it back is a great tool for debugging, making a dynamic form, and so on. Our next examples will take actions based on the user's data, and will build dynamic responses accordingly.

CGI Code Examples

In this section, we're going to apply the **CFormParser** class to some complex forms parsing. We'll start out with some simple cases, and build our way up to some fairly sophisticated form handling. You don't have to be familiar with the internal workings of the **CFormParser** class, but I recommend that you understand how to use **CFormParser** from the FormHandler example in Listing 3.7.

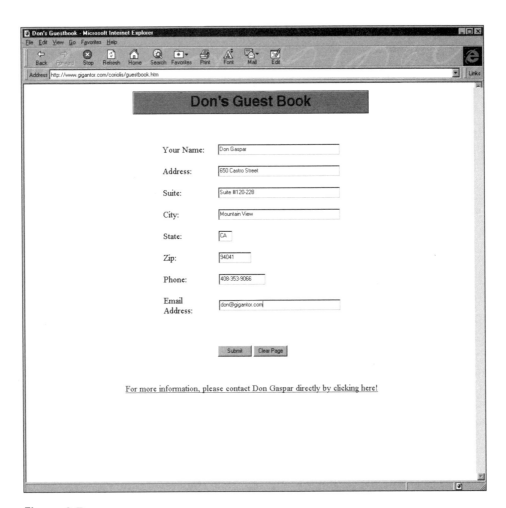

Figure 3.7
The guest book form we fill out and submit.

Hello World Revisited

We created a CGI code fragment at the beginning of this chapter to deal with this simplistic example, but now we're going to take it a step further. Let's intercept the user's choices from a form and display a Hello World response based on user input.

For this example, I've created a form that displays options that will determine our dynamically generated response. Listing 3.8 shows the HTML for the new Hello World page, which offers some input options, such as the user's name,

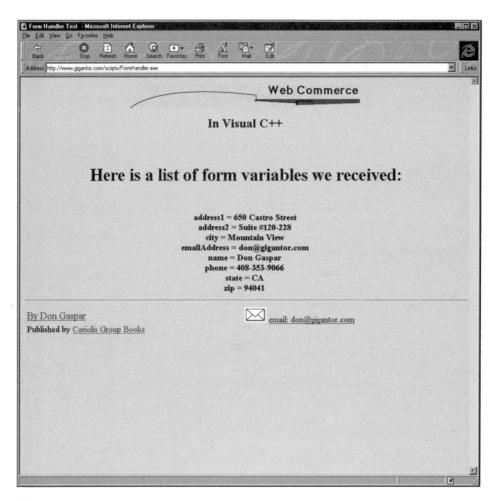

Figure 3.8
Results of submitting the guest book to FormHandler.exe.

and some radio buttons to choose what OS he or she prefers to use. So we need to concern ourselves with only two variables: the user name, which we've cleverly named **userName**, and a computer preference, with an equally clever name, **computerPref**.

LISTING 3.8   HTML SOURCE FOR NEWHELLOWORLD.HTM.

```
<!Chapter 3 New Hello World by Don Gaspar>
<HTML>
```

```
<HEAD>
<!Here's the title of our page. Note the beginning and ending tags>
<TITLE>New Hello World</TITLE>
</HEAD>

<BODY BGCOLOR="#DDDDDD" LINK="#FF0000" VLINK="#800080"
    TEXT="#000000">

<!This is just our fancy border at the top of the page>
<CENTER>
<IMG HEIGHT=48 WIDTH=504 SRC="http://www.gigantor.com/coriolis/
helloworld.gif"
    BORDER=0 >


<FORM ACTION="/scripts/newhelloworld.exe" METHOD=POST>

<BR><H1>New Hello World from Chapter 3</H1><BR><BR>
<P>Please enter your name:<INPUT TYPE="text" NAME="userName" MAXSIZE=32>
    <BR>
<P>Please select your favorite type of personal computer:<BR><BR>

<TABLE BORDER=2>
<TR><TD>
<INPUT TYPE="radio" NAME="computerPref" VALUE="Macintosh">Macintosh
</TR></TD>
<TR><TD>
<INPUT TYPE="radio" NAME="computerPref" VALUE="Windows">Windows 95
</TR></TD>
<TR><TD>
<INPUT TYPE="radio" NAME="computerPref" VALUE="WindowsNT" CHECKED>
    Windows NT
</TR></TD>
<TR><TD>
<INPUT TYPE="radio" NAME="computerPref" VALUE="Next">
    Wintel Box running NeXT OS
</TR></TD>
<TR><TD>
<INPUT TYPE="radio" NAME="computerPref" VALUE="Sun">
    Sun with Solaris OS
</TR></TD>
<TR><TD>
<INPUT TYPE="radio" NAME="computerPref" VALUE="Unix">BSDI Unix
</TR></TD>
</TABLE>
<BR><BR>
```

```
<INPUT TYPE=submit VALUE="Hello World">
<INPUT TYPE=reset VALUE="Reset Form">
</CENTER>
</FORM>

</BODY>
</HTML>
```

To start off, we implement a **main**() that calls **BeginHeader**() and then **StreamFile**() with our header file that's saved on the server machine. Next, we call a function **HandleForm**(), which is where all the action takes place.

HandleForm() instantiates an instance of the **CFormParser** class. Next, to access the variables we mentioned above, **HandleForm**() uses the [] **operator**. To get the **userName** variable and send it to **stdout**, we do:

```
cout << ourFormParser["userName"];
```

To get the radio button that the user selected, we use the variable name **computerPref** in the same way:

```
cout << ourFormParser["computerPref"];
```

Our **CFormParser** has done almost all the work we need for this form. We did add a few extra lines of code in NewHelloWorld.cpp, so be sure to review Listing 3.9.

LISTING 3.9   SOURCE CODE FOR NEWHELLOWORLD.CPP.

```
//
//     File: NewHelloWorld.cpp
//     By: Don Gaspar
//
//     This is the source for the translating and displaying form
//     variables from an example from Chapter 3, the NewHelloWorld sample,
//     in the book Visual Developer Web Commerce Programming With
//     Visual C++.
//     The publisher is The Coriolis Group.
//
//     You may reach the author at: don@gigantor.com
//

// Some standard headers we're going to need in here
```

```
#include <ostream.h>
#include <fstream.h>
#include <stdio.h>
#include <stdlib.h>

// Now, headers we've written
#include "CFormParser.hpp"

// our header and footer file names
const char *cHeaderName = "c:\\inetpub\\gigantor\\
    coriolis\\head.htm";
const char *cFooterName = "c:\\inetpub\\gigantor\\
    coriolis\\foot.htm";

//
//     Function: BeginHeader
//     Purpose: Outputs the appropriate header information to
//        stdout for a
//     Web browser to display.
//     Arguments: inTitle, the title of the dynamic page you are creating.
//
void
BeginHeader(const char* inTitle)
{
    cout << "Content-type:TEXT/HTML\n\n" << "<HTML><HEAD><TITLE>\n" <<
        inTitle << "\n</TITLE></HEAD><BODY>\n";
} // BeginHeader...

//
//     Function: EndHeader
//     Purpose: Outputs the delimiter tags corresponding to those set by
//        PrintHeader() for proper HTML display.
//     Arguments: None
//
void
EndHeader()
{
    cout << "</BODY></HTML>\n";
} // EndHeader...

//
//     StreamFile
//     Input:       char*, which is the name of the file to use with path.
//     Purpose:   Opens the designated file and streams it out through
//     stdout so the client's browser will get this dynamic HTML page.
//
void
```

```
StreamFile(const char* inFile)
{
    try
    {
        ifstream file(inFile);      // file stream

        if (!file)                  // if we don't get the file, then
            throw(-1);              // throw an exception

        char buffer[80];            // just a line of characters

        // Here, we loop through the file line by line until we
        // hit the end
        // sending all the data to cout.
        while (file.getline(buffer,sizeof(buffer)))
            cout << buffer;

        file.close();
    }

    catch(...)
    {
        cout << "<center><b>Couldn't locate the header file.
            <br></center></b>";
    }
} // StreamFile...

//
// function:     HandleForm
// purpose:      Creates a CFormParser object and passes the data
//      received from a POST in cin to CFormParser. Checks length, and
//      so on and throws an exception upon detection of any error.
// returns:      Nothing, exceptions are used for error handling.
//
void
HandleForm()
{
    try
    {
        char *streamSize = getenv("CONTENT_LENGTH");
        THROWIF(!streamSize);
        long dataSize = atol(streamSize);
        THROWIF(!dataSize);

        char *buffer = new char[dataSize];
```

```
        cin >> buffer;
        CFormParser ourParser(buffer);

        cout << "<CENTER><H1> Hello " << ourParser["userName"] << "!<
        H1><BR><BR>";
        cout << "<H3>You prefer to use " << ourParser["computerPref"] <<
        " OS!/CENTER></H3><BR><BR><BR>";

        delete [] buffer;
    }

    catch(...)
    {
        cout << "<B>An unrecoverable error occurred.<BR></B>";
    }
} // HandleForm...

//
//  Well, we gotta start somewhere.
//
void
main()
{
    // As we're streaming a file, we'll need to identify the
    // content type here
    BeginHeader("Form Handler Test");
    StreamFile(cHeaderName);    // fetch, Rover

    HandleForm();

    StreamFile(cFooterName);        // fetch
    EndHeader();
} // main...
```

Guest Book Revisited

We've already written the HTML source for a cool guest book. Now let's fill in the source code so that we can save guest information to disk. In Chapter 7, we'll revisit the guest book in detail and use a database to store user information. For now, we'll save it to a text file on disk.

We need to link the guest book form with a code fragment that uses our **CFormParser** class, much like the New Hello World example, except we'll thank the user and save the information to our text file. It would be really neat to view all the users who have signed the guest book, so we're going to modify the HTML slightly so that we can. Let's add a control called View Users that will be another **submit** button. *"Holy multiple **submit** buttons, Batman! How does it work?"* We'll have to assign a **NAME** for each of our **submit** buttons to distinguish them apart and avoid taking an inappropriate action in our CGI code fragment. Listing 3.10 shows the newly revised HTML, which I've renamed NewGuestBook.cpp.

LISTING 3.10   HTML SOURCE FOR NEWGUESTBOOK.CPP.

```
<!Chapter 3 NewGuestbook HTML by Don Gaspar>
<HTML>

<HEAD>
<!Here's the title of our page. Note the beginning and ending tags>
<TITLE>Don's New Guestbook</TITLE>
</HEAD>

<BODY BGCOLOR="#FFFFFF" LINK="#FF0000" VLINK="#800080"
    TEXT="#000000">

<!This is just our fancy border at the top of the page>
<CENTER>
<IMG HEIGHT=48 WIDTH=504 SRC="http://www.gigantor.com/articles
    /assets/auto_generated_images/img_10b1c001.gif" BORDER=0 >
</CENTER>

<!These place spaces vertically between items>
<BR><BR><BR>

<!Everything from the FORM tag until the /FORM tag is encapsulated
    within the form>
<FORM ACTION="/scripts/NewGuestbook.exe" METHOD="POST">

<!Here, we've placed our items in a table to line them up>
<CENTER>
<TABLE BORDER=0 CELLSPACING=20 WIDTH=400 HEIGHT=18>
<TR><TD><P>Your Name:</TD><TD><INPUT TYPE="text" NAME= "name" SIZE=48>
    </TD></TR>
<TR><TD><P>Address:</TD><TD><INPUT TYPE="text" NAME= "address1" SIZE=48>
    </TD></TR>
<TR><TD><P>Suite:</TD><TD><INPUT TYPE="text" NAME= "address2" SIZE=48>
    </TD></TR>
```

```
<TR><TD><P>City:</TD><TD><INPUT TYPE="text" NAME= "city" SIZE=48>
    </TD></TR>
<TR><TD><P>State:</TD><TD><INPUT TYPE="text" NAME= "state" SIZE=2>
    </TD></TR>
<TR><TD><P>Zip:</TD><TD><INPUT TYPE="text" NAME= "zip" SIZE=10>
    </TD></TR>
<TR><TD><P>Phone:</TD><TD><INPUT TYPE="text" NAME= "phone" SIZE=16>
    </TD></TR>
<TR><TD><P>Email Address:</TD><TD><INPUT TYPE="text" NAME= "emailAddress"
    SIZE=48>
    </TD></TR>
</TABLE>
</CENTER>

<BR><BR><BR>
<CENTER>
<INPUT TYPE="submit" NAME="task VALUE="Submit">
<INPUT TYPE="submit" NAME="task" VALUE="View Other Guests">
<INPUT TYPE="reset" VALUE="Clear Page">
</CENTER>
</FORM>

<BR><BR><BR>
<CENTER>
<P><A HREF="http://www.gigantor.com">For more information, please contact
    Don Gaspar directly by clicking here!</A>
</CENTER>

</BODY>
</HTML>
```

The new guest book looks identical to the old one except for a new button visible at the bottom of the screen. Figure 3.9 shows the Web page with the new addition.

Now, we need to write the code to support the multiple **submit** buttons. To add support for the multiple **submit** buttons, we check for the value of the **submit** button: Here, the task variable will be equal to the name of the button. Because our **CFormParser** class breaks everything into key/value pairs for us, we can use the following code snippet to retrieve the name of the **submit** button that the user selects:

```
string buttonSelected = ourFormParser["task"];
```

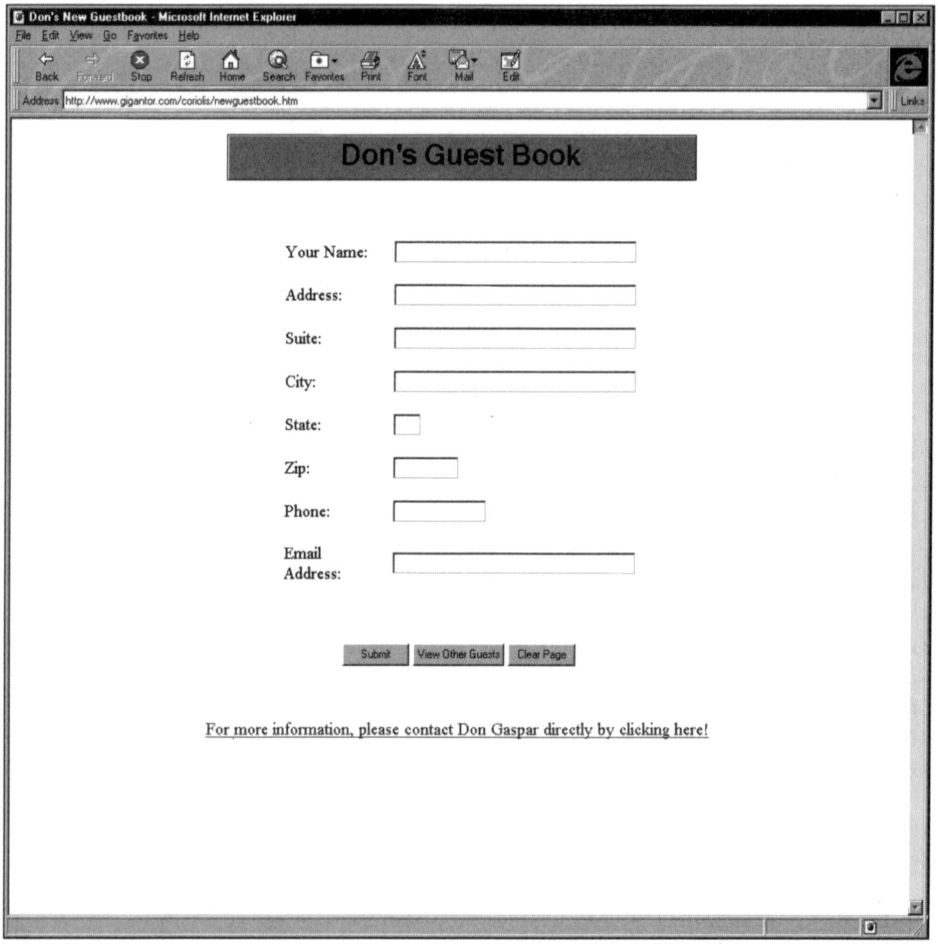

Figure 3.9
The new guest book.

Or, we could just compare the **string**, as it is a class that has a **compare**() member function:

```
if (ourFormParser["task"].compare("submit") == 0 )
```

> *Note: The ANSI **string** class' **compare**() member returns results identical to those of **strcmp**() from the Standard C Library. If the result is zero, the strings are identical. Like **strcmp**(), comparisons are case sensitive.*

After we receive the type of task that was selected, we have two choices: either save your guest information to our guest log or display the names of guests.

The new guest book form (shown in Figure 3.9) looks like a great C++ structure, so I've made a structure based on the information from the form, relying again on the **string** class:

```
struct GuestInfo
{
    string    name;
    string    address1;
    string    address2;
    string    city;
    string    state;
    string    zip;
    string    phone_number;
    string    email_address;
};
```

This structure encapsulates all guest fields into one convenient location. Our **CFormParser** class places everything into a map, so you can access all of the fields and store them in the **GuestInfo** structure. Next, we open an **ofstream** (an output file stream). We're going to save the user data from the **GuestInfo** structure at the end of this file; if this file doesn't exist, we'll create it. I wrote a stream operator for both input and output streams that want to use a **GuestInfo** structure (see Listing 3.11). With these operators, I can append the **GuestInfo** structure into the file simply by doing:

```
outputFile << ourStructure;
```

The **ofstream** class and the stream operator I wrote handled all the work here, so I needed only one line of code to add the structure of guest information to the guest's file. We close the file and thank the user, as Figure 3.10 shows.

When the user wants to see who else has visited the site, we need to read the guest file into memory and display it. Here, I made a vector of **GuestInfo** structures and read them in using a clever approach. We make an **ifstream** (an input file stream), and then we use the STL **istream_iterator**—this will allow us to iterate through the file just like we did previously with our **map** container. Because we now have an **iterator** to our input file, I read the entire file into our vector container with just one line of code! This one line merely calls the **copy()** function.

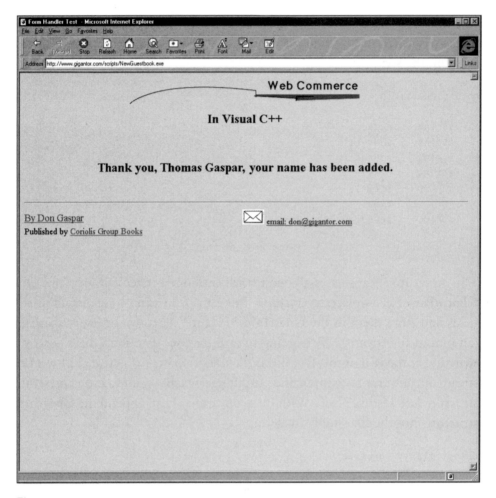

Figure 3.10
Confirmation of user, adding his or her name.

To display the output file, I used a *vector* **iterator** and **cout** for each **GuestInfo** structure in the vector. You can try it out at **www.gigantor.com/coriolis/ newguestbook.htm**.

LISTING 3.11   SOURCE FOR NEWGUESTBOOK.CPP.

```
//
//    File: NewGuestBook.cpp
//    By:   Don Gaspar
//
//    This is the source for the new Guest Book,
//    an example from Chapter 3, the NewHelloWorld sample,
//    in the book Visual Developer Web Commerce Programming With Visual
```

```
//      C++.
//      The publisher is The Coriolis Group.
//
//      You may reach the author at: don@gigantor.com
//

// Some standard headers we're going to need in here
#include <ostream.h>
#include <fstream.h>
#include <stdio.h>
#include <stdlib.h>

// Now, headers we've written
#include "CFormParser.hpp"
#include "NewGuestBook.hpp"

// our header and footer file names
const char *cHeaderName = "c:\\inetpub\\gigantor\\
    coriolis\\head.htm";
const char *cFooterName = "c:\\inetpub\\gigantor\\
    coriolis\\foot.htm";
const char *cGuestFile = "f:\\OurGuestFile";

// Some useful things we've provided

ostream&
operator<< (ostream &inOStream, const GuestInfo &inGuest)
{
    inOStream << inGuest.name << "|";
    inOStream << inGuest.address1 << "|";
    inOStream << inGuest.address2 << "|";
    inOStream << inGuest.city << "|";
    inOStream << inGuest.state << "|";
    inOStream << inGuest.zip << "|";
    inOStream << inGuest.phone_number << "|";
    inOStream << inGuest.email_address << "|";
    return inOStream;
}

istream&
operator>> (istream &inIStream, GuestInfo &outGuest)
{
    char  temp[64];
    inIStream.getline(temp,32,'|');
    outGuest.name = temp;
    inIStream.getline(temp,32,'|');
    outGuest.address1 = temp;
    inIStream.getline(temp,32,'|');
```

```
        outGuest.address2 = temp;
        inIStream.getline(temp,32,'|');
        outGuest.city = temp;
        inIStream.getline(temp,32,'|');
        outGuest.state = temp;
        inIStream.getline(temp,16,'|');
        outGuest.zip = temp;
        inIStream.getline(temp,16,'|');
        outGuest.phone_number = temp;
        inIStream.getline(temp,64,'|');
        outGuest.email_address = temp;
        return inIStream;
}


//
//    Function: BeginHeader
//    Purpose: Outputs the appropriate header information to
//       stdout for a Web browser to display.
//    Arguments: inTitle, the title of the dynamic page you are creating.
//
void
BeginHeader(const char* inTitle)
{
    cout << "Content-type:TEXT/HTML\n\n" << "<HTML><HEAD><TITLE>\n" <<
        inTitle << "\n</TITLE></HEAD><BODY>\n";
} // BeginHeader...


//
//    Function: EndHeader
//    Purpose: Outputs the delimiter tags corresponding to those set by
//         PrintHeader() for proper HTML display.
//    Arguments: None
//
void
EndHeader()
{
    cout << "</BODY></HTML>\n";
} // EndHeader...


//
//    StreamFile
//    Input: char*, which is the name of the file to use with path.
//    Purpose: Opens the designated file and streams it out through stdout
//         so the client's browser will get this dynamic HTML page.
//
void
StreamFile(const char* inFile)
```

```
{
    try
    {
        ifstream  file(inFile);     // file stream

        if (!file)                  // if we don't get the file, then
            throw(-1);              // throw an exception

        char buffer[80];            // just a line of characters

        // Here, we loop through the file line by line until we
        // hit the end
        // sending all the data to cout.
        while (file.getline(buffer,sizeof(buffer)))
            cout << buffer;

        file.close();
    }

    catch(...)
    {
        cout << "<center><b>Couldn't locate the header file.
            <br></center></b>";
    }
} // StreamFile...

//
//      function:     HandleTask
//      purpose:      Because this page has multiple submits, this
//      routine handles the proper one by checking the "task"
//      variable from the
//      HTML form.
//      returns:      Nothing!
//
void
HandleTask(CFormParser &inParser)
{
    // adding his or her name???
    if (inParser["task"].compare("Submit") == 0)
    {
        GuestInfo guest;                // copy to a GuestInfo struct
        guest.name = inParser["name"];
        guest.address1 = inParser["address1"];
        guest.address2 = inParser["address2"];
        guest.city = inParser["city"];
```

```
        guest.state = inParser["state"];
        guest.zip = inParser["zip"];
        guest.phone_number = inParser["phone"];
        guest.email_address = inParser["emailAddress"];


    // append "At The End"
     ofstreamguestFile(cGuestFile,ios::ate | ios::out);
        int count = 0;    // attempts to open the file
    if (guestFile == NULL)
    {
        cout << "Guest File failure...";
        while(count++ < 25 && !guestFile
            guestFile.open(cGuestFile,ios::ate | ios::out);
    }


    if (guestFile && count != 25)
    {
        // put it in our file with our stream operator
        guestFile << guest;                guestFile.close();
        // save our changes
        cout << "<CENTER><H2>Thank you, " << guest.name << " your
            name has
            been added.</CENTER><BR><BR><BR>";
    }
    else
        cout << "<H2>Sorry, an error occurred and your name was
            not added</H2><BR><BR><BR>";
    }
else                           // spying on others!
{
    vector<GuestInfo> theGuests;       // display using a vector
    ifstream  inputFile(cGuestFile);   // the file to use
    if (inputFile)
    {
        // iterator
        istream_iterator<GuestInfo,ptrdiff_t> iter(inputFile),end;
//       copy to our vector
        copy(iter, end, inserter(theGuests,theGuests.begin()));
//       all done for now
        inputFile.close();

        // move through and display the names
        vector<GuestInfo>::iterator  guestIter;
```

```
            cout << "<CENTER><H1>Guest who have signed in:"
             "</H1><BR><BR><BR>";
             for (guestIter = theGuests.begin(); guestIter !=
theGuests.end();
                guestIter++)
            cout << (*guestIter).name << " from " <<
                (*guestIter).city << "<BR>";
           cout << "</CENTER><BR><BR><BR>";
       }
       else
           cout << "<H2>Sorry, the guest file is busy. Please try again
later.
                </H2><BR><BR><BR>";
    }
} // HandleTask...

//
//    function:    HandleForm
//    purpose:     Creates a CFormParser object and passes the data
//    received from a POST in cin to CFormParser. Checks length,
//    and so on and throws an exceptionupon detection of any error.
//    returns:     Nothing, exceptions are used for error handling.
//
void
HandleForm()
{
    try
      {
        char *streamSize = getenv("CONTENT_LENGTH");
        THROWIF(!streamSize);
        long dataSize = atol(streamSize);
        THROWIF(!dataSize);

        char *buffer = new char[dataSize];
        cin >> buffer;
        CFormParser ourParser(buffer);

        // Now we need to find out what task the user wants us to do
        HandleTask(ourParser );
         delete [] buffer;
      }

    catch(...)
      {
```

```
        cout << "<B>An unrecoverable error occurred.<BR></B>";
    }
} // HandleForm...

//
//  Well, we gotta start somewhere.
//
void
main()
{
  // As we're streaming a file, we'll need to identify the
  // content type here
    BeginHeader("Form Handler Test");
    StreamFile(cHeaderName);        // fetch, Rover

    HandleForm();

    StreamFile(cFooterName);        // fetch
    EndHeader();
} // main...
```

Quite a few things are missing here. If you have a busy site and lots of people signing in, or if you want to do something with the guest data, you need to use a database. We did no removal of duplicate names in our example, and the names are not sorted before they're displayed. Figure 3.11 shows a listing of names of people who have signed on. To sort the names, you could use the STL **sort**() routine, and then **unique**() to make sure there were no duplicate names. While there are still some improvements to be made, you'll discover this is a high-performance guest book.

CGI Architecture

We've covered quite a bit of CGI, how a CGI code fragment handles variables, and how data is passed back to the client's browser. We've written several examples, and you should now have a good feel for how CGI works. Figure 3.12 shows the brief process of CGI starting from when the client initiates it.

The CGI flow starts when the client sends a **submit** to the server. The server receives this information, and finds the designated code fragment that the browser requested. The server then launches this code fragment and lets it take over.

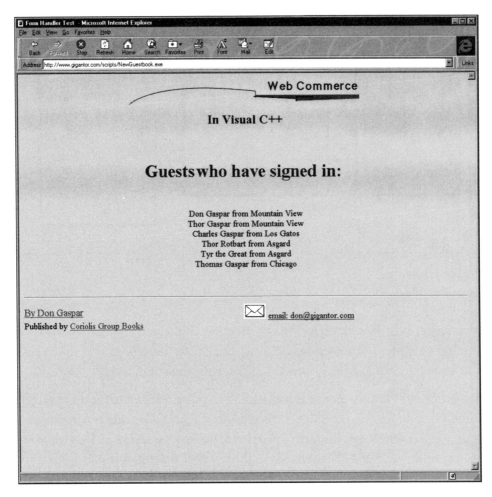

Figure 3.11
Viewing names of other guests who have signed in.

Next, the code fragment processes the data and takes some action, and hopefully, writes back a reply for the user using **stdout**. The server receives the **stdout** data, and passes it to the client, at which point it interprets the HTML and displays it for the user.

Overhead

Launching code fragments is very expensive in terms of CPU cycles. Every user that connects and makes a request via **submit** causes a CGI code fragment to be launched into memory. Some of these code fragments take up lots of individual

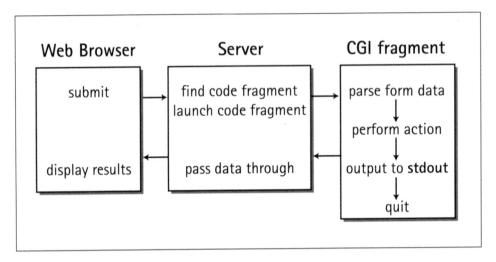

Figure 3.12
Flow of control during a CGI session.

heap space. It is possible that if many users are connected to your site and are sending you forms, your server could run out of free heap space to launch further code fragments. This is something you will need to manage.

A solution that most sites use is statistically keeping track of hits on the pages, and CGI code fragments. You can then assess if your CGI code fragments and your Web server are too slow, or if people are getting turned away because your heap is filling up. One alternative is to buy a faster machine. If you're running out of heap space, you can always upgrade to more memory, but redirection might be a better option.

Some servers can keep track of how many users are connected. After you reach a certain number, you can then direct future connections to another server you have set up. Have you ever connected to a busy site like **www.microsoft.com**? All major sites use redirection for heavy-traffic time periods to prevent potential havoc on a single machine.

To use redirection, you will need to study HTTP a little more. When you make a dynamic HTML page, you can send some header information back to a client that causes his or her browser to connect to another machine.

Advantages Of CGI

CGI applications (code fragments) are substantially faster than CGI scripts. However, what other special advantages does CGI offer? While launching separate code fragments requires significant overhead, each one lives in its own process space, separate from the Web server.

The Web server and each CGI code fragment have their own heaps. If something goes wrong with one of these components, the others won't be affected. Because of protected memory (sorry Mac folks, we've heard promises and promises from Apple, but you still don't have it), a wild pointer in one application will not cause overwrites in other heaps. This protected heap space ensures your code fragments—although it's expensive in terms of heap requirements—won't bring the server down in a crash. This is great to remember when debugging your CGI code fragments.

Summary

We've looked at the CGI mechanism and how forms are handled via CGI code fragments. We wrote some forms, and then some code to handle the variables (parsing, and so on). We wrote the **CFormParser** class to handle all key/value pairs via an STL **map** container, and we used this class in several examples. For all of our examples, we sent dynamic responses back to the client via HTML using **stdout** with streams. Finally, we implemented some more powerful CGI code fragments like the new guest book example.

CGI code fragments are powerful, much faster than interpreted scripts, and relatively efficient. They're also easy to write and debug. However, another standard for writing code fragments, ISAPI, does not have some of CGI's disadvantages, and it speeds things up quite substantially. We'll discuss how ISAPI does this in Chapter 4.

THE ISAPI CRASH COURSE

4

> *I feel the need for expeditious velocity.*
>
> ***Brain, Pinky and the Brain***

SAPI is an acronym for Internet Server Application Programming Interface. Although Microsoft's Internet Information Server supports this standard completely, ISAPI wasn't developed specifically for Microsoft. It's a general specification that allows you to extend a server's capabilities through the use of DLLs, much like CGI allows extension via applications. ISAPI was designed to improve on some of CGI's shortfalls and it has provided some fantastic performance increases as a result: An ISAPI code fragment on a busy server has a fivefold increase in performance over its CGI counterpart.

> *Note: ISAPI has nothing to do with ActiveX, so don't confuse the two. While they were at one time distributed within the same SDK, they are completely different. ActiveX encompasses a large spectrum of technologies to extend applications and services in general. ISAPI merely deals with extending the Web server, much like CGI.*

IIS loads the ISAPI code fragment into its process space once, and keeps it there until the server quits (you can change this option). This eliminates the problem of loading and unloading a code fragment into memory repeatedly that you encounter when using CGI. You can see why ISAPI improves performance when your site is busy. Every request to use the DLL is assigned a thread (that the Web server creates) that resides within the same process space. While creating threads is not nearly as expensive in taxing an operating system's resources and time as loading code fragments, it's even less expensive when you consider that servers like IIS generally allocate a pool of threads at initialization time and then use those threads throughout their runtime cycle. This saves the Web server the overhead of creating threads for every request they receive.

In this chapter, we're going to learn about ISAPI and write ISAPI DLLs. We're going to cover how they work, and how they improve performance over their CGI counterparts. Remember the old saying "You don't get something for nothing?" We'll cover what these performance gains will cost you in terms of extra programming skills.

What Is ISAPI?

ISAPI has its own specifications for how modules should interface with the server, retrieve server variables, and perform input/output. The major difference between ISAPI and CGI is that an ISAPI DLL runs in the process space of the Web server, whereas a CGI code fragment runs in its own separate process space. This is why performance improves.

Instead of going through system calls to get environmental variables, we can now share memory with the server and get this information immediately. Output goes directly through the server (rather than through **stdout**) using an ECB, an Extension Control Block, that is shared between your ISAPI code fragment and the Web server. Listing 4.1 shows the Extension Control Block's structure.

LISTING 4.1   THE EXTENSION CONTROL BLOCK STRUCTURE.

```
typedef struct _EXTENSION_CONTROL_BLOCK {

    DWORD     cbSize;  //IN
    DWORD     dwVersion ;  //IN
    HCONN     ConnID;  //IN
    DWORD     dwHttpStatusCode;  //OUT
```

```
CHAR        lpszLogData[HSE_LOG_BUFFER_LEN];    //OUT
LPSTR       lpszMethod; //IN
LPSTR       lpszQueryString; //IN
LPSTR       lpszPathInfo; //IN
LPSTR       lpszPathTranslated; //IN
DWORD       cbTotalBytes; //IN
DWORD       cbAvailable; //IN
LPBYTE      lpbData; //IN
LPSTR       lpszContentType; //IN

BOOL (WINAPI * GetServerVariable)
    (HCONN      hConn,
    LPSTR       lpszVariableName,
    LPVOID      lpvBuffer,
    LPDWORD     lpdwSize);

BOOL (WINAPI * WriteClient)
    (HCONN      ConnID,
    LPVOID      Buffer,
    LPDWORD     lpdwBytes,
    DWORD       dwReserved);

BOOL (WINAPI * ReadClient)
    (HCONN      ConnID,
    LPVOID      lpvBuffer,
    LPDWORD     lpdwSize);

BOOL (WINAPI * ServerSupportFunction)
    (HCONN      hConn,
    DWORD       dwHSERRequest,
    LPVOID      lpvBuffer,
    LPDWORD     lpdwSize,
    LPDWORD     lpdwDataType);

} EXTENSION_CONTROL_BLOCK, *LPEXTENSION_CONTROL_BLOCK;
```

This ECB structure is the mechanism that allows your ISAPI extension to gather information about the server, and to exchange information with the client's browser and the server. Notice that Listing 4.1 also shows some function pointers within this ECB structure. These function pointers are the routines you use to get a server variable, or read and write data to and from the client. You can do the equivalent with CGI, but the functions you use are system calls.

We're in the same process space as the Web server, so for multiple instances of our DLL to be used, a separate thread must be created for each—which is exactly what the server does automatically. Threads are substantially cheaper (in terms of memory and CPU cycles) than creating and loading new processes from scratch. However, this now requires your code fragment (DLL) to be thread-safe. Thread safety can be very dangerous if you're not familiar with reentrancy issues. Imagine that you're using a global variable, but another thread is using it too and is changing the value: You expect one result, but the other thread expects a different one. You both change the variable. Serious near-fatal bugs such as Deadlock could result from this re-entrancy. Because of issues like this, you'll have to be extra careful when you design portions of your DLL up front. In this chapter, we'll cover these issues and how to deal with them safely.

A Comparison Of ISAPI And CGI

In Listing 4.1, you'll notice that some of the function pointers are very similar to actions we performed with CGI in Chapter 3. Table 4.1 lists the routines that are similar between ISAPI and CGI.

CGI is so easy to learn because it uses **stdio** and streams, which are familiar to all C++ programmers. ISAPI routines like **ReadClient()** and **WriteClient()**are faster than their CGI equivalents, but they're certainly not familiar to C++ programmers. Microsoft has added some classes to simplify your development of ISAPI code fragments. **CHttpServerContext**, **CHtmlStream**, and **CHttpServer** will make writing ISAPI code fragments just as easy as writing ones with CGI— possibly easier. We'll use these classes in the next section, where we develop some ISAPI code fragments.

The **ServerSupportFunction**() has no CGI equivalent. It allows us to pass back a command to the server to perform some specialized tasks, such as redirection. We'll be using this in Chapter 10, where we'll cover it in more detail.

TABLE 4.1

A comparison of ISAPI and CGI routines.

ISAPI	CGI (or C++)
GetServerVariable()	getenv()
WriteClient()	printf() or <<
ReadClient()	scanf() or getc() or >>
ServerSupportFunction()	no equivalent

Creating ISAPI Code Fragments

While we can develop a DLL that uses the ECB directly to interface with our server, it would be much easier to use the special classes that Microsoft provides. To start off, let's open the Microsoft Developer Studio and create a new project. Select the "ISAPI Extension Wizard" and call your project "Hello-ISAPIWorld", as in Figure 4.1, and click the Create button.

Next, you'll get a dialog similar to the one in Figure 4.2. Do not check the "Generate a Filter object" checkbox because we're writing an extension and not an ISAPI filter.

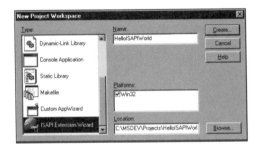

Figure 4.1
Making a new ISAPI extension with the Class Wizard.

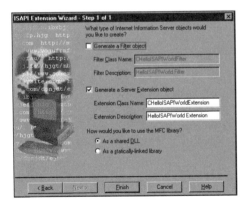

Figure 4.2
Class Wizard options for ISAPI extensions.

>*Note: An ISAPI filter is a special server extension that allows you to do special processing for all connections (hits) that occur on your server. It has no CGI equivalent. We will not be using an ISAPI filter for this book because it will not aid us in form processing.*

Be sure the "Generate a Server Extension object" is selected (as in Figure 4.2), and leave MFC as a shared DLL. If MFC is linked in as a static DLL, your ISAPI code fragment will become over 200K in size! Also, keeping MFC as a shared DLL allows you to replace that component without affecting the other programs that use the shared library.

The Class Wizard created two files for us: HelloISAPIWorldExtension.h and HelloISAPIWorldExtension.cpp. Let's take a look at Listing 4.2, which shows our class declaration for CHelloISAPIWorldExtension.

LISTING 4.2   HELLOISAPIWORLDEXTENSION.H.

```
// HELLOISAPIWORLD.H - Header file for your Internet Server
//    HelloISAPIWorld Extension

#include "resource.h"

class CHelloISAPIWorldExtension : public CHttpServer
{
public:
    CHelloISAPIWorldExtension();
    ~CHelloISAPIWorldExtension();

// Overrides
// ClassWizard generated virtual function overrides
// NOTE:  The ClassWizard will add and
// remove member functions here.
//    DO NOT EDIT what you see in these blocks of generated code!
 //{{AFX_VIRTUAL(CHelloISAPIWorldExtension)
public:
    virtual BOOL GetExtensionVersion(HSE_VERSION_INFO* pVer);
//}}AFX_VIRTUAL

// TODO: Add handlers for your commands here.
// For example:

    void Default(CHttpServerContext* pCtxt);

    DECLARE_PARSE_MAP()
```

```
//{{AFX_MSG(CHelloISAPIWorldExtension)
//}}AFX_MSG
};
```

Our class inherits from **CHttpServer**, which is at the heart of any MFC ISAPI code fragment. This class will manage our tasks for us and delegate how our member functions are called by the server via a member function **CallFunction**(). Listing 4.3 shows the code that the Class Wizard generates.

LISTING 4.3   HELLOISAPIWORLD.CPP, GENERATED BY THE CLASS WIZARD.

```
// HELLOISAPIWORLD.CPP - Implementation file for your
// Internet Server
//    HelloISAPIWorld Extension

#include "stdafx.h"
#include "HelloISAPIWorld.h"

///////////////////////////////////////////////////////////////////////
// The one and only CWinApp object
// NOTE: You may remove this object if you alter your project to no
// longer use MFC in a DLL.

CWinApp theApp;

///////////////////////////////////////////////////////////////////////
// command-parsing map

BEGIN_PARSE_MAP(CHelloISAPIWorldExtension, CHttpServer)
    // TODO: insert your ON_PARSE_COMMAND() and
    // ON_PARSE_COMMAND_PARAMS() here to hook up your commands.
    // For example:

    ON_PARSE_COMMAND(Default, CHelloISAPIWorldExtension, ITS_EMPTY)
    DEFAULT_PARSE_COMMAND(Default, CHelloISAPIWorldExtension)
END_PARSE_MAP(CHelloISAPIWorldExtension)


///////////////////////////////////////////////////////////////////////
// The one and only CHelloISAPIWorldExtension object

CHelloISAPIWorldExtension theExtension;
```

```
/////////////////////////////////////////////////////////////////////
// CHelloISAPIWorldExtension implementation

CHelloISAPIWorldExtension::CHelloISAPIWorldExtension()
{
}

CHelloISAPIWorldExtension::~CHelloISAPIWorldExtension()
{
}

BOOL CHelloISAPIWorldExtension::GetExtensionVersion(HSE_VERSION_INFO* pVer)
{
    // Call default implementation for initialization
    CHttpServer::GetExtensionVersion(pVer);

    // Load description string
    TCHAR sz[HSE_MAX_EXT_DLL_NAME_LEN+1];
    ISAPIVERIFY(::LoadString(AfxGetResourceHandle(),
        IDS_SERVER, sz, HSE_MAX_EXT_DLL_NAME_LEN));
    _tcscpy(pVer->lpszExtensionDesc, sz);
    return TRUE;
}


/////////////////////////////////////////////////////////////////////
// CHelloISAPIWorldExtension command handlers

void CHelloISAPIWorldExtension::Default(CHttpServerContext* pCtxt)
{
    StartContent(pCtxt);
    WriteTitle(pCtxt);

    *pCtxt << _T("This default message was produced by the Internet");
    *pCtxt << _T(" Server DLL Wizard. Edit your
    CHelloISAPIWorldExtension::Default()");
    *pCtxt << _T(" implementation to change it.\r\n");

    EndContent(pCtxt);
}

// Do not edit the following lines, which ClassWizard needs.
#if 0
BEGIN_MESSAGE_MAP(CHelloISAPIWorldExtension, CHttpServer)
    //{{AFX_MSG_MAP(CHelloISAPIWorldExtension)
    //}}AFX_MSG_MAP
END_MESSAGE_MAP()
#endif // 0
```

```
///////////////////////////////////////////////////////////////////////
// If your extension will not use MFC, you'll need this code to make
// sure the extension objects can find the resource handle for the
// module. If you convert your extension to not be dependent on MFC,
// remove the comments around the following AfxGetResourceHandle()
// and DllMain() functions, as well as the g_hInstance global.

/****

static HINSTANCE g_hInstance;

HINSTANCE AFXISAPI AfxGetResourceHandle()
{
    return g_hInstance;
}

BOOL WINAPI DllMain(HINSTANCE hInst, ULONG ulReason,
    LPVOID lpReserved)
{
    if (ulReason == DLL_PROCESS_ATTACH)
    {
        g_hInstance = hInst;
    }

    return TRUE;
}

****/
```

Table 4.2 shows us **CHttpServer** and its members. This class offers so much functionality that it would be hard not to use it. First off, **CHttpServer** offers several attribute member functions that manage a **CHtmlStream** object for us—in fact, we don't even need to call the stream object directly. Before sending output back to the client, we can use **StartContent**(): This member tells the server that we're beginning an HTML stream here. Of course, there's a corresponding **EndContent**() for when we're done with the stream—this tells the server to send our data to the client. In Chapter 3, we wrote our own routines that performed the same tasks, and called them **BeginHeader**() and **EndHeader**(); they behave nearly identically.

	TABLE 4.2

THE CHTTPSERVER CLASS.

Member Function	What Does It Do?
CHttpServer()	Constructs a CHttpServer object.
Overridable	
CallFunction()	Finds and executes the appropriate function associated with the command in the URL. If you will be processing your own variables, you will need to override this member.
OnParseError()	Constructs a description of the error to be returned to the client. Use this to aid with debugging.
HttpExtensionProc()	Uses the callback functions to read client data and decide what action to take.
GetExtensionVersion()	Gets the version number on which the DLL extension is based.
ConstructStream()	Constructs a **CHtmlStream** object.
Attribute	
StartContent()	Inserts opening HTML tags into a **CHtmlStream** object to be returned to the client.
EndContent()	Inserts closing HTML tags into a **CHtmlStream** object to be returned to the client.
WriteTitle()	Inserts the title between the appropriate HTML tags in the **CHtmlStream** object to be returned to the client.
GetTitle()	Gets the title of an HTML document to be sent to the client.
AddHeader()	Adds headers to a response before it is sent to the server. Use this before calling **StartContent()**, or some browsers will break.
InitInstance()	Initializes the **CHttpServer** object.

Another member function to note is **AddHeader**(), which we listed in Table 4.2. This allows us to send information to the browser before the client views the data—in other words, he or she won't see this information; this information could be a cookie for the browser to store away for our later use. We'll be using **AddHeader**() in Chapter 8 when we send and receive cookies from the client's browser.

The **CallFunction**() member is instantiated every time a request is made for your DLL, much like **main**() is called in your CGI code fragment. Chances are that in a simple ISAPI fragment you will not override this; rather, you'll use the default routine from **CHttpServer**. How, then, will **CHttpServer** know what member function to call for a user action? This is where Parsemaps, which we'll cover in the next section, comes in. For now I'll just say that when **CallFunction**() gets a request for any unfamiliar member function, it calls your **Default**() member function (refer back to Listing 4.3) if the arguments are similar.

To send HTML output, each member function that **CallFunction**() calls receives a pointer to a **CHttpServerContext** object, which provides a stream << **operator** for your convenience. **CHttpServerContext** provides many other member functions and even an ECB with a wealth of information to access, and Table 4.3 shows the class listing and descriptions of its member functions. This class is a thin—but extremely convenient—wrapper around the ECB structure. You can tell this because several member functions parallel the ECB function pointers from Listing 4.1.

TABLE 4.3

THE CHTTPSERVERCONTEXT CLASS.

Data Members	What Does It Do?
m_pECB	A pointer to an **EXTENSION_CONTROL_BLOCK** structure. See Listing 4.1 for more detail on this structure.
m_pStream	A pointer to a **CHtmlStream**. We never use this directly in this chapter.
Constructor	**What Does It Do?**
CHttpServerContext()	Constructs a **CHttpServerContext** object.
Operations	**What Does It Do?**
GetServerVariable()	Copies information relating to an HTTP connection, or to the server itself, into a supplied buffer. In CGI, we used the system call, getenv().
WriteClient()	Sends information to the HTTP client immediately.

(continued)

	TABLE 4.3

THE CHTTPSERVERCONTEXT CLASS (*CONTINUED*).

Operations	What Does It Do?
ReadClient()	Reads information from the body of the Web client's HTTP request into the buffer supplied by the caller.
ServerSupportFunction()	Provides ISAs with some general-purpose functions as well as functions that are specific to HTTP server implementation.
Special Operator	What Does It Do?
operator <<	Writes data into a stream, just like we did to **cout** in Chapter 3.

To perform output in the **CHtmlStream**, we can use the pointer we get to the **CHttpServerContext** object and use its stream operator, or **ReadClient**() and **WriteClient**(). Let's modify the **Default**() member function from our CHelloISAPIWorldExtension to say "Hello ISAPI World!"

First, we need to tell the server we're starting an HTML stream, so we call **StartContent**(). Next, we can either use the **CHttpServerContext**'s **WriteClient**() member, or the **<< operator**, which I personally prefer because it parallels the streams we used previously with CGI. Your **Default**() member has already done everything we want, but the text is wrong, so let's change it:

```
// CHelloISAPIWorldExtension command handlers

void CHelloISAPIWorldExtension::Default(CHttpServerContext* pCtxt)
{
    StartContent(pCtxt);
    WriteTitle(pCtxt);

    *pCtxt << _T("<CENTER><H1>Hello ISAPI World!</H1></CENTER>");

    EndContent(pCtxt);
} // CHelloISAPIWorldExtension...
```

> *Note: The _T() macro is for Unicode support, which is something all of us will have to start using eventually. If you're not building a Unicode project, it does nothing, but you might want to get accustomed to the syntax now.*

The **Default**() member now does everything that we need, and is instantiated through the browser with the following modification to our Hello-
World.htm page:

```
<FORM ACTION="/scripts/HelloISAPIWorld.dll" METHOD=POST>
```

Figure 4.3 shows the output from the **submit** action. While this is a fine example of using ISPAI to implement a simple code fragment, we're still missing
some functionality that we developed in Chapter 3 when using CGI. Therefore, let's add some of that functionality to our **CHttpServer** class.

Extending CHttpServer

In Chapter 3, we wrote a couple of useful functions that streamed a header and
footer file out for us. We sent our output results after the header was sent. As a
result, we could use a generic header and footer, and only needed to specify the
file name to our function. For **CHttpServer**, we'll override the **StartContent**()
and **EndContent**() members and add this functionality there. We'll use the
identical header and footer files that we used in Chapter 3.

In Developer Studio, create a new ISAPI extension project and then click on
the Class Wizard icon (we'll name this new class **CCoolHttpServer**). The
CCoolHttpServer class will appear, and in the right-hand list box, you'll see
member functions from its base class, **CHttpServer**. Double-click on **End-
Content**() and **StartContent**(), as shown in Figure 4.4. To add a new member
function, click with the right mouse button on your class view list, shown in
Figure 4.5.

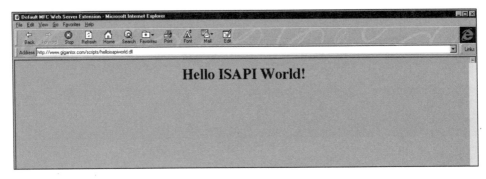

Figure 4.3
Output from HelloISAPIWorld.htm.

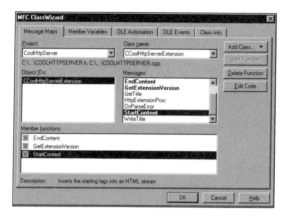

Figure 4.4
Modifying the **CCoolHttpServer** class with the Class Wizard.

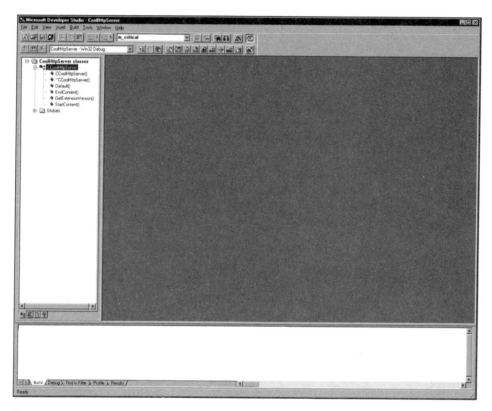

Figure 4.5
Adding a new member function to a class.

Listing 4.4 displays the new sources for CoolHttpServer.cpp. From now on, we'll use this as our base class (instead of **CHttpServer**). Later on in this chapter, we'll expand on using it for error handling and will talk about additional functionality we could use in our ISAPI code fragments. Figure 4.6 shows the output results of HelloISAPIWorld.htm when making the **CHelloISAPIWorld-Extension** class inherit from **CCoolHttpServer**.

LISTING 4.4   SOURCE CODE FOR **CCOOLHTTPSERVER**.

```
// COOLHTTPSERVER.CPP - Implementation file for your Internet Server
//    CoolHttpServer Extension

#include "stdafx.h"
#include "CoolHttpServer.h"


///////////////////////////////////////////////////////////////////////
// The one and only CWinApp object
// NOTE: You may remove this object if you alter your
// project to no
// longer use MFC in a DLL.

CWinApp theApp;

///////////////////////////////////////////////////////////////////////
// command-parsing map

BEGIN_PARSE_MAP(CCoolHttpServer, CHttpServer)
    // TODO: insert your ON_PARSE_COMMAND() and
    // ON_PARSE_COMMAND_PARAMS() here to hook up your commands.
    // For example:

    ON_PARSE_COMMAND(Default, CCoolHttpServer, ITS_EMPTY)
    DEFAULT_PARSE_COMMAND(Default, CCoolHttpServer)
END_PARSE_MAP(CCoolHttpServer)


///////////////////////////////////////////////////////////////////////
// The one and only CCoolHttpServer object

CCoolHttpServer theExtension;


///////////////////////////////////////////////////////////////////////
// CCoolHttpServer implementation
```

```
CCoolHttpServer::CCoolHttpServer()
{
}


CCoolHttpServer::~CCoolHttpServer()
{
}


BOOL CCoolHttpServer::GetExtensionVersion(HSE_VERSION_INFO* pVer)
{
    // Call default implementation for initialization
    CHttpServer::GetExtensionVersion(pVer);

    // Load description string
    TCHAR sz[HSE_MAX_EXT_DLL_NAME_LEN+1];
    ISAPIVERIFY(::LoadString(AfxGetResourceHandle(),
        IDS_SERVER, sz, HSE_MAX_EXT_DLL_NAME_LEN));
    _tcscpy(pVer->lpszExtensionDesc, sz);
    return TRUE;
}


/////////////////////////////////////////////////////////////////////
// CCoolHttpServer command handlers

void CCoolHttpServer::Default(CHttpServerContext* pCtxt)
{
    StartContent(pCtxt);
    WriteTitle(pCtxt);

    *pCtxt << _T("This default message was produced by the Internet");
    *pCtxt << _T(" Server DLL Wizard. Edit your
        CCoolHttpServer::Default()");
    *pCtxt << _T(" implementation to change it.\r\n");

    EndContent(pCtxt);
}


// Do not edit the following lines, which are needed by ClassWizard
#if 0
BEGIN_MESSAGE_MAP(CCoolHttpServer, CHttpServer)
  //{{AFX_MSG_MAP(CCoolHttpServer)
  //}}AFX_MSG_MAP
END_MESSAGE_MAP()
#endif // 0
```

```
/////////////////////////////////////////////////////////////////
// If your extension will not use MFC, you'll need this code to make
// sure the extension objects can find the resource handle for the
// module. If you convert your extension to not be dependent on MFC,
// remove the comments around the following AfxGetResourceHandle()
// and DllMain() functions, as well as the g_hInstance global.

/****

static HINSTANCE g_hInstance;

HINSTANCE AFXISAPI AfxGetResourceHandle()
{
    return g_hInstance;
}

BOOL WINAPI DllMain(HINSTANCE hInst, ULONG ulReason,
    LPVOID lpReserved)
{
    if (ulReason == DLL_PROCESS_ATTACH)
    {
        g_hInstance = hInst;
    }

    return TRUE;
}

****/

void CCoolHttpServer::EndContent(CHttpServerContext* pCtxt) const
{
    StreamFile(pCtxt, cFooterFile);
    CHttpServer::EndContent(pCtxt);
}


void CCoolHttpServer::StartContent(CHttpServerContext* pCtxt) const
{
    CHttpServer::StartContent(pCtxt);
    StreamFile(pCtxt, cHeaderFile);
}


//
//     function: CCoolHttpServer::StreamFile
```

```
//     purpose: streams the designated file via CHttpServerContext.
//     returns: nothing.
//
void
CCoolHttpServer::StreamFile(CHttpServerContext *pCtxt, const char
  *inFileName)
{
    try
    {
        ifstream    file(inFile); // file stream

        if (!file)              // if we don't get the file, then
            throw(-1);          // throw an exception

        char buffer[80];            // just a line of characters

        // Here, we loop through the file line by line until we hit the
        //    end
        // sending all the data to the CHttpServerContext ptr
        while (ile.getline(buffer,sizeof(buffer)))
            *pCtxt << buffer;

        file.close();
    }

    catch(...)
    {
        *pCtxt << "<center><b>Couldn't locate the header file.
           <br></center></b>";
    }
} // CCoolHttpServer::StreamFile
```

Figure 4.6 shows the results, and they look substantially better than the basic example we started with. The code for **CHelloISAPIWorldExtension** is identical to what it was earlier, except that we changed the base class to use the new **CCoolHttpServer** class.

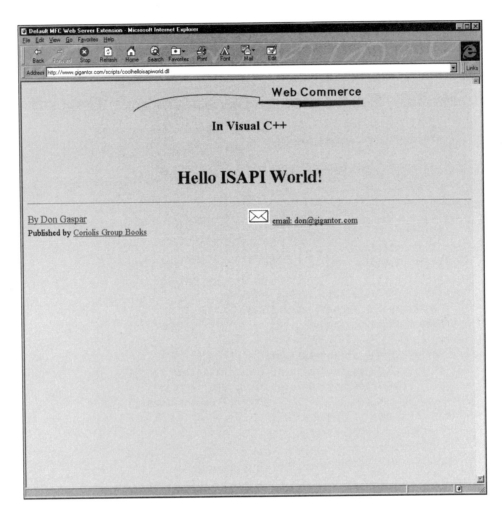

Figure 4.6
New output from CoolHelloISAPIWorld.htm.

Server Variables

We did an example with CGI that retrieved and displayed server variables, and now we're going to do it with an ISAPI extension. Again, we'll create a new project and change our main class to inherit from **CCoolHttpServer** instead of **CHttpServer**. Next, we'll add the table we used for getting the CGI variables so that our code doesn't span 10 pages as it does in most other books about this subject. Instead, it fits within a few lines—like it should.

Listing 4.5 shows the source code changes we've made. It uses the table of character pointers to retrieve all the environmental variables, but uses **GetServer-Variable**() from the **CHttpServerContext** class.

LISTING 4.5   SOURCE CODE FOR CISAPISERVERVARS::DEFAULT().

```
/////////////////////////////////////////////////////////////////////////////
// CIsapiServerVars command handlers

void CIsapiServerVars::Default(CHttpServerContext* pCtxt)
{
    char          buffer[256];
    unsigned long   bufferSize;

    StartContent(pCtxt);
    WriteTitle(pCtxt);

    *pCtxt << _T("<CENTER><H1>Here are your
        ISAPI Server Variables!</H1><BR><BR><BR>");
    for(short index=0; index != cNumberOfVars; index++)
    {
        bufferSize = sizeof(buffer);
      if (pCtxt->GetServerVariable(const_cast<char *>
            (cEnvironment[index]),buffer, &bufferSize))
            *pCtxt << _T("<B>") << _T(cEnvironment[index])
                << _T(" = </B>") <<
                _T(buffer) << _T("<BR>");
    }
    *pCtxt << _T("<BR><BR><BR></CENTER>");

    EndContent(pCtxt);
}
```

Figure 4.7 shows the results of the output. Note that so far, we've only used the **Default**() member function. In order to use other member functions that we write, we can either override the **CallFunction**() member—which we'll have to do sometime anyway—or we can use the MFC Parsemaps.

We could have used **getenv**() like we did in Chapter 3, but using **GetServer-Variable**() is much faster because we're calling a routine from the server within the server's context, whereas **getenv**() is a system call that has slightly more overhead.

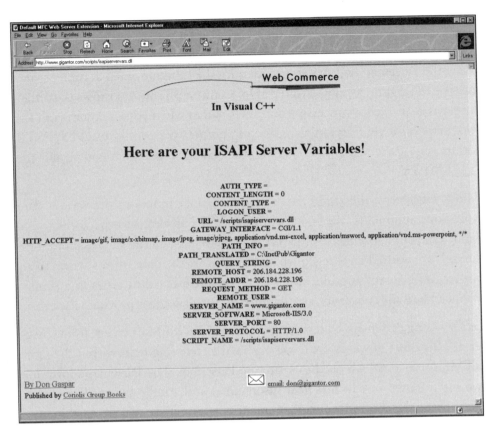

Figure 4.7
Environmental variables retrieved via CHttpServerContext's GetServerVariable() member.

Parsemaps And NewHelloISAPIWorld

A Parsemap is a set of macros provided with MFC that allows us to tell our ISAPI code fragment what we call our function in the outside world (our HTML form, for example), and what its parameters are. To call your function from one routine, you would use something like:

```
<FORM ACTION="/scripts/yourDll?functionName METHOD="POST">
```

In this case, when the **submit** action is selected on the client browser, **functionName** will be called, and all the HTML variables from your form will be passed to your **functionName**. In ISAPI, there's no need to parse the variables from the stream that the browser sends: It's done automatically for you when you use a Parsemap. There's also no need to worry about whether you're using **GET** or **POST**, because that's handled for you too (except when you transfer large amounts of data, like greater than 48K).

Using the Parsemap requires you to identify the function, each argument, and the type the argument can be (integer, for example). Table 4.4 shows the different types available for processing and their names when you use them with the Parsemap. So if your argument is a string pointer you would use **ITS_PSTR** within your Parsemap macro, and if you had no arguments you would use **ITS_EMPTY**.

Before you receive the arguments to your member function, the various data types your arguments can be are automatically converted to the correct type defined in your Parsemap. With CGI, we had to parse all the variables and store them. If we wanted an integer, we had to convert the data from a string to an integer using something like **atoi()**, and convert other data types in a similar manner. Here, the conversions are handled for us; all we do is provide a Parsemap.

Let's try using Parsemaps by revisiting the NewHelloWorld.htm page from Chapter 3. This time, however, we'll use our ISAPI code fragment within the same HTML form. First, we need to write the Parsemap. The Parsemap's form has two input items: an edit text field (**userName**) and a radio button (**computerPref**). Using the above Parsemap argument types, we'll use two string pointers.

The Parsemap contains everything within a **BEGIN_PARSE_MAP** and an **END_PARSE_MAP** macro. We need to tell the macros what our function is called, and then identify its arguments on a separate line. For our case, we provide something like:

TABLE 4.4

PARSEMAP ARGUMENT TYPES.

Datatype	Description
ITS_PSTR	string pointer
ITS_I2	two-byte integer
ITS_I4	four-byte integer (long)
ITS_R4	float
ITS_R8	double
ITS_EMPTY	no arguments being used

```
BEGIN_PARSE_MAP(CNewHelloISAPIWorld, CCoolHttpServer)
    ON_PARSE_COMMAND(DoHelloWorld,CNewHelloISAPIWorld,
        ITS_PSTR  ITS_PSTR)
    ON_PARSE_COMMAND_PARAMS("userName computerPref")
    ON_PARSE_COMMAND(Default, CNewHelloISAPIWorld, ITS_EMPTY)
    DEFAULT_PARSE_COMMAND(Default, CNewHelloISAPIWorld)
END_PARSE_MAP(CNewHelloISAPIWorld)
```

 ### HTML Variables Are Case Sensitive

When declaring a variable in your Parsemap, be sure its case is identical to that in your form. If it's not, you'll find yourself in a debugging marathon trying to find out why your member function isn't being called, but the **Default()** member is.

For our member function **DoHelloWorld**() to be properly instantiated, we must identify the function and the class, and its arguments with the **ON_PARSE _COMMAND** macro. We then define the variable names with the **ON_PARSE_COMMAND_PARAMS** macro. This macro now identifies our function name with those variables for the base class, **CHttpServer**, to use its **CallFunction**() member to instantiate us. The data will be parsed and passed in to our arguments so we don't have to process anything.

ON_PARSE_COMMAND will not accept a comma in between the argument types; likewise, the compiler will give you an error if you provide one. Also, **ON_PARSE_COMMAND_PARAMS** contains all the variable names within a quoted string with only a space separating them. Neither macro takes a semicolon at the end of its statement, so watch your syntax.

If it's possible that your variables could be equal to any default value, put your variables in your **ON_PARSE_COMMAND_PARAMS** macro in the following way:

```
ON_PARSE_COMMAND_PARAMS("userName=Don computerPref=AIX")
```

When you provide default argument values, your function will still be called, even if the browser does not send you the data for that item on the form. Check boxes are a good example of something that requires default values. Remember that check-box variables are not sent over unless they've been selected.

Notice both the default member function called **Default**() and the
DEFAULT_PARSE_COMMAND macro. These identify who **CallFunction**()
should instantiate if the variables and function name do not match anyone. I
usually insert some obnoxious debugging message for myself—a customer will
never see the error message, and it tells me to fix the problem when I see it.

When your function is instantiated, the first argument is always a pointer to
a **CHttpServerContext** object, but this object is not included in the Parsemap.
So for the above **DoHelloWorld**() member function, we would have an interface like

```
void
CNewHelloISAPIWorldExtension::DoHelloWorld(
    CHttpServerContext* pCtxt,
    LPCTSTR userName, LPCTSTR computerPref)
```

where an **LPCTSTR** data type is just a fancy name for a "const long pointer c-
style Unicode string." You could use a **char** * if you prefer.

Listing 4.6 contains the sources for the NewHelloISAPIWorld code fragment,
with a new Parsemap so that the member function **DoHelloWorld**() is used
rather than the **Default**() member.

LISTING 4.6   NEWHELLOISAPIWORLD.CPP.

```
// NEWHELLOISAPIWORLD.CPP - Implementation file for your
// Internet Server
//    NewHelloISAPIWorld Extension

#include "stdafx.h"
#include "NewHelloISAPIWorld.h"


///////////////////////////////////////////////////////////////////////
// The one and only CWinApp object
// NOTE: You may remove this object if you alter your project to no
// longer use MFC in a DLL.

CWinApp theApp;


///////////////////////////////////////////////////////////////////////
// command-parsing map


BEGIN_PARSE_MAP(CNewHelloISAPIWorldExtension, CHttpServer)
    ON_PARSE_COMMAND(DoHelloWorld,
```

```
        CNewHelloISAPIWorldExtension,
            ITS_PSTR ITS_PSTR)
    ON_PARSE_COMMAND_PARAMS("userName computerPref")
    ON_PARSE_COMMAND(Default, CNewHelloISAPIWorldExtension,
        ITS_EMPTY)
    DEFAULT_PARSE_COMMAND(Default,
        CNewHelloISAPIWorldExtension)
END_PARSE_MAP(CNewHelloISAPIWorldExtension)


/////////////////////////////////////////////////////////////////////
// The one and only CNewHelloISAPIWorldExtension object

CNewHelloISAPIWorldExtension theExtension;


/////////////////////////////////////////////////////////////////////
// CNewHelloISAPIWorldExtension implementation

CNewHelloISAPIWorldExtension::CNewHelloISAPIWorldExtension()
{
}

CNewHelloISAPIWorldExtension::~CNewHelloISAPIWorldExtension()
{
}

BOOL CNewHelloISAPIWorldExtension::GetExtensionVersion(HSE_VERSION_INFO*
pVer)
{
    // Call default implementation for initialization
    CHttpServer::GetExtensionVersion(pVer);

    // Load description string
    TCHAR sz[HSE_MAX_EXT_DLL_NAME_LEN+1];
    ISAPIVERIFY(::LoadString(AfxGetResourceHandle(),
        IDS_SERVER, sz, HSE_MAX_EXT_DLL_NAME_LEN));
    _tcscpy(pVer->lpszExtensionDesc, sz);
    return TRUE;
}

/////////////////////////////////////////////////////////////////////
// CNewHelloISAPIWorldExtension command handlers

void CNewHelloISAPIWorldExtension::Default(CHttpServerContext* pCtxt)
{
```

```
        StartContent(pCtxt);
        WriteTitle(pCtxt);

        *pCtxt << _T("This default message was produced by the Internet");
        *pCtxt << _T(" Server DLL Wizard. Edit your
                CNewHelloISAPIWorldExtension::Default()");
        *pCtxt << _T(" implementation to change it.\r\n");

        EndContent(pCtxt);
}

// Do not edit the following lines, which ClassWizard needs.
#if 0
BEGIN_MESSAGE_MAP(CNewHelloISAPIWorldExtension, CHttpServer)
    //{{AFX_MSG_MAP(CNewHelloISAPIWorldExtension)
    //}}AFX_MSG_MAP
END_MESSAGE_MAP()
#endif // 0


/////////////////////////////////////////////////////////////////////
// If your extension will not use MFC, you'll need this code to make
// sure the extension objects can find the resource handle for the
// module. If you convert your extension to not be dependent on MFC,
// remove the comments around the following AfxGetResourceHandle()
// and DllMain() functions, as well as the g_hInstance global.
/****

static HINSTANCE g_hInstance;

HINSTANCE AFXISAPI AfxGetResourceHandle()
{
    return g_hInstance;
}

BOOL WINAPI DllMain(HINSTANCE hInst, ULONG ulReason,
    LPVOID lpReserved)
{
    if (ulReason == DLL_PROCESS_ATTACH)
    {
        g_hInstance = hInst;
    }

    return TRUE;
}

****/
```

```
void
CNewHelloISAPIWorldExtension::DoHelloWorld(CHttpServerContext* pCtxt,L
    PCTSTR userName, LPCTSTR computerPref)
{
    StartContent(pCtxt);
    WriteTitle(pCtxt);

    *pCtxt << _T("<CENTER><H1>Hello, ") << _T(userName) <<
        _T("</H1><BR>");
            *pCtxt << _T("<H3>You prefer to use ") << _T(computerPref) <<
            _T(" OS!</CENTER></H3><BR><BR><BR>");

    EndContent(pCtxt);
} // CNewHelloISAPIWorldExtension::DoHelloWorld...
```

While these Parsemaps have simplified our tasks substantially, how about a Parsemap for a form that contains 20 items? What about a form with an unknown number of items? A classic example is the contents of a customer's shopping cart, because we never know what's going to be in it until he or she views the contents. How do we handle that form data?

You could write a member function that contains one of every item you sell and list each one as an argument to your function with default values set to zero. This way, only items that were in the shopping cart would be correctly processed. I said that you *could* do this. You could also get shot for doing it—by your fellow programmers. On most projects I've worked on, the penalty for writing such a bad function would usually be the public firing squad—with your teammates shooting you with Nerf guns. And it would be justified.

The solution for such a case is to override **CallFunction**() from **CHttpServer**, and use something like the **CFormParser** class that we wrote in Chapter 3. In this version of **CallFunction**(), you check for special function names that could contain an unknown number of variables. If there are any, you use the **CFormParser** class and then call the function yourself. For other cases, you call the base class' member so that all your other functions take advantage of their Parsemaps. Later on in Chapter 5, when we start processing dynamic HTML contents, we'll do just that.

Some More ISAPI Examples

Our study of ISAPI wouldn't be complete without looking again at some of the examples we created with CGI and redoing them with ISAPI. Let's take a look at each example we've written so far, and provide the equivalent ISAPI code fragment. This is an excellent exercise for getting familiar with Parsemaps, **CHttpServer**, and **CHttpServerContext**.

Debugging

Debugging an ISAPI code fragment can be even worse than debugging one in CGI. An ISAPI code fragment is, after all, a DLL. A few tools can help you out with debugging: If you've programmed with MFC, you've seen the **TRACE()** macros and how to use them. Essentially, they allow you to place comments in your code, and data at certain spots in your code. They are compiled out when you build non-debug code, so don't worry about something like **TRACE()** being functional in a released version of your product. The **ISAPITRACE()** macro accomplishes the same task, so be sure to try it out. Both of these macros take formatted input just like Standard C Library functions **printf()**, **sprintf()**, and so on. They're easy to use as well as versatile.

Develop Code Fragments On A Web Server

Well, not on *the* Web server, but on a server nonetheless. This will allow you to debug your code with a debugger. If you don't use a debugger, you run the risk of crashing the production server, not to mention wasting valuable time, which can be very frustrating.

CHttpServer has a member function called **OnParseError()**, and it makes sense to override this member if you're having any trouble with debugging. **OnParseError()** takes a pointer to a **CHttpServerContext** object, so you can stream results back out to a browser to view them for debugging. The other argument that **OnParseError()** takes is a value to the error that has occurred (integer), so this error valuewill help you isolate the problem you're experiencing. Table 4.5 shows the possible values **OnParseError()** can receive for its **nCause** argument.

Something else you should note is that there are some simple applications that allow you to load your DLL into memory, pass a command string to it, and view the results. One is called EyeSapi and it's in the public domain. The only

	TABLE 4.5

NCAUSE VALUES FOR CHTTPSERVER::ONPARSEERROR().

Error Values	Meaning
callOK	OnParseError() handled the error.
callParamRequired	A required parameter was missing.
callBadParamCount	There were too many or too few parameters.
callBadCommand	The command name was not found.
callNoStackSpace	No stack space was available.
callNoStream	No **CHtmlStream** was available.
callMissingQuote	A parameter is missing a quotation mark.
callMissingParams	No parameters were available.
callBadParam	A parameter had a bad format.

problem with using such tools is that you have to understand how the command string is passed to the server, and do the same with this tool. This requires you to think like a Web browser, and type your arguments just like the browser would pass them to the Web server.

Other tools are becoming available all the time. We'll place links to them on our support page for this book (**www.gigantor.com/coriolis**) to keep you up to date, so please be sure to take a look there periodically.

Guest Book Revisited With ISAPI

Again, we revisit another classic: the guest book. Listing 4.7 provides the sources. The code to handle the guest book is nearly identical to what we wrote in NewGuestBook.cpp for the CGI code fragment (Chapter 3). The main difference is that in ISAPI, we use Parsemap to break up the variables for us automatically (instead of using **CFormParser**). Therefore, to access the variables, we use the names of the arguments in our member function.

Be Careful When Mixing MFC And STL

When you use anything from STL with MFC, be sure to define the preprocessor symbol NOMINMAX. If you don't, you'll find yourself getting various compiler errors in some template files of STL that could be very difficult and time-consuming to debug.

As for passing in a lot of arguments for a member function, this member, **Sign-GuestBook**(), is probably about as large as you would ever want one to be, or close to it. In Chapter 5, we'll override **CallFunction**() and use the **CFormParser** in an ISAPI Code fragment to handle any number of arguments passed to us independent of the Parsemap limitation.

LISTING 4.7   SOURCE FOR ISAPIGuestBook.cpp.

```
// ISAPIGUESTBOOK.CPP - Implementation file for your Internet Server
//     ISAPIGuestBook Extension

#include "stdafx.h"

// Headers we need, but are provided with the compiler
#include <ostream.h>
#include <fstream.h>
#include <stdio.h>
#include <stdlib.h>

// and from wondeful STL
#include <function.h>
#include <algo.h>
#include <bstring.h>

// our header file
#include "ISAPIGuestBook.h"

// the name of our guest book file
const char *cGuestFile  = "f:\\ISAPIGuestFile";

// some useful things we've provided

ostream&
operator<< (ostream &inOStream, const GuestInfo &inGuest)
{
    inOStream << inGuest.name << "|";
    inOStream << inGuest.address1 << "|";
    inOStream << inGuest.address2 << "|";
    inOStream << inGuest.city << "|";
    inOStream << inGuest.state << "|";
    inOStream << inGuest.zip << "|";
    inOStream << inGuest.phone_number << "|";
    inOStream << inGuest.email_address << "|";
    return inOStream;
}
```

```
istream&
operator>> (istream &inIStream, GuestInfo &outGuest)
{
    char    temp[64];
    inIStream.getline(temp,32,'|');
    outGuest.name = temp;
    inIStream.getline(temp,32,'|');
    outGuest.address1 = temp;
    inIStream.getline(temp,32,'|');
    outGuest.address2 = temp;
    inIStream.getline(temp,32,'|');
    outGuest.city = temp;
    inIStream.getline(temp,32,'|');
    outGuest.state = temp;
    inIStream.getline(temp,16,'|');
    outGuest.zip = temp;
    inIStream.getline(temp,16,'|');
    outGuest.phone_number = temp;
    inIStream.getline(temp,64,'|');
    outGuest.email_address = temp;
    return inIStream;
}


/////////////////////////////////////////////////////////////////////
// The one and only CWinApp object
// NOTE: You may remove this object if you alter your project to no
// longer use MFC in a DLL.

CWinApp theApp;

/////////////////////////////////////////////////////////////////////
// command-parsing map

BEGIN_PARSE_MAP(CISAPIGuestBook, CHttpServer)
  ON_PARSE_COMMAND(SignGuestBook,CISAPIGuestBook,
    ITS_PSTR ITS_PSTR ITS_PSTR ITS_PSTR ITS_PSTR
    ITS_PSTR ITS_PSTR ITS_PSTR ITS_PSTR)
  ON_PARSE_COMMAND_PARAMS("name=none address1=none
    address2=none city=none state=none zip=none phone=none
    emailAddress=none task=none")

    ON_PARSE_COMMAND(Default, CISAPIGuestBook, ITS_EMPTY)
    DEFAULT_PARSE_COMMAND(Default, CISAPIGuestBook)
END_PARSE_MAP(CISAPIGuestBook)
```

```
/////////////////////////////////////////////////////////////////////
// The one and only CISAPIGuestBook object

CISAPIGuestBook theExtension;


/////////////////////////////////////////////////////////////////////
// CISAPIGuestBook implementation

CISAPIGuestBook::CISAPIGuestBook()
{
}

CISAPIGuestBook::~CISAPIGuestBook()
{
}

BOOL CISAPIGuestBook::GetExtensionVersion(HSE_VERSION_INFO* pVer)
{
    // Call default implementation for initialization
    CHttpServer::GetExtensionVersion(pVer);

    // Load description string
    TCHAR sz[HSE_MAX_EXT_DLL_NAME_LEN+1];
    ISAPIVERIFY(::LoadString(AfxGetResourceHandle(),
        IDS_SERVER, sz, HSE_MAX_EXT_DLL_NAME_LEN));
    _tcscpy(pVer->lpszExtensionDesc, sz);
    return TRUE;
}


/////////////////////////////////////////////////////////////////////
// CISAPIGuestBook command handlers

void CISAPIGuestBook::Default(CHttpServerContext* pCtxt)
{
    StartContent(pCtxt);
    WriteTitle(pCtxt);

    *pCtxt << _T("This default message was produced by the Internet");
    *pCtxt << _T(" Server DLL Wizard. Edit your
    CISAPIGuestBook::Default()");
    *pCtxt << _T(" implementation to change it.\r\n");

    EndContent(pCtxt);
}
```

```
// Do not edit the following lines, which ClassWizard needs.
#if 0
BEGIN_MESSAGE_MAP(CISAPIGuestBook, CHttpServer)
    //{{AFX_MSG_MAP(CISAPIGuestBook)
    //}}AFX_MSG_MAP
END_MESSAGE_MAP()
#endif // 0




/////////////////////////////////////////////////////////////////////////
// If your extension will not use MFC, you'll need this code to make
// sure the extension objects can find the resource handle for the
// module. If you convert your extension to not be dependent on MFC,
// remove the comments around the following AfxGetResourceHandle()
// and DllMain() functions, as well as the g_hInstance global.

/****

static HINSTANCE g_hInstance;

HINSTANCE AFXISAPI AfxGetResourceHandle()
{
    return g_hInstance;
}

BOOL WINAPI DllMain(HINSTANCE hInst, ULONG ulReason,
    LPVOID lpReserved)
{
    if (ulReason == DLL_PROCESS_ATTACH)
    {
        g_hInstance = hInst;
    }

    return TRUE;
}

****/

void
CISAPIGuestBook::SignGuestBook(CHttpServerContext *pCtxt, LPCTSTR inName,
  LPCTSTR
    inAddress1, LPCTSTR inAddress2, LPCTSTR inCity, LPCTSTR inState,
    LPCTSTR inZip, LPCTSTR inPhone,
    LPCTSTR inEmailAddress, LPCTSTR inTask )
{
```

```
    StartContent(pCtxt);
    WriteTitle(pCtxt);

    if (strcmp(inTask,"Submit") == 0)    // adding their name???
    {
        if (strcmp(inName,"none") && strcmp(inAddress1,"none")&&
         strcmp(inCity,"none") &&
          strcmp(inState,"none") && strcmp(inZip,"none") &&
            strcmp(inPhone,"none") &&
            strcmp(inEmailAddress,"none") )
        {
            GuestInfo guest;    // copy to a GuestInfo struct
            guest.name = inName;
             guest.address1 = inAddress1;
            guest.address2 = inAddress2;
            guest.city = inCity;
            guest.state = inState;
            guest.zip = inZip;
            guest.phone_number = inPhone;
            guest.email_address = inEmailAddress;

            ofstream  guestFile(cGuestFile,ios::ate | ios::out);    //
             append "At The End"
            int count = 0;    // attempts to open the file
            if (guestFile == NULL)
            {
                cout << "Guest File failure...";
            while(count++ < 25 && !guestFile)
                    guestFile.open(cGuestFile,ios::ate | ios::out);
            }

            if (guestFile && count != 25)
            {
                guestFile << guest;    // put it in our file with our
                 //stream operator
                guestFile.close();    // save our changes
                *pCtxt << "<CENTER><H2>Thank you, " << guest.name.c_str()
                << ", your name has been added.</   CENTER><BR><BR><BR>";
            }
             else
                *pCtxt << "<H2>Sorry, an error occurred and your name
                        was not added</H2><BR><BR><BR>";
```

```
        }
    else
        *pCtxt << "<H2>Sorry, an error occurred and your name
                         was not added</H2><BR><BR><BR>";
    }
else    // spying on others!
{
    vector<GuestInfo>  theGuests;        // display using a vector
    ifstream inputFile(cGuestFile);      // the file to use
    if (inputFile)
    {
        istream_iterator<GuestInfo,ptrdiff_t> iter(inputFile),end;
          // iterator
        copy(iter, end, inserter(theGuests,theGuests.begin()));
          // copy to our vector
        inputFile.close();      // all done for now

        vector<GuestInfo>::iterator guestIter;     // move through and
          display the names
        *pCtxt << "<CENTER><H1>Guest who have signed in:</
          H1><BR><BR><BR>";
        for (guestIter = theGuests.begin(); guestIter !=
          theGuests.end(); guestIter++)
            *pCtxt << (*guestIter).name.c_str() << " from " <<
              (*guestIter).city.c_str() << "<BR>";
         *pCtxt << "</CENTER><BR><BR><BR>";
    }
    else
        *pCtxt << "<H2>Sorry, the guest file is busy. Please try
          again later.
                    </H2><BR><BR><BR>";
}

    EndContent(pCtxt);
} // CISAPIGuestBook::SignGuestBook...
```

The **SignGuestBook**() member does everything for us. Figure 4.8 shows the results of adding a name to the guest book. There are entire textbooks on ISAPI and the climactic result is just a guest book, but with a little practice, you'll see this become a programming task that you can do from scratch in under a half an hour with some 50 or so lines of familiar code.

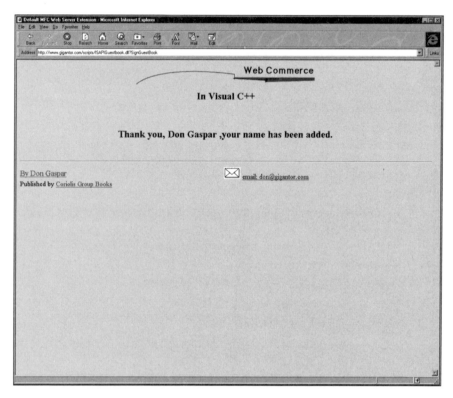

Figure 4.8
Results of signing the guest book.

Order Taking

In Chapter 3, we tested out the **CFormParser** class using CGI. Here, we'll redo
the example to work with ISAPI. We need one function that will output the
results the user has selected, and we'll call that member function **DoOrder()**.
Listing 4.8 shows the source code for the ISAPI code fragment.

LISTING 4.8   SOURCE FOR ISAPIORDER.CPP.

```
// ISAPIOrder.CPP - Implementation file for your Internet Server
//     ISAPIOrders Extension

#include "stdafx.h"
#include "ISAPIOrders.h"


///////////////////////////////////////////////////////////////////////
// The one and only CWinApp object
// NOTE: You may remove this object if you alter your project to no
// longer use MFC in a DLL.
```

```
CWinApp theApp;

/////////////////////////////////////////////////////////////////////
// command-parsing map
BEGIN_PARSE_MAP(CISAPIOrdersExtension, CHttpServer)
    ON_PARSE_COMMAND(DoOrder, CISAPIOrdersExtension, ITS_PSTR ITS_PSTR
            ITS_PSTR ITS_PSTR ITS_PSTR ITS_PSTR ITS_PSTR ITS_PSTR ITS_PSTR
            ITS_PSTR
            ITS_PSTR ITS_PSTR)
    ON_PARSE_COMMAND_PARAMS("name phone pizzaSize crust extraCheese=no
    garlic=no
            anchovies=no olives=no pepperoni=no sausage=no footFungus=no
            peppers=no")

    ON_PARSE_COMMAND(Default, CISAPIOrdersExtension, ITS_EMPTY)
    DEFAULT_PARSE_COMMAND(Default, CISAPIOrdersExtension)
END_PARSE_MAP(CISAPIOrdersExtension)


/////////////////////////////////////////////////////////////////////
// The one and only CISAPIOrdersExtension object

CISAPIOrdersExtension theExtension;


/////////////////////////////////////////////////////////////////////
// CISAPIOrdersExtension implementation

CISAPIOrdersExtension::CISAPIOrdersExtension()
{
}

CISAPIOrdersExtension::~CISAPIOrdersExtension()
{
}

BOOL CISAPIOrdersExtension::GetExtensionVersion(HSE_VERSION_INFO* pVer)
{
    // Call default implementation for initialization
    CHttpServer::GetExtensionVersion(pVer);

    // Load description string
    TCHAR sz[HSE_MAX_EXT_DLL_NAME_LEN+1];
    ISAPIVERIFY(::LoadString(AfxGetResourceHandle(),
        IDS_SERVER, sz, HSE_MAX_EXT_DLL_NAME_LEN));
```

```
    _tcscpy(pVer->lpszExtensionDesc, sz);
    return TRUE;
}


/////////////////////////////////////////////////////////////////
// CISAPIOrdersExtension command handlers

void CISAPIOrdersExtension::Default(CHttpServerContext* pCtxt)
{
    StartContent(pCtxt);
    WriteTitle(pCtxt);

    *pCtxt << _T("This default message was produced by the Internet");
    *pCtxt << _T(" Server DLL Wizard. Edit your
CISAPIOrdersExtension::Default()");
    *pCtxt << _T(" implementation to change it.\r\n");

    EndContent(pCtxt);
}

// Do not edit the following lines, which ClassWizard needs.
#if 0
BEGIN_MESSAGE_MAP(CISAPIOrdersExtension, CHttpServer)
    //{{AFX_MSG_MAP(CISAPIOrdersExtension)
    //}}AFX_MSG_MAP
END_MESSAGE_MAP()
#endif // 0



/////////////////////////////////////////////////////////////////
// If your extension will not use MFC, you'll need this code to make
// sure the extension objects can find the resource handle for the
// module. If you convert your extension to not be dependent on MFC,
// remove the comments around the following AfxGetResourceHandle()
// and DllMain() functions, as well as the g_hInstance global.

/****

static HINSTANCE g_hInstance;

HINSTANCE AFXISAPI AfxGetResourceHandle()
{
    return g_hInstance;
}

BOOL WINAPI DllMain(HINSTANCE hInst, ULONG ulReason,
    LPVOID lpReserved)
```

```
{
    if (ulReason == DLL_PROCESS_ATTACH)
    {
        g_hInstance = hInst;
    }

    return TRUE;
}

****/

void
CISAPIOrdersExtension::DoOrder(CHttpServerContext *pCtxt, LPCTSTR inName,
    LPCTSTR inPhone, LPCTSTR inPizzaSize,LPCTSTR inCrust,  LPCTSTR
      inExtraCheese,
    LPCTSTR inGarlic, LPCTSTR inAnchovies,LPCTSTR inOlives, LPCTSTR
      inPepperoni,
    LPCTSTR inSausage, LPCTSTR inFootFungus, LPCTSTR inPeppers)
{
    StartContent(pCtxt);
    WriteTitle(pCtxt);

    if (*inName && *inPhone)
    // make sure their name and number were provided
    {
        *pCtxt << "<CENTER><H1>Here's your order:</H1><BR><BR><BR>";
        *pCtxt << "Pizza Size = " << inPizzaSize << "<BR>";
        *pCtxt << "Crust = " << inCrust << "<BR>";
        if (strcmp(inExtraCheese,"no"))
            *pCtxt << "Extra Cheese = " << inExtraCheese << "<BR>";
        if (strcmp(inGarlic,"no"))
            *pCtxt << "Garlic = " << inGarlic << "<BR>";
        if (strcmp(inAnchovies,"no"))
            *pCtxt << "Anchovies = " << inAnchovies << "<BR>";
        if (strcmp(inOlives,"no"))
            *pCtxt << "Olives = " << inOlives << "<BR>";
        if (strcmp(inPepperoni,"no"))
            *pCtxt << "Pepperoni = " << inPepperoni << "<BR>";
        if (strcmp(inSausage,"no"))
            *pCtxt << "Sausage = " << inSausage << "<BR>";
        if (strcmp(inFootFungus,"no"))
            *pCtxt << "Mushrooms = " << inFootFungus << "<BR>";
        if (strcmp(inPeppers,"no"))
            *pCtxt << "Bell Peppers = " << inPeppers << "<BR>";
```

```
    *pCtxt << "You are :<B>" << inName << "<BR></B>";
    *pCtxt << "Your phone number is :<B>" << inPhone << "<BR></B></
        CENTER><BR><BR><BR>";
}
else
    *pCtxt << "<CENTER><H1>Name and phone number are required for all
        orders.

                    </CENTER></H1><BR><BR><BR>";


    EndContent(pCtxt);
} // CISAPIOrdersExtension::DoOrder...
```

Disadvantages Of ISAPI

ISAPI offers many performance advantages over CGI. However, it does bring
in a new set of problems because it runs in the process space of the server. An
ISAPI code fragment can crash the Web server, whereas a CGI code fragment
cannot (sorry Mac folks, you don't qualify here) because protected memory
keeps separate processes from writing into one another's heaps.

Use A Leak Checker

To make darn sure your code fragment is not filling up the server's
heap, use a debug version of **new()** that supports tracking allocations. Such **new()** operators are in plentiful supply, and after your
member function has completed, you can check and see if any allocations were not freed. SmartHeap from MicroQuill Systems
(www.microquill.com) is an excellent tool for such debugging.

Another problem that results from being in the same process space is memory
leaks. Any allocations we perform with an ISAPI code fragment must be freed
from the same thread that created it. Otherwise, you'll leave dangling pointers
behind—pointers that have no code referencing them. In a CGI code fragment, this wouldn't be an issue because once the fragment is done, its process
space (heap) becomes invalidated and the memory manager frees up any space
it had allocated. If your fragment keeps allocating and no one frees up the
space, once the server's available memory partition is either fragmented or filled,
it will crash. Figure 4.9 shows a block of memory with dangling pointers left
behind. Once these blocks are left, the heap becomes fragmented and then the

largest contiguous block of free space available to the Web server becomes diminished. On Windows or Unix, this might take some time to happen, but for a busy Web site, it'll be sooner rather than later.

Another issue is reentrancy, where multiple threads are accessing the same variables at the same time. If you have global variables, you'll need to lock certain part of your code to prevent other threads from accessing it. While this is not difficult, it's something else that you must deal with in your design phase.

Summary

ISAPI offers incredible performance advantages over CGI, has a small learning curve, and involves a few additional programming design and implementation issues. We've applied ISAPI code fragments to various form examples in this chapter. MFC offers three classes to help simplify our development of ISAPI code fragments: **CHttpServer**, **CHtmlStream**, and **CHttpServerContext**. Our fragment uses **CHttpServer** as a base class, and each member function gets a

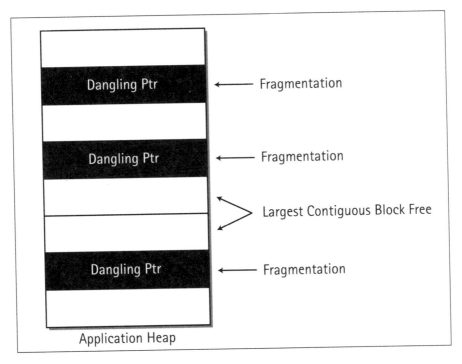

Figure 4.9
A fragmented application heap.

pointer to a **CHttpServerContext** object passed in as an argument. While we didn't use the **CHtmlStream** class directly, we did access it via member functions and a **<< operator** with the **CHttpServerContext** class.

Parsemaps automatically allow **CHttpServer**'s **CallFunction**() to instantiate the correct member function that we designate from our HTML form. The variables in Parsemaps are case sensitive. **CHttpServer** doesn't care what order the arguments are listed in, because the server never guarantees the order anyway. It also doesn't matter if we use **GET** or **POST**; the correct member function is called, and its data is passed as arguments rather than as a contiguous stream. What's missing? We haven't linked anything to a database yet. We've implemented some powerful functionality in ISAPI (and CGI earlier), but all our data was embedded within our code, or directly gathered from an HTML form. We need to abstract this data away from not only our code fragment, but away from the Web server as well. We need to use a datastore (collection of databases and their associated tables), generate dynamic content, and save the information back in the same storage facility. Let's move on to Chapter 5, and see how we create the tables that compose a datastore, and add them to a powerful database application like MS SQL Server.

5

USING THE DATASTORE FOR ORDERS

Flight reservation systems decide whether or not you exist.
If your information isn't in their database,
then you simply don't get to go anywhere.

Arthur Miller

The *datastore* refers to multiple data tables you implement and "store" away within your database, hence its name. Storing away your data allows you to separate your program from the data, and allows many programs to interact with the same sets of data and perform different tasks and services for your various clients.

In the '60s, the programming style was information-based; we designed what type of data we were going to use and then implemented code around the data. In the '70s, we implemented structure-based programming, in which the architecture of the program was paramount and the data was ancillary. In the '80s, our design was object-oriented, in which the data and the functions that manipulate the data were encapsulated within a container we call an *object*. Now, we are expanding upon the object mindset of the previous decade, and are taking the object-oriented design across multiple programs running on multiple machines.

 ### Even Databases Have Standards

All major relational databases now support SQL, an acronym for *Structured Query Language*. This is an English-like language that allows you to type simple queries. The database then returns results based upon those structured queries. SQL 92 is the specification that all major database manufacturers use: Oracle, Sybase, and Microsoft are fully SQL 92-compliant. Don't use a database that is not SQL 92-compliant, because it will be difficult to maintain, hard to hire someone who knows how it works, and impossible to locate a textbook on it or a class to instruct you on its use. Using a database without SQL ensures that you'll paint yourself into a corner with no clean path out.

By designing your data as an object that is separate from your source code, you can interface different programs with it and share the data between separate processes. The programs can even be written at different times, and depend solely upon your needs. Interfacing your sources with the data binds the two together and makes both data and code the functional datastore.

A typical Internet store will have a Web server that distributes HTML pages for customers. Some will order merchandise; others will want to search for items that they can't find on the home pages. Figure 5.1 shows a typical layout. To allow a customer to search your site via the Web, you write a CGI/ISAPI code fragment that will interface between the user and the datastore, get the information from this datastore, and provide output via HTML for the user to review. Your code fragment is the Web server's link to your datastore.

A shopping cart is usually a table of items that the user has selected, but is present in your datastore. When the buyer is ready to order, your CGI/ISAPI code fragment will retrieve the shopping cart information and output it into an HTML form. The user can then change the quantity of the items ordered, remove some of them, and possibly order them immediately. The information is always stored in a central location so that it can be accessible from multiple access points. Storing it in a location separate from your Web server also allows your server to do what it's supposed to: serve HTML documents to clients.

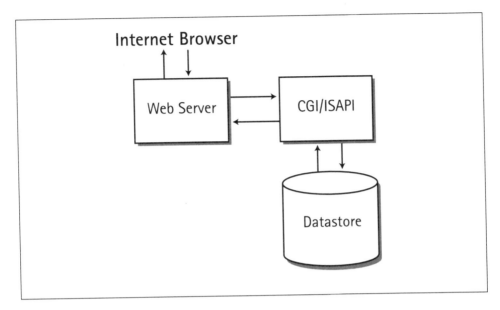

Figure 5.1
The relationship between database, Web server, and CGI/ISAPI.

In this chapter, we're going to implement some database tables that make up a datastore and learn how to use them. We're going to use the **CFormParser** class from Chapter 3 to handle dynamic forms, and we will propose a design scheme for implementing dynamic HTML forms from the datastore. We're also going to modify our **CCoolHttpServer** class from Chapter 4 to handle dynamic forms using **CFormParser**. Finally, we'll use MS SQL Server to make some live data tables.

Tables

A *table* is a set of data, while a *database* is a collection of various tables. A datastore is your database with live data stored within it. Think of a single set of data as an instance of an object. In Chapter 6, this becomes object-oriented when we bind the member functions that manipulate the data with the specific data itself.

In Chapter 2, we mentioned how forms resembled a C/C++ structure. This analogy is perfect when you are thinking of creating a table for a database. First, think of the data that you need and the C type (or a C++ class in some cases) the data should be stored as. For example, small numbers might be integers, a dollar amount might be a float, and a name might be a string. These C data types correspond to the database types that we can store things with. Table 5.1 shows the various SQL data types.

Not all values match directly with a C counterpart (in this chapter, we'll point out the ones that don't, and in Chapter 6, we'll use these data types frequently). In some cases, it makes sense to match an SQL data type with a C++ object type, like the MFC class **CString**, or the ANSI **string** class.

TABLE 5.1

SQL DATA TYPES.

Data Type	Value Range	Example
char[n]	<= 255 characters	"Don Gaspar"
varchar[n]	<= 255 characters	"Michelle Stroup"
text	BLOB <= 2x10^9 in 2K chunks	Lots and lots of text!
binary[n]	<= 255 characters	0x3889087
varbinary[n]	<= 255 characters	0x1414213
image	BLOB <= 2x10^9 in 2K chunks	0x1732050... on and on
bit	0 or 1 (true or false)	0
int	+- 2,147,483,647 (4 bytes)	3,889,087
smallint	+- 32,767 (2 bytes)	31,141
tinyint	0 to 255 (1 byte)	15
float	N/A (80 bytes)	3.889087297
double	N/A (120 bytes)	3.339087E23
real	N/A	123.45
numeric	+- 10^38	12.34E10
money	+-$922,337,203,685,477.5807	$15.13
smallmoney	+-$214,748.3647	$15.13
datetime	Jan 1, 1753–Dec 31, 9999	"August 8, 1963 05:22"
smalldatetime	Jan 1, 1900–June 6, 2079	"August 8, 1963 05:22"
timestamp	N/A (just time, no date)	12:44.12

How To Use Tables

Your design depends on whether you have a static form with non-changing items, or a dynamic one, in which you don't know how many items there will be. For right now, let's look at designing with static forms. Later in this chapter, we'll develop some code to dynamically handle any generic form without knowing what data is present on the form.

Is your data numeric, text, binary, currency, or time? Evaluate what data types the items on your HTML form are, and design the CGI/ISAPI code fragment to handle such types. The C structure you will implement is your database table, but use the data types from Table 5.1 rather than your C types.

To access the tables from your datastore, we'll use SQL statements via ODBC (Open DataBase Connectivity) or subclass an MFC class, **CRecordset**—we'll use both of these approaches in Chapter 6.

Table Examples

Let's apply some of the SQL data types to a few examples that we'll be using. As we are discussing stores on the Internet, our examples would not be complete without some database tables of inventory items and order tables.

Remember that a table needs some kind of key so that we can find the correct table. Using a key allows us to search through a set of tables (a datastore) until we find one that matches our criteria. A key can be a name or a number, and it doesn't have to be singular. We could have a number and a name and both could represent a single unique key.

Using a key also allows us to reference other tables. For example, you can use the same key to link together several tables. The key becomes our search term to find a table we need, and bind tables together, as shown in Figure 5.2.

Inventory Storage

Let's say that we have some merchandise that we want to sell on the Web. We could just create a custom page that displays the merchandise, hard-code a CGI/ISAPI code fragment to keep track of how many of each item we have, and generate a form. A major drawback to such a solution is that the code fragment and the data are bound together but cannot be dynamic. If we changed our

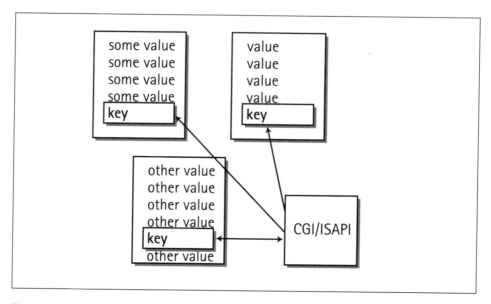

Figure 5.2
CGI/ISAPI interaction with a key.

inventory, we'd have to rebuild our code fragment and our Web pages! However, if we separate our inventory data from our code fragment, we can maintain both independently.

Using a table allows us to keep track of inventory and orders in a central location. We can also vary what we sell. If we write a generic form-handling CGI/ISPAI code fragment, our code will remain constant even when the data from our store changes. We could even implement multiple stores with various merchandise, and use the same code fragment (we'd use different HTML, though!). This is the design philosophy we've been following in this book: When we can implement a general solution with excellent performance, we will. Separating the data then allows us to reuse code later on, and possibly reuse entire code fragments for various stores.

If we opened a comic book store, what kind of information would we need in our datastore? We would first consider what buyers would want to know about the comics we are selling. Then we would implement a table that encapsulates this data.

A collector may want to know a lot of information about a comic: the publisher, the title, the issue number, its condition, the main characters in it, the illustrator, and/or the writer. On the seller's end, we need to know how many copies of that comic we have in stock, and we must mark the inventory counter down when a customer places one inside his or her virtual shopping cart (we implement this in Chapter 9). We left out the most important piece of information—at least the most important one to someone in business—the cost of the comic! If we stored all the necessary information about this item, we could also build a dynamic form that allows the user to order it.

The text items for the comic are very clear; we'll make sure we store them as **char** data types. The issue number and quantity should be integer values. Why not a **smallint**? Because issue numbers and the quantity of the items might exceed the value capability of a **smallint**, which is only 1 byte in length and not large enough for a value greater than 255. The price for the comic can be any of the following types: **money**, **smallmoney**, or **numeric**. Table 5.2 shows the table we've implemented for a comic book store.

This table contains everything we need to know about comic books in our inventory. We used the **char**[n] data type (always a fixed size), but we could have used a **varchar** type, a variable-length character array stored in the database. As performance for reads and writes is generally better for fixed-sized fields,

TABLE 5.2

COMIC BOOK SQL TABLE.

Field	SQL Data Type	Example
Publisher	char[32]	"DC," "Marvel"
Title	char[32]	"Batman"
Condition	char[16]	"Mint," "Fine"
Characters	char[128]	"Robin," "Mr. Freeze"
Author	char[64]	"Don Gaspar"
Illustrator	char[64]	"Michelle Stroup"
IssueNum	int	298
InStock	int	2,045
Incart	int	23
Price	money, smallmoney, or numeric	$345.27

I've opted to use the **char** type here. For the price field, we have several choices. For large ranges of dollars, the **money** type is appropriate. However, I can't think of a comic book that even approaches those ranges, so using **money** to store a comic price would be a waste of space. A numeric data type, or **smallmoney**, would be best.

An equivalent C++ structure for the comic book table is shown in Listing 5.1.

LISTING 5.1   COMIC BOOK C++ STRUCTURE.

```
typedef struct comicBook
{
    string      publisher;
    string      title;
    string      condition;
    string      characters;
    string      author;
    string      illustrator;
    short       issueNum;
    short       inStock;
    short       inCarts;
    float       price;
};
```

The C++ structure parallels the database table identically. The **string** class handles character data in the C++ structure for us; otherwise, this would be a simple C structure. The **string** class gives us extra capabilities that an ordinary character array would lack.

Database Conversions to C/C++

Something to note on database type conversions when going to C/C++: The **money** and **smallmoney** types will be strings with a "$" and a decimal, so translating these types to a float or double will require you to remove the "$" and convert the remaining value yourself. You will also have to convert it back to store it in the database.

Orders

When a customer orders merchandise, we need to store that information somewhere—that's what the datastore is for. We don't need to store all the information, just enough to link an item to a certain user via what database programmers call a key. In Chapter 3, we developed the **CFormParser** class that used an STL **map** container and worked with key/value pairs—the key was used to find a value that the **map** had stored away for us. With a database, the key performs the same lookups, but it also binds different tables within the same database together.

Although our table contains the information for merchandise that we have in our inventory, we need another table that contains all the items a customer will order later on. When the consumer reviews his or her order, we use both tables together to build a dynamic form that displays the order (the items the customer selected) with the descriptions from the inventory table.

We'll need to know how many items were ordered, and a key that links back to the inventory item itself. A good key to use is usually some kind of inventory ID, like a bar code or a serial number. For the comic book table, the title and issue number make up a unique key. Let's continue with the comic book example and use it for the order table as well. The order table uses two fields to link with the comic book inventory table, which leads to the table shown in Table 5.3.

Wait a minute! If we have a table that contains only comic book titles, issue numbers, and quantity, how does this get linked back to the user? It can't unless we create another key. Chances are that when the customer adds the first item to his or her shopping cart, we'll generate a cookie and use it as the key. This new cookie will require yet another table so that we maintain unique keys for each user. For now, we'll look at Table 5.4 as our final table and visit the cookie table in Chapter 9. Think of the cookie as a 4-byte integer that is unique for every customer.

TABLE 5.3

COMIC BOOK ORDER TABLE.

Field	SQL Data Type	Example
Title	char[n]	"Spiderman"
Issue	int	345
Quantity	int	1

TABLE 5.4		
CORRECT COMIC BOOK ORDER TABLE.		
Field	SQL Data Type	Example
Title	char[n]	"Sooperman"
Issue	int	9,234
Quantity	int	3
Cookie	int	3,023

The order table is also a temporary table. It's not something we permanently store away, but we will use it until orders are placed, then we'll clear it out from the datastore. We use it to keep track of items a person wants to order. If those items aren't ordered within a certain time period, we delete the table and adjust the inventory table to contain any items that weren't purchased.

We can use this table to link the inventory table fairly easily. By searching the inventory table for a case where the title fields and issue numbers are equal, we can find the exact inventory item. Using the inventory item, we can then display the publisher, author, and any other information we associated with that table. We will display this information when the consumer wants to review his or her order.

Handling Dynamic Order Forms

We built dynamic forms in Chapter 3 to show what we could do with CGI and **stdout**. When the customer orders some items and we've stored them in an order table, he or she will want to review them at some point. Therefore, we need to be flexible to allow him or her to change quantities (for new merchandise), or use a check box (for limited-stock items). This leaves us with a form in which there are a variable number of controls on an HTML page that we need to parse.

The **CFormParser** class is versatile enough to handle any form thrown at us, but we'll have to use it with an iterator provided with STL in something like the following:

```
map<string,string,less<string>>::iterator    mapIter;
for(mapIter = map.begin(); mapIter != map.end(); mapIter++)
   AddToDatabase(*iter)
```

Another elegant approach is to use the ANSI routine (part of STL) **for_each**() with a simple function that's called for each item:

```
for_each(map.begin(), map.end(), ptr_fun( AddToDatabase));
```

Both of these approaches start at the beginning of your form data, and iterate through until the last item, adding each to the database. Right now, we're not adding the items to the database, but are using an empty function that we'll implement in Chapter 6.

 ### Take Advantage Of STL

STL was designed with performance in mind, and the iterators are treated as first-class entities. Use them. They will allow you to implement fast, tight code without re-implementing containers and iterators for each project. Spend time designing your algorithms and implementing features, not rewriting data containers and iterators.

The **ptr_fun**() function is another STL routine that converts the name of a routine into a function pointer that STL can use. Adding a few lines of code to the **CFormParser** class shows how versatile our design was; we'll need to extend ISAPI to take advantage of this class.

CHttpServer has a member function called **CallFunction**() that we covered in detail in Chapter 4. This function uses the Parsemaps and knows what function to call automatically, based on the arguments we specified and the name of the member function. To instantiate a member function that contains a variable number of arguments, we need to override this member.

We overrode a few member functions and called our class **CCoolHttpServer**, so this is where we'll start as our base class. First, we'll get the name of the member function we're supposed to call, and then we'll separate the data stream to get all the variables from the arguments passed into **CallFunction**()—these will vary slightly depending on whether this is a **GET** or a **POST**. We'll tell **CHttp-Server::CallFunction**() that we have no variables and we'll call it. This requires that our member function be declared in the Parsemap as **ITS_EMPTY**, as no variables are passed over directly to it. We move these variables to the ECB's (from Chapter 4) **lpszQueryString** member, which we'll restore later when we've completed our task.

We'll add the **CFormParser** instance to our **CHttpServer** derived class in the member function we call. This will bind the form data to our **CHttpServer** derived class, and allow our member functions to access it without using global variables, which wouldn't work anyway because they wouldn't be thread-safe. Listing 5.2 shows the source code for the new **CallFunction**() replacement. Note that we need to know the name of the member function when we write this replacement routine, unless we use it for all member functions in our **CHttpServer** subclass.

LISTING 5.2   CCOOLHTTPSERVER::CALLFUNCTION().

```
//
//    function:    CCoolHttpServer::CallFunction
//    purpose:     overrides CHttpServer's member to facilitate
//        variable input arguments.
//    returns:     whatever CHttpServer::CallFunction normally returns
//
int
CCoolHttpServer::CallFunction ( CHttpServerContext* pCtxt,
    LPTSTR pszQuery,  LPTSTR pszCommand )
{
    string    functionToCall;
    LPTSTR    tempStorage;

    // check to see if we're using a GET method
    if ( !pszCommand )
    {
        // now we just want to get the name of the member function to call
        functionToCall = pszQuery;
        int index = functionToCall.find('?',0);
        functionToCall[index+1] = '\0';

        // now get the variables and pass them via the ECB
        tempStorage = pCtxt->m_pECB->lpszQueryString;
        pCtxt->m_pECB->lpszQueryString = pszQuery + index;
    }
    else// must be a POST
    {
        functionToCall = pszCommand;
        // Note: we must know the name of the function we're handling
        // variables for, unless we're handling all the cases.
        if ( functionToCall.compare("StoreUserData") == 0 )
        {
            tempStorage = pCtxt->m_pECB->lpszQueryString;
            pCtxt->m_pECB->lpszQueryString = pszQuery;
            functionToCall += "?";
```

```
        }
    }

    // call base member and let it use the Parsemaps for us
    if ( functionToCall.compare("StoreUserData?") == 0 /*||
        functionToCall.compare("DoGuestBook") == 0*/)
    {
        int result = CHttpServer::CallFunction( pCtxt, const_cast<char *>
            (functionToCall.c_str()), NULL );
        pCtxt->m_pECB->lpszQueryString = tempStorage;
        return result;
    }
    else
        return CHttpServer::CallFunction( pCtxt, pszQuery, pszCommand );
} // CCoolHttpServer::CallFunction...
```

The **CallFunction**() member's definition is as follows:

```
int CallFunction(CHttpServerContext* pCtxt, LPTSTR pszQuery, LPTSTR
    pszCommand);
```

If the data is sent over from the client via a **GET** method, then the **pszCommand** item is **NULL**, and the **pszQuery** is a pointer to the **ECB** query string. If the method of sending the data over is by a **POST**, then **pszCommand** is a pointer to the **ECB** query string and **pszQuery** is a pointer to the body of the query string sent over from the browser. The trick here is to write a general **CallFunction**() replacement that uses the **parsemap** macros, but puts our form variables into a **CFormParser** class in which we can access them.

To perform this miracle, we have to intercept the values of **pszQuery** and **pszCommand**, get the variables passed over, and store them into our in the **lszQueryString** member of the ECB. We then need to get the member function to call, and allow the base class **CHttpServer** to call it without using any arguments (remember that we declared its **PARSE_MAP** as **ITS_EMPTY**). We change the values of **pszQuery** to be the member function name and **pszCommand** is NULL. This approach, by the way, is the way Microsoft recommends working around this problem. When our member function is called, we use the **lpszQueryString** of the ECB and pass that to an instance of our **CFormParser** class, that parses and isolates the variables for us automatically.

A major weakness of ISAPI is that it lacks the ability to handle variable arguments within the provided MFC framework. We extended the framework using a few lines of STL, and eliminated the weakness all together.

Generating Dynamic HTML Forms

Generating forms requires more database knowledge than handling the forms and their data. When the information from a database is displayed, we'll want to use various fields from the database table to create an order form where the customer can mark what he or she wants to place inside the virtual shopping cart.

The form is database table-specific, so we'll need to have specialized functions to handle the creation of a dynamic form for us. This requires innate knowledge of the table itself.

The best advice here is to display a form item first. Use a check box only if you have a one-of-a-kind item. Use an edit text field so that the user can change the quantity for items that you can order or have plenty of in stock.

Handling the order with **CFormParser** will be quite simple.

Back To The Guest Book

The guest book represents a static table with a fixed number of items that we'll receive input from. In Chapters 3 and 4, we used STL stream iterators and saved the guest information in a simple text file. This was great for our purpose at that time, but there are some advantages to using a database.

We can easily search a database to see if the customer has already been added, and display a message that alerts them if not. We could do that with our text file too, but we would have to load the entire text file into memory and then search for the customer's name (and probably his or her phone number too). Using the database is preferable because it was designed to do this type of search with a variety of tables.

STL Functions

If you don't want to use the database for your guest book, you can use the file we developed in Chapters 3 and 4 and add a few STL functions to give it the same functionality as the database solution. First, read the file into memory using a vector<> container of GuestInfo structures. Add your new guest to the vector<>, then use the **unique()** function to guarantee different records. To sort your list, use the STL **sort()** function. You will be required to write your own comparators for **unique()** and **sort()** to use, and you're going to take a lot of memory for a CGI/ISAPI code fragment, but it may meet your requirements. You will also have to save your unique file in its entirety rather than just append guests to the end.

Using the database for just a guest book would be overkill, but if the database is already there for other information on your system, you might as well take advantage of it. For our guest book, we can create a table like that shown in Table 5.5.

Once again, when you view the new database table, we have an ensemble of fixed size character arrays. If we wanted to make a key so that we knew these were unique users, we would use the name and email fields.

TABLE 5.5

GUEST BOOK TABLE.

Field	SQL Data Type	Example
Name	char[64]	"Don Gaspar"
Address1	char[32]	"650 Castro Street"
Address2	char[32]	"Suite #120-228"
City	char[32]	"Mountain View"
State	char[16]	"CA"
Zip	char[16]	"94041"
Phone	char[16]	"408-353-9066"
Email	char[32]	"don@gigantor.com"

The Foosball Datastore

The Foosball datastore represents a virtual store—it has no inventory to speak of. It takes orders, and upon receiving and validating the payment, places an order with the distributor. For large items like Foosball tables, the distributor ships directly to the client for us. There is no limit to the quantity of merchandise in stock because we order directly from the distributor.

 Design Your Datastore For Performance

The biggest thief of time cycles when using a database is the disk you use to store information. Always get the fastest, most reliable disk you can afford. Currently, Ultra-wide SCSI is the best on the market, and seek times on that disk are about 8 ms. Using a drive like this will allow users to search for merchandise and review shopping carts fast.

This virtual store may seem quite unique, but it's the ultimate way many companies conduct business on the Internet. In the next section, we'll design our database tables. In the following section, we'll implement them on Microsoft's SQL Server.

The Shopping Cart Table

We've already created a basic order table for a comic-book business, but not for the virtual Foosball store. The order table we created was in reality the contents of a virtual shopping cart. For typical merchandise, we merely need a key that links the item to the inventory table, or a products table.

Here, *products* refers to merchandise that is available for sale, but not actually in stock; we have to order it from a distributor. The *inventory* table contains in-stock goods. Some businesses will implement both tables. When a user orders some merchandise, your CGI/ISAPI code fragment will search your datastore to see if it's in stock. If it's not, it will search the products table. This allows your virtual store to sell virtually an unlimited quantity of items.

We need to know how many items the consumer put into his or her cart. We also need two keys: one to link us to the customer, and the other to link us to the product or inventory table. (Remember that the user key will be a cookie, and we'll develop a class to implement these in Chapter 8.) Table 5.6 shows the SQL table based on this information.

		TABLE 5.6

SHOPPING CART TABLE.

Field	SQL Data Type	Example
cookieID	int	3,895
productID	char[n]	1234-ABX
Quantity	int	3

Our table is simple because it contains only three fields. With the two keys present, we could then get other information, as the keys link us to other database tables. The **productID** key will allow us to retrieve information using the product table, while the **cookieID** will link all the items in the shopping cart to the customer ordering them.

The Product Table

Again, the product table contains merchandise we're selling but do not have on hand. This table needs to contain enough information about the product so that we can use it to make a dynamic form for the user; it also needs to contain information about pricing, vendor, discounts, and so on. We can even use the product table to display our merchandise using the dynamic HTML generation we've been using throughout this book.

When we order merchandise from a vendor, the merchandise item typically has a part ID (or product ID) associated with it, so we'll need that for each item, as well as the vendor name. Besides a description of the merchandise, we need to display the name of the item and the associated cost. Table 5.7 stores this information.

		TABLE 5.7

PRODUCT TABLE.

Field	SQL Data Type	Example
Vendor	char[n]	"Marvel Comic Distributors"
PartID	char[n]	"312A-XCV4"
Cost	smallmoney or numeric	$123.14

(continued)

		TABLE 5.7

PRODUCT TABLE (*CONTINUED*).

Field	SQL Data Type	Example
Discount	int	10
InStock	int	32,000
Description	char[n]	"Contains Spiderman and the Hulk"

The Customer Table

When the customer orders some merchandise, we need to know where to send it, and whom to bill. The customer table will contain information just like our guest book did, but probably with a little more detail. For performance reasons, we won't even use this table unless the consumer wants to order the contents of his or her shopping cart.

We keep a cookie (a key that links us to the customer's browser) for every shopping cart, so we know who the buyer is. We can link this **cookieID** to a customer table that will store away his or her information. Table 5.8 shows what we've come up with.

		TABLE 5.8

CUSTOMER TABLE.

Field	SQL Data Type	Example
FirstName	char[n]	"Don"
LastName	char[n]	"Gaspar"
Address1	char[n]	"650 Castro Street"
Address2	char[n]	"Suite #120-228"
City	char[n]	"Mountain View"
State	char[n]	"CA"
Zip	char[n]	"94041"
Phone	char[n]	"408-353-9066"
Email	char[n]	"don@gigantor.com"
WorkPhone	char[n]	"408-353-9066"
cookieID	int	3,897

Almost all the table fields are character arrays, except **cookieID**, which is a 4-byte integer. The cookie is stored on the browser, so we can get that value and create this table accurately. We then use the cookie to link the various tables together.

The Payment Table

We need to maintain information on how the customer paid for the order, along with approval codes and a timestamp that we get from the credit card authentication company. Chapter 10 will cover how to check for the correct types of cards using the Luhn algorithm. Normally, the credit card information that you need is the card number and the expiration date. Some cards, such as American Express, will require you to gather additional information like the beginning valid date of the card, and even a fraud control number on the card. Here, we'll cover the most likely cases.

An order has a total, possibly sales tax, and a description that will appear on the buyer's charge card statement. Table 5.9 builds a payment table based upon this information.

TABLE 5.9

PAYMENT INFORMATION TABLE.

Field	SQL Data Type	Example
CardNumber	char[n]	"1234454545" up to 16 digits
ExpDate	char[n]	"1299"
BeginDate	char[n]	"1295"
Amount	smallmoney or numeric	$120.12
SalesTax	smallmoney or numeric	$12.13
ApprovalCode	char[n]	"1234VBXFR1234"
Description	char[n]	"Foosball Face Mask"
TimeStamp	char[n]	"6:02:12.12"
cookieID	int	3,990

The table we've just designed should store information about any customer and payment details for a particular order. We use **cookieID** as our universal key that links this table to the customer table and the shopping cart table.

The Order Table

So far, we've covered every table except the order table, which is a record that we use to order our merchandise from the distributor: It tells us how much of each item we need to order. It's identical to the shopping cart table, except that this is to remain static—that is, this table does not change until the merchandise is ordered, at which point we set a flag so we know not to order it again.

We also need a flag to identify whether or not we've shipped the merchandise the order refers to. Table 5.10 shows the simple table we've designed with this in mind.

Linking The Tables Together

All the tables are linked together through keys we've specified. When using one table, you can access the others via their keys. The **cookieID** is the most-used key within our tables, and then the **partID**. Given the **cookieID** key, you could find any table from the entire datastore. This **cookieID** will bind the user, their shopping cart contents, their credit card information, shipping address, and—in different database tables—all in the datastore.

TABLE 5.10

THE ORDER TABLE.

Field	SQL Data Type	Example
cookieID	int	3,881
partID	int	123
Qty	int	3
Ordered	flag	1 (true)
Shipped	flag	0 (false)

Using MS SQL Server

I've used all the major databases on the market and am currently using MS SQL Server. It's simple to set up, powerful, fast, and easy to configure various options. Most databases will require you to have one person dedicated to working with just your database, which can become very expensive.

Although I've used SQL Server, you could use any ODBC database product on the market: MS Access, FoxPro, Sybase, or Oracle. The databases and their ODBC drivers need to be thread-safe. This will allow tables to be modified correctly by multiple processes, and they will remain intact.

Don't Use A Macintosh For Your Database

The Mac is a great machine, but the OS hasn't evolved since 1989. It still does not offer protected memory or real multitasking. As a result, you put your database at risk and subject to corruption when you run it on a machine that doesn't protect processes from one another. While you probably wouldn't have a problem, it's not worth taking the risk. If you are dead set on using a Mac, wait until Rhapsody arrives; it'll be worth the wait.

SQL Server employs a few methods of entering new tables into your database. You could use a text window and use SQL commands, or you could use the SQL Server Enterprise Manager (an applicant provided by MS to configure your database) and a point-and-click interface. We've chosen the latter for simplicity.

You must first create a database that will store all of your tables. Open the Enterprise Manager for SQL Server, and find the database that you have created, as shown in Figure 5.3.

Open Tables and with the right mouse button, and select the Create Table drop-down list item. Next, enter your data and use the pop-up menu to select the appropriate SQL data type for each field of your new database table, as shown in Figure 5.4. Now be careful, because once you set a type in your table, you can't come back in later and edit it—you have to literally throw away the table and make a new one with your corrections.

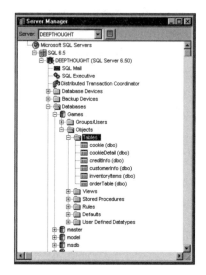

Figure 5.3
The SQL Enterprise Manager.

 ### Design First

Design your database tables before entering them on your database. Work everything out on paper first because once you've made a table, you can't change the number of fields in that table, and you can't change the data types. If you were to have information saved away and found you needed a change, it would require major database changes, and you would have to change your code as well! A design change before you implement actual code is 10 times cheaper in terms of your time. It's easier to change things before you actually start implementation, and will save you from substantial hair loss doing so. Use some paper up front and discuss the design with others, and ask them to look for problems with the design.

You can also set up access permissions for your table, so be sure to set access to the level you want. Generally, you do not want anyone to access your database; you will want to secure it behind a firewall. Your CGI/ISAPI code fragments can connect via ODBC with a login account and password for security reasons.

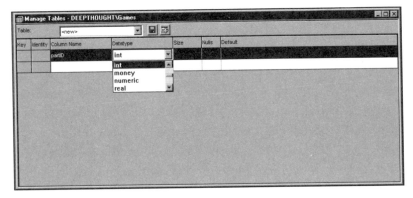

Figure 5.4
The table creator window.

ODBC And Sharing Tables

Just because your database has been set up doesn't mean you can use it. You will need to open your control panel folder, and select the ODBC control panel. Here, you will have to select your database, and allow it to be shared via ODBC, as shown in Figure 5.5. While this might sound silly, you will spend—literally—hours trying to track down a malfunctioning database when all you needed to do was set up permissions and access for your tables correctly.

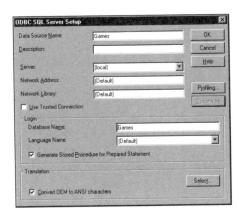

Figure 5.5
The ODBC control panel.

Summary

We can use our universal HTML form handling class, **CFormParser**, to deal with variable forms whose contents we do not know. With minor additions of a few lines of code, **CFormParser** can be iterated through—that is to say, move through each form item incrementally (we'll discuss iterators later). During this iteration of its members, we can add them to a database, output to **stdout** to build a dynamic HTML form, and do just about anything else you can think of. Some changes were required to use our **CFormParser** class with ISAPI.

We extended ISAPI's capabilities to handle variable forms by using the **CFormParser** class. We overrode the **CallFunction**() member function, and had to declare our functions as **ITS_EMPTY** in their designated Parsemaps. The base class we've used for our ISAPI code fragments has been **CCool-HttpServer**, and that's where we overrode **CallFunction**().

Finally, we built several database tables, the ensemble that comprises our datastore. We succinctly showed how to add a table to MS SQL Server. We've done everything with our data except access the datastore from CGI and ISAPI, and to do that we'll need to use ODBC and an MFC class, **CRecordset**, which we'll explore in Chapter 6.

ODBC AND LINKING THE DATASTORE

6

A well-written program is its own heaven; a poorly written program is its own hell.

The Tao of Programming

O nce your business is in full swing, your datastore will contain gigabytes of information. In order to retrieve it quickly via your database application (SQL Server, Oracle, or Sybase, for example), you will need fast and wide ultra SCSI drives with optimal seek times. Although all the data is stored and available, it's truly worthless if we don't write an efficient interface for our code to access it. This is where ODBC comes in.

ODBC, as we said in Chapter 5, stands for Open DataBase Connectivity, and is a general-purpose interface that lets programs access information from their database. You will use it from CGI and/or ISAPI to store information (such as shopping cart data) and to retrieve information (such as a search or a shopping cart total). Figure 6.1 illustrates how the ODBC interface links your code fragment to the database.

Your database includes an ODBC driver that accesses the database from software you write. No matter which database you use, you will make the same ODBC function calls; the interface

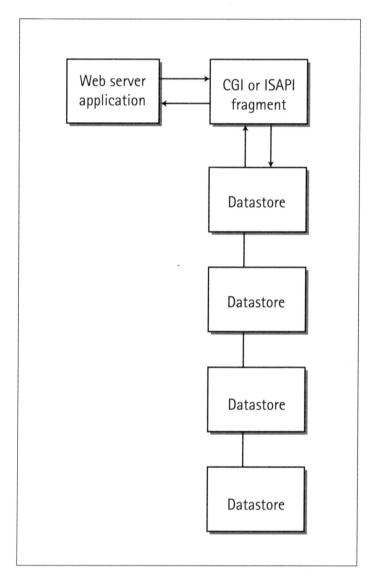

Figure 6.1
ODBC interfacing with a database.

to the database that you program remains constant even if you switch databases later on. This enables you to work with an entire spectrum of different databases, and all you need to learn is ODBC.

Don't Use A Non-ODBC Database

While some non-ODBC databases offer tremendous performance benefits, they're still not standard. Trying to find information on how to use them is difficult, and any interface you write to them will be proprietary and non-expandable. If you use an ODBC-compliant database, you can change databases and your code will still work: This scalability is nearly free.

ODBC is already such a standard that even Java's interfaces to databases are based on it. Figure 6.2 shows how Java's JDBC talks with a database; it's layered on top of the ODBC driver! Of course, if you found a JDBC network driver, and a JDBC database, you could skip the layering over ODBC, but learning ODBC will not only help you store and retrieve information with C++, it will also teach you how Java performs the same task. Let's see how we can use ODBC in our code fragments.

ODBC And CRecordset

ODBC's functional interfaces allow you to connect, retrieve, and submit information to your database from your C or C++ code fragments. Because the interfaces remain identical (even if you change databases), if you write your code fragment to work with MS Access and decide to use the Sybase SQL Server a year later, your code won't change. All ODBC-compliant databases contain a driver that your CGI/ISAPI code fragment will use to help you maintain consistencies in your code while using various databases.

The designers of your database wrote a compliant set of routines to be compatible with ODBC, and also provide a driver to enable you to interface with their database. Changing databases merely requires that the provider is ODBC compliant and has a driver for the machine your CGI/ISAPI code fragment will execute on.

Another approach to using ODBC is with an MFC class, **CRecordset**, which insulates you from using the ODBC calls directly. You build **CRecordset** with the Class Wizard that links with your data table from your datastore. It will encapsulate your database table with ODBC functionality, so the data and its manipulators are one object. We'll cover this class later in this chapter.

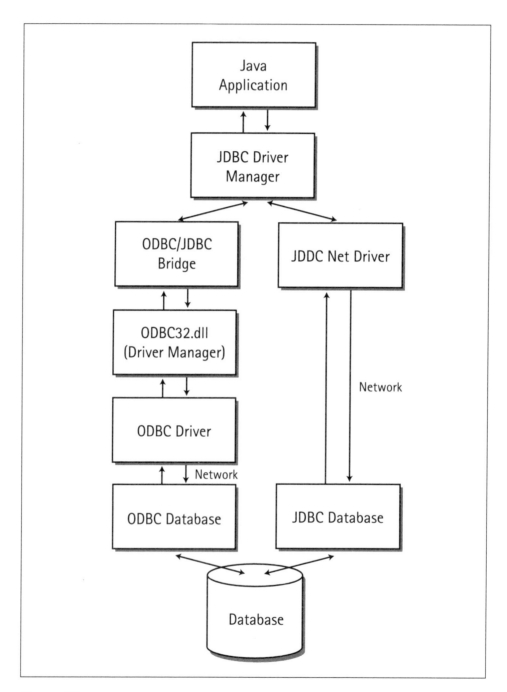

Figure 6.2
JDBC and the database.

Using ODBC

ODBC has several calls, but in order to use them you must have some understanding of SQL (Structured Query Language), which offers English-like commands to interface with and query your database. While we're not going to cover how to write SQL in substantial detail, we should at least see a few queries and how they're structured. This will be enough SQL for us to store and retrieve information from our database, which is all we'll do for now.

Using SQL

To insert information into a database via SQL, you will need to form an SQL command. You can use a command cleverly named **INSERT** to tell the database what to insert, and how. Let's look at a couple of insertions based on some tables we created in Chapter 5. Remember the Shopping Cart table? Figure 6.3 shows the table we've created with SQL Server.

To add a new shopping cart item to the database, you would use the SQL **INSERT** command

```
INSERT INTO shoppingCart (cookieID, productID, quantity)
    VALUES(3890, "1234-ABX", 3)
```

where the **VALUES** command-word contains the values for the items **cookieID**, **productID**, and **quantity** respectively.

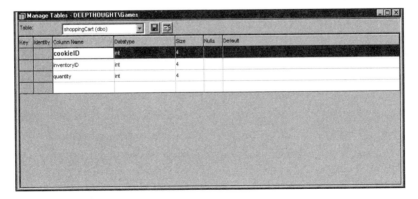

Figure 6.3
Shopping Cart table.

To modify a record that already exists, we can use the **UPDATE** command in combination with the **WHERE** directive as follows:

```
UPDATE shoppingCart SET quantity=5 WHERE cookieID=3890
    AND productID="1234-ABX"
```

This command line would take the existing record with the specified **cookieID** and **productID**, and adjust **quantity** to 5.

To retrieve data from your database, you use the **SELECT** command with various options. For example, if we wanted to select all of the items that we've stored in our database and that belong to a single user's virtual shopping cart, we would do something like:

```
SELECT * FROM shoppingCart WHERE cookieID=3890
```

To select everything from a table in the database, we would leave out the **WHERE** directive:

```
SELECT * FROM shoppingCart
```

This would show us the shopping carts of all users on our system. This might not be very useful for shopping carts, but it is extremely valuable for an Order table, as it tells us how many of each item to buy from our distributor using:

```
SELECT * FROM orderTable
```

You can see why SQL became the standard of database languages in 1992: its simple English-like commands. In this book, we've only briefly touched on SQL—just enough for us to become proficient using it to insert, update, and retrieve. SQL offers report generation features, sorting, and an armada of other features that you can take advantage of. If you're interested in SQL, there are several good books at your local computer book store, and companies like Learning Tree International offer courses on it as well (**www.learningtree.com**).

ODBC AND TABLE INSERTIONS

Before we can access the database, ODBC requires us to take several steps. Let's take a look at them. Table 6.1 lists a few of the ODBC routines, some of which we'll be using right here. The basic steps in using ODBC are:

• Allocate an environment handle for ODBC

- Allocate a connection handle

- Connect to the database

- Allocate a statement handle using your SQL command

- Send the statement

- Close the connection

- Deallocate the connection and environment handles

While the sheer volume of these routines might seem overwhelming at first, a large portion of them set up storage and initialization items for ODBC; others free up storage allocations. It ends up that we only need to concern ourselves with a few new routines. With them, we'll pass our SQL statements and gather results from the database. They will allow us to perform powerful SQL queries, insertions, and retrievals from our program with just a few lines of code.

TABLE 6.1

LIST OF **ODBC** FUNCTIONS.

ODBC Function Name	Description
SQLAllocConnect()	Allocates a connection handle to the ODBC driver we specify.
SQLAllocEnv()	Allocates a handle to the SQL routines we need.
SQLAllocStmt()	Allocates a handle for the SQL statement you specify for sending to the database.
SQLBindCol()	Lets you bind a data type with a record item from a database table.
SQLConnect()	Actually uses the connection handle and connects us to a specified datasource we provide.
SQLExecute()	Executes the statement specified by the handle created by SQLAllocStmt().
SQLFetch()	Retrieves data specified from the statement you made with SQLAllocStmt() and bound the data with SQLBindCol().
SQLFreeConnect()	Deallocates the connection handle made with SQLAllocConnect().
SQLFreeEnv()	Deallocates the SQL environment handle created with SQLAllocEnv().
SQLFreeStmt()	Frees allocation of the statement handle from SQLAllocStmt().

Now on to the code to perform the first two steps we listed above. Something like the following sample code will suffice:

```
HENV    ourEnvH;
HDBC    ourConnH;
If (SQLAllocEnv(&ourEnvH) == SQL_SUCCESS )
{
    if (SQLAllocConnect(&ourConnH) == SQL_SUCCESS )
    {
        //  now do something!
        // here you would do various things with the
        // data before freeing the connection and
        // environment handles.
        SQLFreeConnect(ourEnvH);      // give a hoot,
                                      //don't pollute (the heap)
    }
    SQLFreeEnv(ourEnvH);             // give a hoot, don't pollute
}
```

This code snippet will allocate the connection and environmental handles needed to maintain your connection with an ODBC source. To physically connect to the database, we need to call:

```
If (  SQLConnect( ourEnvH, ourConnH) == SQL_SUCCESS  )
    Then get/put data inside the database.
```

How about actually inserting a new record? Listing 6.1 shows the source for a CGI code fragment that when instantiated inserts a new record into the database table that was specified from an HTML form. In this example, you specify a **cookieID**, the **productID**, and the **quantity**. In Chapter 8, we'll show how to automatically insert cookies in the user's browser and how to retrieve them for processing from CGI and ISAPI. For now, let's do this manually so that we can cover database usage with ODBC.

LISTING 6.1   SOURCE FOR ODBCSAMPLE1.CPP.

```
//
//    File: ODBCSample1.cpp
//    By:    Don Gaspar
//
//    This example tests ODBC from CGI and is from
//    Chapter 6 in the book Visual Developer Web Commerce
//    Programming With Visual C++.
//    The publisher is The Coriolis Group.
//
```

```
//    You may reach the author at: don@gigantor.com
//

// some standard headers we're going to need in here
#include <ostream.h>
#include <fstream.h>
#include <stdio.h>
#include <stdlib.h>
#include <SQL.h>

// now headers we've written
#include "CFormParser.hpp"

// our header and footer file names
const char *cHeaderName =
    "c:\\inetpub\\gigantor\\coriolis\\head.htm";
const char *cFooterName =
    "c:\\inetpub\\gigantor\\coriolis\\foot.htm";
const char *cSQLInsertCmd =
    "INSERT INTO shoppingCart (cookieID,"
    " inventoryID, quantity) VALUES(%s,%s,%s)";


//
//    Function: BeginHeader
//    Purpose: Outputs the appropriate header information to stdout
//    for a Web browser to display.
//    Arguments: inTitle, the title of the dynamic page
//    you are creating.
void
BeginHeader(const char* inTitle)
{
    cout << "Content-type:TEXT/HTML\n\n" << "<HTML><HEAD><TITLE>\n" <<
    inTitle << "\n</TITLE></HEAD><BODY>\n";
} // BeginHeader...


//
//    Function: EndHeader
//    Purpose: Outputs the delimiter tags corresponding to those set by
//        PrintHeader() for proper HTML display.
//    Arguments: None
//
void
EndHeader()
{
    cout << "</BODY></HTML>\n";
} // EndHeader...

    //
```

```cpp
//      StreamFile
//      Input: char*, which is the name of the file to use with path.
//      Purpose: Opens the designated file and streams it out
//           through the CHttpServerContext
//           so the client's browser will get this dynamic HTML page.
//
void
StreamFile( const char* inFile )
{
try
    {
        ifstream file( inFile );     // file stream

        if ( !file ) // if we don't get the file, then
          throw(-1); // throw an exception

    char buffer[80];     // just a line of characters

    // here we loop through the file line by line until we hit
    // the end of our data buffer stream,
    // sending all the data to cout.
    while ( file.getline(buffer,sizeof(buffer)) )
        cout << buffer;

    file.close();
    }

    catch(...)
    {
        cout << "<center><b>Couldn't locate the header file."
            "<br></center></b>";
}
} // StreamFile...

//
//      function: DoDatabaseStuff
//      purpose: Creates a CFormParser object and passes the data
//      received from a POST in cin to CFormParser.
//      Checks length, etc. and throws an exception
//      upon detection of any error.
//      returns: Nothing, exceptions are used for error handling.
//
void
DoDatabaseStuff()
{
    // Why is this variable here?
    // If it was in our try{} block and an exception was thrown
```

```
// it wouldn't get deallocated. Another trick is to use the
// ANSI auto_ptr() class.
char *buffer = NULL;
HENV envH = NULL; // environmental ODBC handle
HDBC dbH = NULL;  // ODBC connection handle
HSTMT stmtH;   // statement handle

try
            {
                char *streamSize = getenv("CONTENT_LENGTH");
        THROWIF(!streamSize);
        long dataSize = atol(streamSize);
        THROWIF(!dataSize);

        buffer = new char[dataSize];
        cin >> buffer;

        CFormParser ourParser(buffer);
       // get outta here if we can't find this variable
        string cookie = ourParser["cookieID"];
        THROWIF( !cookie.length() );

        // now to make our database connections, etc.
        // notice how using exceptions cleans the code up.
        // if we were checking error codes, this could get
        // nested fairly deep and become difficult to
        // understand.
        THROWIF( SQLAllocEnv( &envH ) != SQL_SUCCESS );
        THROWIF( SQLAllocConnect( envH, &dbH ) != SQL_SUCCESS );

        RETCODE result = SQLConnect( dbH,(unsigned char *)"Games",6,
        (unsigned char *)"sa",3,NULL,0 );
        THROWIF( result != SQL_SUCCESS && result != SQL_SUCCESS_WITH_INFO);
        SQLAllocStmt( dbH, &stmtH );

        // now add our string
        char command[512];
            sprintf( command, cSQLInsertCmd,
                ourParser["cookieID"].c_str(),
                ourParser["productID"].c_str(),
                ourParser["quantity"].c_str() );
        SQLPrepare( stmtH, (unsigned char *)command,
            strlen( command ) + 1 );
        THROWIF( SQLExecute( stmtH ) != SQL_SUCCESS );

            // give a hoot, don't pollute
        delete [] buffer;
```

```
SQLFreeStmt( stmtH, SQL_CLOSE );
SQLFreeConnect( dbH );
        SQLFreeEnv( envH );

        // to get here, we had to be successful, so respond!
cout << "<CENTER><H1>Item successfully added to database"
" table!</H1><BR><BR><BR></CENTER>";
}

    catch(...)
    {
        // give a hoot, don't pollute
    delete [] buffer;
    SQLFreeStmt( stmtH, SQL_CLOSE );
    SQLFreeConnect( dbH );
            SQLFreeEnv( envH );
            cout << "<B>An unrecoverable error occurred.<BR></B>";
    }
} // HandleForm...

//
//    well, we gotta start somewhere
//
void
main()
{
// since we're streaming a file, we'll need to identify the
// content type here.
BeginHeader( "Form Handler Test");
StreamFile( cHeaderName );    // fetch, Rover

    try
    {
        DoDatabaseStuff();    // everything we do here

    catch(...)
    {
        cout << "<H1><CENTER>An error occurred!</H1></CENTER>";
    }

    StreamFile( cFooterName );    // fetch
    EndHeader();
} // main...
```

The code from Listing 6.1 is deceptively simple. It hides a few changes we had to make for the CGI code fragment to actually work with ODBC, and to build correctly with Developer Studio. Figure 6.4 shows the project settings we made within Developer Studio: Note that we defined a preprocessor symbol **USING_CGI**. We had to use this symbol because one of the header files that was included in our project when we included SQL.h was defining some SQL data type as an HWND! We're not using an HWND for CGI, but rather **stdio**.

You will also notice a **NOMINMAX** preprocessor symbol that is used to keep MFC from conflicting with STL. You do not need to use this with CGI code fragments unless you're using MFC. I used it here in case I wanted to add MFC later. The Microsoft file SqlTypes.h was modified, as shown in Figure 6.5, in order to link under Developer Studio. While the SQLHWND was defined as a FAR*, we are not using it here. We just did this change in order to build the project and get around various compiler errors that are really not errors but rather data types that we're not using, and which the compiler doesn't understand while building our project.

The routine that does almost everything is **DoDatabaseStuff**(), which opens the connection via **SQLConnect**(). Then an SQL statement is prepared by calling **SQLAllocStmt**(), and is actually set using **SQLPrepare**() and our SQL command string. The **SQLExecute**() function sends the statement we've prepared to the SQL Server, which causes the SQL string we made to be executed by the server and to generate a new record for storage

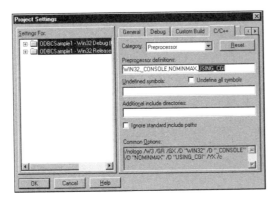

Figure 6.4
Project settings.

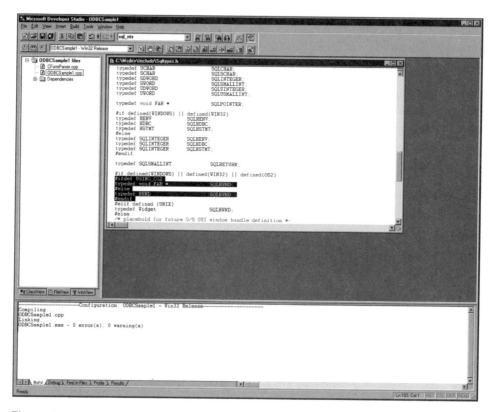

Figure 6.5
Modified SqlTypes.h.

in the database. The remainder of the code is for cleanup purposes, and is simply a good coding style to enforce. That's all—four functions plus a few for setup and cleanup.

Deallocate All Storage You've Allocated

It's really easy to assume that memory you've allocated is freed when your application quits, as with a CGI code fragment. And you're right! However, depending on your task, you might be allocating system memory to configure a driver, or something else, and these items would not be getting freed. Also, you might haphazardly make the same assumption when writing a DLL, in which case it would be a blatant memory leak—and eventually pollute your heap beyond use.

Figure 6.6 shows the HTML form that we used to interface with the CGI code fragment. While this form and the code fragment are relatively simple, you can see that with some minor customization, it could easily become an order entry form for a business that takes phone orders. Wait a minute! Aren't we doing *Web* commerce? We sure are, but sometimes you might get an order by fax, or even by phone; this form just shows a simple interface to an existing Web ordering system you can construct. You could create a form that your company would use internally and where manual orders would be entered—that way your entire business would use the same datastore.

> *Note: We're not listing the HTML for this site because it's just a variation of earlier examples on form processing. If you would like to review it, you'll find it on the CD-ROM enclosed with this book and on our Web site that supports this book (**www.gigantor.com/coriolis**).*

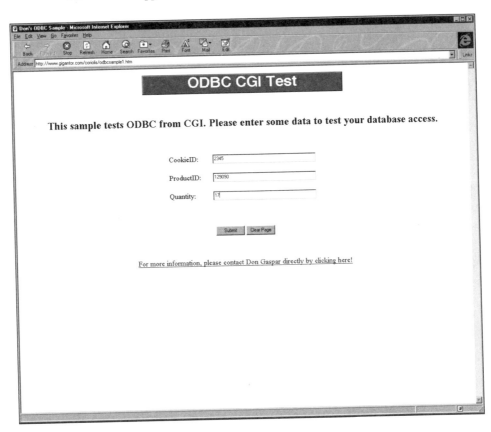

Figure 6.6
HTML interface to ODBC sample.

ODBC AND RETRIEVING RECORDS

We've just seen how to insert records in a database that we've created. Now it's time to retrieve data that we added previously. Let's use the Shopping Cart table from the previous section as an example. In this instance, the customer stores away several items for purchasing. When he or she is ready to view the items, he or she will most likely select the Review Order button from your HTML form.

Our code here will be nearly identical to our insertion code from Listing 6.1, except that we'll be sending an SQL command to search for all items using the customer's **cookieID** (which we automate in Chapter 8). The SQL statement becomes:

```
SELECT * FROM shoppingCart WHERE cookieID=something
```

The only other difference is a call to **SQLBindCol**() and **SQLFetch**(). **SQLBindCol**() allows us to bind a particular item in a database row with a particular data type, and a specified buffer to receive the data. That is, you tell ODBC what type each item in a database row is: string, integer, and so on. What's a database row? When we execute a **SELECT** statement, the results of that query are one row for each match. Iterating over each row of data until we hit the end retrieves all the rows that had matching data. We then use **SQLFetch**() to "fetch" the data into the buffers specified with the **SQLBindCol**() function. Making a loop that calls **SQLFetch**() repeatedly for the previous SQL statement will allow you to retrieve (fetch) all shopping cart items for the specified **cookieID** by moving through one row at a time. Table 6.2 lists the various data types you can bind with **SQLBindCol**(). The data types should be fairly obvious from their names, but we provide a description next to each for convenience.

TABLE 6.2

SQLBINDCOL() ODBC DATA TYPES.

Type	Description
SQL_C_BINARY	A binary item, such as image data.
SQL_C_BIT	A bit value, like a bool flag, true, or false.
SQL_C_BOOKMARK	Used for bookmark retrieval with SQLExtendedFetch.
SQL_C_CHAR	Character data.
SQL_C_DATE	Date item.

(continued)

TABLE 6.2

SQLBindCol() ODBC data types (*continued*).

Type	Description
SQL_C_DEFAULT	Tells ODBC to figure out what the type is.
SQL_C_DOUBLE	64-bit floating point value.
SQL_C_FLOAT	32-bit floating point value.
SQL_C_SLONG	Signed long integer, 32-bit value.
SQL_C_SSHORT	Signed short integer, 16-bit value.
SQL_C_STINYINT	Signed byte, 8-bit value.
SQL_C_TIME	Time value.
SQL_C_TIMESTAMP	Data and time value.
SQL_C_ULONG	Unsigned long integer, 32-bit value.
SQL_C_USHORT	Unsigned short integer, 16-bit value.
SQL_C_UTINYINT	Unsigned byte, 8-bit value.

Listing 6.2 shows the source for reviewing items that are already in the database. We've used a few additional ODBC SQL routines that we'll explain after you review the code listing. All of the code that uses ODBC is provided in the **DoDatabaseStuff**() function, and this example was created by modifying the **INSERT** demo from Listing 6.1.

LISTING 6.2   SOURCE FOR ODBCSAMPLE2.CPP.

```
//
//      File: ODBCSample2.cpp
//      By: Don Gaspar
//
//      This example tests ODBC from CGI and is from
//      Chapter 6 in the book Visual Developer Web Commerce
//      Programming With  C++.
//      The publisher is The Coriolis Group.
//
//      You may reach the author at: don@gigantor.com
//

// some standard headers we're going to need in here
#include <ostream.h>
```

```cpp
#include <fstream.h>
#include <stdio.h>
#include <stdlib.h>
#include <SQL.h>

// now headers we've written
#include "CFormParser.hpp"

// our header and footer file names
const char *cHeaderName =
    "c:\\inetpub\\gigantor\\coriolis\\head.htm";
const char *cFooterName =
    "c:\\inetpub\\gigantor\\coriolis\\foot.htm";
const char *cSQLInsertCmd =
    "INSERT INTO shoppingCart (cookieID,"
    " inventoryID, quantity) VALUES(%s,%s,%s)";
const char *cSQLRetrieveCmd =
    "SELECT * FROM shoppingCart WHERE "
    " cookieID=%s";

//
//    Function: BeginHeader
//    Purpose: Outputs the appropriate header information to
//         stdout for a Web browser to display.

//    Arguments: inTitle, the title of the dynamic page you
//         are creating.
//
void
BeginHeader(const char* inTitle)
{
    cout << "Content-type:TEXT/HTML\n\n" << "<HTML><HEAD><TITLE>\n" <<
    inTitle << "\n</TITLE></HEAD><BODY>\n";
} // BeginHeader...

//
//    Function: EndHeader
//    Purpose: Outputs the delimiter tags corresponding to those
//         set by PrintHeader() for proper HTML display.

//    Arguments: None
//
void
EndHeader()
{
    cout << "</BODY></HTML>\n";
} // EndHeader...
```

```
//
//    StreamFile
//    Input: char*, which is the name of the file to use with path.
//    Purpose: Opens the designated file and streams it out
//        through the CHttpServerContext
//        so the client's browser will get this dynamic HTML page.
//
void
StreamFile(const char* inFile)
{
try
    {
        ifstream file( inFile );    // file stream

            if ( !file )   // if we don't get the file, then
    throw(-1);    // throw an exception

    char buffer[80];    // just a line of characters

    // here we loop through the file line by line until we hit
    // the end of the stream buffer's data
    // sending all the data to cout.
    while ( file.getline(buffer,sizeof(buffer)) )
    cout << buffer;

    file.close();
    }

    catch(...)
    {
        cout << "<center><b>Couldn't locate the header file."
            "<br></center></b>";
} // StreamFile...

//
//    function: DoDatabaseStuff
//    purpose: Creates a CFormParser object and passes the data
//        received from a POST in cin to CFormParser.
//        Checks length, etc. and throws an exception
//        upon detection of any error.
//    returns: Nothing, exceptions are used for error handling.
//
void
DoDatabaseStuff()
{
```

```
// Why is this variable here?
// If it was in our try{} block and an exception was thrown
// it wouldn't get deallocated. Another trick is to use the
// ANSI auto_ptr() class.
    char *buffer = NULL;
    HENV envH = NULL; // environmental ODBC handle
    HDBC dbH = NULL;  // ODBC connection handle
    HSTMT stmtH;         // statement handle

    try
    {
        char *streamSize = getenv("CONTENT_LENGTH");
        THROWIF( !streamSize );
        long dataSize = atol( streamSize );
        THROWIF( !dataSize );

        buffer = new char[dataSize];
        cin >> buffer;

        CFormParser ourParser( buffer );
        // get outta here if we can't find this variable
        string cookie = ourParser["cookieID"];
        THROWIF( !cookie.length() );

        // now to make our database connections, etc.
        // notice how using exceptions cleans the code up.
        // if we were checking error codes, this could get
        // nested fairly deep and become difficult to
        // understand.
        THROWIF( SQLAllocEnv( &envH ) != SQL_SUCCESS );
        THROWIF( SQLAllocConnect( envH, &dbH ) != SQL_SUCCESS );

        RETCODE result = SQLConnect( dbH,(unsigned char *)"Games",6,
            (unsigned char *)"sa",3,NULL,0 );
        THROWIF( result != SQL_SUCCESS && result !=
            SQL_SUCCESS_WITH_INFO);
        SQLAllocStmt( dbH, &stmtH );

        // now add our string
        char command[512];
        sprintf( command, cSQLRetrieveCmd,
            ourParser["cookieID"].c_str() );
        SQLPrepare( stmtH, (unsigned char *)command,
            strlen( command ) + 1 );
        result = SQLExecute( stmtH );
        THROWIF( result != SQL_SUCCESS && result !=
            SQL_SUCCESS_WITH_INFO);
```

```
// now bind the columns and the data type
SDWORD dwTypeLen;
unsigned long cookieID, productID, quantity;
SQLBindCol( stmtH,1,SQL_C_ULONG, &cookieID,
    sizeof(cookieID), &dwTypeLen );
SQLBindCol( stmtH,2,SQL_C_ULONG, &productID,
    sizeof(productID), &dwTypeLen );
SQLBindCol( stmtH,3,SQL_C_ULONG, &quantity,
    sizeof(quantity), &dwTypeLen );

// display output as a table
cout << "<CENTER><H2>Shopping cart contents:</H2><BR><BR>";
cout << "<TABLE BORDER=1 CELLSPACING=3>";
cout << "<TR><TH>cookieID</TH><TH>productID"
    "</TH><TH>quantity</TH></TR>";
// fetch and display all shopping cart items using
// the cookie ID
do
{
    result = SQLFetch( stmtH );
    if ( result != SQL_SUCCESS && result !=
        SQL_SUCCESS_WITH_INFO )
        break;

    cout << "<TR><TD>" << cookieID << "</TD><TD>" <<
        productID << "</TD><TD>" << quantity <<
            "</TD></TR><BR>";
}
while(true);

// give a hoot, don't pollute
delete [] buffer;
SQLFreeStmt(stmtH, SQL_CLOSE);
SQLFreeConnect(dbH);
SQLFreeEnv(envH);

// to get here, we had to be successful, so respond!
cout << "</TABLE></CENTER><BR><BR><BR>";
}

catch(...)
{
    // give a hoot, don't pollute
    delete [] buffer;
    SQLFreeStmt( stmtH, SQL_CLOSE );
    SQLFreeConnect( dbH );
    SQLFreeEnv( envH );
```

```
            cout << "<B>An unrecoverable error occurred.<BR></B>";
        }
} // HandleForm...

//
//    well, we gotta start somewhere
//
void
main()
{
    // since we're streaming a file, we'll need to identify the
    // content type here
    BeginHeader( "Form Handler Test");
    StreamFile( cHeaderName );    // fetch, Rover

    try
    {
    }    DoDatabaseStuff();    // everything we do here

    catch(...)
    {
        cout << "<H1><CENTER>An error occurred!</H1></CENTER>";
    }

    StreamFile( cFooterName );    // fetch
    EndHeader();
} // main...
```

All the statements in **DoDatabaseStuff**() are very similar to those in the **IN-SERT** demo until you pass the **SQLExecute**() function. Here, we have to bind the data types with **SQLBindCol**(), which are long integers, so we use **SQL_C_ULONG** and identify each item that we have to bind starting with the leftmost column as "1," then "2," and so on. Binding the data indicates two things: It tells ODBC what type the data should be converted to and tells the storage location for the same data. We have to call **SQLBindCol**() for each column we expect to receive as part of our query, in this case, three times. Then we loop calling **SQLFetch**(), retrieving each row individually and always checking for the result. If you want to save this data away, you should do it here because the next time you call **SQLFetch**(), it will use the same memory locations you specified with **SQLBindCol**(), so all will be lost if you don't save it away. I personally would make an STL vector of structures that parallel the database table and add one record after each **SQLFetch**() call. For our output, we create an HTML table to format the output, view the shopping cart contents based on a specified **cookieID**, and display each row in the database as a row in our HTML table. We'll use this exact code in Chapter 11 for our full-blown shopping cart functions, so get familiar with it here. Figure 6.7 shows the formatted results.

Using CRecordset

CRecordset is an MFC class that adds all the ODBC functionality and encapsulates your database table—all in one class. The ODBC routines and functionality need a class, or even a class wrapper to group their functionality within an object, and **CRecordset** does just that. You use **CRecordset** by subclassing it and using it with a specific data table.

ODBC is very powerful because it allows us to use SQL statements directly. With **CRecordset**, you can access its database object and still do SQL if you want to, but you now have member functions that can enable quite a bit of database functionality. Table 6.3 shows the **CRecordset** class members and contains a description of what each item does.

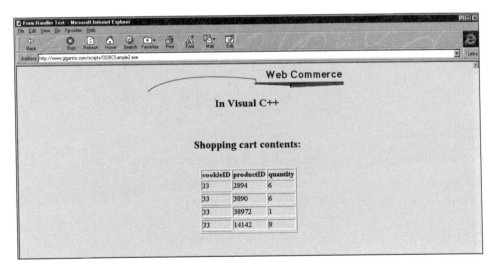

Figure 6.7
Output from ODBCSample2.cpp.

TABLE 6.3

CRECORDSET CLASS.

Member Function	Description
Construction	
CRecordset	Constructs a CRecordset object. Your derived class must provide a constructor that calls this one.
Open	Opens the recordset by retrieving the table or performing the query that the recordset represents. You can provide a CDatabase pointer if you are handling your own database directly.
Close	Closes the recordset and the ODBC statement handle associated with it.
Recordset Attributes	
CanAppend	Returns nonzero if new records can be added to the recordset via the AddNew member function.
CanBookmark	Returns nonzero if the recordset supports bookmarks.
CanRestart	Returns nonzero if Requery can be called to run the recordset's query again.
CanScroll	Returns nonzero if you can scroll through the records.
CanTransact	Returns nonzero if the data source supports transactions.
CanUpdate	Returns nonzero if the recordset can be updated (you can add, update, or delete records).
GetODBCFieldCount	Returns the number of fields in the recordset.
GetRecordCount	Returns the number of records in the recordset.
GetStatus	Gets the status of the recordset: the index of the current record and whether a final count of the records has been obtained.
GetTableName	Gets the name of the table on which the recordset is based.
GetSQL	Gets the SQL string used to select records for the recordset. This is a default string, so if you want anything specialized you will need to add it here.
IsOpen	Returns nonzero if Open has been called previously.
IsBOF	Returns nonzero if the recordset has been positioned before the first record. There is no current record.

(continued)

TABLE **6.3**

CRECORDSET CLASS (*CONTINUED*).

Member Function	Description
IsEOF	Returns nonzero if the recordset has been positioned after the last record. There is no current record.
IsDeleted	Returns nonzero if the recordset is positioned on a deleted record.

Recordset Update Operations

AddNew	Prepares for adding a new record. Call Update to complete the addition and make sure it's properly updated in the database.
CancelUpdate	Cancels any pending updates due to an AddNew or Edit operation.
Delete	Deletes the current record from the recordset. You must explicitly scroll to another record after the deletion.
Edit	Prepares for changes to the current record. Call Update to complete the edit.
Update	Completes an AddNew or Edit operation by saving the new or edited data on the data source.

Recordset Navigation Operations

GetBookmark	Assigns the bookmark value of a record to the parameter object.
Move	Positions the recordset to a specified number of records from the current record in either direction.
MoveFirst	Positions the current record on the first record in the recordset. Test for IsBOF first.
MoveLast	Positions the current record on the last record or on the last rowset. Test for IsEOF first.
MoveNext	Positions the current record on the next record or on the next rowset. Test for IsEOF first.
MovePrev	Positions the current record on the previous record or on the previous rowset. Test for IsBOF first.
SetAbsolutePosition	Positions the recordset on the record corresponding to the specified record number.
SetBookmark	Positions the recordset on the record specified by the bookmark.

(continued)

TABLE 6.3

CRECORDSET CLASS (*CONTINUED*).

Member Function	Description
Other Recordset Operations	
Cancel	Cancels an asynchronous operation or a process from a second thread.
FlushResultSet	Returns nonzero if there is another result set to be retrieved, when using a predefined query.
GetFieldValue	Returns the value of a field in a recordset.
GetODBCFieldInfo	Returns specific kinds of information about the fields in a recordset.
GetRowsetSize	Returns the number of records you wish to retrieve during a single fetch.
GetRowsFetched	Returns the actual number of rows retrieved during a fetch.
GetRowStatus	Returns the status of the row after a fetch.
IsFieldDirty	Returns nonzero if the specified field in the current record has been changed.
IsFieldNull	Returns nonzero if the specified field in the current record is Null (has no value).
IsFieldNullable	Returns nonzero if the specified field in the current record can be set to Null (has no value).
RefreshRowset	Refreshes the data and status of the specified row(s).
Requery	Runs the recordset's query again to refresh the selected records.
SetFieldDirty	Marks the specified field in the current record as changed.
SetFieldNull	Sets the value of the specified field in the current record to Null (has no value).
SetLockingMode	Sets the locking mode to "optimistic" locking (the default) or "pessimistic" locking. Determines how records are locked for updates.
SetRowsetCursorPosition	Positions the cursor on the specified row within the rowset.
Check	Called to examine the return code from an ODBC API function.

(continued)

TABLE 6.3

CRECORDSET CLASS (*CONTINUED*).

Member Function	Description
Recordset Overridables	
CheckRowsetError	Called to handle errors generated during record fetching.
DoBulkFieldExchange	Called to exchange bulk rows of data from the data source to the recordset. Implements bulk record field exchange (bulk RFX).
DoFieldExchange	Called to exchange data (in both directions) between the field data members of the recordset and the corresponding record on the data source. Implements record field exchange (RFX).
GetDefaultConnect	Called to get the default connect string.
GetDefaultSQL	Called to get the default SQL string to execute.
OnSetOptions	Called to set options for the specified ODBC statement.
SetRowsetSize	Specifies the number of records you wish to retrieve during a fetch.

You can see that **CRecordset** contains all of the ODBC functionality if you look at its various member functions in detail, and additional items for manipulating data members for your database table. It binds your database table with a subclass of **CRecordset**, but how does it do this? Support for **CRecordset** is provided with the Developer Studio Class Wizard, shown in Figure 6.8. We

Figure 6.8
Using Class Wizard for **CRecordset** subclassing.

create a new class within our project and select **CRecordset** as the base class. We then choose dynaset for our option because the data here will not be static (see the MFC Developer Help files for more information). Next, we get a dialog box asking us to select our data source and data table.

After selecting the various project options with the Class Wizard, the source and header files are generated automatically for the data table we selected (from the ODBC data source), as shown in Figure 6.9. Clicking OK will bring up active data sources for you to select, and then tables within the database to choose from. This binds the database table with a new subclass of **CRecordset**.

We've made a simple class called **CShoppingCartSet** to use with the same database table we used directly with ODBC earlier in this chapter. Our functionality earlier included adding items to the database, and then retrieving multiple records given a **cookieID**. We'll duplicate the same functionality here using an ISAPI code fragment with the **CShoppingCartSet** class. Listing 6.3 shows the source code for the newly generated subclass of **CRecordset**, CShoppingCartSet.

LISTING 6.3   SOURCE CODE FOR CSHOPPINGCARTSET.CPP.

```cpp
// ShoppingCartSet.cpp : implementation file
//

#include "stdafx.h"
#include "FoosballDB.h"
#include "ShoppingCartSet.h"

#ifdef _DEBUG
#define new DEBUG_NEW
#undef THIS_FILE
static char THIS_FILE[] = __FILE__;
#endif

/////////////////////////////////////////////////////////////////
// CShoppingCartSet

IMPLEMENT_DYNAMIC(CShoppingCartSet, CRecordset)

CShoppingCartSet::CShoppingCartSet(CDatabase* pdb)
: CRecordset(pdb)
{
//{{AFX_FIELD_INIT(CShoppingCartSet)
    m_cookieID = 0;
    m_productID = 0;
```

```
    m_quantity = 0;
    m_orderCounter = 0;
    m_nFields = 4;
    //}}AFX_FIELD_INIT
    m_nDefaultType = dynaset;
}


CString CShoppingCartSet::GetDefaultConnect()
{
    return _T("ODBC;DSN=Games");
}


CString CShoppingCartSet::GetDefaultSQL()
{
    return _T("[dbo].[shoppingCart]");
}


void CShoppingCartSet::DoFieldExchange(CFieldExchange* pFX)
{
//{{AFX_FIELD_MAP(CShoppingCartSet)
    pFX->SetFieldType(CFieldExchange::outputColumn);
    RFX_Long(pFX, _T("[cookieID]"), m_cookieID);
RFX_Long(pFX, _T("[productID]"), m_productID);
RFX_Long(pFX, _T("[quantity]"), m_quantity);
RFX_Long(pFX, _T("[orderCounter]"), m_orderCounter);
//}}AFX_FIELD_MAP
}


/////////////////////////////////////////////////////////////////////
// CShoppingCartSet diagnostics

#ifdef _DEBUG
void CShoppingCartSet::AssertValid() const
{
    CRecordset::AssertValid();
}

void CShoppingCartSet::Dump(CDumpContext& dc) const
{
    CRecordset::Dump(dc);
}
#endif //_DEBUG
```

Adding a new item from **CRecordset** requires you to call the **AddNew()** member; you also need to call **Update()** to make sure that your changes hold and are

Figure 6.9
Class settings for database options.

saved on the database. An error condition for most of the **CRecordset** member functions is usually a **CDBException** being thrown, so be sure to have a catch to intercept errors. Additionally, design your program around exceptions, as we've been doing in this book where applicable. So is that it? Almost. We need to make a few changes to our new class.

First off, open stdafx.h and add:

```
#include <afxdb.h>
```

This adds every database item needed in an MFC-based database project. Now we need to add specific changes to our class, such as locating the data source. Let's change **GetDefaultConnection**() to use our password and user name when connecting. Changes you need to make here will depend on your database settings.

```
CString CShoppingCartSet::GetDefaultConnect()
{
    return _T("ODBC;DSN=Games;UID=sa;PWD=");
}
```

Finally, if you want to make any changes to your default SQL statement that will be called when this class is instantiated, you will need to modify **GetDefaultSQL**(); here, we didn't need to make any changes. Now we need to make some ISAPI member functions that we'll specify in our HTML pages to access the database. When we used CGI earlier, we created two separate fragments to handle this case, but here we can keep one DLL resident in memory, so it makes sense to add both new member functions to the same DLL. Let's call the first one **InsertCartItem**() and the other **RetrieveCartContents**().

*Note: Remember that when writing an ISAPI fragment you will have
to provide a Parsemap so that **CallFunction()** will find the correct member function to execute.*

Some books will tell you that you need to use a database class, open it, pass the
handle from it to the **CRecordset** instance you made, and so on. It's not really
necessary to do all of that unless you want phenomenal performance, so right
now we'll just use **CRecordset**'s member functions without accessing the database class at all. When you create a new **CRecordset** class (or subclass), if a
database class is not specified, it will make one for you automatically, and will
dispose of it when your **CRecordset** destructor is called. Listing 6.4 shows the
source for the entire ISAPI code fragment.

LISTING 6.4   SOURCE CODE FOR ISAPIDB1 EXTENSION.CPP.

```
// ISAPIDB1.CPP - Implementation file for your Internet Server
//     ISAPIDB1 Extension

#include "stdafx.h"
#include "ISAPIDB1.h"
#include "ShoppingCartSet.h"

/////////////////////////////////////////////////////////////////////
// The one and only CWinApp object
// NOTE: You may remove this object if you alter your project to no
// longer use MFC in a DLL.

CWinApp theApp;

/////////////////////////////////////////////////////////////////////
// command-parsing map

BEGIN_PARSE_MAP(CISAPIDB1Extension, CHttpServer)
ON_PARSE_COMMAND( InsertCartItem,
    CISAPIDB1Extension, ITS_I4 ITS_I4 ITS_I4 )
ON_PARSE_COMMAND_PARAMS( "cookieID productID quantity" )

ON_PARSE_COMMAND( ReceiveCartContents,
    CISAPIDB1Extension, ITS_I4 )
ON_PARSE_COMMAND_PARAMS( "cookieID" )

ON_PARSE_COMMAND(Default, CISAPIDB1Extension,
    ITS_EMPTY)
DEFAULT_PARSE_COMMAND(Default, CISAPIDB1Extension)
END_PARSE_MAP(CISAPIDB1Extension)
```

```
//////////////////////////////////////////////////////////////////
// The one and only CISAPIDB1Extension object

CISAPIDB1Extension theExtension;


//////////////////////////////////////////////////////////////////
// CISAPIDB1Extension implementation

CISAPIDB1Extension::CISAPIDB1Extension()
{
}

CISAPIDB1Extension::~CISAPIDB1Extension()
{
}

BOOL CISAPIDB1Extension::GetExtensionVersion(HSE_VERSION_INFO* pVer)
{
    // Call default implementation for initialization
    CHttpServer::GetExtensionVersion(pVer);

        // Load description string
    TCHAR sz[HSE_MAX_EXT_DLL_NAME_LEN+1];
    ISAPIVERIFY(::LoadString(AfxGetResourceHandle(),
            IDS_SERVER, sz, HSE_MAX_EXT_DLL_NAME_LEN));
    _tcscpy(pVer->lpszExtensionDesc, sz);
        return TRUE;
}

//////////////////////////////////////////////////////////////////
// CISAPIDB1Extension command handlers

void CISAPIDB1Extension::Default(CHttpServerContext* pCtxt)
{
    StartContent(pCtxt);
    WriteTitle(pCtxt);

    *pCtxt << _T("This default message was produced by the Internet");
    *pCtxt << _T(" Server DLL Wizard. Edit your "
        _T("CISAPIDB1Extension::Default()");
    *pCtxt << _T(" implementation to change it.\r\n");

EndContent(pCtxt);
}

// Do not edit the following lines, which are needed by ClassWizard.
```

```
#if 0
BEGIN_MESSAGE_MAP(CISAPIDB1Extension, CHttpServer)
//{{AFX_MSG_MAP(CISAPIDB1Extension)
    //}}AFX_MSG_MAP
END_MESSAGE_MAP()
#endif // 0




/////////////////////////////////////////////////////////////////////
// If your extension will not use MFC, you'll need this code to make
// sure the extension objects can find the resource handle for the
// module.  If you convert your extension to not be dependent on MFC,
// remove the comments around the following
// AfxGetResourceHandle()and DllMain() functions,
// as well as the g_hInstance global.

/****

static HINSTANCE g_hInstance;

HINSTANCE AFXISAPI AfxGetResourceHandle()
{
return g_hInstance;
}

BOOL WINAPI DllMain(HINSTANCE hInst, ULONG ulReason,
LPVOID lpReserved)
{
    if (ulReason == DLL_PROCESS_ATTACH)
    {
            g_hInstance = hInst;
    }

    return TRUE;
}

****/

//
//    function: CISAPIDB1Extension::InsertCartItem
//    purpose: inserts a new item using the specified
//        cookieID, productID
//        and quantity into the database.
//    returns: nothing; generates HTML page to respond to user
//
void
```

```
CISAPIDB1Extension::InsertCartItem(CHttpServerContext *pCtxt,
    unsigned long inCookieID, unsigned long inProductID,
    unsigned long inQuantity)
{
    StartContent( pCtxt );
    // the item to add to our cart
    CShoppingCartSet item;

    try
    {
        // open our db table
        item.Open();

            // make sure the table is not empty
        item.AddNew();
            item.m_cookieID = inCookieID;
        item.m_productID = inProductID;
        item.m_quantity = inQuantity;

        // commit the change if we're allowed to add
        if ( item.CanUpdate() )
        item.Update();

            // close the db table since we're done
        item.Close();

            // now tell them the result was successful
        *pCtxt << "<H2><CENTER>Thank you, your item has been added to" <<
            " your shopping cart.</CENTER></H2><BR><BR><BR>";
    }

    // danger Will Robinson, danger, danger
catch(CDBException *ex)
{
        item.Close();

            // get and display any error result
        TCHAR errorMsg[1024];
            *pCtxt << "<B><CENTER>Sorry, an error occurred " <<
                "with the cookie details." <<
                "<BR></CENTER></B>";
        if ( ex->GetErrorMessage(errorMsg,sizeof(errorMsg)) )
        *pCtxt << "<CENTER>" << errorMsg << "</CENTER><BR><BR><BR>";

        EndContent( pCtxt );
    }
```

```
    EndContent( pCtxt );
} // CISAPIDB1Extension::InsertCartItem...


//
//    function: CISAPIDB1Extension::ReceiveCartContents
//    purpose: searches the database for and displays all
//       items with the specified cookieID
//    returns: nothing; generates HTML page to respond to user
//
void
CISAPIDB1Extension::ReceiveCartContents(CHttpServerContext *pCtxt,
    unsigned long inCookieID)
{
StartContent( pCtxt );

// the database item
CshoppingCartSet item;

    try
    {
        // open the database table
    item.Open();
            // is the table empty?
    if ( item.IsEOF() )
    *pCtxt << "<H2><CENTER>The database is empty!"
        "</CENTER></H2><BR><BR><BR>";
    else
            {
                // display ouput as a table
    *pCtxt << "<CENTER><H2>Shopping cart contents:</H2><BR><BR>";
    *pCtxt << "<TABLE BORDER=1 CELLSPACING=3>";
    *pCtxt << "<TR><TH>cookieID</TH><TH>productID"
        "</TH><TH>quantity</TH></TR>";

    // move to the first item in the table
    item.MoveFirst();
                while ( !item.IsEOF() )
    {
                    // does it belong to this cookie?
    if ( item.m_cookieID == inCookieID )
    *pCtxt << "<TR><TD>" << item.m_cookieID << "</TD><TD>" <<
        item.m_productID << "</TD><TD>" << item.m_quantity <<
        "</TD></TR><BR>";
    // move to the next item
    item.MoveNext();
                    }
```

```
                    // to get here, we had to be successful, so respond!
    *pCtxt << "</TABLE></CENTER><BR><BR><BR>";
    }
        item.Close();
    }

    // danger Will Robinson, danger, danger
catch(CDBException *ex)
{
        item.Close();

        // get and display any error result
TCHAR errorMsg[1024];
        *pCtxt << "<B><CENTER>Sorry, an error occurred with "
            "the cookie details.<BR></CENTER></B>";
if ( ex->GetErrorMessage(errorMsg,sizeof(errorMsg)) )
*pCtxt << "<CENTER>" << errorMsg << "</CENTER><BR><BR><BR>";

        EndContent(pCtxt);
    }


    EndContent(pCtxt);
} // CISAPIDB1Extension::ReceiveCartContents...
```

The member function **InsertCartItem**() first opens the database table using **Open**(), and then calls the **AddNew**() member to create a new record for addition into our database. **AddNew**() makes a new record that is blank, so we must insert our values after calling it. The next step is to call **Update**() to make sure the changes hold in the database, and finally a **Close**() for the database table. While there's a little less code than in our CGI sample where we used ODBC, we had to do some additional setup before using the **CShoppingCartSet** class. Also note that most of the code here was generated for us automatically using the Developer Studio Class Wizard, so we actually ended up about even.

The **ReceiveCartContents**() item takes a **cookieID** and displays all items within the shopping cart table that contain that cookie identifier. It moves to the first database row (first item) with **MoveFirst**(), and iterates through the rows one by one using **MoveNext**(). The entire time it iterates through the database table, it compares the **cookieID** it receives with the one from the database, which is the member variable **m_cookieID**. When they are equal, we obviously have a match, so we output items to our HTML table when they correspond to items in the **cookieID** shopping cart.

Your datastore will be an ensemble of several database tables, and using **CRecordset** as a base class for database objects could really simplify some of your tasks. Each database table then becomes a separate, distinct class, which makes changing your databases and maintaining your source code easier. Having separate classes for each table also allows you to use those tables in other programs that you develop with very little extra coding.

Using The CDatabase Class

When we used ODBC, we created a SQL statement and sent it to the server. SQL is a standard, so why not use it with **CRecordset** too? It does make a lot of sense to do this: We can then concentrate on SQL, and not have to worry about having to learn very much about **CRecordset**.

In ODBC, we created a statement that passed a string that was an actual SQL command into **SQLAllocStmt()**. If we use **CRecordset** and want to use SQL directly, we have to use another MFC class, **CDatabase**. This has a member function, **ExecuteSQL()**, that will take a string as input, allocate the statement with ODBC, and send it to the database server for processing.

While we don't need to use the **CDatabase** class directly, because **CRecordset** handles that for us, doing so can improve performance even more. Opening the connection to the database (in general) will be the most time-consuming CPU task in your database transaction, so why not maintain some open connections all the time? You can do this by making a vector of **CDatabase** objects and keeping them in your ISAPI fragment. This will require some management overhead for the database connections, but the performance increases will make it worth your while.

In CGI, you will not be able to do this. Do you remember why? Each CGI fragment is actually a miniature application that is launched and terminated, so you wouldn't be able to maintain connection information to the database. Is there a workaround? Yes. We could make a miniature server that maintains the connections and contains all of our ODBC commands; we could send it a TCP query that handles connections to the database for us and it would send us the response. This approach removes the ODBC from our fragment, but adds another program that we would have to develop that included it. We would also have to develop a client/server model, so using CGI could actually get quite involved. Remember that the more components you have in a project, the more can go wrong.

Summary

ODBC links your CGI or ISAPI code fragments to a datastore so that you can store, remove, and retrieve information from your database tables. Learning the functions to use ODBC is not difficult, and we use standard SQL to pass commands to the database.

CRecordset is an MFC class we can use for ISAPI projects that is built using the Class Wizard, and contains all of the ODBC functionality in one class bound with the database record information. It's relatively simple to set up a project to use this class, but if we want to use SQL from **CRecordset**, we need to use another MFC class, **CDatabase**, and its member function **ExecuteSQL()**.

Any serious Web project will use an SQL database for storing information, retrieving information, or most likely both. ODBC or **CRecordset** will let you add powerful database functions to your code fragments rapidly, and has a small learning curve. Using either ODBC or **CRecordset** will allow your Web pages to be more dynamic when they display information like the contents of an individual customer's shopping cart, or when they build custom pages of "hits" for a user who searched your site. With only a few extra lines of code, you've added some extremely powerful capabilities to your Web site. Now that we've learned how to use ODBC and **CRecordset**, we're going to apply it to an example we've used throughout our book, namely the guest book. Chapter 7 will build upon the guest book we've used in earlier chapters, and do so with both CGI and ISAPI.

FINISH THAT GUEST BOOK 7

The only reason for making honey is so I can eat it.

Winnie the Pooh

The only reason your database exists is so that people can use it. With it, you store and retrieve gigabytes of data that has nowhere else to go. One example we've followed throughout this book has been the guest book, which was great for showing how to process an HTML form and its associated data, and in Chapters 3 and 4, we even saved information into a file for later retrieval. Now, instead of using a file for our storage, we're going to use a database to stash away guest information.

Keeping the database as a central repository for all your information is a great idea, and allows you to extend your code fragment's capabilities by using the functionality that your database provides. You may use this information at another time as a mailing list, and a mailer program that you write will contact all of your guests and advertise a special promotional offer.

We're going to expand on this example in two ways: We will link information to the database first with ODBC for our CGI sample, then with **CGuestset**, a subclass of **CRecordset** that we'll derive for our ISAPI example. When linking our sample code fragments to the database we'll provide additional functionality: viewing previous guests, sorting names, and increased error handling. Performing these tasks will further demonstrate how to generate dynamic HTML forms.

The Guest Book HTML

We originally wrote this in Chapter 2 and have provided it in Listing 7.1 for your convenience. The only differences here are that the **<FORM>** tag calls the CGI or ISAPI code fragment, and we've added a button to view previous guests who have signed our book.

LISTING 7.1   GUESTBOOK.HTM.

```
<!Chapter 7 Guestbook HTML by Don Gaspar>
<HTML>

<HEAD>
<!Here's the title of our page. Note the beginning and ending tags>
<TITLE>Don's Guestbook</TITLE>
</HEAD>

<BODY BGCOLOR="#FFFFFF" LINK="#FF0000" VLINK="#800080"
    TEXT="#000000">

<!This is just our fancy border at the top of the page>
<CENTER>
<IMG HEIGHT=48 WIDTH=504 SRC=
    "http://www.gigantor.com/articles/assets/
    auto_generated_images/img_10b1c001.gif"  BORDER=0 >
</CENTER>

<!These place spaces vertically between items>
<BR><BR><BR>

<!Everything from the FORM tag until the /FORM tag is
    encapsulated within the form>
<FORM ACTION="/scripts/ODBCGuestBook.exe" METHOD="POST">

<!Here we've placed our items in a table to align them >
<CENTER>
<TABLE BORDER=0 CELLSPACING=20 WIDTH=400 HEIGHT=18>
<TR><TD><P>Your Name:</TD><TD><INPUT TYPE="text"
    NAME= "name" SIZE=48></TD></TR>
```

```
<TR><TD><P>Address:</TD><TD><INPUT TYPE="text"
    NAME= "address1" SIZE=48></TD></TR>
<TR><TD><P>Suite:</TD><TD><INPUT TYPE="text"
    NAME= "address2" SIZE=48></TD></TR>
<TR><TD><P>City:</TD><TD><INPUT TYPE="text"
    NAME= "city" SIZE=32></TD></TR>
<TR><TD><P>State:</TD><TD><INPUT TYPE="text"
    NAME= "state" SIZE=2></TD></TR>
<TR><TD><P>Zip:</TD><TD><INPUT TYPE="text"
    NAME= "zip" SIZE=10></TD></TR>
<TR><TD><P>Phone:</TD><TD><INPUT TYPE="text"
    NAME= "phone" SIZE=12></TD></TR>
<TR><TD><P>Email Address:</TD><TD><INPUT TYPE="text"
    NAME= "email" SIZE=48></TD></TR>
</TABLE>
</CENTER>

<BR><BR><BR>
<CENTER>
<INPUT TYPE="submit" Name="task" VALUE="Sign Guestbook">
<INPUT TYPE="submit" Name="task" VALUE="See Other Guests">
<INPUT TYPE="reset" VALUE="Clear Page">
</CENTER>
</FORM>

<BR><BR><BR>
<CENTER>
<P><A HREF="http://www.gigantor.com">For more information,
    please contact Don Gaspar directly by clicking here!</A>
</CENTER>

</BODY>
</HTML>
```

Figure 7.1 shows what the guest book page looks like now; the HTML page will definitely look familiar: Remember that the form is similar, but the back end to our code fragment is going to use the database instead of a streamed file as we did in Chapter 3.

Because we're using the same database and database table for the guest book, our CGI and ISAPI code fragments will share the same database and table too. Don't worry, the database can handle multiple requests from different processes—make sure that your code fragment is thread-safe if you're using ISAPI. If you're not sure how to deal with thread safety, we'll show you in

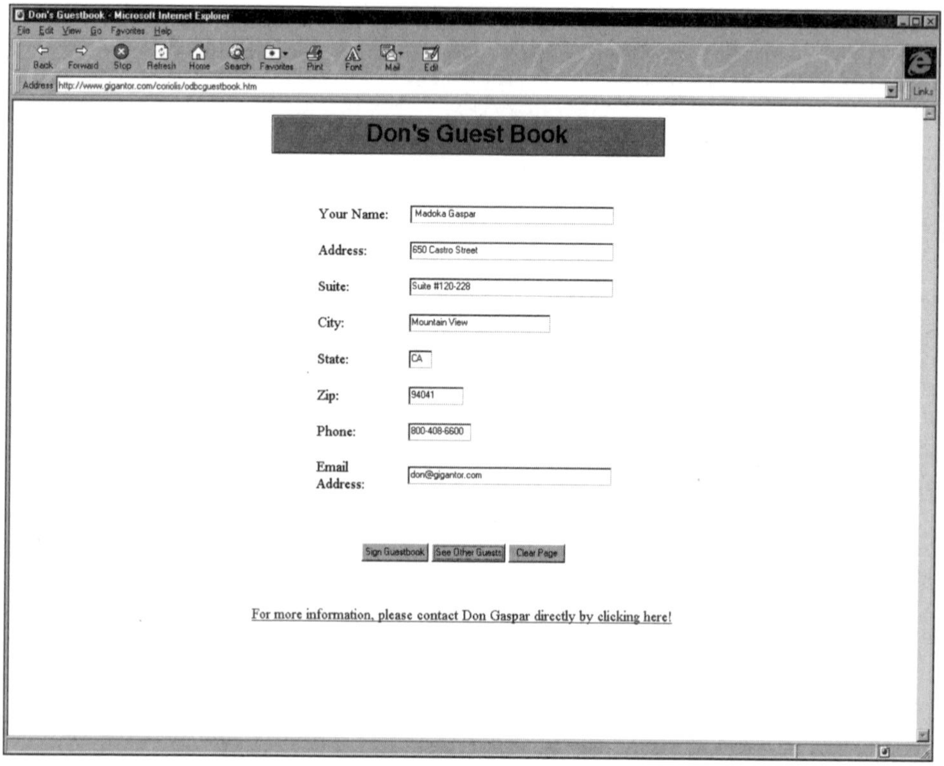

Figure 7.1
The final guest book.

detail later in this chapter. Be sure your database can handle situations when multiple processes access it simultaneously.

The Guest Book Database Table

The table is quite simple, and is shown in Table 7.1. It took just a few minutes to add this to MS SQL Server. The C++ structure that we create will be just a collection of objects.

The CGI Guest Book

Here we are again—another CGI fragment. We need to be able to add new users to the database, and also display guests who have previously signed our guest book. We should now make sure that the user doesn't already exist in the

TABLE 7.1

THE GUEST BOOK DATABASE TABLE.

Field Name	Data Type	Description
Name	varchar[64]	The name of our guest
Address1	varchar[64]	The street address of our guest
Address2	varchar[64]	The apartment or suite number
City	varchar[48]	The city where the guest lives
State	char[2]	What state the guest is in
Zip	varchar[10]	The zip code
Phone	varchar[16]	The guest's phone number
Email	varchar[64]	The guest's email address

database. If we don't, there will be redundant entries; I'm also sure your customer won't appreciate it if he or she receives two emails about each of your special offers, which would happen if you used such a database.

Let's jump right into the source code and see what we've done to make this CGI guest book functional with the database, as shown in Listing 7.2.

LISTING 7.2   CGIGUESTBOOK.CPP.

```
//
//      File: ODBCGuestBook.cpp
//      By: Don Gaspar
//
//      This example tests ODBC from CGI and is from
//      Chapter 7 in the book Visual Developer Web Commerce
//      Programming With Visual C++.
//      The publisher is The Coriolis Group.
//
//      You may reach the author at: don@gigantor.com
//

// some standard headers we're going to need in here
#include <ostream.h>
#include <fstream.h>
#include <stdio.h>
#include <stdlib.h>
#include <SQL.h>
```

```
// now headers we've written
#include "CFormParser.hpp"

// our header and footer file names
const char *cHeaderName =
    "c:\\inetpub\\gigantor\\coriolis\\head.htm";
const char *cFooterName =
    "c:\\inetpub\\gigantor\\coriolis\\foot.htm";
const char *cSQLInsertCmd = "INSERT INTO GuestTable(name,"
    " address1, address2, city, state, zip, phone, email) "
    "VALUES('%s','%s','%s','%s','%s','%s','%s','%s')";
const char *cSQLRetrieveCmd = "SELECT name, city FROM GuestTable";
const char *cSearchForName = "SELECT * FROM GuestTable "
    "WHERE name='%s' AND email='%s'";

//
//    Function: BeginHeader
//    Purpose: Outputs the appropriate header information
//                  to stdout for a Web browser to display.
//    Arguments: inTitle, the title of the dynamic
//        page you are creating.
//
void
BeginHeader(const char* inTitle)
{
    cout << "Content-type:TEXT/HTML\n\n" <<
        "<HTML><HEAD><TITLE>\n" <<
        inTitle << "\n</TITLE></HEAD><BODY>\n";
} // BeginHeader...


//
//    Function: EndHeader
//    Purpose: Outputs the delimiter tags corresponding to those
//                  set by PrintHeader() for proper HTML display.
//    Arguments: None
//
void
EndHeader()
{
    cout << "</BODY></HTML>\n";
} // EndHeader...


//
//    StreamFile
//    Input:    char*, which is the name of the file to use with path.
//    Purpose:  Opens the designated file and streams it out
```

```
//              through the CHttpServerContext
//              so the client's browser will get this dynamic HTML page.
//
void
StreamFile( const char* inFile )
{
    try
    {
        ifstream    file( inFile );    // file stream

        if ( !file )                   // if we don't get the file, then
            throw(-1);                 // throw an exception

        char buffer[80];               // just a line of characters

        // here we loop through the file line by
        //    line until we hit the end
        //    sending all the data to cout.
        while ( file.getline(buffer,sizeof(buffer)) )
            cout << buffer;

        file.close();
    }

    catch(...)
    {
        cout << "<center><b>Couldn't locate the header file."
            "<br></center></b>";
    }
} // StreamFile...

//
//    function:    AddName
//    purpose:     Adds names to the Guest Book SQL Server database!
//    returns:     Nothing since we use exceptions for errors
void
AddName( CFormParser &inParser )
{
    HENV envH = NULL;      // environmental ODBC handle
    HDBC dbH = NULL;       // ODBC connection handle
    HSTMT stmtH = NULL;    // statement handle

    try
    {
        // make sure all the required fields are present:
        // everything but address2 is required.
```

```cpp
THROWIF( inParser["name"].c_str()[0] == '\0' ||
    inParser["address1"].c_str()[0] == '\0' ||
    inParser["city"].c_str()[0] == '\0' ||
    inParser["state"].c_str()[0] == '\0' ||
    inParser["zip"].c_str()[0] == '\0' ||
    inParser["phone"].c_str()[0] == '\0' ||
    inParser["email"].c_str()[0] == '\0' );

// now to make our database connections, etc.
// notice how using exceptions cleans the code up.
// if we were checking error codes, this could get
// nested fairly deep and become difficult to
// understand.
THROWIF( SQLAllocEnv( &envH ) != SQL_SUCCESS );
THROWIF( SQLAllocConnect( envH, &dbH ) != SQL_SUCCESS );

RETCODE result = SQLConnect( dbH,(unsigned char *)"Games",6,
    (unsigned char *)"sa",3,NULL,0 );
THROWIF( result != SQL_SUCCESS &&
    result != SQL_SUCCESS_WITH_INFO);
SQLAllocStmt( dbH, &stmtH );

// used for our SQL statements
char    command[512];

// check to see if they already exist in the database
sprintf( command, cSearchForName, inParser["name"].c_str(),
    inParser["email"].c_str() );
result = SQLPrepare( stmtH, (unsigned char *)command,
    strlen( command ) + 1 );
THROWIF(result == SQL_ERROR);
// execute the SQL statement we made
result = SQLExecute( stmtH );
THROWIF( result != SQL_SUCCESS &&
    result != SQL_SUCCESS_WITH_INFO);

char name[64], email[64];
SDWORD      dwTypeLen;
SQLBindCol( stmtH,1,SQL_C_CHAR,
    &name,sizeof(name), &dwTypeLen );
SQLBindCol( stmtH,2,SQL_C_CHAR,
    &email,sizeof(email), &dwTypeLen );

result = SQLFetch( stmtH );
SQLFreeStmt( stmtH, SQL_CLOSE );
// are they actually there????
```

```
if ( result == SQL_SUCCESS ||
    result == SQL_SUCCESS_WITH_INFO )
{
    // to get here, we had to be successful, so respond!
    cout << "<CENTER><H1>Thanks, but you're already listed!"
        "</H1><BR><BR><BR></CENTER>";
}
else//not there, so add them
{
    // now add our string
    sprintf( command, cSQLInsertCmd,
        inParser["name"].c_str(),
        inParser["address1"].c_str(),
        inParser["address2"].c_str() .
        inParser["city"].c_str(),
        inParser["state"].c_str(),
        inParser["zip"].c_str(),
        inParser["phone"].c_str(),
        inParser["email"].c_str());

    // prepare our actual data now
    SQLAllocStmt( dbH, &stmtH );
    result = SQLPrepare( stmtH, (unsigned char *)command,
        strlen( command ) + 1 );
    THROWIF(result == SQL_ERROR);

    // execute the SQL statement we made
    result = SQLExecute( stmtH );
    THROWIF( result != SQL_SUCCESS &&
        result != SQL_SUCCESS_WITH_INFO);

    // to get here, we had to be successful, so respond!
    cout << "<CENTER><H1>Thank you for signing our"
        " Guest Book!"
        "</H1><BR><BR><BR></CENTER>";

}

// commit the addition to the database
SQLTransact( envH, dbH, SQL_COMMIT );

// give a hoot, don't pollute
SQLFreeStmt( stmtH, SQL_CLOSE );
SQLFreeConnect( dbH );
SQLFreeEnv( envH );
}
```

```
    catch(...)
    {
        SDWORD    err;
        char text[512], errText[512];;
        SQLError(envH,dbH,stmtH,(unsigned char *)text,&err,
            (unsigned char *)errText,sizeof(errText),0);
        cout << "<CENTER>" << errText << ": err = " <<
            text << "<BR></CENTER>";

        // give a hoot, don't pollute
        SQLTransact( envH, dbH, SQL_ROLLBACK );
        SQLFreeStmt( stmtH, SQL_CLOSE );
        SQLFreeConnect( dbH );
        SQLFreeEnv( envH );
        cout << "<CENTER><H2>Please complete all fields<BR></H2></CENTER>";
        throw(-1);    // propagate up to the next catch in the chain...
    }
} // AddName...

//
//    function:    ViewGuestBook
//    purpose:     Allows visitors to view the names of other guests who
//                 have signed our guest book.
//    returns:     Nothing, since we have exceptions thrown for errors
//
void
ViewGuestBook( )
{
    HENV envH = NULL; // environmental ODBC handle
    HDBC dbH = NULL;  // ODBC connection handle
    HSTMT stmtH;      // statement handle

    try
    {
        // now to make our database connections, etc.
        // notice how using exceptions cleans the code up.
        // if we were checking error codes, this could get
        // nested fairly deep and become difficult to
        // understand.
        THROWIF( SQLAllocEnv( &envH ) != SQL_SUCCESS );
        THROWIF( SQLAllocConnect( envH, &dbH ) != SQL_SUCCESS );

        RETCODE result = SQLConnect( dbH,(unsigned char *)"Games",6,
            (unsigned char *)"sa",3,NULL,0 );
        THROWIF( result != SQL_SUCCESS && result != SQL_SUCCESS_WITH_INFO);
        SQLAllocStmt( dbH, &stmtH );

        // now add our string
```

```
    result = SQLPrepare( stmtH, (unsigned char *)cSQLRetrieveCmd,
        strlen( cSQLRetrieveCmd ) + 1 );
    THROWIF( result == SQL_ERROR );

    result = SQLExecute( stmtH );
    THROWIF( result != SQL_SUCCESS && result != SQL_SUCCESS_WITH_INFO);

    // now bind the columns and the data type
    SDWORD    dwTypeLen;
    char name[64], city[64];
    SQLBindCol( stmtH,1,SQL_C_CHAR, &name,sizeof(name), &dwTypeLen );
    SQLBindCol( stmtH,2,SQL_C_CHAR, &city,sizeof(city), &dwTypeLen );

    // display output as a table
    cout << "<CENTER><H2>Guests who have signed in:</H2><BR><BR>";
    cout << "<TABLE BORDER=1 CELLSPACING=3>";
    cout << "<TR><TH>Name</TH><TH>Home Town</TH></TR>";

    // fetch and display all shopping cart items using the cookie ID
    do
    {
        result = SQLFetch( stmtH );
        if ( result != SQL_SUCCESS && result != SQL_SUCCESS_WITH_INFO )
            break;

        cout << "<TR><TD>" << name << "</TD><TD>" <<
            city << "</TD></TR><BR>";
    }
    while( true );

    // give a hoot, don't pollute
    SQLFreeStmt( stmtH, SQL_CLOSE );
    SQLFreeConnect( dbH );
    SQLFreeEnv( envH );

    // to get here, we had to be successful, so respond!
    cout << "</TABLE></CENTER><BR><BR><BR>";
}

catch(...)
{
    SDWORD    err;
    char text[512], errText[512];;
    SQLError(envH,dbH,stmtH,(unsigned char *)text,&err,
        (unsigned char *)errText,sizeof(errText),0);
    cout << "<CENTER>" << errText << ": err = " <<
        text << "<BR></CENTER>";
```

```
        // give a hoot, don't pollute
        SQLFreeStmt( stmtH, SQL_CLOSE );
        SQLFreeConnect( dbH );
        SQLFreeEnv( envH );
        throw(-1);     // propagate to next catch...
    }
} // ViewGuestBook...

//
//    function:   DoDatabaseStuff
//    purpose:    Creates a CFormParser object and passes the data received
//                from a POST
//                in cin to CFormParser. Checks length, etc. and throws an
//                exception
//                upon detection of any error.
//    returns:    Nothing, exceptions are used for error handling.
//
void
DoDatabaseStuff()
{
    // Why is this variable here?
    // If it was in our try{} block and an exception was thrown
    // it wouldn't get deallocated. Another trick is to use the
    // ANSI auto_ptr() class.
    char *buffer = NULL;

    try
    {
        char *streamSize = getenv("CONTENT_LENGTH");
        THROWIF( !streamSize );
        long dataSize = atol( streamSize );
        THROWIF( !dataSize );

        buffer = new char[dataSize];
        cin >> buffer;

        CFormParser    ourParser( buffer );

        // see what submit button the user selected
        string whatToDo = ourParser["task"];

        //add the guest, or display other guests
        if ( whatToDo.compare("Sign Guestbook") == 0 )
            AddName( ourParser );
        else
            ViewGuestBook( );
    }
```

```
    catch(...)
    {
        delete [] buffer;
        cout << "<CENTER><B>An unrecoverable error occurred.<BR></B></
            //CENTER>";
    }

    delete [] buffer;
} // HandleForm...

//
//    well, we gotta start somewhere
//
void
main()
{
    // since we're streaming a file, we'll need to identify the content
    // type here
    BeginHeader( "Form Handler Test");
    StreamFile( cHeaderName );          // fetch, Rover

    try
    {
        DoDatabaseStuff();                  // everything we do here
    }

    catch(...)
    {
        cout << "<H1><CENTER>An error occurred!</H1></CENTER>";
    }

    StreamFile( cFooterName );          // fetch
    EndHeader();
} // main...
```

We need to make sure that each guest's name and email address are distinct,
that is, no other name/email combination exactly matches the one we've just
received. For example, if we had multiple Thor Rotbarts connected, hopefully their email addresses would be different in order for this schema to work.
Using ODBC, we set up a query with the following SQL statement to accomplish the task:

```
SELECT (name,email) FROM GuestTable WHERE name='%s' AND email='%s'
```

This statement is missing the name and email address! Previously, we created generic SQL statements in our code fragments and used them as char *s throughout. Here, we've provided another SQL statement, and we fill in the missing **%s** items using **sprintf()**. The values that we fill this in with are from our HTML form, which we retrieve and parse with our **CFormParser** class:

```
inParser["name"] and inParser["email"]
```

If the code for **CFormParser** looks unfamiliar, please review Chapters 3 and 6 again. It's a powerful technique for getting form variables and for associating values with them rapidly and efficiently. We then use an **SQLFetch()** (after we set up proper access to the ODBC environment and connection handles as we showed in Chapter 6), and query the database. If we get a response back, then the matching pair (name and email address) is present. We just thank the user, and tell him or her that he or she is already listed, as in Figure 7.2. If the user is not in the guest book (we get no match from the SQL search query), then we need to add him or her.

Adding a user record here is just like when we added other records in Chapter 6. The only difference here is that there are more fields for the guest book. We fill in the SQL string, prepare a statement, and call **SQLExecute()**. If all goes well, the user has been added to the database and will see the Web page response shown in Figure 7.3.

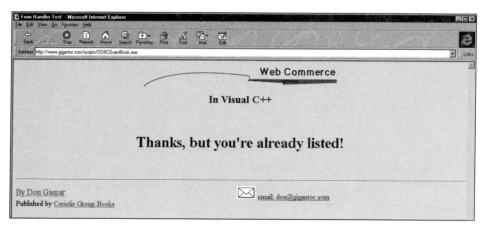

Figure 7.2
Response page for a user already in the database.

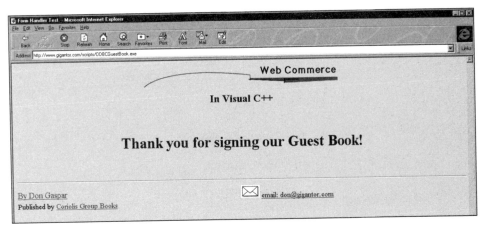

Figure 7.3
Response page for a user after we add his or her name to the database.

Now we've also added a new button that allows a guest to see which other guests have signed our site. Wait a minute! Won't the spammers find the site, copy the data, and torment your guests? They might if that were possible, but here we're only going to display the guest's name and the city where the guest is from: This will keep would-be spammers distant and alleviate any fears our guests might have that their name will be sold or misused. For the SQL query to view the guests who have already signed the guest book, we've sorted the names before displaying them and placed them in a table like we did in Chapter 6 with the shopping cart items. Figure 7.4 shows the results.

The SQL query to sort the guests' names in order was:

```
SELECT name, city FROM GuestTable ORDER BY name, city
```

That's all. You've got a high-powered guest book that is driven by your Web server and an SQL database. How would we write the same code fragment in ISAPI?

The ISAPI Guest Book

We're going to finish this chapter rather quickly. A picture can be worth a thousand words, and a few lines of good code is worth pages of text. We're going to use the same database table we used earlier in this chapter, and the same HTML file. but we'll change the <FORM> tag to:

```
<FORM ACTION="/scripts/ISAPIGuestBook.dll?DoGuestBook" METHOD="POST">
```

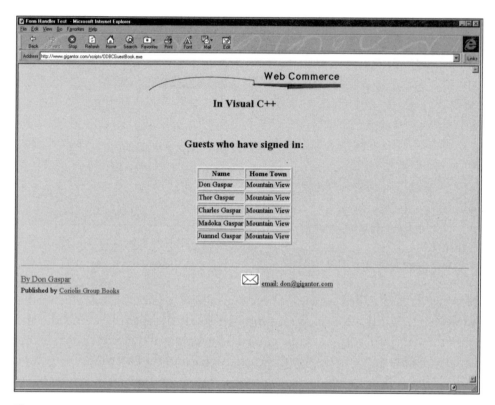

Figure 7.4
Results of viewing other guests.

Hold on! We're going to handle two options (view and add, remember) but provide only one entry point (function)? The guest book has quite a few form fields on it, so we're going to use **CFormParser** and our overridden **CallFunction**() from Chapter 5. This simplifies our Parsemaps, as they have no arguments (the view-other-guests option wouldn't have any arguments anyway), and simplifies our code. It also allows our code to resemble our CGI fragment to a degree.

Instead of using ODBC, we'll subclass **CRecordset** for our GuestTable database and call it **CGuestset**. Listing 7.3 shows the source code generated by MS Developer Studio Class Wizard, along with some slight modifications to login to our database.

LISTING 7.3 GUESTSET.CPP.

```
// Guestset.cpp : implementation file
//
```

```
#include "stdafx.h"
#include "FoosballDB.h"
#include "GuestSet.h"

#ifdef _DEBUG
#define new DEBUG_NEW
#undef THIS_FILE
static char THIS_FILE[] = __FILE__;
#endif

/////////////////////////////////////////////////////////////////
// CGuestset

IMPLEMENT_DYNAMIC(CGuestset, CRecordset)

CGuestset::CGuestset(CDatabase* pdb)
    : CRecordset(pdb)
{
    //{{AFX_FIELD_INIT(CGuestset)
    m_name = _T("");
    m_address1 = _T("");
    m_address2 = _T("");
    m_city = _T("");
    m_state = _T("");
    m_zip = _T("");
    m_phone = _T("");
    m_email = _T("");
    m_guestNumber = 0;
    m_nFields = 9;
    //}}AFX_FIELD_INIT
    m_nDefaultType = dynaset;
}


CString CGuestset::GetDefaultConnect()
{
    return _T("ODBC;DSN=Games;UID=sa;PWD=");
}


CString CGuestset::GetDefaultSQL()
{
    return _T("[dbo].[GuestTable]");
}


void CGuestset::DoFieldExchange(CFieldExchange* pFX)
{
```

```
//{{AFX_FIELD_MAP(CGuestSet)
pFX->SetFieldType(CFieldExchange::outputColumn);
RFX_Text(pFX, _T("[name]"), m_name);
RFX_Text(pFX, _T("[address1]"), m_address1);
RFX_Text(pFX, _T("[address2]"), m_address2);
RFX_Text(pFX, _T("[city]"), m_city);
RFX_Text(pFX, _T("[state]"), m_state);
RFX_Text(pFX, _T("[zip]"), m_zip);
RFX_Text(pFX, _T("[phone]"), m_phone);
RFX_Text(pFX, _T("[email]"), m_email);
RFX_Long(pFX, _T("[guestNumber]"), m_guestNumber);
//}}AFX_FIELD_MAP
}


/////////////////////////////////////////////////////////////////////////////
//
// CGuestset diagnostics

#ifdef _DEBUG
void CGuestset::AssertValid() const
{
    CRecordset::AssertValid();
}

void CGuestset::Dump(CDumpContext& dc) const
{
    CRecordset::Dump(dc);
}
#endif //_DEBUG
```

The final item is our ISAPI fragment's code, so let's review the source in Listing 7.4 in some detail.

LISTING 7.4   ISAPIGUESTBOOK.CPP.

```
// ISAPIGUESTBOOK.CPP - Implementation file for your Internet Server
//     ISAPIGuestBook Extension

#include "stdafx.h"
#include "CFormParser.hpp"
#include "Guestset.h"
#include "ISAPIGuestBook.h"


/////////////////////////////////////////////////////////////////////
// The one and only CWinApp object
// NOTE: You may remove this object if you alter your project to no
// longer use MFC in a DLL.
```

```
CWinApp theApp;

/////////////////////////////////////////////////////////////////////
// command-parsing map

BEGIN_PARSE_MAP(CISAPIGuestBookExtension, CCoolHttpServer)
    ON_PARSE_COMMAND(DoGuestBook, CISAPIGuestBookExtension,
        ITS_EMPTY)

    ON_PARSE_COMMAND(Default, CISAPIGuestBookExtension, ITS_EMPTY)
    DEFAULT_PARSE_COMMAND(Default, CISAPIGuestBookExtension)
END_PARSE_MAP(CISAPIGuestBookExtension)


/////////////////////////////////////////////////////////////////////
// The one and only CISAPIGuestBookExtension object

CISAPIGuestBookExtension theExtension;


/////////////////////////////////////////////////////////////////////
// CISAPIGuestBookExtension implementation

CISAPIGuestBookExtension::CISAPIGuestBookExtension()
{
}

CISAPIGuestBookExtension::~CISAPIGuestBookExtension()
{
}

BOOL CISAPIGuestBookExtension::GetExtensionVersion(
    HSE_VERSION_INFO* pVer)
{
    // Call default implementation for initialization
    CHttpServer::GetExtensionVersion(pVer);

    // Load description string
    TCHAR sz[HSE_MAX_EXT_DLL_NAME_LEN+1];
    ISAPIVERIFY(::LoadString(AfxGetResourceHandle(),
            IDS_SERVER, sz, HSE_MAX_EXT_DLL_NAME_LEN));
    _tcscpy(pVer->lpszExtensionDesc, sz);
    return TRUE;
}

/////////////////////////////////////////////////////////////////////
// CISAPIGuestBookExtension command handlers
```

```
void CISAPIGuestBookExtension::Default(CHttpServerContext* pCtxt)
{
    StartContent(pCtxt);
    WriteTitle(pCtxt);

    *pCtxt << _T("This default message was produced by "
        "the Internet");
    *pCtxt << _T(" Server DLL Wizard. Edit your "
        "CISAPIGuestBookExtension::Default()");
    *pCtxt << _T(" implementation to change it.\r\n");

    EndContent(pCtxt);
}

// Do not edit the following lines, which are needed by Class Wizard.
#if 0
BEGIN_MESSAGE_MAP(CISAPIGuestBookExtension, CHttpServer)
    //{{AFX_MSG_MAP(CISAPIGuestBookExtension)
    //}}AFX_MSG_MAP
END_MESSAGE_MAP()
#endif    // 0



///////////////////////////////////////////////////////////////////////
// If your extension will not use MFC, you'll need this code to make
// sure the extension objects can find the resource handle for the
// module. If you convert your extension to not be dependent
// on MFC, remove the comments
// around the following AfxGetResourceHandle()
// and DllMain() functions, as well as the g_hInstance global.

/****

static HINSTANCE g_hInstance;

HINSTANCE AFXISAPI AfxGetResourceHandle()
{
    return g_hInstance;
}

BOOL WINAPI DllMain(HINSTANCE hInst, ULONG ulReason,
                    LPVOID lpReserved)
{
    if (ulReason == DLL_PROCESS_ATTACH)
    {
        g_hInstance = hInst;
    }
```

```
    return TRUE;
}

****/

//
//    function:    DoGuestBook
//    purpose:     Calls member functions to add or view guests
//                 from our database.
//    returns:     nada
//
void
CISAPIGuestBookExtension::DoGuestBook( CHttpServerContext *pCtxt )
{
    StartContent(pCtxt);

    // make sure no one else passes this point
    // until we unlock things
    CSingleLock     lock(&m_guestSection, TRUE);
    try
    {
        // let CFormParser get our variables
        CFormParser     ourVars( pCtxt->m_pECB->lpszQueryString );

        // do we want to view guests, or add our name?
        string whatToDo = ourVars["task"];
        if (  whatToDo.compare("Sign Guestbook") == 0 )
            ViewGuestBook( pCtxt );
        else
        {
            // make sure all the required fields are present:
            // everything but address2 is required.
            THROWIF( ourVars["name"].c_str()[0] == '\0' ||
                ourVars["address1"].c_str()[0] == '\0' ||
                ourVars["city"].c_str()[0] == '\0' ||
                ourVars["state"].c_str()[0] == '\0' ||
                ourVars["zip"].c_str()[0] == '\0' ||
                ourVars["phone"].c_str()[0] == '\0' ||
                ourVars["email"].c_str()[0] == '\0' );

            // our guest record
            CGuestSet       guestRec;
            bool            dontAdd = false;

            // open links to our database table
            guestRec.Open();
```

```cpp
    // see if the guest is in our database already
    if ( !guestRec.IsEOF() )
    {
        // start with the first entry
        guestRec.MoveFirst();while( !guestRec.IsEOF() )
        {
            // what are they doing there already?
            {
            if ( !guestRec.m_name.Compare(
                    ourVars["name"].c_str())
                && !guestRec.m_name.Compare(
                    ourVars["email"].c_str()) )
                // they already entered the info
                // but ended up here again?
                dontAdd = true;
                break;
            }
            guestRec.MoveNext();
        }
    }

    // don't add them?
    if ( dontAdd )
    {
        *pCtxt << "<CENTER><H1>Thanks, but you're"
            " already listed!"
            "</H1><BR><BR><BR></CENTER>";
    }
    else    // stuff them in the database!
    {
        guestRec.AddNew();                  // new blank record
        guestRec.m_name = ourVars["name"].c_str();
        guestRec.m_address1 = ourVars["address1"].c_str();
        guestRec.m_address2 = ourVars["address2"].c_str();
        guestRec.m_city = ourVars["city"].c_str();
        guestRec.m_state = ourVars["state"].c_str();
        guestRec.m_zip = ourVars["zip"].c_str();
        guestRec.m_phone = ourVars["phone"].c_str();
        guestRec.m_email = ourVars["email"].c_str();

        // update the entry in the db
        if ( guestRec.CanUpdate() )
            guestRec.Update();
        // make sure the changes hold
        guestRec.Requery();
```

```
                *pCtxt << "<CENTER><H1>Thank you for signing"
                    " our Guest Book!"
                    "</H1><BR><BR><BR></CENTER>";
            }

        guestRec.Close();

        // better unlock things, or we'll keep threads out and
        // our dll will look dead—and might as well be!
        if ( lock.IsLocked() )
            lock.Unlock();
        }
    }

    catch(CDBException *ex)
    {
        if ( lock.IsLocked() )
            lock.Unlock();
        TCHAR    errorMsg[1024];
        *pCtxt << "<b><center>Sorry, an error occurred with"
            " the database.<br></center></b>";

        if ( ex->GetErrorMessage(errorMsg,sizeof(errorMsg)) )
        {
            *pCtxt << "<center>";
            *pCtxt << errorMsg;
            *pCtxt << "</center><br>";
        }
        EndContent( pCtxt );
    }

    catch(...)
    {
        if ( lock.IsLocked() )
            lock.Unlock();
        *pCtxt << "<H1><CENTER>Please fill out <B>all</B>"
            " information completely and resubmit."
            "</CENTER></H1><BR><BR><BR>";
        EndContent( pCtxt );
    }

    EndContent(pCtxt);

} // DoGuestBook...


//
//    function:    ViewGuestBook
```

```
//      purpose:    Displays the members from our Guest Book.
//      returns:    nada
//
void
CISAPIGuestBookExtension::ViewGuestBook( CHttpServerContext *pCtxt )
{
    CGuestSet      guestInfo;

    // open DB table, find item if it's there
    guestInfo.Open();

    // not an empty table?
    if ( !guestInfo.IsEOF() )
    {
                // display ouput as a table
        *pCtxt << "<CENTER><H2>Guests who have signed in:"
           "</H2><BR><BR>";
        *pCtxt << "<TABLE BORDER=1 CELLSPACING=3>";
        *pCtxt << "<TR><TH>Name</TH><TH>Home Town</TH></TR>";

        // start at beginning
        guestInfo.MoveFirst();

          // loop until we find our item
        do
        {
            *pCtxt << "<TR><TD>" << guestInfo.m_name <<
                "</TD><TD>" <<
                 guestInfo.m_city <<
                "</TD></TR><BR>";
            guestInfo.MoveNext();
        }
        while ( !guestInfo.IsEOF() );

        // to get here, we had to be successful, so respond!
        *pCtxt << "</TABLE></CENTER><BR><BR><BR>";
    }

    guestInfo.Close();
} // ViewGuestBook...
```

Our ISAPI project has once again inherited from **CCoolHttpServer**, which provides some additional functionality that we seem to duplicate everywhere. Now we're not using SQL queries in this extension, but taking advantage of the **CRecordset** member functions directly. To view guests, we retrieve the first record from the database, iterate through all of them, and send the output to **pCtxt**, our pointer to the **CHttpServerContext** object.

To add a new guest record in the database, we start out by looking for the user—much like we did earlier for the CGI example. Here, we get the first record by calling **MoveFirst()**, and we compare the name and email fields to those of the user; if they match, the user is already in the database, so we send the exact message we did earlier with the CGI example. If we don't find a match, we add the user and thank him or her.

Adding the user requires us to call **AddNew()**, which creates an empty GuestTable database record that we access via **CGuestset**. We fill in the fields, and then call **Update()** to make sure the changes hold.

There are two additional programming tasks that we've neglected so far: threads and re-entrancy. We need to prevent two threads from changing the same record in the database from the same process. If they were different processes, then SQL Server could handle it for us correctly, like it does for CGI. An ISAPI code fragment runs in the process space of the Web server, so we're going to have to protect this code.

The only code we protected was where we added a GuestTable record, not where we searched. When we're searching, we're not changing the data, so we're not worried about a change from our process space at that time—as long as we restrict multiple changes from the same process space to the same database record, we'll be safe. MFC provides a **CSingleLock** class that should solve that problem for us.

CSingleLock will lock down a section of code and keep other threads "frozen" at their current line of code executing, not allowing the next line of code to be executed until the **CSingleLock** object specifies an **Unlock()** call. Figure 7.5 shows this concept in a graph. Multiple threads are entering the same code to modify the same database record: Here, **CSingleLock** locks them out, so they become idle until this section of code is Unlocked(). When it becomes Unlocked(), the next thread destined to change the database record enters this section of code and **Lock()**s the code from the other threads. This process repeats until all the threads have gotten their chance. The section of code that is locked is called a "critical section."

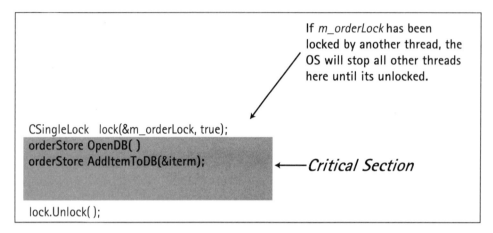

Figure 7.5
Threads being blocked.

We make a static member variable in our **CISAPIGuestBookExtension** class that is a critical section, and pass it on to the **CSingleLock** object. This means we have one copy of this member, and we share it among multiple threads that IIS creates. Using this approach maintains process integrity, and prevents us from causing a potential problem with our database.

Summary

Our guest book can add new guests and view those who have already signed in. We store this information in SQL Server, our central data repository. Much like Pooh Bear stashes away buckets of honey, we store our information in the database. This allows us to "eat" (use) our data when it is required, such as for a mailing list, or even where we allow guests to review each other.

The techniques we've covered in developing the guest book are extremely powerful. You've just linked together a high-powered database and HTML forms from your Web server using ODBC and **CRecordset**. This is the exact technique we'll be using throughout the remainder of this book for storing orders, displaying merchandise, and processing credit card transactions. The only subject we haven't covered is cookies, what they do, and how they work. We're talking about HTTP cookies, and we're going to need to use the datastore to maintain them, just like we used it for maintaining guest information in this chapter. Let's rocket into Chapter 8 and see how we can make these cookies.

COOKIES

A cookie store is a bad idea. Besides, the market research reports say America likes crispy cookies, not soft and chewy cookies like you make.

Response to Debbi Fields' idea of starting Mrs. Fields' Cookies

When we discuss cookies on the Internet, we don't mean chocolate chip, Oreo, or what have you. We're talking about HTTP cookies, tokens up to 4K in size that you can send the Web browser in an HTTP stream from your CGI or ISAPI code fragment. The browser then saves them to a cache (cookie jar). Cookies let you store some data, and save the state of a user's actions in between sessions with your Web server. A state might be what merchandise a user has added to their shopping cart, like *Batman* comics, or if the user is playing a *Star Trek* game, how many photon torpedoes remain in their arsenal.

The cookies also come with a time expiration date, meaning that you can specify that the cookie becomes stale at some time in the future: five minutes from creation time, a year, or whatever you want. For my online Foosball store, the cookies expire in 24 hours; I figure that I don't need to preserve the shopping cart contents beyond that. What user is going to shop one day, then come back a whole day later to finish up? You can force a cookie to be deleted immediately by setting its expiration date to some time in the past. If the cookie cache is full, however, a cookie will be deleted anyway, even if its expiration date hasn't been reached. The cookie cache is much like Mom's cookie jar—

241

it can only have so much in it. When the jar is full, someone has to eat a cookie in order for another cookie to fit. In cache terms, the disk space allocated for the cookies is filled, and when a request for a new cookie comes in, something has to be deleted. Which one will go? It's up to the browser's programmer.

If you can save a user's state when he or she has visited your Web site, you open up the door of opportunity for what you can now do with your code fragments. How about creating a *Star Trek* game with multiple users? You can achieve this by saving users' status information, where they are, how many photon torpedoes they have left, and so on. You can do just about anything; only your imagination restricts you.

In this chapter, we're going to discuss cookies in detail, specifically how to implement them from your code fragments. We're going to write a new class, **CCookieMonster**, that you can use from CGI and ISAPI to create, manage, update, and send cookies to a client's browser. While cookies may sound complex with all these expiration dates and states, you'll find they are quite simple—so simple, in fact, that baking cookies in the kitchen is more complex than making a cookie store information in a client's browser.

Storing Information

Information that you will need to store about your users is the merchandise in their shopping cart. In Chapter 9, we'll cover this implementation in detail, but keep examples like this in mind when thinking of cookies. We're storing information for later that needs to be preserved between client-server interactions, even when this connection is discontinued for some time.

What other kind of information would be useful to store away? You could keep track of searches a user does on your site. This would then provide you with a cookie that could tell which items interest the user, and you could pull the appropriate advertisement for display while he or she is searching—much like some of the larger search engines on the Net!

For stores, I recommend that you assign the user a unique-value ID. This will let you identify him or her when he or she connects to your CGI/ISAPI fragment. You could store the customer's shopping cart contents, but that should be considered poor *netiquette*. A shopping cart can get quite large, and storing the contents could force lots of other useful cookies to be expunged from the client's cookie cache on his or her browser. Therefore, a stored unique ID is a key to your database tables that store the shopping cart contents. When you retrieve information via this key—like we did in Chapter 6—the shopping cart contents are easily displayed. The combination of using your database and cookies this way makes a formidable Internet store.

Besides holding values and specifying an expiration date, what else can cookies do? We can name the cookie, much like a variable name, and assign a value to it. We can also give a cookie a URL, the only location at which it will be valid, and other URLs would never see this cookie because the user's browser will only allow access to it when our URL is the active site. The cookie will be secure, and a path for its usage, much like the URL, can be specified; it will be valid only at the specified path, at the URL provided. These options are great for larger sites because they permit you to have different cookies for different pages, and even make them secure.

Let's take a look at some examples before diving into the cookie jar of **CCookieMonster**.

Search Engine Pages

I'm not going to bother to ask you if you've been to Yahoo!; everyone has at one time or another. However, have you noticed that when you do a search, advertisements that deal with the subject material of your search start appearing? This is an absolutely brilliant application of cookies. It appears that your search terms are matched against paid advertisements, and when there's a match, an ad appears. The same is true when you do a search on Lycos, as shown in Figure 8.1.

Now where do cookies fit in? Some of the search engine sites—along with lots of regular sites you visit—will save a cookie after some searches. The next time you connect to their site, they start pasting advertisements all over your browser that deal with your search subject. To see this for yourself at various sites, turn on your browser's setting to notify you when a cookie is being added to it. You will be amazed at how many sites are doing this. Figure 8.2 shows an Excite search in action.

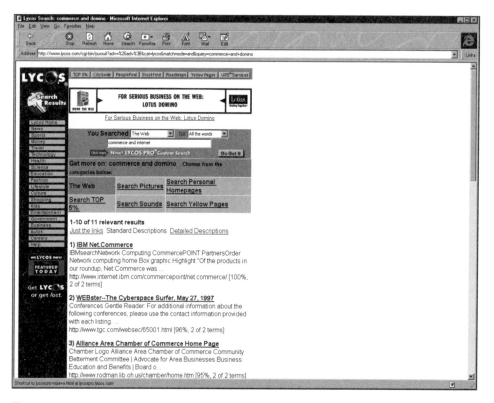

Figure 8.1
Search at Lycos.

The Foosball Shop

Let's return to our textbook example, the Foosball shop. Here we create a cookie when the user first adds an item to the shopping cart. In our CGI/ISAPI code fragment, we first check for a valid cookie and see if we can find it in our database. If we don't find it, we make a new one and replace the user's cookie. We then create a Shopping Cart table record, and use the cookie ID as the database key. We also have a Cookie table in the database that allows us to search for valid cookie IDs, and so on, and is a good place to start when we need to reference older cookies and delete associated database tables. A timestamp helps us keep only fresh cookies in our database, and removes stale ones that were never really valid orders anyway (whose time expires beyond what we allocated).

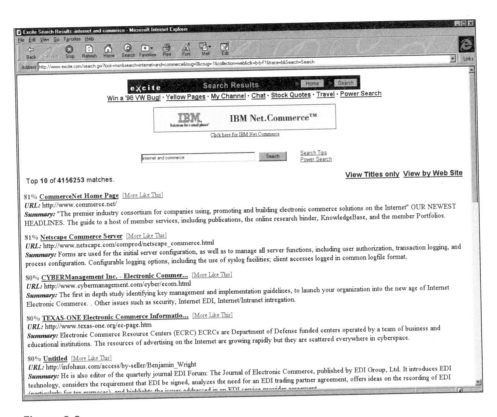

Figure 8.2
Search at Excite.

Figure 8.3 shows the shopping cart contents when the client views everything he or she has been stashing away. Each cart item is a Shopping Cart table entry in the database and represents a single record. The cookie keeps one user's shopping cart items separate from those of everyone else.

We've looked at enough cookies, so now it's time to design our new C++ class to handle these cookies for us.

CCookieMonster

CFormParser is a useful class for handling variables and their associated values. Here we're going to develop a class that is just as useful, perhaps even more so. We'll use the **CCookieMonster** class throughout the remainder of this book, so please study it here and become familiar with it. It also leverages off of **CFormParser** by subclassing from it.

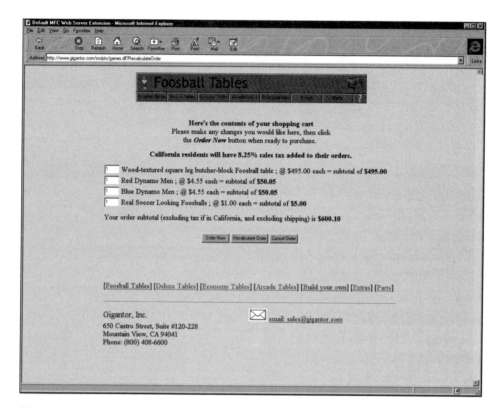

Figure 8.3
Shopping Cart contents.

It's difficult to find any written material, let alone a book, on cookies. Here, we'll not only explain them in detail and provide examples, but we'll also provide a class that handles the intricacies of retrieving, sending, and creating cookies.

Retrieving Cookies

Retrieving cookies from a browser is a little simpler than creating them, so let's see how it's done. Cookies have values, and when users are at our URL, we can request those particular cookies that deal only with our site. The cookie has a variable name associated with up to 4K of data. The cookies associated with our site are returned as system environment variables, separate from the form data. We can have multiple cookies too, so how do multiple variables with associated values look?

Cookies are displayed much like the HTML form variables with some minor differences. The browser sends over cookies separated by a ";" rather than an "&"; they're transmitted in the header information before the HTML variables and associated information are sent to the server via HTTP. An example of cookies is:

```
Cookie: var1=value1; var2=value2; var3=value3; var4=value4...
```

This is just asking us to use the **CFormParser** class to parse the variables, and provide them in an associative container for us to use. Doing this requires that we make **CFormParser** slightly more flexible, and add the capability to use a different variable/value separator, not just an "&". Thanks to polymorphism, we can create an alternate constructor to handle this, or we can modify the default constructor to do the same thing and make a default variable that equals the "&" character. This will mean that if you don't specify a separator character, the "&" will be used. We'll save the separator as a member variable of type **char**. Once we've made these changes, we have a new, slightly more versatile **CFormParser** class, as shown in Listing 8.1. The source code for the class is shown in Listing 8.2. The **CFormParser** class here is a little different than the one from Chapter 3, where you first encountered it. In Chapter 5, we decided to use the **CFormParser** to get around some ISAPI problems, so we changed some stream operations to use **CHttpServerContext** rather than **cout**. We've broken the parsing code from the constructor when the **inputString** argument is NULL; this will allow us to parse data without necessarily using the constructor, such as in a subclass.

LISTING 8.1   CFORMPARSER.HPP.

```
//
//     File: CFormParser.hpp
//     By:   Don Gaspar
//
//     This is the source for the translating and displaying
//     form variables from an example from Chapter 8
//     in the book Visual Developer Web Commerce
//     Programming With Visual C++.
//     The publisher is The Coriolis Group.
//
//     You may reach the author at: don@gigantor.com
//

#ifndef __CFORMPARSER__
#define __CFORMPARSER__
```

```
// some standard headers we're going to need in here

// some goodies provided by the STL
#include <map.h>
#include <function.h>
#include <algo.h>
#include <bstring.h>
#include <pair.h>

// cool exception macros that help simplify tasks around here
#define THROWIFNULL(value)     \
    if ( value == NULL ) throw(-1)

#define THROWIF(condition)     \
    if (condition) throw(-1)

// now for our class declaration
class CFormParser
{
    public:
        CFormParser( const char *inStringToParse = NULL,
            const char inSeparator = '&' );

        ~CFormParser();

        void ParseVars( const char *inputString );

#ifdef USING_CGI
        void OutputMap();
#else
        void OutputMap(CHttpServerContext *pCtxt);
#endif

        string& operator[] (string& inKey)
            { return GetMap()[inKey]; }

        string& operator[] (const char* inKey)
            { return GetMap()[inKey]; }

        string& GetVariable( string& inKey )
            { return GetMap()[inKey]; }

    private:
                // copy of the input string we can manipulate
        string   m_InputString        char    m_separator;
        // here's our map for storing things
        map< string, string, less<string> >   m_StorageMap;
```

```
        // some internally used member functions
        void    CleanupString();
        void    MakeVariables();
        int        hextoi( const char inChar );

        // convenient accessors
        string& GetInputString() { return m_InputString; }

        char    GetSeparator()    { return m_separator; }

        map< string, string, less<string> >& GetMap()
            { return m_StorageMap; }


}; // class CFormParser...

#endif
```

LISTING 8.2   CFORMPARSER.CPP.

```
//
//    File: CFormParser.cpp
//    By:    Don Gaspar
//
//    This is the source for the CFormParser class from Chapter 8
//    in the book Visual Developer Web Commerce
//    Programming With Visual C++. The publisher
//    is The Coriolis Group.
//
//
//    You may reach the author at: don@gigantor.com
//

// headers we've written and need

#ifndef USING_CGI
#include "stdafx.h"
#endif
#include "CFormParser.hpp"

//
//    function:    CFormParser::CFormParser
//    purpose:    A constructor for our forms parsing class.
//                Breaks the form
//                input string into an associative map
//                container for fast access.
```

```
//                  If no input string is provided it assumes
//                  you will call it later
//                  via ParseVars.
//    returns:    Constructors can't return anything
//
CFormParser::CFormParser( const char *inputString,
    const char inSeparator )
{
    m_separator = inSeparator;


    if ( inputString )
    {
        GetInputString() = inputString;
        // remove ctrl characters, etc.
        CleanupString();        // fill our map with the goodies
        MakeVariables();
    }
} // CFormParser::CFormParser...

//
//    function:    CFormParser::ParseVars
//    purpose:    Breaks the form input string into an associative
//                  map container for fast access
//    returns:    Constructors can't return anything
//

void
CFormParser::ParseVars( const char *inputString )
{
    THROWIFNULL( inputString );
    THROWIF( !strlen( inputString ) );

    GetInputString() = inputString;
    // remove ctrl characters, etc.
    CleanupString();
    MakeVariables();
} // CFormParser::ParseVars...

//
// function:    CFormParser::~CFormParser
// purpose:    CFormParser destructor – our own chance to clean up
//                  after ourselves.
// returns:        destructors can't return things
//
CFormParser::~CFormParser()
{
```

```
} // CFormParser::~CFormParser...

//
//      function:    CFormParser::hextoi()
//      purpose:     Takes a character as input and if it's a hex number,
//                   returns the appropriate ASCII value.
//      returns:     mentioned above.
//
int
CFormParser::hextoi( const char inChar )
{
    int        result;
    char       charToCompare = inChar;

    if ( isdigit( inChar ) )                        // check for base 10 digits
        result = inChar - '0';
    else                                            // check for hex number a-f
    {
// we can work with the lowercase here
        charToCompare = tolower( inChar );
        if ( charToCompare >= 'a' && charToCompare <= 'f' )
            result = charToCompare - 'a' + 10;
    }

    return result;                                  // all we really wanted
} // CFormParser::hextoi...

//
//      function:    CFormParser::CleanupString
//      purpose:     Cleans up the input string by removing the browser's
//      encoded      %XX characters, and translates '+' to whitespace.
//
//      returns:     Nothing
//
void
CFormParser::CleanupString()
{
    try
    {
        // start at the string's beginning
        int    index = 0;
        // get outta here if it's empty
        THROWIF( !GetInputString().length() );

        while ( index < GetInputString().length() )
        {
            // remember browsers translate a space to '+'
            if ( GetInputString()[index] == '+' )
```

```
                    GetInputString()[index] = ' ';
            else if ( GetInputString()[index] == '%' &&
                ( index + 2 < GetInputString().length() ))
            {
                int value = hextoi( GetInputString()[index + 1] );
                GetInputString()[index] = static_cast<char>( value * 16 |
                    hextoi( GetInputString()[index + 2] ));
                GetInputString().remove(index+1,2);
            }
            index++;                            // check next character
        } // while...
    } // try...

    catch(...)
    {
#ifdef USING_CGI
        cout << "Error in CFormParser::CleanupString()<BR>";
#endif
        throw(-1);                 // propagate exception up the chain
    } // catch...
} // CFormParser::CleanupString...


//
// function:    CFormParser::MakeVariables
// purpose:      Converts a form input string and converts it into a map
//               of key/value pairs. Uses internal map
// return:       Nothing
//
void
CFormParser::MakeVariables()
{
    try
    {
        int index = 0, pos;
        string    key, value;   // we'll use these for map insertion
        GetInputString() += ' ';

        // go through the entire string and get the key/value pairs
        while ( index < GetInputString().length() )
        {
            // remember: values are after the '='
              // get up to the variable name
            pos = GetInputString().find('=', index);
            if ( pos == NPOS )                        // paranoia
                break;
```

```
            key.resize(pos-index,0);
            copy(&GetInputString()[index], &GetInputString()[pos],
              &key[0]);
            index = pos + 1;

            // remember: next variable starts with a separator char
            // get up to the variable's value
            pos = GetInputString().find( GetSeparator(), index );
            if ( pos == NPOS )
                pos = GetInputString().length() - 1;
                  // go until we hit the end

            if ( pos-index != 0 )
            {
                value.resize(pos-index,0);
                copy( &GetInputString()[index], &GetInputString()[pos],
                    &value[0] );
            }
            else
                value = " ";                        // empty variable
            index = pos + 1;
            GetMap()[key] = value;     // insert into our map container!
        } // while...
    }

    catch(...)
    {
#ifdef USING_CGI
        cout << "Error in CFormParser::MakeVariables()...<BR>";
#endif
        throw(-1);
    }
} // CFormParser::MakeVariables...



//
//    function:    CFormParser::OutputMap...
//    purpose:     Takes our map container and iterates through all the
//                 items outputting them
//                 to stdout.
//    returns:     Nothing
//

#ifdef USING_CGI
void
CFormParser::OutputMap()
{
```

```
    map< string, string, less<string> >::iterator iter;

    if ( !GetMap().empty() )
        for( iter = GetMap().begin(); iter != GetMap().end(); iter++ )
            cout << "<B>" << (*iter).first << "</B> = <B>" <<
            (*iter).second << "</B><BR>";
    else
        cout << "Error: map container is empty.<br>";
} // CFormParser::OutputMap...
#else
void
CFormParser::OutputMap(CHttpServerContext *pCtxt)
{
    map< string, string, less<string> >::iterator iter;

    if ( !GetMap().empty() )
        for( iter = GetMap().begin(); iter != GetMap().end(); iter++ )
            *pCtxt << "<B>" << (*iter).first << "</B> = <B>" <<
            (*iter).second << "</B><BR>";
    else
        *pCtxt << "Error: map container is empty.<br>"; */
} // CFormParser::OutputMap...
#endif
```

C++ was designed with the concept of subclassing to reuse good code that you write, rather than requiring you to rewrite code for every project. While our **CFormParser** is now slightly more accommodating for parsing different data pairs, it still doesn't do everything we want it to do, nor should it! This is a job for subclassing, and the **CCookieMonster** class.

CFormParser now breaks variables up and can use different separators, but how do we apply this to cookies? Pass in a data input buffer just like you would with **CFormParser**, but make it a cookie buffer. You can do this with either of the following:

```
From CGI:       cookieBuffer = getenv("HTTP-COOKIE");
From ISAPI:     pCtxt->GetServerVariable("HTTP-COOKIE",
    &buffer[0], sizeof(buffer));
```

Make the separator character the ";" and you've got your cookies. While this is convenient, we need to make it still easier to use.

Making Cookies

CFormParser needs some modifications for cookie support, and because the logical functionality is now going to be different than it was originally designed for, it makes sense to make a subclass, called **CCookieMonster**. This new functionality can hide the **getenv**() or **GetServerVariable**() calls, and thus simplifies our programming by a few lines of code, which is what object-oriented code is supposed to do.

Logical Components As Separate Classes

It makes sense that when the functionality of a class has been expanded, maybe that new functionality belongs in its own class. This keeps code object-oriented, and makes reading and maintaining it easier. Programmers always prefer to have small base classes with specific functionality; that way you choose what you want to use with each project, and roll the classes you've previously written into your project. If you have one Godzilla-sized class with lots of functionality, it will be much more difficult to maintain, expand, understand, and so on. It's also expensive in terms of memory to instantiate large objects when you probably wouldn't need all the capabilities Godzilla has anyway.

Let's look at a Godzilla class. Suppose we're writing a reptile class and we want those cool Godzilla scales. Why do we need the overhead of laser breath and giant height when all we want are the scales? Wouldn't a better monster design contain small classes like scales, height, laser breath, and so on? This way if someone wanted to make Godzilla, he or she could multiply inherit from all the small classes; if we wanted just some scales, we wouldn't have the entire baggage associated with Godzilla. Make small classes based on functionality, and you will be a much happier programmer.

The constructor will pass NULL to the parent class for inputString during creation. Next, we get the HTTP_SERVER value and pass it to **CForm Parser::ParseVars**() for parsing and setting up the associative storage container. We're going to pass in the separator as a ";" because that's what the cookie specification requires; we did this from our default **CCookieMonster** constructor. This allows us to have a constructor that does exactly what we need. CGI and ISAPI access server variables differently, so we need to create some conditional code in the constructor to handle this for us. We'll add that conditional code shortly.

We've parsed some existing cookies, but that's not going to be very useful unless we can also create cookies. We now need to see how to create cookies for the Web browser. The browser accepts a "SET-COOKIE" command in the header that is the part of our data we send to it before the HTML tags. We specify the name of the cookie, the expiration date, a path where it is valid on our server, a domain that it is valid with, and a boolean option to tell if it should be secure or not. A typical cookie transmission to the browser from your code fragment that includes all of this would resemble the following string:

```
"SET-COOKIE: CookieName = CookieValue; expires=when;
    path=/someDirectory; domain=www.gigantor.com;
    secure or not secure"
```

Paths are always specified as Unix style, and the expires variable is formatted as:

```
"Weekday, DD-Mon-YYYY HH:MM:SS GMT"
```

An actual cookie for the Foosball store when sent to the browser would look like:

```
"SET-COOKIE: GigantorFoosball = 3889087297;
    expires Tuesday, 15-Jul-1997 12:10:08 GMT".
```

When we receive cookie data from the browser to our code fragment via **getenv**() or **GetServerVariable**(), it would look like a variable value pair such as:

```
"GigantorFoosball=3889087297"
```

To make cookies, it makes sense for our class to be able to create a new cookie for us with all of this information passed in as arguments to the member function. We've cleverly named this member function **MakeCookie**(). The source code is shown in Listing 8.3. Here, we receive all the data and use an ANSI string object as the destination cookie string.

LISTING 8.3   SOURCE FOR CCOOKIEMONSTER::MAKECOOKIE().

```
//
//    function:      CCookieMonster::CreateCookie
//    purpose:       makes a cookie with the specified data; outCookie
//                   is the resultant string.
//    returns:       nothing; throws an exception on failure
//
void
CCookieMonster::MakeCookie( char *inCookieName, char *inCookieValue,
    char *inDomainName, char *inPath, int inDays, bool inSecure,
    string &outCookie )
{
    // if the string is being used, truncate to nothing
    if ( outCookie.length() )
        outCookie.resize(0);

    // add the cookie and its value
    outCookie = "SET-COOKIE: ";
    outCookie += inCookieName;
    outCookie += "=";
    outCookie += inCookieValue;

    // add the expiration date
    if ( inDays )
    {
        char    buffer[64];
        time_t        now = time(NULL), later;
        tm            *timeInfo;

        timeInfo = gmtime(&now);
        timeInfo->tm_mday += inDays;
        later = mktime(timeInfo);

        strftime( buffer, sizeof(buffer), "%A, %d-%b-%Y %H:%M:%S"
            " GMT",
            gmtime(&later));
        outCookie = outCookie + "; expires=" + buffer;
    }

    // now add the path if needed
    if ( inPath )
    {
        outCookie += "; path=";
        outCookie += inPath;
    }
```

```
    // now the domain
    if ( inDomainName )
    {
        outCookie += "; domain=";
        outCookie += inDomainName;
    }

    // is it supposed to be secure?
    if ( inSecure )
        outCookie += "; secure";
} // CCookieMonster::MakeCookie...
```

MakeCookie() takes advantage of ANSI, not MFC, so that the sources will be portable to Unix and other operating systems. The **strftime**() function is part of ANSI, takes an input character array, and allows us to use date and time formatting much like **printf**() and **sprintf**() let us format regular strings. Be sure to look this up in your ANSI C book. We also use the **string** class for portability, convenience, and its power; however, if you're using MFC you may want to use the more powerful **CString** class.

We just learned how to make cookies; now we need to send them to the client to save.

Sending Cookies

After we make a cookie, we need to pass the information from the cookie to the browser before we send any HTML tags. In ISAPI, there's a member function of **CHttpServer** called **AddHeader**() that does this if and when it's called before **StartContent**(). When using CGI, send this information via a stream before calling **BeginHeader**(). Once, I mixed up the order of these items and literally spent all night trying to find the missing cookie. It was as frustrating debugging this as asking a two-year-old what he or she did with a cookie and getting an *"I don't know"* answer—it was really hard to find out what the problem was because all the code worked perfectly—you just lost a cookie intermittently.

Making Cookies Stale

How do we make a cookie expire with a browser, that is, make it stale? We make it stale by setting its expiration date to the day before the current time. The browser follows this metaphor and then deletes the bad cookie from its internal cookie cache (cookie jar). Passing a value of −1 in the inDays argument of **MakeCookie**() will make it stale automatically.

Why would we ever want to make a stale cookie? Let's suppose a user shops at your site, orders, confirms everything, and pays. How would you empty his or her shopping cart? When the order is confirmed, you would make his or her cookie stale, so that he or she no longer has a cart full of merchandise—he or she has already checked out. Similarly, after you check out at a grocery store, your cart is empty. The virtual shopping cart is referenced by a cookie value, so it makes perfect sense to let this value become stale when a user is finished with it.

Listing 8.4 shows the complete source for CCookieMonster.cpp. Note that some conditional code is present for ISAPI and CGI; this allows us to use the same class for either type of code fragment we write.

LISTING 8.4 SOURCE FOR COOKIEMONSTER.CPP.

```
//
//    File: CFormParser.cpp
//    By:   Don Gaspar
//
//    This is the source for the CFormParser class from Chapter 8
//    in the book Visual Developer Web Commerce
//    Programming With Visual C++. The publisher
//    is The Coriolis Group.
//
//
//    You may reach the author at: don@gigantor.com
//

// headers others have written and we need
#include <stddef.h>
#include <time.h>

// headers we've written and need
#ifndef USING_CGI
#include "stdafx.h"
#endif
#include "CookieMonster.hpp"

//    function:   CCookieMonster::CCookieMonster
//    purpose:    Constructs a CCookieMonster object,
//                gets the HTTP_COOKIE
```

```
//                  data from the server and parses it for our use.
//      returns:    constructors don't return things!
//
#ifdef USING_CGI
CCookieMonster::CCookieMonster()
#else
CCookieMonster::CCookieMonster( CHttpServerContext *pCtxt )
#endif
: CFormParser( NULL, ';' )
{
#ifdef USING_CGI
    char    *buffer = getenv("HTTP_COOKIE");
    if ( buffer )
        ParseVars( buffer );
#else
    // remember cookies can be 4K in size
    char tempString[BUFSIZ];
    DWORD cookieSize =sizeof(tempString);

        if ( pCtxt->GetServerVariable("HTTP_COOKIE",tempString,&cookieSize)
        {
            m_stringCookie = szTemp;
            return;
        }

#endif

} // CCookieMonster::CCookieMonster...

//
//      function:   CCookieMonster::CreateCookie
//      purpose:    makes a cookie with the specified data; outCookie
//                  is the resultant string.
//      returns:    nothing; throws an exception on failure
//
void
CCookieMonster::MakeCookie( char *inCookieName, char *inCookieValue,
    char *inDomainName, char *inPath, int inDays, bool inSecure,
    string &outCookie )
{
    // if the string is being used, truncate to nothing
    if ( outCookie.length() )
        outCookie.resize(0);
```

```
    // add the cookie and its value
    outCookie = "SET-COOKIE: ";
    outCookie += inCookieName;
    outCookie += "=";
    outCookie += inCookieValue;

    // add the expiration date
    if ( inDays )
    {
        char     buffer[64];
        time_t        now = time(NULL), later;
        tm            *timeInfo;

        timeInfo = gmtime(&now);
        timeInfo->tm_mday += inDays;
        later = mktime(timeInfo);

        strftime( buffer, sizeof(buffer),
            "%A, %d-%b-%Y %H:%M:%S GMT",
            gmtime(&later));
        outCookie = outCookie + "; expires=" + buffer;
    }

    // now add the path if needed
    if ( inPath )
    {
        outCookie += "; path=";
        outCookie += inPath;
    }

    // now the domain
    if ( inDomainName )
    {
        outCookie += "; domain=";
        outCookie += inDomainName;
    }

    // is it supposed to be secure?
    if ( inSecure )
        outCookie += "; secure";
} // CCookieMonster::MakeCookie...
```

Summary

This chapter helped you to understand those mysterious cookies that you hear about everywhere. We discussed how they work, why they work, how the browser deals with them, and so on. We then developed a new class we can use with our CGI and ISAPI code fragments called **CCookieMonster**. This class handles all of the details of creating, removing (expiring), receiving, and parsing cookies using **CFormParser** as a base class.

We've covered quite a bit of material in a few pages, but we haven't seen how to actually use cookies in a powerful example. The best example to demonstrate how to use cookies is the shopping cart we've talked so much about. Let's move on now to Chapter 9.

THE SHOPPING CART 9

When a program is being tested, it is too late to make design changes.

Thus spake the master programmer

The Tao of Programming

We need to design a versatile shopping cart to use with various CGI and ISAPI code fragments. It needs to be extendable and powerful, and should connect to our database with ease. When we design this shopping cart correctly, we'll be able to use it on multiple code fragments and hopefully on multiple commercial Web sites. This duplication of our results is the best productivity gain we could imagine. To estimate the time we'll save by this reuse, multiply the time it took to write the code by the number of times the code is reused.

Code evolution—adding and removing data members and functions over time—is normal. We want to prevent having to rewrite large sections of code, or changing the architecture of a base class after the initial design. The costs of making changes in a project increases exponentially, so during the design phase a correction or change in the architecture will cost us our normal rate—the employee's standard salary. If we make a correction or change during the coding phase, it's 10 times more expensive —software testers have to stop what they're doing, and engineers have to make significant changes to something that might have required only a minor change if detected during the design phase. After code is in production, it's 100-fold more expensive. For example, if you detect a defect in your shopping cart design, you'll have to bring your Web server down, lose business until the problem is fixed, test it, retest it, and then reconfigure your server. Avoid this situation with proper up-front analysis and design.

Your server will encounter problems that you are going to have to deal with anyway, so it's better not to create new ones with your code architecture along the way. While all of this might sound comical, coding is serious business and there's a lot of money involved. Time spent in the design phase is a worthwhile investment, even if your schedule slips slightly. All schedules are flexible—unless your company will go out of business, or your country is at war. Consider this time-critical war project: Engineers had 48 hours to break the Iraqi radar system—before the squadrons of fighters flew in to attack. A slipped schedule would have cost billions of dollars per day! Not to mention thousands of lives that might have been lost if the Iraqi military had operational radar and computer systems. As far as your Web-based business, adjusting your schedule a bit for quality's sake will make your customers more satisfied with your site's performance and stability. Yes, the slight delay might send your customer's business elsewhere, but you won't lose billions. And it's better than turning them completely off to Internet shopping with a site that doesn't work correctly at all.

Let's start designing our shopping cart, and let's design it right the first time.

Forms And Orders

In Chapters 2 and 3, we covered creating HTML forms and processing the variables on them. We need to process these HTML forms and link everything into the database for storage. We're also going to make cookies, and apply everything we've covered in the book up to now to a shopping cart design.

Virtual Shopping Carts

The concept is simple: A user browses merchandise on your site, and when he or she is interested in one of the items (or hopefully, more!), he or she clicks on a control that adds the item to the shopping cart. Behind the scenes, we create a cookie when the customer first adds an item to the cart, and store the cookie in his or her browser's cookie cache (cookie jar). We then use this cookie as the key in our database when we add items to the buyer's virtual shopping cart, which is just a database record. When the merchandise on the page is submitted to us, we never know how many items are on the HTML order page, so our **CFormParser** class parses the order correctly and our code fragment adds the information to the database.

We conveniently provide a button to click on when the user wants to view the items in the shopping cart. At this point, our code fragment will retrieve the user's cookie with our **CCookieMonster** class, use the cookie to do a database search, retrieve each item row by row, and output the items in an HTML form that the customer can edit. The customer will then approve the order, or maybe adjust the quantity of the items to purchase. For example, maybe the buyer doesn't want one *Lost in Space* Robot, but three. This form should then provide a Recalculate button that allows the customer to adjust the order and see what the new order total will be.

There are two different tasks that we need to isolate: receiving an order and reviewing an order. Although the tasks are similar, the subtle differences will affect our design. When we receive an HTML form's data after a submit action, we don't know the number of variables or all of their names. This is why we designed the **CFormParser** class in Chapter 3. It uses an associative container to retrieve all of the variables and values and store them away for us to access. We'll continue to use this approach because it's going to be tough to find a better and more efficient one. We can then iterate through the **CFormParser** instance and store each item the user selected (ordered) into our database.

Reviewing an order is a little different. Our code fragment will connect to the database, retrieve the information, build a form dynamically, and send this information back to the customer. We don't need to parse any data in this case, but we do have variables and values associated with the HTML form we generate as we create the edit text fields. The data will be in variables that we specify when we use CGI; with ISAPI, we'll subclass **CRecordset**, and the variables there will be member variables of that class. **CFormParser** would be additional overhead in this case and offers no real value except for its associative container for storing information. Why not just use an associative container directly within our class? The STL map container will group everything in variable/value pairs for us, and store this data for later fast associative lookup. This is a fine approach, but not the best for displaying the shopping cart contents (retrieving) from our database.

C++ Class Design

When designing any C++ class, think in terms of actions and names of items that the actions manipulate. This means breaking down your design into nouns (names of items) and verbs (actions). The nouns then become member variables and the verbs become member functions. The design technique is also language independent, so you can apply the same technique to other OO languages.

We're adding data sequentially, and creating the form sequentially. We could sort information while storing it in the container, but why bother? The variable names will most likely be inventory IDs, so sorting won't necessarily make sense on the form. We can also sort with an SQL statement before retrieving the data, which saves our code fragment from doing it manually. A vector container would be ideal here. It offers the best performance for linear access and storage, where insertions of data are at the end of the vector.

A vector is a sequential container, much like a dynamic array. We add structures, data, classes, and so on to it; if it doesn't have space, it will allocate new space for the added items. How would we associate the variable name and value? We're not doing this when we retrieve the contents of a shopping cart—we're going to retrieve more information than a variable/value pair can store, so a structure makes sense. We then use a vector of structures and use a vector iterator to move through the container in a linear fashion and display each item within an HTML form we send back to the user.

We get each database row in a loop and call **vector<struct>.push_back()** to keep adding our shopping cart items to our vector container. Adding each item is sequential, so our time requirements are *linear* in this case, which we can call *n*. Displaying the items within an HTML form will require that we use the **vector::iterator**, which we'll cover briefly here and in substantial detail later in this chapter.

STL ITERATORS ARE COOL

When you use STL, you get iterators for free. Well, we don't benefit from the "free" part unless we take advantage of them. Iterators allow you to move through a storage container and access your data elements. It's just like accessing elements of an array using the [] operator through a **for{}** loop, but easier.

Most STL containers have a **begin()** and an **end()** member function that returns an iterator that points to right before the first item in your container, and right past the last item. Moving through a container of ints, for example, would then use that same **for{ }** loop without the indexing with the **[]** operator:

```
Vector<int>::iterator iter;
for( iter = ourContainer.begin(); iter != ourContainer.end();
     iter++ )
{
    // iter is now a pointer to our ints!
    if ( *iter == whatWeAreLookingFor )
        break; // or do something else
}
```

Some of the STL containers contain an [] operator, which means that they allow random access to container members. The vector container offers a bracket operator, so you can access container members with a normal indexed loop:

```
int stop = ourContainer.size();
for( int index = 0; index != stop; index++ )
{
    //use the container directly here
    if ( ourContainer[index] == whatWeAreLookingFor )
        break;    // or do something else
}
```

Because we have an [] operator for the container we're using, why bother using an iterator? Style preference is one reason. Another reason is that when you use iterators, you gain access to several ANSI functions that perform powerful tasks—tasks that you will no longer have to code.

Let's say that you want to remove all items that equal 8 from your int container, or find an item that's negative 47. Loop and search, right? Wrong. Take a look at the ANSI C++ specification and the new STL functions. Some are:

```
replace_if()
find_if()
count()
sort()
unique()
```

There are tons of useful functions that you can take advantage of, and nearly all of them use iterators! A great book to look all of these items up, and also gather information on STL containers, is Graham Glass' *The STL Primer*, published by Prentice-Hall PTR.

Adding all of the items sequentially, our time requirement will be *1n*, but if we add them to a container like a vector and then output the HTML, our time will also be *1n*, so we've just designed a dynamic form maker that's *2n*! We then have *1m* time added because we have to match each cart entry we maintain for the user with a product of *m* items in our database. Can we improve on this? We can make the time requirement just *1n* if we make the form display only the order, but we'll need those items again for other processing, which can make our requirements even slower if we design our code incorrectly. We'll need to total the order, and add sales tax. Why not do all of these in a loop while accessing the information from the database? You can do that with one large loop, but you will still have to do the same calculations and totals—so while your time is linear, it won't be *1n* but some larger value, like *1N*, where *N* will probably equal *2n*, give or take a few microseconds. No matter how we look at this scenario, our time requirements are going to be proportional to the number of items in the cart multiplied by the number of items we maintain in our online catalog.

It's easier to maintain smaller code blocks that have specific, logical functionality rather than trying to maintain one Godzilla-sized function. Part of maintenance is future expandability. With one hard-coded loop, there's little future modifications we can do with the data from that loop later on—like email the information to us! Using a vector places data in a container for future use, which is a better coding style anyway. As the time requirements here are not great, we're breaking the functionality into smaller chunks, making the code easier to maintain.

Later in this chapter, we'll cover the full implementation of our shopping cart, but right now let's take a break and look at a few examples. While there are a lot of commercial products out there to perform shopping cart tasks (for thousands of dollars), you'll see later in this chapter how easily it is to roll out your own in just a few hours.

Shopping Cart Examples

This is nothing new, so why bother revisiting it? Well, we need to group the logical functionality into something we can code easily. Although we've already covered the code storage containers and iterators, we do need to examine each task that the user performs and review the action we'll perform on the back end with our code fragment. Our code fragments need to be responsive to the user, or customers will leave our site and visit another.

The *add* action takes a form and sends the data to your server for processing. You will check for a browser cookie, and if there isn't one, you'll create one. Figure 9.1 shows the Foosball pages after the consumer adds an item: For convenience, we've activated the browser's alert to notify us when a cookie is added.

Next, the customer reviews the cart contents, shown in Figure 9.2. Here, we generate an HTML form that uses an edit text field for data. This item should restrict quantities to the maximum you want the user to have, using the MAXLENGTH attribute.

Then, the user either changes the quantity of the ordered items and has the merchandise recalculated, or actually orders the goods. Figure 9.3 shows the form we create when the user recalculates an order. This form is then sent back to the server when the user submits it and our code fragment updates the database's record of the shopping cart contents. We then retrieve all this information again and create another dynamic HTML form. If this sounds complicated, relax, only a few functions will handle all of these actions.

When the order is actually placed, we'll want to get information on the user, including how he or she will pay. We'll cover this in detail in Chapter 10, along with security. If we've covered any of these examples too fast for you or if you want to test them out, be sure to visit **www.gigantor.com/games**.

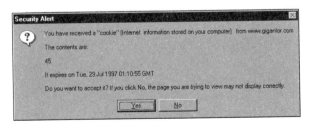

Figure 9.1
Receiving a cookie from our code fragment.

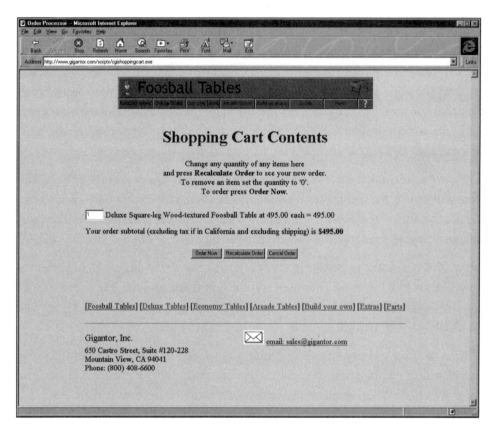

Figure 9.2
Reviewing the cart.

Design And Implementation

Let's review the database tables that we'll need. First, we need to keep track of cookies that are in use and timestamp them. Let's set them to expire in one day, and store them in the database so we don't generate duplicates. If the user switches browsers, he or she will not be able to view the order—the concept is just as if you switched shopping carts in a grocery store. However, the cookie will let us maintain the order without asking for a user ID and password, which quite a few brain-dead sites require. How many people can remember a user ID and password for multiple stores? We'd better use cookies.

Our cookie table will then be something like Table 9.1. When we create a new cookie, we'll get the highest value cookie out there and increment it by one.

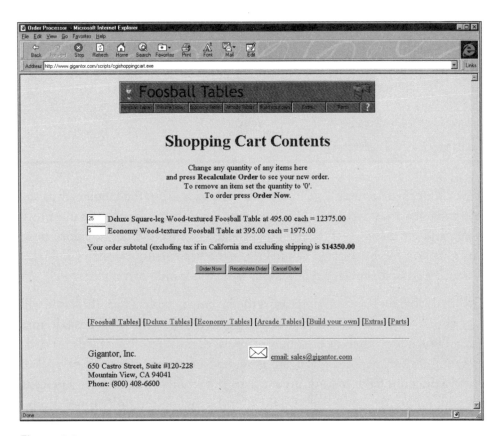

Figure 9.3
A recalculated order.

We'll also need a flag to tell us if the cookie has expired. We expire the cookie when an order is placed, cancelled, or just becomes too old. We've also added a date/time stamp, which opens the door for us to then write a process that goes through our database and cleans out old cookie entries and keeps unnecessary data out of the database. When adding the date/time stamp in SQL Server, be sure to use the **getdate** () function to make the database automatically generate this for you when adding a new record. If you're using SQL Server, Sybase, or Oracle, you can have your cookie values automatically generated for you using *seed* values—a feature of most high-powered databases. In our actual code, this is the technique I use.

		TABLE 9.1

THE COOKIE TABLE.

Field	Type	Example
CookieID	integer	388908
Expired	boolean	false
TimeStamp	datetime	Aug 8, 1998:06:43

How about the shopping cart items? This requires using the CookieID as the key, and then the inventory ID of the item (as another key to the inventory table), and the quantity of the item that the user wants to order. We don't need a date/time stamp because we can reference that information from a CookieID in another database table. Table 9.2 shows the Shopping cart table.

The final table for the shopping cart is the inventory table. Now, this table will vary from store to store, but I've provided a generic one here. The Foosball store orders from a few different distributors, so we've provided some fields for that, as well as a short description of the item, and of course, the retail price. I've added a discount field that I didn't use here, but it allows you to place a percent discount for an item and then give the user the discount at order time; adding this field in the database table allows you to discount various items differently. In my comic book store, I offer 10 percent off on Terminator Heads (from the movie *Terminator 2*), and 20 percent off on *Lost in Space* Robots. I can't offer an equal discount on all items because the items are from different distributors and have different markups. Table 9.3 provides our inventory table.

Be sure to add the tables to your database just as we have them here; if you make a change for your particular needs, you may need to modify your code as well. After you've added these tables, let's move on to coding each action.

		TABLE 9.2

SHOPPING CART TABLE.

Field	Type	Example
CookieID	integer	388908
InventoryID	varchar[32]	1256xcB88
Quantity	integer	3

TABLE 9.3

THE INVENTORY TABLE.

Field	Type	Example
InventoryID	varchar[32]	1256xcB88
Description	varchar[64]	"Deluxe Wood-Textured Foosball Table"
Cost	float	495.00
Discount	float	5.5
Vendor	varchar[32]	"Don's Foosball Supplies"

Shopping Cart Cookies

In this chapter, we'll write a new class, **CShoppingCart**, that's just as easy to use as other classes we've developed so far. To start off, we need to maintain the state of a user's session with our Web server and database, so we know we have to use a cookie for that. We'll add the cookie when the customer adds an item to the shopping cart, provided the cookie doesn't exist when we initially check.

In our **CShoppingCart** constructor, we'll check for the presence of a cookie. If the cookie doesn't exist, then we'll create a new one, send it back to the user's browser, and store it in our database as a reference to his or her shopping cart table. The **CShoppingCart** class is only instantiated when a CGI/ISAPI action for adding or reviewing items has occurred, so our logic here should suffice. What if the user already has a cookie? Never assume it's valid—you're dealing with money here! Verify the cookie with your database before proceeding; it only takes a few lines of code.

> *Note: The CShoppingCart constructor takes a CFormParser class as an argument so that it can process any HTML form orders that may have been submitted, so remember to do this. Our design is centered on exception handling for error conditions, so be sure to use your **try** and **catch** blocks.*

To implement the functionality we've discussed so far, the **CShoppingCart** constructor calls a member function **CheckCookie()** to verify the user's cookie. If a cookie is present, it calls **VerifyCookieInDB()**. If there's a problem, **MakeCookieInDB()** is called, which uses the **CCookieMonster** class to actually create the cookie for it. Listing 9.1 shows the source code for our constructor and these member functions.

LISTING 9.1   MEMBER FUNCTIONS FROM CSHOPPINGCART.

```
//
//      function:    CShoppingCart::CShoppingCart
//      purpose:     Constructor for the CShoppingCart class.
//                   Takes a CFormParser as input.
//                   Propagates exceptions out after
//                   displaying any appropriate errors.
//      returns:     Constructors can't return anything
//
CShoppingCart::CShoppingCart( CFormParser &inParser )
{
    try
    {
        m_parser = inParser;
        m_cookie = 0;
        m_envH = NULL;
        m_dbH = NULL;

        THROWIF( SQLAllocEnv( &m_envH ) != SQL_SUCCESS );
        THROWIF( SQLAllocConnect( m_envH, &m_dbH ) != SQL_SUCCESS );

        RETCODE result = SQLConnect( m_dbH,(unsigned char *)
            "Games",6,
            (unsigned char *)"sa",3,NULL,0 );
        THROWIF( result != SQL_SUCCESS &&
            result != SQL_SUCCESS_WITH_INFO);
        SQLAllocStmt( m_dbH, &m_stmtH );

        // make sure user has one, if not make a new one
        CheckCookie();
    }

    catch(...)
    {
        ShowSQLError();
        throw(-1);    // propagate to next catch...
    }
} // CShoppingCart::CShoppingCart...

//
//      function:    CShoppingCart::VerifyCookieInDB
//      purpose:     Verified m_cookie to make sure it's
//                   also in our database.
//      returns:     true if m_cookie is in the DB.
//
bool
```

```
CShoppingCart::VerifyCookieInDB()
{
    bool    memberResult = false;     //always the pessimist

    try
    {
        // if no exception is thrown, it's in the DB
        char command[256];
        sprintf( command, cSQLCheckCookieCmd, m_cookie );
        cout << command << "<BR>";
        RETCODE result = SQLPrepare( m_stmtH,
            (unsigned char *)command,
            strlen( command ) + 1 );
        THROWIF( result == SQL_ERROR );

        result = SQLExecute( m_stmtH );
        THROWIF( result != SQL_SUCCESS &&
            result != SQL_SUCCESS_WITH_INFO);

        // now bind the columns and the data type
        SDWORD    dwTypeLen;
        long    cookieID;
        SQLBindCol( m_stmtH,1,SQL_C_LONG,
            &cookieID,sizeof(cookieID), &dwTypeLen );

        result = SQLFetch( m_stmtH );
        memberResult = ( result == SQL_SUCCESS ||
            result == SQL_SUCCESS_WITH_INFO )?
            true: false;
    }

    catch(...)
    {
        ShowSQLError();
        throw(-1);     // propagate to next catch...
    }

    return memberResult;
} // CShoppingCart::VerifyCookieInDB...


//
//    function:    CShoppingCart::MakeCookieInDB
//    purpose:     Makes a new cookie in the DB and
//                 sets outCookieString to contain the same
//                 value.
//    returns:     Nothing. Throws an exception on failure.
```

```
//
void
CShoppingCart::MakeCookieInDB( string &outCookieString )
{
    try
    {
        // now make our SQL insert command
        RETCODE result = SQLPrepare( m_stmtH,
            (unsigned char *)cSQLNewCookieCmd,
            strlen( cSQLNewCookieCmd ) + 1 );
        THROWIF( result == SQL_ERROR );

        result = SQLExecute( m_stmtH );
        THROWIF( result != SQL_SUCCESS &&
            result != SQL_SUCCESS_WITH_INFO);

        // need a new statement, use old handle
        SQLFreeStmt( m_stmtH, SQL_CLOSE );
        SQLAllocStmt( m_dbH, &m_stmtH );

        // now add our string
        result = SQLPrepare( m_stmtH,
            (unsigned char *)cSQLMaxCookieCmd,
            strlen( cSQLMaxCookieCmd ) + 1 );

        result = SQLExecute( m_stmtH );
        THROWIF( result != SQL_SUCCESS &&
            result != SQL_SUCCESS_WITH_INFO );

        // now bind the columns and the data type
        SDWORD    dwTypeLen;
        SQLBindCol( m_stmtH,1,SQL_C_SLONG,
            &m_cookie,sizeof(m_cookie), &dwTypeLen );

        result = SQLFetch( m_stmtH );
        THROWIF( result != SQL_SUCCESS &&
            result != SQL_SUCCESS_WITH_INFO );

        char    temp[32];
        sprintf(temp,"%ld",m_cookie);
        // copy the cookie to a string
        outCookieString = temp;
    }

    catch(...)
    {
```

```
            ShowSQLError();
            throw(-1);    // propagate to next catch...
    }
} // CShoppingCart::MakeCookieInDB...

//
//    function:    CShoppingCart::CheckCookie
//    purpose:     Makes sure the user has a cookie and
//                 that it's in the DB, and creates one
//                 if there's a problem, or it's missing.
//    returns:     Nothing.
//
void
CShoppingCart::CheckCookie()
{
    // used for fetching cookies
    CCookieMonster    cookie;
    // a general purpose string
    string    cookieStr;

    try
    {
        // did we get a cookie?
        cookieStr = cookie["FoosballCookie"];

        // extra level of paranoia in case it's bad
        if ( cookieStr.length() )
        {
            m_cookie = atol( cookieStr.c_str() );

            // always make sure we have a record in the
            // db that matches it.
            THROWIF( !VerifyCookieInDB() );
        }
        else
            throw(-1);
    }

    catch(...)
    {
        // let this member do the dirty work
        MakeCookieInDB( cookieStr );

        // make a format browsers understand
        cookie.MakeCookie("FoosballCookie",
            (char *)cookieStr.c_str(),
            "www.gigantor.com","",
            1,false, cookieStr);
```

```
        // send it to their browser
        // DO NOT forget the "\r\n" or
        // you will have debugging nightmares
        cout << cookieStr.c_str() << "\r\n";
    }
} // CShoppingCart::CheckCookie...
```

The source code should be easy to follow, and you should see familiar code from Chapters 6 and 8 with cookies and ODBC. The **CShoppingCart** class automatically handles cookies for you via **CCookieMonster** and also stores and retrieves the cookies from the database for later reference—and all you do is instantiate a **CShoppingCart** object. Now, how about adding items to the cart?

Adding Items To The Cart

Several actions will require us to add or update information to our database, so why not group all of this functionality into one place? I've written a few member functions for dealing with all of these actions within the **CShoppingCart** class. We need to concern ourselves with only one functional entry point, which we'll see later in this chapter.

To add items to the cart, a member function, **RecalcOrder**(), iterates through the **CFormParser** class that was passed into our constructor. It starts at the beginning of the **CFormParser**, and goes until the end, adding each item to the database by calling the **AddItemToDB**() member function. Listing 9.2 shows the source for this member function.

LISTING 9.2   CSHOPPINGCART::ADDITEMTODB().

```
//
//     function:    CShoppingCart::AddItemToCart
//     purpose:     Adds the item inItem to the user's
//                  shopping cart in the DB.
//     returns:     Nothing. Throws an exception on failure.
//
void
CShoppingCart::AddItemToCart( CartItem &inItem )
{
    try
    {
        // used for our SQL statements
        char    command[512];
        // check to see if they already exist in the database
        sprintf( command, cSQLGetCartCmd, inItem.cookieID,
            inItem.inventoryID.c_str() );
```

```
RETCODE result = SQLPrepare( m_stmtH,
    (unsigned char *)command, strlen( command ) + 1 );
THROWIF(result == SQL_ERROR);

// execute the SQL statement we made
result = SQLExecute( m_stmtH );
THROWIF( result != SQL_SUCCESS &&
    result != SQL_SUCCESS_WITH_INFO);

SDWORD    dwTypeLen;
long    quantity = 0;
SQLBindCol( m_stmtH,1,SQL_C_LONG,
    &quantity,sizeof(quantity), &dwTypeLen );

result = SQLFetch( m_stmtH );
SQLFreeStmt( m_stmtH, SQL_CLOSE );
SQLAllocStmt( m_dbH, &m_stmtH );

// are they actually there????
if ( result == SQL_SUCCESS ||
    result == SQL_SUCCESS_WITH_INFO )
    sprintf( command, cSQLUpdateCartCmd, inItem.quantity,
        inItem.cookieID, inItem.inventoryID.c_str() );
else//not there, so add them
    // now add our string
    sprintf( command, cSQLInsertCmd, inItem.cookieID,
        inItem.inventoryID.c_str(), inItem.quantity );

// prepare our actual data now
result = SQLPrepare( m_stmtH, (unsigned char *)command,
    strlen( command ) + 1 );
THROWIF(result == SQL_ERROR);

// execute the SQL statement we made
result = SQLExecute( m_stmtH );
THROWIF( result != SQL_SUCCESS &&
    result != SQL_SUCCESS_WITH_INFO);

// commit the addition to the database
SQLTransact( m_envH, m_dbH, SQL_COMMIT );
}

catch(...)
{
    ShowSQLError();
    throw(-1);
}
} // CShoppingCart::AddItemToCart...
```

We also use this member function to change the quantity of an item the user has requested. Our design now accommodates changing an order and adding items to a new order, so let's explore removing items.

Removing Items From The Cart

To remove items, we'll follow the same steps with **AddItemToCart**(), except we'll use a different SQL statement. Again, this is called from **RecalcOrder**(), and is only called if the order quantity is set to zero by the user. If the quantity of an item a user is ordering is greater than zero, we'll call **AddItemToCart**() and if the item is already present in the database, we'll change the order quantity. To empty a user's shopping cart, we'll call **CancelOrder**(), a member function shown in Listing 9.3.

LISTING 9.3   CSHOPPINGCART::CANCELORDER().

```
//
//      function:   CShoppingCart::CancelOrder
//      purpose:    Deletes all items in the user's
//                  shopping cart.
//      returns:    Nothing. Throws an exception on failure.
//
void
CShoppingCart::CancelOrder()
{
    try
    {
        // need a new statement, use old handle
        SQLFreeStmt( m_stmtH, SQL_CLOSE );
        SQLAllocStmt( m_dbH, &m_stmtH );

        char    command[128];
        sprintf( command, cSQLDeleteCartCmd, m_cookie );
        // now make our SQL insert command
        RETCODE result = SQLPrepare( m_stmtH,
            (unsigned char *)command,
            strlen( command ) + 1 );
        THROWIF( result == SQL_ERROR );

        result = SQLExecute( m_stmtH );
        THROWIF( result != SQL_SUCCESS &&
            result != SQL_SUCCESS_WITH_INFO);

        // commit the addition to the database
        SQLTransact( m_envH, m_dbH, SQL_COMMIT );
```

```
        cout << "<H1><CENTER>Your shopping cart has been "  <<
            "emptied.</H1><BR>\n";
        cout << "Thank you for visiting our site!<BR><BR><BR>";
    }

    catch(...)
    {
        ShowSQLError();
        throw(-1);    // propagate to next catch...
    }
} // CShoppingCart::CancelOrder...
```

CancelOrder() is normally called when a user's browser indicates that he or she wishes to cancel. We'll explain how we parse that information shortly.

Reviewing Orders

Let's take a common request—a user wants to see everything in the shopping cart. Here, another member function, **ReviewOrder**(), displays the entire contents. It retrieves each item and stores it into a vector container via the member function **GetCart**(). We then retrieve the catalog of merchandise we're selling online with **GetCatalog**(), which makes a vector of products and has a description and price for each item.

We iterate through each item of the cart and match the corresponding item from our catalog. If something doesn't match, we'll throw an error to break out of the **ReviewOrder**() member function. Such an error would generally be caused by a bug, but it could be someone modifying your database or your Web pages. We create an HTML text item and display each item's description; at the end of the page, we add controls to let the user Order Now, Recalculate, or Cancel Order. Listing 9.4 shows the **ReviewOrder**() member.

LISTING 9.4   CSHOPPINGCART::REVIEWORDER().

```
//
//    function:   CShoppingCart::ReviewOrder
//    purpose:    Gets the shopping cart contents and
//                cross-references every item with our
//                inventory DB table. Outputs all items
//                as an HTML form the user can edit.
//    returns:    Nothing.
//
void
CShoppingCart::ReviewOrder()
{
```

```cpp
vector<CartItem>        cartContents;
vector<InventoryItem>    catalog;
vector<float>            orderCost;
char    tempStr[256];

GetCartContents( cartContents );
GetCatalog( catalog );

cout << "<H1><CENTER>Shopping Cart Contents</H1><BR>\n";
cout << "Change any quantity of any items here<BR>\n" <<
    "and press <B>Recalculate Order</B> to see your " <<
    "new order.<BR>\n" <<
    "To remove an item set the quantity to '0'.<BR>\n" <<
    "To order press <B>Order Now</B>.<BR><BR><BR>\n";

cout << "<FORM ACTION=/scripts/cgishoppingcart.exe  " <<
    "METHOD=POST>\n";


if ( !cartContents.empty() && !catalog.empty() )
{
    vector<CartItem>::iterator     iter;
    vector<InventoryItem>::iterator catIter;

    // display each item in the user's cart
    for( iter = cartContents.begin();
        iter != cartContents.end();
        iter++ )
    {
        cout << "<TR><INPUT TYPE=text SIZE=5 MAXLENGTH=2 NAME="
            << iter->inventoryID.c_str() <<
            " VALUE = " <<
            iter->quantity << ">\n";

        // another loop! ouch!
        for ( catIter = catalog.begin();
            catIter != catalog.end();
            catIter++ )
        {
            if ( !iter->inventoryID.compare(
                catIter->inventoryID) )
            {
                float lineTotal = catIter->cost *
                    iter->quantity;
                sprintf(tempStr, "%s at %.2f each = %.2f<BR>\n",
                    catIter->description.c_str(),
```

```
                        catIter->cost,
                        lineTotal );
                cout << tempStr;

                // add the order up
                orderCost.push_back( lineTotal );
                break;
            }
        }
    } // for...
}
else
    cout << "<CENTER>Nothing found!</CENTER><BR><BR><BR>\n";

sprintf(tempStr,"<P>Your order subtotal \
    (excluding tax if in California \
    and excluding shipping) is <B>$%.2f</B><BR><BR><BR>",
        accumulate( orderCost.begin(), orderCost.end(),0.0 ) );
cout << tempStr;

    // add buttons and end the form's scope
cout<< "<CENTER><INPUT TYPE=submit NAME=task " <<
    "VALUE='Order Now'>" <<
    "<INPUT TYPE=submit NAME=task VALUE='Recalculate Order'>" <<
    "<INPUT TYPE=submit NAME=task " <<
    "VALUE='Cancel Order'></CENTER>" <<
    "</FORM><BR><BR><BR>\n";
} // CShoppingCart::ReviewOrder...
```

The **FORM ACTION** action attribute uses the same code fragment that this code is present in for all cart actions, thereby keeping the shopping cart functionality in one location, as it should be.

Using CShoppingCart

To use **CShoppingCart**, you must first specify the name of the code fragment in your HTML page, as shown in Listing 9.5, from the Deluxe Foosball page. Here, you specify the name of your code fragment for the action. To tell the fragment what action to perform internally, we set up the **task** variable for each submit control—the value tells us what action to take. The actions I've defined are: **ReviewOrder()**, **RecalcOrder()**, **CancelOrder()**, and one we'll implement in Chapter 10, **OrderNow()**.

LISTING 9.5   DELUXE.HTM.

```
<!DOCTYPE HTML PUBLIC "-//W3C//DTD HTML 3.2//EN">
<HTML>
<HEAD>
<TITLE>Deluxe Tables</TITLE>
</HEAD>

<BODY BGCOLOR="#DDDDDD" LINK="#0000EE" VLINK="#EE0000"
     TEXT="#000000">
<FORM ACTION="/scripts/cgishoppingcart.exe" METHOD=POST>

<CENTER>
<TABLE BORDER=0 CELLSPACING=0 CELLPADDING=0>
<TR>
<TD COLSPAN=8>
<IMG HEIGHT=48 WIDTH=595 SRC="Header2.gif" BORDER=0
    ALT="Deluxe Tables">
</TD>
</TR>

<TR>
<TD WIDTH=80>
<A HREF="default.htm">
<IMG HEIGHT=24 WIDTH=80 SRC="OneOff.gif" BORDER=0
    ALT="Foosball Tables">
</A>
</TD>

<TD WIDTH=80>
<A HREF="deluxe.htm">
<IMG HEIGHT=24 WIDTH=80 SRC="TwoOn.gif" BORDER=0
    ALT="Deluxe Tables">
</A>
</TD>

<TD WIDTH=80>
<A HREF="economy.htm">
<IMG HEIGHT=24 WIDTH=80 SRC="ThreeOff.gif" BORDER=0
    ALT="Economy Tables">
</A>
</TD>

<TD WIDTH=80>
<A HREF="arcade.htm">
```

```
<IMG HEIGHT=24 WIDTH=80 SRC="FourOff.gif" BORDER=0
    ALT="Arcade Tables">
</A>
</TD>

<TD WIDTH=80>
<A HREF="build.htm">
<IMG HEIGHT=24 WIDTH=80 SRC="FiveOff.gif" BORDER=0
    ALT="Build your own">
</A>
</TD>

<TD WIDTH=80>
<A HREF="extras1.htm">
<IMG HEIGHT=24 WIDTH=80 SRC="SixOff.gif" BORDER=0
    ALT="Extras">
</A>
</TD>

<TD WIDTH=80>
<A HREF="parts.htm">
<IMG HEIGHT=24 WIDTH=80 SRC="SevenOff.gif" BORDER=0
    ALT="Parts">
</A>
</TD>

<TD WIDTH=35>
<A HREF="fooshelp.htm">
<IMG HEIGHT=24 WIDTH=35 SRC="HelpOff.gif" BORDER=0
    ALT="Help!">
</A>
</TD>
</TR>
</TABLE>
</CENTER>

<CENTER>
<P>Just click on the buttons above for the type of Foosball
Championship Table you might be interested in.
<br>
<br>
<br>

<FONT SIZE="+3">Premier Championship Soccer Table</FONT>
<br>
</CENTER>
```

```
<TABLE CELLPADDING=0 CELLSPACING=0 BORDER=0 WIDTH=100%>
   <TR>
    <TD HEIGHT=10></TD>
   </TR>

<TR VALIGN="top" ALIGN="left">
<TD>
<IMG HEIGHT=300 WIDTH=340 SRC="FB1.jpg" BORDER=0
    ALT="Deluxe Foosball Picture" >
<p>
<CENTER>
<B>

<FONT SIZE="+2">
Our Best Seller $495
</FONT>
</B>
</CENTER>
</TD>

<TD>
<UL TYPE="DISC">
<LI>
14&quot; Burn Resistant Mica Laminated Gray Butcher Block Cabinet
</LI>

<LI>
Solid Rods, Double Chromed
</LI>

<LI>
Non-Glare Gray Playfield with contrasting
    Light Gray Corners and Sides
</LI>

<LI>
Large Rubber Grips
</LI>

<LI>
Side Ball Return
</LI>

<LI>
Solid Hardwood Legs
</LI>
```

```
<LI>
1 1/2&quot; Thick Plywood Side Walls
</LI>

<LI>
Decorative Racing Stripe &quot;Premier Soccer -
    Table of Champions&quot; Imprinted
</LI>



<LI>
New Style Color Wide Shoulder-Rounded Foot Players
</LI>

<LI>
Triple Reinforced Cabinet
</LI>

<LI>
Weight: 150 lbs
</LI>

<LI>
Regulation Sized: 55&quot; x 29 3/4&quot; x 34 7/8&quot;
</LI>
</UL>

<P>
<TABLE>
<TR>
<TD WIDTH=20></TD>
<TD><IMG HEIGHT=32 WIDTH=32 SRC="swatchg.jpg"
    BORDER=0 ALT="Gray-colored swatch"></TD>
<TD>Gray-colored deluxe table<br>Enter how many</TD>
<TD><INPUT TYPE="text" NAME="26-131" VALUE=""
    SIZE=5 MAXLENGTH=1></TD>
</TR>

<TR>
<TD WIDTH=20></TD>
<TD><IMG HEIGHT=32 WIDTH=32 SRC="swatchw.jpg" BORDER=0
    ALT="Wood-colored swatch"></TD>
<TD>Wood-colored deluxe table<br>Enter how many</TD>
<TD><INPUT TYPE="text" NAME="26-130" VALUE="1"
    SIZE=5 MAXLENGTH=1></TD>
</TR>
</TABLE>
```

```
<p>
<! Here's our form submit buttons and their associated values>
<INPUT TYPE="submit" NAME="task" VALUE="Add To Shopping Cart">
<INPUT TYPE="submit" NAME="task" VALUE="Review Order" >
<INPUT TYPE="reset" NAME="" VALUE="Reset Form">
</TD>
</TR>
</TABLE>

<br>
<br>

[<A HREF="default.htm">Foosball Tables</A>]

[<A HREF="deluxe.htm">Deluxe Tables</A>]

[<A HREF="economy.htm">Economy Tables</A>]

[<A HREF="arcade.htm">Arcade Tables</A>]

[<A HREF="build.htm">Build your own</A>]

[<A HREF="extras1.htm">Extras</A>]
[<A HREF="parts.htm">Parts</A>]
<p>

<HR>

<TABLE CELLPADDING=0 CELLSPACING=0 BORDER=0 WIDTH=100%>
   <TR VALIGN="middle" ALIGN="left"
    <TD WIDTH=50%>
        <FONT SIZE="+1">Gigantor, Inc.</FONT>
    </TD>
    <TD WIDTH=50%><IMG HEIGHT=31 WIDTH=47 SRC="Envelope.gif" BORDER=0
      ALT="Envelope Picture">
    <A HREF="mailto:sales@gigantor.com">email: sales@gigantor.com</A></TD>
   </TR>

    <TR>
    <TD>650 Castro Street, Suite #120-228</TD>
    </TR>

    <TR>
    <TD>Mountain View, CA 94041</TD>
    </TR>
```

```
    <TR>
    <TD>Phone: (800) 408-6600</TD>
    </TR>
</TABLE>

</FORM>
</BODY>
</HTML>
```

Your HTML form needs to use the task variable, as we showed in Listing 9.5. This variable is then passed in via **CFormParser** to our **CShoppingCart** class, which then figures out what action to take. I've written a member called **HandleCart()** that performs all of these actions. If you want to add a new action and have it automatically handled for you, this is the place. This is also a great place to look at if you plan on writing your own dispatcher rather than using the ISAPI Parsemap macros—you have to do this anyway if you are using CGI. Listing 9.6 shows the cart in action. There's a call to the constructor after we've created a **CFormParser** class, and then a call to **HandleCart()**. That's it—just a few lines of code for a fully functional shopping cart.

LISTING 9.6   USING CSHOPPINGCART.

```
void
HandleAction()
{
    char *buffer;

    try
    {
        char *streamSize = getenv("CONTENT_LENGTH");
        THROWIF( !streamSize );
        long dataSize = atol( streamSize );
        THROWIF( !dataSize );

        buffer = new char[dataSize];
        cin >> buffer;

        // get our form data and parse
        CFormParser    ourParser( buffer );

        // let the cart do what is needed
        CShoppingCart    cart( ourParser );

        BeginHeader( "Order Processor");
        StreamFile( cHeaderName );        // fetch, Rover
```

```
        // let the shopping cart handle things
        cart.HandleCart();

        delete [] buffer;
    }

    catch(...)
    {
        cout << "<B>An unrecoverable error occurred.<BR></B>";
        delete [] buffer;
    }
} // HandleForm...
```

When you use this class, you only need to be concerned about when you send the header information over to the user's browser. To make a cookie for the user's browser, we need to send the cookie variable over with **CCookieMonster** before any other information is sent. Listing 9.6 shows **BeginHeader**() being called after this happens, which is in the **CShoppingCart** constructor. Listing 9.7 shows the class declaration for **CShoppingCart**. You will notice that mostly everything is a *private* member, as no one outside of this class will ever need access.

LISTING 9.7   SHOPPINGCART.HPP.

```
//
//      File: ShoppingCart.hpp
//      By:    Don Gaspar
//
//      This is the source for the ShoppingCart class
//      from Chapter 9 in the book
//      Visual Developer Web Commerce
//      Programming With Visual C++.
//      The publisher is The Coriolis Group.
//
//      You may reach the author at: don@gigantor.com
//

// some headers from STL that we'll need
#include <vector.h>
#include <iterator.h>
#include <algo.h>
#include <function.h>
#include <bstring.h>

#include <SQL.h>
```

```cpp
// now to represent each shopping cart item
// with a structure that parallels our database
// ShoppingCart Table
struct CartItem
{
    long    cookieID;
    string  inventoryID;
    long    quantity;
};

// this structure parallels our cookie Table
struct Cookie
{
    long        cookieID;
    bool        expired;
    //DateTime  validTo;
};

// now to represent the inventory Table
struct InventoryItem
{
    string  inventoryID;
    string  description;
    float   cost;
    float   discPercent;
    string  vendor;
};

// gotta encapsulate all of this into one class
class CShoppingCart
{
public:
    CShoppingCart( CFormParser &inParser );
    ~CShoppingCart();

    // the only public routine we need to know
    void    HandleCart();

private:
    CFormParser     m_parser;
    long            m_cookie;
     // environmental ODBC handle
    HENV            m_envH;
    // handle to db connection
    HDBC            m_dbH;
    // statement handle
    HSTMT           m_stmtH;
```

```
void     ShowSQLError();

// cookies
bool     VerifyCookieInDB();
void     CheckCookie();
void     MakeCookieInDB( string &outCookieString );

void     GetCatalog( vector<InventoryItem> &outCatalog );

    // for dealing with the shopping cart...
void     AddItemToCart( CartItem &inItem );
void     RemoveItemFromCart( CartItem &inItem );
void     GetCartContents( vector<CartItem> &outCart );

// now for viewing the order contents
void     RecalcOrder();
void     ReviewOrder();
void     CancelOrder();
};
```

Note: Hiding members within a class is a key C++ feature that you should use. It's called encapsulation.

The **HandleCart**() member checks the string of the task variable to determine what action to perform, and does this using the string class' member **compare**(). The **compare**() member behaves just like the C library function **strcmp**(). Listing 9.8 completes this chapter by showing the source for the entire **CShoppingCart** class.

LISTING 9.8   SHOPPINGCART.CPP.

```
//
//    File: CFormParser.hpp
//    By:   Don Gaspar
//
//    This is the source for the translating and displaying
//    form variables from an example from Chapter 9
//    in the book Visual Developer Web Commerce
//    Programming With Visual C++.
//    The publisher is The Coriolis Group.
//
//    You may reach the author at: don@gigantor.com
//
```

```c
// standard headers we need all over
#include <stdio.h>
#include <stdlib.h>

// headers we've written and need
#include "CFormParser.hpp"
#include "ShoppingCart.hpp"
#include "CookieMonster.hpp"

// these are the various SQL queries we perform from
// this class, from this file only.
const char *cSQLInsertCmd = "INSERT INTO "
    "shoppingCart(cookieID,"
    " inventoryID, quantity) VALUES(%ld,'%s',%ld)";
const char *cSQLGetCartCmd = "SELECT quantity FROM "
    "shoppingCart WHERE cookieID=%ld AND inventoryID='%s'";
const char *cSQLUpdateCartCmd = "UPDATE shoppingCart"
    " SET quantity = %ld"
    " WHERE cookieID=%ld AND inventoryID='%s'";
const char *cSQLDeleteCartCmd = "DELETE FROM shoppingCart "
    " WHERE cookieID=%ld";
const char *cSQLDeleteCartItemCmd = "DELETE FROM shoppingCart "
    " WHERE cookieID=%ld AND inventoryID='%s'";
const char *cSQLDeleteCartQtyCmd = "DELETE FROM shoppingCart "
    " WHERE cookieID=%ld AND quantity < %ld";

const char *cSQLNewCookieCmd = "INSERT INTO "
    "cookie(expired) VALUES(0)";
const char *cSQLMaxCookieCmd = "SELECT MAX(cookieID) FROM cookie";
const char *cSQLCheckCookieCmd = "SELECT cookieID FROM "
    "cookie WHERE cookieID=%ld";

const char *cSQLSelectCartCmd = "SELECT inventoryID, "
    "quantity FROM shoppingCart WHERE cookieID=%ld";

const char *cSQLSelectCatalogCmd = "SELECT * FROM inventory";

// code begins here


//
//    function:    CShoppingCart::CShoppingCart
//    purpose:     Constructor for the CShoppingCart class.
//                 Takes a CFormParser as input.
//                 Propagates exceptions out after
//                 displaying any appropriate errors.
//    returns:     Constructors can't return anything
//
```

```
CShoppingCart::CShoppingCart( CFormParser &inParser )
{
    try
    {
        m_parser = inParser;
        m_cookie = 0;
        m_envH = NULL;
        m_dbH = NULL;

        THROWIF( SQLAllocEnv( &m_envH ) != SQL_SUCCESS );
        THROWIF( SQLAllocConnect( m_envH, &m_dbH ) != SQL_SUCCESS );

        RETCODE result = SQLConnect( m_dbH,
            (unsigned char *)"Games",6,
            (unsigned char *)"sa",3,NULL,0 );
        THROWIF( result != SQL_SUCCESS &&
            result != SQL_SUCCESS_WITH_INFO);
        SQLAllocStmt( m_dbH, &m_stmtH );

        // make sure user has one, if not make a new one
        CheckCookie();
    }

    catch(...)
    {
        ShowSQLError();
        throw(-1);    // propagate to next catch...
    }
} // CShoppingCart::CShoppingCart...

//
//    function:    CShoppingCart::~CShoppingCart
//    purpose:     Destructor. Closes and frees any
//                 ODBC connections, etc. that we
//                 may have allocated
//    returns:     Constructors can't return anything
//
CShoppingCart::~CShoppingCart()
{
    // give a hoot, don't pollute
    if ( m_stmtH )
        SQLFreeStmt( m_stmtH, SQL_CLOSE );
    if ( m_dbH )
        SQLFreeConnect( m_dbH );
    if( m_envH )
        SQLFreeEnv( m_envH );
} // CShoppingCart::~CShoppingCart...
```

```
//
//      function:    CShoppingCart::ShowSQLError
//      purpose:     Sends the appropriate SQL error
//                   via cout.
//      returns:     Nothing
//
void
CShoppingCart::ShowSQLError()
{
    SDWORD    err;
    char text[512], errText[512];
    SQLError(m_envH,m_dbH,m_stmtH,(unsigned char *)text,&err,
        (unsigned char *)errText,sizeof(errText),0);

    // show the error message
    cout << "<CENTER>" << errText << ": err = " <<
        text << "<BR></CENTER>";
} // CShoppingCart::ShowSQLError...


//
//      function:    CShoppingCart::VerifyCookieInDB
//      purpose:     Verified m_cookie to make sure it's
//                   also in our database.
//      returns:     true if m_cookie is in the DB.
//
bool
CShoppingCart::VerifyCookieInDB()
{
    bool    memberResult = false;    //always the pessimist

    try
    {
        // if no exception is thrown, it's in the DB
        char command[256];
        sprintf( command, cSQLCheckCookieCmd, m_cookie );
        cout << command << "<BR>";
        RETCODE result = SQLPrepare( m_stmtH,
            (unsigned char *)command,
            strlen( command ) + 1 );
        THROWIF( result == SQL_ERROR );

        result = SQLExecute( m_stmtH );
        THROWIF( result != SQL_SUCCESS &&
            result != SQL_SUCCESS_WITH_INFO);

        // now bind the columns and the data type
        SDWORD    dwTypeLen;
```

```
        long    cookieID;
        SQLBindCol( m_stmtH,1,SQL_C_LONG,
            &cookieID,sizeof(cookieID), &dwTypeLen );

        result = SQLFetch( m_stmtH );
        memberResult = ( result == SQL_SUCCESS ||
            result == SQL_SUCCESS_WITH_INFO )?
            true: false;
    }

    catch(...)
    {
        ShowSQLError();
        throw(-1);    // propagate to next catch...
    }


    return memberResult;
} // CShoppingCart::VerifyCookieInDB...



//
//    function:    CShoppingCart::MakeCookieInDB
//    purpose:     Makes a new cookie in the DB and
//                 sets outCookieString to contain the same
//                 value.
//    returns:     Nothing. Throws an exception on failure.
//
void
CShoppingCart::MakeCookieInDB( string &outCookieString )
{
    try
    {
        // now make our SQL insert command
        RETCODE result = SQLPrepare( m_stmtH,
            (unsigned char *)cSQLNewCookieCmd,
            strlen( cSQLNewCookieCmd ) + 1 );
        THROWIF( result == SQL_ERROR );

        result = SQLExecute( m_stmtH );
        THROWIF( result != SQL_SUCCESS &&
            result != SQL_SUCCESS_WITH_INFO);

        // need a new statement, use old handle
        SQLFreeStmt( m_stmtH, SQL_CLOSE );
        SQLAllocStmt( m_dbH, &m_stmtH );
```

```
        // now add our string
        result = SQLPrepare( m_stmtH,
            (unsigned char *)cSQLMaxCookieCmd,
            strlen( cSQLMaxCookieCmd ) + 1 );

        result = SQLExecute( m_stmtH );
        THROWIF( result != SQL_SUCCESS &&
            result != SQL_SUCCESS_WITH_INFO );

        // now bind the columns and the data type
        SDWORD      dwTypeLen;
        SQLBindCol( m_stmtH,1,SQL_C_SLONG,
            &m_cookie,sizeof(m_cookie), &dwTypeLen );

        result = SQLFetch( m_stmtH );
        THROWIF( result != SQL_SUCCESS &&
            result != SQL_SUCCESS_WITH_INFO );

        char    temp[32];
        sprintf(temp,"%ld",m_cookie);
        // copy the cookie to a string
        outCookieString = temp;
    }

    catch(...)
    {
        ShowSQLError();
        throw(-1);    // propagate to next catch...
    }
} // CShoppingCart::MakeCookieInDB...

//
//    function:    CShoppingCart::CheckCookie
//    purpose:     Makes sure the user has a cookie and
//                 that it's in the DB, and creates one
//                 if there's a problem, or it's missing.
//    returns:     Nothing.
//
void
CShoppingCart::CheckCookie()
{
    // used for fetching cookies
    CCookieMonster    cookie;
    // a general purpose string
    string    cookieStr;
```

```
    try
    {
        // did we get a cookie?
        cookieStr = cookie["FoosballCookie"];

        // extra level of paranoia in case it's bad
        if ( cookieStr.length() )
        {
            m_cookie = atol( cookieStr.c_str() );

            // always make sure we have a record in the
            // db that matches it.
            THROWIF( !VerifyCookieInDB() );
        }
        else
            throw(-1);
    }

    catch(...)
    {
        // let this member do the dirty work
        MakeCookieInDB( cookieStr );

        // make a format browsers understand
        cookie.MakeCookie("FoosballCookie",
            (char *)cookieStr.c_str(),
            "www.gigantor.com","",
            1,false, cookieStr);

        // send it to their browser
        // DO NOT forget the "\r\n" or
        // you will have debugging nightmares
        cout << cookieStr.c_str() << "\r\n";
    }
} // CShoppingCart::CheckCookie...

//
//    function:    CShoppingCart::AddItemToCart
//    purpose:     Adds the item inItem to the user's
//                 shopping cart in the DB.
//    returns:     Nothing. Throws an exception on failure.
//
void
CShoppingCart::AddItemToCart( CartItem &inItem )
{
    try
    {
```

```
// used for our SQL statements
char    command[512];
// check to see if they already exist in the database
sprintf( command, cSQLGetCartCmd, inItem.cookieID,
    inItem.inventoryID.c_str() );

RETCODE result = SQLPrepare( m_stmtH,
    (unsigned char *)command, strlen( command ) + 1 );
THROWIF(result == SQL_ERROR);

// execute the SQL statement we made
result = SQLExecute( m_stmtH );
THROWIF( result != SQL_SUCCESS &&
    result != SQL_SUCCESS_WITH_INFO);

SDWORD    dwTypeLen;
long    quantity = 0;
SQLBindCol( m_stmtH,1,SQL_C_LONG,
    &quantity,sizeof(quantity), &dwTypeLen );

result = SQLFetch( m_stmtH );
SQLFreeStmt( m_stmtH, SQL_CLOSE );
SQLAllocStmt( m_dbH, &m_stmtH );

// are they actually there????
if ( result == SQL_SUCCESS ||
    result == SQL_SUCCESS_WITH_INFO )
    sprintf( command, cSQLUpdateCartCmd, inItem.quantity,
        inItem.cookieID, inItem.inventoryID.c_str() );
else//not there, so add them
    // now add our string
    sprintf( command, cSQLInsertCmd, inItem.cookieID,
        inItem.inventoryID.c_str(), inItem.quantity );

// prepare our actual data now
result = SQLPrepare( m_stmtH,
    (unsigned char *)command, strlen( command ) + 1 );
THROWIF(result == SQL_ERROR);

// execute the SQL statement we made
result = SQLExecute( m_stmtH );
THROWIF( result != SQL_SUCCESS &&
    result != SQL_SUCCESS_WITH_INFO);

// commit the addition to the database
SQLTransact( m_envH, m_dbH, SQL_COMMIT );
}
```

```
        catch(...)
        {
            ShowSQLError();
            throw(-1);
        }
} // CShoppingCart::AddItemToCart...

//
//    function:    CShoppingCart::RemoveItemFromCart
//    purpose:     Removes the item inItem to the user's
//                 shopping cart in the DB.
//    returns:     Nothing. Throws an exception on failure.
//
void
CShoppingCart::RemoveItemFromCart( CartItem &inItem )
{
    try
    {
        // used for our SQL statements
        char    command[512];

        // check to see if they already exist in the database
        sprintf( command, cSQLGetCartCmd, inItem.cookieID,
            inItem.inventoryID.c_str() );
        RETCODE result = SQLPrepare( m_stmtH,
            (unsigned char *)command, strlen( command ) + 1 );
        THROWIF(result == SQL_ERROR);
        // execute the SQL statement we made
        result = SQLExecute( m_stmtH );
        THROWIF( result != SQL_SUCCESS &&
            result != SQL_SUCCESS_WITH_INFO);

        char inventoryInDB;
        SDWORD    dwTypeLen;
        long    cookieInDB;
        SQLBindCol( m_stmtH,1,SQL_C_LONG,
            &cookieInDB,sizeof(cookieInDB), &dwTypeLen );
        SQLBindCol( m_stmtH,2,SQL_C_CHAR,
            &inventoryInDB,sizeof(inventoryInDB), &dwTypeLen );

        result = SQLFetch( m_stmtH );
        SQLFreeStmt( m_stmtH, SQL_CLOSE );
        SQLAllocStmt( m_dbH, &m_stmtH );

        // are they actually there????
        if ( result == SQL_SUCCESS ||
            result == SQL_SUCCESS_WITH_INFO )
```

```
                sprintf( command, cSQLDeleteCartItemCmd,
                    inItem.cookieID, inItem.inventoryID.c_str() );
            else//not there, so add them
                // now add our string
                sprintf( command, cSQLDeleteCartQtyCmd,
                    inItem.cookieID, inItem.quantity );

            // prepare our actual data now
            result = SQLPrepare( m_stmtH,
                (unsigned char *)command, strlen( command ) + 1 );
            THROWIF(result == SQL_ERROR);

            // execute the SQL statement we made
            result = SQLExecute( m_stmtH );
            THROWIF( result != SQL_SUCCESS &&
                result != SQL_SUCCESS_WITH_INFO);

            // commit the addition to the database
            SQLTransact( m_envH, m_dbH, SQL_COMMIT );
        }

    catch(...)
    {
        ShowSQLError();
        throw(-1);
    }
} // CShoppingCart::RemoveItemFromCart...

//
//    function:   CShoppingCart::RecalcOrder
//    purpose:    Adds an item from an HTML form
//                to the user's existing shopping cart.
//                Also removes the items if the quantity
//                specified is zero or less. Calls
//                ReviewOrder() to display results when
//                finished.
//    returns:    Nothing.
//
void
CShoppingCart::RecalcOrder()
{
    CartItem    item;
    vector<InventoryItem>    catalog;

    // need a new statement, use old handle
    SQLFreeStmt( m_stmtH, SQL_CLOSE );
    SQLAllocStmt( m_dbH, &m_stmtH );
```

```
    map< string, string, less<string> >::iterator    iter;
    for ( iter = m_parser.begin();
        iter != m_parser.end();
        iter++ )
    {
        item.cookieID = m_cookie;
        item.inventoryID = (*iter).first;
        item.quantity = -1L;

        if ( (*iter).second.length() )
            item.quantity = (long)atol( (*iter).second.c_str() );

        if ( item.quantity > 0 )
            AddItemToCart( item );
        else if ( item.quantity == 0 )
            RemoveItemFromCart( item );
    } // for...

    ReviewOrder();
} // CShoppingCart::RecalcOrder...

//
//    function:    CShoppingCart::ReviewOrder
//    purpose:     Gets the shopping cart contents and
//                 cross-references every item with our
//                 inventory DB table. Outputs all items
//                 as an HTML form the user can edit.
//    returns:     Nothing.
//
void
CShoppingCart::ReviewOrder()
{
    vector<CartItem>        cartContents;
    vector<InventoryItem>   catalog;
    vector<float>           orderCost;
    char    tempStr[256];

    GetCartContents( cartContents );
    GetCatalog( catalog );

    cout << "<H1><CENTER>Shopping Cart Contents</H1><BR>\n";
    cout << "Change any quantity of any items here<BR>\n" <<
        "and press <B>Recalculate Order</B>" <<
        " to see your new order.<BR>\n" <<
        "To remove an item set the quantity to '0'.<BR>\n" <<
        "To order press <B>Order Now</B>.<BR><BR><BR>\n";
```

```cpp
cout << "<FORM ACTION=/scripts/cgishoppingcart.exe  " <<
    "METHOD=POST>\n";


if ( !cartContents.empty() && !catalog.empty() )
{
    vector<CartItem>::iterator     iter;
    vector<InventoryItem>::iterator catIter;

    // display each item in the user's cart
    for( iter = cartContents.begin();
        iter != cartContents.end();
        iter++ )
    {
        cout << "<TR><INPUT TYPE=text SIZE=5 MAXLENGTH=2 "
            "NAME=" << iter->inventoryID.c_str() <<
            " VALUE = " <<
            iter->quantity << ">\n";

        // another loop! ouch!
        for ( catIter = catalog.begin();
            catIter != catalog.end();
            catIter++ )
        {
            if ( !iter->inventoryID.compare(
                catIter->inventoryID) )
            {
                float lineTotal = catIter->cost *
                    iter->quantity;
                sprintf(tempStr, "%s at %.2f each = %.2f<BR>\n",
                    catIter->description.c_str(),
                    catIter->cost,
                    lineTotal );
                cout << tempStr;

                // add the order up
                orderCost.push_back( lineTotal );
                break;
            }
        }
    } // for...
}
else
    cout << "<CENTER>Nothing found!</CENTER><BR><BR><BR>\n";

sprintf(tempStr,"<P>Your order subtotal "
    "(excluding tax if in California "
```

```
        "and excluding shipping) is <B>$%.2f</B><BR><BR><BR>",
            accumulate( orderCost.begin(), orderCost.end(),0.0 ) );
    cout << tempStr;

        // add buttons and end the form's scope
    cout<< "<CENTER><INPUT TYPE=submit NAME=task"
        " VALUE='Order Now'>" <<
        "<INPUT TYPE=submit NAME=task VALUE='Recalculate Order'>" <<
        "<INPUT TYPE=submit NAME=task "
        "VALUE='Cancel Order'></CENTER>" <<
        "</FORM><BR><BR><BR>\n";
} // CShoppingCart::ReviewOrder...


//
//    function:    CShoppingCart::CancelOrder
//    purpose:     Deletes all items in the user's
//                 shopping cart.
//    returns:     Nothing. Throws an exception on failure.
//
void
CShoppingCart::CancelOrder()
{
    try
    {
        // need a new statement, use old handle
        SQLFreeStmt( m_stmtH, SQL_CLOSE );
        SQLAllocStmt( m_dbH, &m_stmtH );

        char    command[128];
        sprintf( command, cSQLDeleteCartCmd, m_cookie );
        // now make our SQL insert command
        RETCODE result = SQLPrepare( m_stmtH,
            (unsigned char *)command,
            strlen( command ) + 1 );
        THROWIF( result == SQL_ERROR );

        result = SQLExecute( m_stmtH );
        THROWIF( result != SQL_SUCCESS &&
            result != SQL_SUCCESS_WITH_INFO);

        // commit the addition to the database
        SQLTransact( m_envH, m_dbH, SQL_COMMIT );

        cout << "<H1><CENTER>Your shopping cart "
            "has been emptied.</H1><BR>\n";
        cout << "Thank you for visiting our site!<BR><BR><BR>";
    }
```

```
    catch(...)
    {
        ShowSQLError();
        throw(-1);    // propagate to next catch...
    }
} // CShoppingCart::CancelOrder...

//
//   function:   CShoppingCart::GetCatalog
//   purpose:    Gets all items we have in our product catalog
//               and adds them to the vector<> outCatalog.
//   returns:    Nothing. Throws an exception on failure.
//
void
CShoppingCart::GetCatalog( vector<InventoryItem> &outCatalog )
{
    try
    {
        // need a new statement, use old handle
        SQLFreeStmt( m_stmtH, SQL_CLOSE );
        SQLAllocStmt( m_dbH, &m_stmtH );

        // now add our string
        RETCODE result = SQLPrepare( m_stmtH,
            (unsigned char *)cSQLSelectCatalogCmd,
            strlen( cSQLSelectCatalogCmd ) + 1 );
        THROWIF( result == SQL_ERROR );

        result = SQLExecute( m_stmtH );
        THROWIF( result != SQL_SUCCESS &&
            result != SQL_SUCCESS_WITH_INFO);

        // now bind the columns and the data type
        SDWORD    dwTypeLen;
        char id[32], description[128],vendor[32];
        float cost, discount;
        SQLBindCol( m_stmtH,1,SQL_C_CHAR, &id,sizeof(id),
            &dwTypeLen );
        SQLBindCol( m_stmtH,2,SQL_C_CHAR, &description,
            sizeof(description), &dwTypeLen );
        SQLBindCol( m_stmtH,3,SQL_C_FLOAT, &cost,sizeof(cost),
            &dwTypeLen );
        SQLBindCol( m_stmtH,4,SQL_C_FLOAT,
            &discount,sizeof(discount),
            &dwTypeLen );
        SQLBindCol( m_stmtH,5,SQL_C_CHAR, &vendor,sizeof(vendor),
            &dwTypeLen );
```

```
            // fetch and add each item to the catalog vector...
            InventoryItem    item;
            do
            {
                result = SQLFetch( m_stmtH );
                if ( result != SQL_SUCCESS &&
                     result != SQL_SUCCESS_WITH_INFO )
                    break;

                // copy info from the database
                item.inventoryID = id;
                item.description = description;
                item.cost = cost;
                item.discPercent = discount;
                item.vendor = vendor;

                // add the item to our vector
                outCatalog.push_back(item);
            }
            while( true );
        }

    catch(...)
    {
        ShowSQLError();
        throw(-1);
    }
} // CShoppingCart::GetCatalog...

//
//    function:    CShoppingCart::GetCartContents
//    purpose:     Gets everything from the user's shopping cart
//                 and adds them to the vector<> outCart.
//    returns:     Nothing. Throws an exception on failure.
//
void
CShoppingCart::GetCartContents( vector<CartItem> &outCart )
{
    try
    {
        // need a new statement, use old handle
        SQLFreeStmt( m_stmtH, SQL_CLOSE );
        SQLAllocStmt( m_dbH, &m_stmtH );

        // now add our string
        char command[128];
        sprintf( command, cSQLSelectCartCmd, m_cookie );
```

```
        RETCODE result = SQLPrepare( m_stmtH,
            (unsigned char *)command,
            strlen( command ) + 1 );
        THROWIF( result == SQL_ERROR );

        result = SQLExecute( m_stmtH );
        THROWIF( result != SQL_SUCCESS &&
            result != SQL_SUCCESS_WITH_INFO);

        // now bind the columns and the data type
        SDWORD    dwTypeLen;
        char id[32];
        long quantity;
        SQLBindCol( m_stmtH,1,SQL_C_CHAR, &id,sizeof(id),
            &dwTypeLen );
        SQLBindCol( m_stmtH,2,SQL_C_LONG, &quantity,
            sizeof(quantity), &dwTypeLen );

        // get each item from the virtual shopping cart
        CartItem    item;
        do
        {
            result = SQLFetch( m_stmtH );
            if ( result != SQL_SUCCESS &&
                result != SQL_SUCCESS_WITH_INFO )
                break;

            // copy info from the database
            item.cookieID = m_cookie;
            item.inventoryID = id;
            item.quantity = quantity;

            // add the item to our vector
            outCart.push_back(item);
        }
        while( true );
    }

    catch(...)
    {
        ShowSQLError();
        throw(-1);
    }
} // CShoppingCart::GetCartContents...

//
//    function:    CShoppingCart::HandleCart
```

```
//    purpose:     Based on the "task" variable specified on
//                 an HTML form, takes the appropriate shopping
//                 cart action.
//    returns:     Nothing.
//
void
CShoppingCart::HandleCart()
{
    if ( !m_parser["task"].compare("Order Now") )
        cout << "<H1><CENTER>Wait until Chapter 10!</H1></CENTER>";
    else if ( !m_parser["task"].compare("Recalculate Order") ||
        !m_parser["task"].compare("Add To Shopping Cart"))
        RecalcOrder();
    else if ( !m_parser["task"].compare("Review Order") )
        ReviewOrder();
    else if ( !m_parser["task"].compare("Cancel Order") )
        CancelOrder();
    else
        cout << "<H1><CENTER>Unklnown task directive...<H1>"
            "</CENTER><BR><BR><BR>\n";
} // CShoppingCart::HandleCart...
```

Summary

In this chapter, we applied everything we've learned in this book and created a new, powerful class that leveraged from previous class designs. **CShoppingCart** handles form processing (via **CFormParser**), and cookie creation/management (via **CCookieMonster**), and links everything into the database for storage, retrieval, and verification. The **CShoppingCart** class requires that we pass a **CFormParser** class to its constructor, and then call the **HandleCart()** member to dispatch the appropriate action: We also have to make sure our HTML form has the **task** variable properly set. We only need a few lines of code to implement a fully functional high-performance shopping cart using **CShoppingCart**.

A shopping cart doesn't do anyone any good unless the merchandise is actually ordered, and to do that we need to integrate a few more database tables, and only a few more lines of code. We need to make sure the orders are secure, that is, keep net-spies from seeing the information being transmitted. In Chapter 10, we'll do all of this.

SECURE ORDERING

Freedom of opinion can only exist when the government thinks itself secure.

Bertrand Russell

Freedom to order merchandise on the Internet will become widespread when consumers understand that it is secure, and most sites offer only secure connections. Secure sites are safe thanks to Netscape and its well-designed Secure Socket Layer (SSL) protocol. This protocol negotiates a key between browser (client) and the Web server; the key changes for every data exchange and the encryption makes sure the data is indecipherable (using the rotating key).

There are still sites out there that do not promote using SSL, and therefore consumers are reluctant to provide their credit card numbers, or their names and addresses to such companies. Providing a secure site is relatively easy, and we're going to expand on the shopping cart example to provide secure sockets for our data collection. Doing this will tell your customers that you want to protect their information, and guarantee it will remain confidential.

Secure Sockets

To provide SSL, you will need to configure your server to use what is called a *digital certificate*. To get a certificate, you will have to use your Web server to generate an encryption key that uniquely identifies you as a merchant, and send this to a

309

certification company like Verisign (**www.verisign.com**). Generating such a key pair is child's play, so be sure to check your server instructions or even look at the Verisign site for more information.

After you have generated the key and signed up with a certification company, the company will check you out. It will make sure you are in business and have a license by checking your articles of corporation and so on; it will verify your address and phone number, look you up with Dun and Bradstreet, and perform a ton of other inspections. While this doesn't guarantee that you are an honest business, it allows the customer to find out who you are, and where to find you. The customer can inspect your certificate, and check with the certification company to see your business information.

The certification company will send a key back to you so that you can activate SSL on your server, and you should be able to do this fairly quickly. I had some problems doing this with Microsoft's IIS, so I used Netscape's Enterprise Server 3.0 for my secure server. You will most likely run two servers once you install your secure key: one for unsecured HTTP and the other for secure HTTPs.

> *Note: Microsoft's IIS has some known problems with SSL certificates. When I initially contacted Verisign and ordered my certificate, the IIS Key Manager never recognized a single key, even after five attempts. Verisign told me that the IIS is the only server to have such problems with digital certificates. I bought Netscape Enterprise Server 3.0 and installed the certificate with no problems on the first try. If you're using IIS for unsecured HTML, I suggest using Netscape for secure HTML.*

Now that you know what is involved in getting SSL on your server, how in Hades do you redirect an unsecured HTML document to a secured one?

Redirection

HTTP will let us send some header information back to the browser to tell it what actions to take. Remember that we sent header information to get the browser to store cookies for us? Here, we can tell the browser to do other tasks, and merely need to send this information before we send the HTTP header over to the browser. Table 10.1 shows the various HTTP numerical response codes that the server generates; in our case, we'll intercept an action and create the HTTP response code ourselves.

TABLE 10.1

HTTP RESPONSE CODES.

Response Value	Response Text
200	OK
202	Accepted
204	No content
301	URL moved permanently
302	URL moved temporarily
304	Not modified
400	Bad request
403	Access forbidden
404	Item not found
500	Internal server error
501	Not implemented
503	Service unavailable

The server always sends *200—OK* to the browser when no errors have been encountered. The 300 codes specify redirection for cases in which the URL has changed permanently, or perhaps it has moved for a day or so. We'll send back one of these codes to redirect the user's browser to a secure page on a secure server (SSL) from the unsecured page (unsecured server). In our case, a page from IIS is redirected upon a submit action to the Netscape server with a secure page.

When the user's browser receives a 300 code, a URL is specified in the header tells the browser where to go. All browsers today will automatically jump to the new page without displaying anything you may have sent after the redirect command.

In Chapter 9, we implemented a powerful shopping cart class, and provided an example to order merchandise; however, we didn't take the next steps. When the user wants to order, he or she will click on the Order Now button, or the Submit button in the case of customer information gathering, as shown in Figure 10.1. Doing this in Chapter 9 would have brought up a dialog box telling

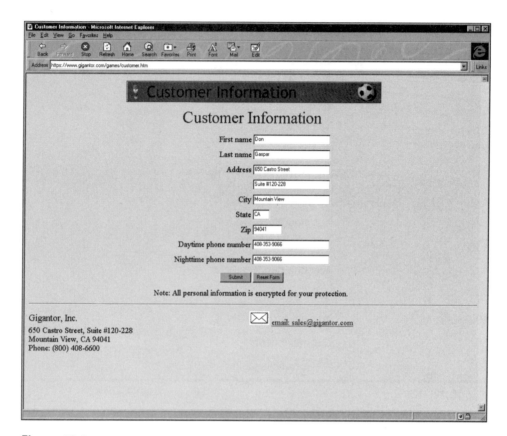

Figure 10.1
Customer Information HTML form.

the user to wait until Chapter 10! The correct action (now that we've made it to
Chapter 10) is to request customer information securely, after a redirection.
Listing 10.1 shows the source code for the shopping cart example from Chapter
9 with the redirection modification in the **HandleCart**() function. Note that
this information is sent to the browser before any header data. If you don't do
this, you will not get redirection. For convenience, we've highlighted the new
code that performs the redirection.

LISTING 10.1   CGISHOPPINGCART.CPP.

```
//
//    File: ShoppingCart.cpp
//    By:   Don Gaspar
//
```

```
//      This is the source for the Shopping Cart
//      an example from Chapter 10
//      in the book Visual Developer Web Commerce
//      Programming With Visual C++.

//      The publisher is The Coriolis Group.
//
//      You may reach the author at: don@gigantor.com
//

// some standard headers we're going to need in here
#include <ostream.h>
#include <fstream.h>
#include <stdio.h>
#include <stdlib.h>

// now headers we've written
#include "CFormParser.hpp"
#include "CookieMonster.hpp"
#include "ShoppingCart.hpp"

// our header and footer file names
const char *cHeaderName =
    "c:\\inetpub\\gigantor\\games\\head.htm";
const char *cFooterName =
    "c:\\inetpub\\gigantor\\games\\foot.htm";

//
//      Function: BeginHeader
//      Purpose: Outputs the appropriate header information
//                   to stdout for a
//                   Web browser to display.
//      Arguments: inTitle, the title of the dynamic
//                   page you are creating.
//
void
BeginHeader(const char* inTitle)
{
    cout << "Content-type:TEXT/HTML\n\n" <<
        "<HTML><HEAD><TITLE>\n" <<
        inTitle << "\n</TITLE></HEAD><BODY>\n";
} // BeginHeader...

//
//      Function: EndHeader
//      Purpose: Outputs the delimiter tags corresponding
//                   to those set by
```

```
//                     PrintHeader() for proper HTML display.
//      Arguments:    None
//
void
EndHeader()
{
    cout << "</BODY></HTML>\n";
} // EndHeader...


//
//      StreamFile
//      Input:     char*, which is the name of the file to
//                 use with path.
//      Purpose:   Opens the designated file and streams it out
//                 through the ChttpServerContext so the
//                 client's browser will get this dynamic HTML page.
//
void
StreamFile( const char* inFile )
{
    try
    {
        ifstream    file( inFile ); // file stream

        if ( !file )                // if we don't get the file, then
            throw(-1);              // throw an exception

        char buffer[80];            // just a line of characters

        // here we loop through the file line by line
        //    until we hit the end
        //    sending all the data to cout.
        while ( file.getline(buffer,sizeof(buffer)) )
            cout << buffer;

        file.close();
    }

    catch(...)
    {
        cout << "<center><b>Couldn't locate the header file." <<
            <br></center></b>";
    }
} // CGamesExtension::StreamFile...
```

```
//
//    function:    HandleCart
//    purpose:     Creates a CFormParser object and passes
//                 the data received from a POST
//                 in cin to CFormParser. Passes this to the
//                 CShoppingCart class for
//                 handling there.
//    returns:     Nothing, exceptions are used for error handling.
//
void
HandleCart()
{
    char *buffer;

    try
    {
        char *streamSize = getenv("CONTENT_LENGTH");
        THROWIF( !streamSize );
        long dataSize = atol( streamSize );
        THROWIF( !dataSize );

        buffer = new char[dataSize];
        cin >> buffer;

        // get our form data and parse
        CFormParser     ourParser( buffer );
        if ( ourParser["task"].compare("Order Now") == 0 )
        {
            cout << "HTTP/1.0 302 Object Moved\n" <<
                "Location: https://www.gigantor.com/games" <<
                "/customer.htm\r\n";
            BeginHeader("Order Redirect");
        }
        else
        {
            // let the cart do what is needed
            CShoppingCart     cart( ourParser );

            BeginHeader( "Order Processor");
            StreamFile( cHeaderName );          // fetch, Rover

            // let the shopping cart handle things
            cart.HandleCart();
        }
```

```
        delete [] buffer;
    }

    catch(...)
    {
        cout << "<B>An unrecoverable error occurred.<BR></B>";
        delete [] buffer;
    }
} // HandleForm...

//
//    well, we gotta start somewhere
//
void
main()
{
        // since we're streaming a file, we'll need to
        // identify the content type here
    HandleCart();

    StreamFile( cFooterName );        // fetch
    EndHeader();
} // main...
```

To achieve the same result in ISAPI, we can send the same information over to the browser before the **ISAPIExtension::BeginHeader**() call, or we can use the **CHttpServer**'s **ServerSupportFunction**() to handle this redirection the same way. The various values for redirection that can be passed to **CHttpServer::Server-SupportFunction**() are shown in Table 10.2.

We implement every example in this book in CGI and ISAPI, so please refer to either the CD-ROM enclosed with this book or our Web support site (**www.gigantor.com/coriolis**) for more details. For redirection via ISAPI, I have been using **HSE_REQ_SEND_URL_REDIRECT_RESP** for the examples.

Using the modified source code from Listing 10.1, we now retrieve and display our secure customer information form, shown in Figure 10.1. When the user wants to order and selects the Submit button, we redirect him or her with a secure URL (https), which in this case sends the customer to the other server (Netscape here) over a different socket (443 for secure connections). At this stage, we collect customer information, which will tell us who is ordering

TABLE 10.2

SERVERSUPPORTFUNCTION() REQUESTS.

Request	What It Does
HSE_REQ_SEND_URL_REDIRECT_RESP	Sends a 302(URL Redirect) message to the client. No further processing is needed after the call. This operation is similar to specifying "URI: <URL>" in a CGI code fragment header. The variable *lpvBuffer* should point to a null terminated URL string. Variable *lpdwSize* should have the size of *lpvBuffer*. Variable *lpdwDataType* is ignored.
HSE_REQ_SEND_URL	Sends the data specified by the URL to the client as if the client had requested that URL. The null terminated URL that *lpvBuffer* points to MUST be on the server and must not specify protocol information (for example, it must begin with a "/"). No further processing is required after this call. Variable *lpdwSize* points to a **DWORD** that holds the size of *lpvBuffer*. Variable *lpdwDataType* is ignored.

and where to send the merchandise. The next steps are getting the customer's credit card information and validating the purchase (we'll validate the cards in Chapter 11). We've stored information in the database numerous times so far, so instead of boring you with yet another table being added to the database, I've provided merely the source code in Listing 10.2, which shows the code fragment for review purposes. This code runs in its own code fragment and is instantiated by the secure server; the function is **AddCustomerToDB**(). There is also code to store the credit card information, but you normally wouldn't store that until after the card and amount have been verified—we provided it here for convenience.

The code represents another code fragment that executes on the secure server. The secure server will be running scripts and code fragments from different directories than your unsecured server—or at least it should be. This separates your secure and unsecured code fragments properly, so that one doesn't get instantiated incorrectly, or even mischievously by some prankster.

LISTING 10.2   ADDCUSTOMERTODB().

```
//
//      function:   AddCustomerToDB
//      purpose:    Adds the item inCust to the
//                  customer table in the DB.
//      returns:    Nothing. Throws an exception on failure.
//
void
AddCustomerToDB( CustomerInfo &inCust )
{
    try
    {
        // used for our SQL statements
        char     command[512];
        // check to see if they already exist in the database
        sprintf( command, cSQLGetCust, inCust.cookieID );

        RETCODE result = SQLPrepare( m_stmtH,
            (unsigned char *)command, strlen( command ) + 1 );
        THROWIF(result == SQL_ERROR);

        // execute the SQL statement we made
        result = SQLExecute( m_stmtH );
        THROWIF( result != SQL_SUCCESS &&
            result != SQL_SUCCESS_WITH_INFO);

        SQLFreeStmt( m_stmtH, SQL_CLOSE );
        SQLAllocStmt( m_dbH, &m_stmtH );

        // are they actually there????
        if ( result == SQL_SUCCESS ||
            result == SQL_SUCCESS_WITH_INFO )
        {
            sprintf( command, cSQLUpdateUser, inCust.cookieID,
                inCust.firstName.c_str(),
                inCust.lastName.c_str(),
                inCust.address1.c_str(),
                inCust.address2.c_str(),
                inCust.city.c_str(),
                inCust.state.c_str(),
                inCust.zip.c_str(),
                inCust.dayPhone.c_str(),
                inCust.nightPhone.c_str() );
        }
```

```
        // prepare our actual data now
        result = SQLPrepare( m_stmtH,
            (unsigned char *)command, strlen( command ) + 1 );
        THROWIF(result == SQL_ERROR);

        // execute the SQL statement we made
        result = SQLExecute( m_stmtH );
        THROWIF( result != SQL_SUCCESS &&
            result != SQL_SUCCESS_WITH_INFO);

        // commit the addition to the database
        SQLTransact( m_envH, m_dbH, SQL_COMMIT );
    }

    catch(...)
    {
        ShowSQLError();
        throw(-1);
    }
} // AddCustomerToDB...
```

The Luhn Algorithm

We'll collect the credit card information, and send it off to a server process that will validate it and tell us if it is being accepted. However, why bog down your credit card server process when you can easily inspect a few pieces of information up front while collecting the form data?

After the customer submits his or her information, we bring up the credit information form shown in Figure 10.2. This form will ask the user for his or her credit card, and we'll use this information to verify the card and validate the charge amount (Chapter 11). Before we do that, we can validate the card type and make sure that our site accepts that type of card; we can also validate the credit card number using what is known as the Luhn Algorithm. This algorithm checks the digits of the card and lets us validate the authenticity of the card. It tells us the type of card, and whether or not the number on the card is valid.

Your site will accept various cards—most likely the ones that a credit card processing clearing house gives you a good deal on. You can check the prefix of the card against the prefixes of the types you accept, and you can also check the length of the credit card number. This will be a quick check to see if the card is

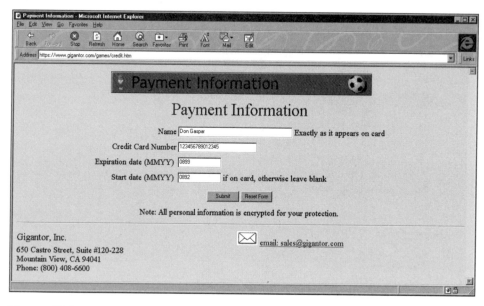

Figure 10.2
Credit card HTML form.

valid. Table 10.3 shows the prefix for each major credit card, and the length of the card number. If your data doesn't match this information, you should send a message back to the user telling him or her that the card is not a valid number and request that he or she re-enter it. The customer's credit card will also register as invalid if you don't accept that kind of card, but your site should display the cards you accept.

TABLE 10.3

CREDIT CARD NUMBER INFORMATION.

Card	Prefix	Length
MasterCard	51 through 55	16
Visa	4	13 or 16
American Express	34 or 37	15
Diner's Club/Carte Blanche	300 through 305 or 36 or 38	14
Discover	6011	16
JCB	3	16
JCB	2131 or 1800	15

This information is frequently updated, so always be aware of any recent changes to it if you plan to reference it. There's nothing more annoying to a potential customer than a rejected credit card when it should be valid. To retrieve the latest data, perform an Internet search with one of the larger search engines, like www.hotbot.com.

Use A Credit Card Number Validation Script In Your HTML

In Chapter 2, we used VBScript to process some items before sending them to the server. A case such as this is perfect for validating credit card information before you transmit it to your secured server. This way, the processing is done on the client and your server will not get bothered with simple things such as typos, or even the mischievous case of someone entering bogus card numbers. JavaScript is also perfect for this task.

How do we verify the actual card number? The Luhn Algorithm uses the following formula:

1. Double the value of alternate digits of the account number beginning with the second digit from the right (the first right-hand digit is the check digit).

2. Add the digits that comprise the products from Step 1 to each of the unaffected digits of the original number. Numbers in the tens column from Step 1 become shifted right to the ones column (18 would then become 1+8=9).

3. The total obtained from Step 2 must be zero when modulo 10. That is, the resultant sum ends in zero, such as 30, 40, and so on when divided by 10.

I implemented a simple code fragment that works for MasterCard and Visa verification; I have provided this in Listing 10.3. I highly recommend that you provide this extra level of checking for your credit card processing, because you can never be too safe when dealing with financial information from your customers.

LISTING 10.3   THE LUHN ALGORITHM IN C.

```
//    function:   CheckCreditCard()
//    purpose:    checks the card type and number, first validating
```

```
//              the card type by its prefix
//              and the number of digits, then
//              the checksum by cal DoCheckSum()
//              returns true on approval, false on failure
//
bool
CheckCreditCard( const char *inCardType, const char *inCardNumber )
{
    bool    result = false;

    // Note: Versions only takes MasterCard and VISA for now...
    // is it a MasterCard???
    if ( strcmp(inCardType, "MasterCard") == 0 )
    {
        if ( strlen( inCardNumber ) == 16 )
        {
            short number;
            char  value[2];
            strncpy(value, inCardNumber,sizeof(value));
            number = atoi( value );
            if ( number >=51 && number <=55 )
                result = DoCheckSum( inCardNumber );
        }
    }
    else if ( strcmp( inCardType, "VISA") == 0 )
    {
        // simplest check is size
        short len = strlen( inCardNumber );
        if ( len == 13 || len == 16 )
        {
            short number = inCardNumber[0] - '0';
            if ( number == 4 )
                result = DoCheckSum( inCardNumber);
        }
    }


    // all we ever needed
    return result;
} // CheckCreditCard...

//
//    function:    DoCheckSum()
//    purpose:     Checks the credit card digits via the
//                 Luhn modulus checksum 10 Algorithm
//    returns:     true if digits are valid, false otherwise
//
bool
```

```
DoCheckSum( const char *inCardNumber )
{
    // always be a pessimist with money involved
    bool    result = false;
    vector<short>    digitArray;
    short            dummy;

    for( short index = 0; index < strlen(inCardNumber); index ++ )
    {
        // convert to an integer
        dummy = inCardNumber[index] - '0';
        // array keeps track of everything
        digitArray.push_back( dummy );
    }

    // now total the reverse digits and double them -
    // part of the Luhn algorithm
    vector<short>::reverse_iterator    iter;
    bool skip = true;
    short sum = 0;
    for ( iter = digitArray.rbegin(); iter != digitArray.rend();
        iter++ )
    {
        if ( skip )
            // total the digits
            sum += *iter;
        else
        {
            short value = *iter * 2;
            if ( value >= 10 )
            {
                sum += 1;
                value -= 10;
            }
            sum += value;
        }
        skip = !skip;                        // toggle every number
    }

    return ( sum %10 == 0 );
}   // DoCheckSum...
```

Summary

This chapter showed us how to use SSL from an unsecured HTML page via redirection. When it's possible for someone to abuse information such as customer's name and address, or credit card number, always use a SSL. We also learned how to check credit card numbers with a simple numerical algorithm called Luhn modulus checksum 10. This validation will keep the credit card server processor free from mundane number checks and so on, and lets it focus solely on verifying the amount of the transaction with the bank. We could also write a VBScript or JavaScript to perform the simple checking credit card number validation, and free our server from such mundane tasks.

So far in this book, we've done everything an online store could want except for validating the actual transaction and getting the money for a sale transferred electronically into our bank account. We'll use everything we've written and learned thus far to write another code fragment that will connect to a credit card server that validates transactions with a bank or a credit card clearing house. Don't close your book right now, because in Chapter 11, we're going to provide validation for realtime credit card transactions.

11

REALTIME CREDIT CARD PROCESSING

COMMERCE, n. A kind of transaction in which A plunders from B the goods of C, and for compensation B picks the pocket of D of money belonging to E.

Ambrose Bierce (1842-1914), **The Devil's Dictionary,** *1911*

Now that we've presented a shopping cart class, **CShoppingCart**, and provided an approach to gather information from the client securely, we need to get paid or our entire effort here is in vain. We need to collect payment for goods that a user will purchase, and in our case, perform that action in realtime—that is, while the user is waiting.

Realtime characterizes an immediate action, without delay on the part of the code fragment or another program. While some realtime programmers may define this term differently, realtime is the proper word here. The customer will wait between 3 and 15 seconds for this transaction to clear, and if something drastic goes wrong, then the wait could extend to possibly 20 seconds or so—not realtime any more, but still close.

We could provide batch processing of credit cards and orders, and notify the customer of errors or acceptance via email. However, this approach is a good way to potentially lose a customer. Let's say that your customer has typed in his or her credit card number incorrectly. Would it be appropriate to tell him or her hours later via email? If you think so, you'll be out of business real quick. Realtime is the best approach we can take for merchandise on the Net—it's immediate and accurate. The only situation where realtime is not desirable is when you are not going to ship your order out quickly, in which case you shouldn't bill the client until the goods actually ship.

In this chapter, we're going to show how to interface with some popular credit card verification software applications. Although all of them claim to be servers, in the sense of "real" servers (multithreaded, fast architectures), we'll let you decide which are servers and which are simple applications. We'll also provide our own server as a workaround for their shortcomings, and write CGI and ISAPI code fragments to interface with them. We'll store the verification information in our datastore for later reference, and then show an SMTP mailing class we use to send status information to us about orders on our server. (You can find the source code for the SMTP mailing class, CPonyExpress, in Appendix E.)

Credit Card Servers

These days, there are very few commerce options that I can use for my Web server. I can buy the Netscape Commerce Server for several thousand dollars or use Microsoft's Merchant program, buy vPos, and get all of it for under $25,000. After looking at the cost of these various approaches, I decided to search for other alternatives that could provide the same performance, or even better performance, and cost around $500. Three low-cost solutions I've found are ICVerify, PCAuthorize, and the Gigantor Commerce Server. While these products don't perform everything the more expensive solutions do, with a little code that we'll write here combined with the classes we've written throughout this book, we'll end up with a high-performance site that exceeds the expensive commerce solutions in terms of features and performance.

ICVerify (**www.icverify.com**) offers an entire spectrum of credit card processing solutions. One of these is a method of processing credit cards from your

PC. The cost is low—which means around $500 or so for a single-user version. Another hot item that ICVerify offers is a developer program that includes a SDK and training on using their product—both are big plusses in my book. ICVerify will dial a bank over a modem and verify your transaction in realtime. Because it's using a modem to dial out and is not sending this information over the Net, it's secure (unless your phone lines are tapped). It processes transactions using files that our code fragments will have to create and save, a poor design that should be improved. To use ICVerify, our code fragment will have to generate a file with transaction data; ICVerify then polls the directory, finds the file, performs necessary actions, and saves the results in a file. Figure 11.1 shows the process. While this is an outdated technique in the age of network coding, it is fast, and ICVerify provides support for all major banking protocols. Versions for DOS, Windows, NT, and several Unix flavors (prices vary for various Unix platforms) are available. ICVerify also has an X.25 version for high-speed transactions where you have a leased line with a bank.

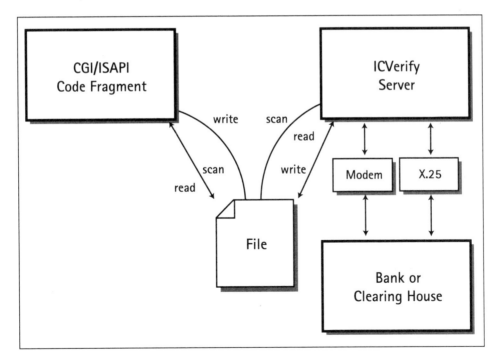

Figure 11.1
CGI/ISAPI to ICVerify.

PCAuthorize is from Tellan (**www.tellan.com**), which also provides a Mac product, cleverly called MacAuthorize. This product runs about the same price as ICVerify, and offers a different design than ICVerify: It uses DDE for communication with it or AppleEvents if you're using the Mac product. I have some problems with DDE and AppleEvents. For example, sometimes the events don't always get to the process that I've sent them to, which is unacceptable for commerce solutions. Tellan has advertised a newer version that will work over Winsock, which will be a great improvement, but this product is still in beta as of mid-1997. PCAuthorize also dials the banks, so the credit card information is transmitted securely from your server. We'll explore this product and show how to interface with it from our CGI/ISAPI code fragments. With DDE and AppleEvents, we send a message to PCAuthorize and await a response; programmatically, this is better than using a file and scanning directories if we weren't using CGI or ISAPI. Figure 11.2 shows the PCAuthorize approach. What else is wrong with DDE? Well, you can't use it from CGI or ISAPI, so we cannot use their server for our transactions. Tellan is advertising a PCAuthorize Hub (due out in late 1997) that will use TCP/IP, but for now we'll have to find

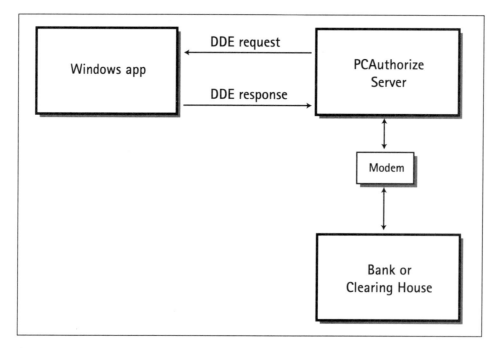

Figure 11.2
CGI/ISAPI to PCAuthorize.

a workaround. PCAuthorize supports almost as many banking protocols as ICVerify. Versions for Windows and Mac are available.

Another product, which is being completed by yours truly, is the Gigantor Commerce Server (**www.gigantor.com**). This server uses the same approach of dialing the banks securely, but you interface with it using TCP/IP. Figure 11.3 shows the model to connect to the Gigantor server from your code fragment. The user administrative interfaces to it are strictly in HTML, so you can configure it from anywhere if you have a Web browser available. This server only uses a few standard protocols, so you won't have the large variety of merchants to select from that you would get with ICVerify or PCAuthorize, but there are several samples of interfacing with it using ISAPI and CGI. While it only supports a few major banking protocols, remember that all the current protocols will be obsolete by mid-1998 when SET (Secure Electronic Transaction) arrives. Versions for various Unix platforms, Windows, and NT will be available in late October 1997. A version that uses X.25 instead of a modem will also be available in late 1997 for high-speed transactions.

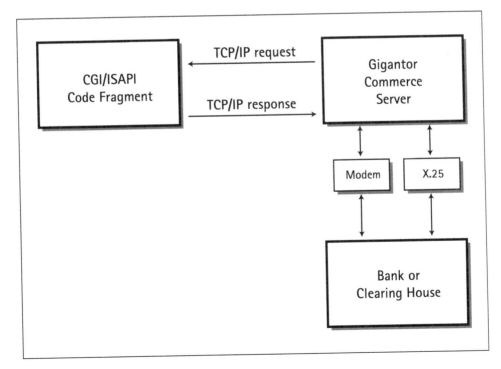

Figure 11.3
CGI/ISAPI to the Gigantor Commerce Server.

Note: SET is a new standard for commerce on the Web. The protocol was developed by MasterCard, Visa and IBM. American Express, First Data Corp. and others participated in the design. SET will become the new banking protocol in 1998 for all commerce transactions because all the major players developed it, and are endorsing it completely. To look at the specification and evaluate it for yourself, check out MasterCard's home page at www.mastercard.com.

The Gigantor Commerce Server uses TCP directly and the interface is quite easy to develop CGI and ISAPI code fragments with. ICVerify offers a file API that will work with CGI and ISAPI, but PCAuthorize presents an API that is quite different from using TCP directly, so we'll write a server application that uses TCP to talk with PCAuthorize. You can find the source code for using all the servers on the CD-ROM enclosed with this book, and at our support site (**www.gigantor.com/coriolis**).

We'll write this server to talk with ICVerify and handle the files for us, thereby enabling us to apply any of these solutions (ICVerify, PCAuthorize, Gigantor) with nearly identical CGI/ISAPI code fragments. We'll write this application so that switching from PCAuthorize to ICVerify or to another server shouldn't matter too much—our CGI/ISAPI code fragments should remain constant even if we change the back end (the credit card server).

Our Server

We need to listen on a known TCP socket for incoming connections, and when we receive one, we need to process this information and pass it on to ICVerify or PCAuthorize for processing (Gigantor's server does this automatically, so we don't use this extra server when using their commerce server). In this case, our server should create a thread that listens for this connection, and when it receives one, accept it and make a new thread that then will listen for other connections. This design method always keeps a listening thread available for any incoming connections. We then need to design a way to receive a response back from the credit card server that our server is interfacing with, process the results and display an appropriate HTML form to our customer.

*Note: If you're designing on a Unix system, you might just want to simplify the process and use the **fork()** call after a synchronous **listen()** call* *completes. This is a fine approach if you can afford to generate a new process for each connection. Process creation is much more expensive than thread creation—something to consider with whatever approach you choose.*

Designing our server to listen over TCP now gives us the added capability that even if these servers require Windows or DOS, we can use a Unix or even a Mac server (heaven forbid) to negotiate the transaction approval. TCP is a standard, and I cannot think of any standard in wider use today. Let's imagine you're using Netscape's Enterprise Server, or the Apache Server at **www.apache.com** (this is a public domain HTTP server—free and fast, and the source code is included), either of which is running on SCO's Unixware OS. In this case, we would target our TCP server for the machine that the credit card server runs on, and our CGI code fragment could be on the Web server machine and can talk with it as it's over TCP—it becomes location independent. Because we're using TCP and not files or DDE, our credit card server (with TCP server) can be located on a different machine, even in a different part of the world.

Encryption

Use encryption for all broadcasted data if your credit card server and Web server are on different CPUs.

If you do put your credit card server on a different machine than your Web server, be sure to use encryption between your code fragment and the TCP server. The packets are not encrypted automatically, so you would be broadcasting customers' credit card numbers to the entire world. In Chapter 15 we'll cover Blowfish— a high performance encryption algorithm that still has not been broken by hackers (or the NSA!).

Missing Threads

If kernel-level threads are missing, do several **fork()** calls at initialization time.

If you don't have kernel-level threads in your OS, consider using **fork()**, and have some initialization routine create several processes using **fork()** when your server first starts up. Although process creation is expensive, the performance usually doesn't matter at initialization time. You can then pass a file descriptor when your connection process calls **accept()** to one of your child processes using a bureaucrat class you design. Another approach is to use pThreads (Posix Threads), which are implemented with lots of changes to system and library calls, but they offer nearly the same functionality as regular threads. You can find pThreads at the MIT site **www.mit.edu/ people/proven/pthreads.html.**

Threads are fairly similar across operating systems, and essentially you always have a **create**() or **beginthread**() call, and sometimes a **run**() call or an equivalent. Listing 11.3 (shown later in this chapter) shows our server source, and we're using NT threads that are similar to Unix threads.

Always Choose Kernel-Level Threads Where Available

If you have a choice, always prefer kernel-level threads as opposed to user-level ones. Kernel threads are *real* threads—that is, the kernel provides the switching and time slicing between the threads. In user-level threads, the implementation must use a **select()** or something similar to switch between tasks—or even worse, you might have to provide explicit yields for CPU time to be given to another task. NT, Solaris, and SCO's Unixware provide kernel threads.

Some user-level threads are decent, so don't throw threads out just because you don't have kernel threads: I said to choose them if they're available. If they're not, look for pThreads, and make sure they're Posix .4a-compliant, or later. This is the next best thing and works well for networking, even if it's not as good as kernel threads.

Threads on a Macintosh are a nightmare. The Mac is a non-preemptive OS, so you must provide explicit time yields. This means that threads must be "cooperative," or the OS could possibly hang.

Now that we've decided to use threads and listen for a connection, we need to handle multiple connections and delegate our tasks to a thread to process the credit card transaction with the credit card server. Figure 11.4 shows the new model—here we've provided a new server that our code fragment will talk with. This server will spawn a thread that will talk with either ICVerify or PCAuthorize and handle the transaction negotiation for us. The main thread will then listen for more connections, and also spawn a child thread when a new connection arrives.

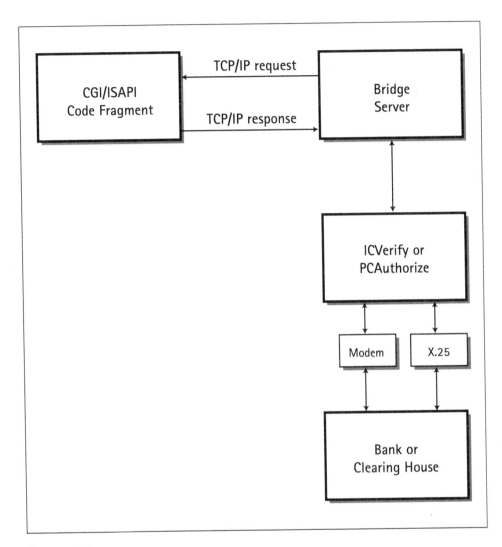

Figure 11.4
New interface to ICVerify and PCAuthorize.

The new design permits a clean client interface via CGI/ISAPI since we're using one protocol (not file I/O or DDE), TCP, that receives a string with all the credit card information. The strings for both ICVerify and PCAuthorize are very similar, but as an example, I've provided the source code for interfacing with PCAuthorize. Both the CD-ROM enclosed with this book and our support site (**www.gigantor.com/coriolis**) contain sources for all of the commerce server interfaces we've just described here.

To talk with PCAuthorize, we'll send a string to our server via TCP, and then make a thread that creates a DDE message and sends it to PCAuthorize. We'll then wait synchronously (we're on a thread, remember) until we get a result code back. Listing 11.1 shows the source code for this new interfacing server that I've called the "Credit Card Bridge."

LISTING 11.1   SOURCE CODE FOR THE BRIDGE.CPP.

```
//
//      File: Bridge.cpp
//      By:    Don Gaspar
//
//      This is the source for the TCP bridge to
//      Tellan's PCAuthorize product.
//      The book is Visual Developer Web Commerce Programming
//          With Visual C++.
//      The publisher is The Coriolis Group.
//
//      Author is Don Gaspar
//      July 1997
//      You may reach the author at: don@gigantor.com
//

// typical headers for this project
#include <windows.h>
#include <string.h>
#include <stdio.h>

// some STL headers needed
#include <vector.h>
#include <map.h>
#include <bstring.h>

// some networking headers
// note there are no Unix items here
// since PCAuthorize uses DDE
#include <WinSock.h>
#include <Process.h>
#include <io.h>
#include <ctype.h>

const int cBridgeListenPort =    1070;

// some useful things only accessed here
struct connInfo
{
```

```
    UINT              connsNow;
    UINT              totalConns;
    UINT              successfulConns;
    UINT              failedConns;
    UINT              errors;
    vector<UINT>      timeVec;
};


const UINT             cCreditPort = 1090;

// globals -- not encouraged to use too many of these
connInfo    gConnInfo;
DWORD         idInst;
map< string, string, less<string> > gTransactions;


// forward declarations

// function to initialize the application window class
BOOL
InitApplication(HINSTANCE);

// function to initialize this instance of the application
BOOL
InitInstance(HINSTANCE, int);

// misc.
int
SendCreditInfo( char *inCreditString );

void
SetupListens();

// DDE stuff
HDDEDATA CALLBACK
DdeCallback( UINT iType, UINT iFmt, HCONV hConv,
    HSZ topic, HSZ service, HDDEDATA hData,
    DWORD dwData1, DWORD dwData2 );

// function that is the window callback for message receipt
LRESULT CALLBACK
WndProc(HWND, UINT, WPARAM, LPARAM);

// WinMain — the guts of all Windows applications
int APIENTRY
WinMain(HINSTANCE hInstance, HINSTANCE hPrevInstance,
        LPSTR lpCmdLine, int nCmdShow)
{
```

```
    // initialize the application and register the window class
    if ( InitApplication(hInstance) )
    {
        // initialize this instance -- create the window
        if ( InitInstance(hInstance, nCmdShow) )
        {
            MSG    msg;
            // while there are messages to process
            while ( GetMessage(&msg,NULL ,0 , 0) )
            {
                // translate and dispatch the window procedure?
                TranslateMessage(&msg);
                DispatchMessage(&msg);
            }

            DdeUninitialize( idInst );
            // end the application
            return msg.wParam;
        }
    }

    return 0;    // some problem occurred
} // WinMain...

// set Winders environment up
BOOL
InitApplication( HINSTANCE hInstance)
{
    WNDCLASS    wc;

    // initialize our data structure
    memset(&gConnInfo,0,sizeof(connInfo));

    // stuff the structure
    // unique application class name
    wc.lpszClassName = "CreditCardBridge";
    // redraw on resize
    wc.style = CS_HREDRAW | CS_VREDRAW;
    // the callback for messages
    wc.lpfnWndProc = (WNDPROC)WndProc;
    // no extra class data
    wc.cbClsExtra = 0;
    // no extra window data
    wc.cbWndExtra = 0;
    // instance handle
    wc.hInstance = hInstance;
```

```
    // default icon
    wc.hIcon = LoadIcon(NULL, IDI_APPLICATION);
    // default cursor
    wc.hCursor = LoadCursor(NULL, IDC_ARROW);
    // some default?
    wc.hbrBackground = (HBRUSH)(COLOR_WINDOW + 1);
    // guess there's no menu tonight
    wc.lpszMenuName = NULL;

    // register struct class with Winders
    return RegisterClass(&wc);
} // InitApplication...

// set up our main window
BOOL
InitInstance( HINSTANCE hInstance, int nCmdShow)
{
    HWND    hWnd;

    // now create a window
    hWnd = CreateWindow( "CreditCardBridge", "Credit Card Bridge",
        WS_OVERLAPPEDWINDOW,
            CW_USEDEFAULT, CW_USEDEFAULT,
            CW_USEDEFAULT, CW_USEDEFAULT,
            NULL, NULL, hInstance, NULL);

    if ( !hWnd )
        return FALSE;           // we failed, return an error

    // a window doesn't do much good unless we can show it
    ShowWindow( hWnd, nCmdShow );

    // make sure it's painted and displayed correctly
    UpdateWindow(hWnd);

    // now set up DDE
    if ( DdeInitialize(&idInst, (PFNCALLBACK)&DdeCallback,
        CBF_FAIL_EXECUTES | CBF_FAIL_POKES |
        CBF_SKIP_REGISTRATIONS |
        CBF_SKIP_UNREGISTRATIONS, 0) )
    {
        MessageBox( hWnd, "Couldn't initialize our bridge!",
            "CreditCardBridge", MB_ICONEXCLAMATION | MB_OK );
        DestroyWindow( hWnd );
        return FALSE;
    }
```

```
    return TRUE;              // success
} // InitInstance...

// handle the events to this window
LRESULT CALLBACK
WndProc( HWND hWnd, UINT message, WPARAM wParam, LPARAM lParam)
{
    // find out what message we received
    switch ( message )
    {
case WM_PAINT:          // another name for an update event
        {
            RECT    r;
            HDC     hdc;    // device context — area to repaint
            PAINTSTRUCT    ps;
            char    outString[128];

            UINT          oldTextSettings = GetTextAlign( hdc );

            // get a device context handle
            hdc = BeginPaint( hWnd, &ps );
            GetClientRect( hWnd, &r );
            SetTextAlign( hdc, TA_CENTER );

            // display our status information
            sprintf(outString,
                "Connection in progress:      %d",
                gConnInfo.connsNow);
            TextOut( hdc, r.right/2, 25, outString,
                strlen(outString));

            sprintf(outString,
                "Total connections since restart:      %d",
                gConnInfo.totalConns);
            TextOut( hdc, r.right/2, 50, outString,
                strlen(outString));

            sprintf(outString,
                "Successful connections:      %d",
                gConnInfo.successfulConns);
            TextOut( hdc, r.right/2, 75, outString,
                strlen(outString));

            sprintf(outString,
                "Failed connections:      %d",
                gConnInfo.failedConns);
            TextOut( hdc, r.right/2, 100, outString,
                strlen(outString));
```

```
            sprintf(outString,
                "Errors:    %d",
                gConnInfo.errors);
            TextOut( hdc, r.right/2, 125, outString,
                strlen(outString));

            SetTextAlign( hdc, oldTextSettings );
            // release device context and let Windows
            // know we're done with the update
            EndPaint( hWnd, &ps );
        }
        break;

    case WM_DESTROY:    // handle application shutdown
        {
            // since this is the main window, post a
            // quit message to terminate us
            PostQuitMessage(0);
        }
        break;

    default:// let Windows handle all other messages for us
        return DefWindowProc( hWnd, message, wParam, lParam );

    } // switch...

    // return control to Windows
    return 0;
} // WndProc...

// DDE Callback function — standard
HDDEDATA CALLBACK
DdeCallback( UINT iType, UINT iFmt, HCONV hConv,
    HSZ topic, HSZ service, HDDEDATA hData,
    DWORD dwData1, DWORD dwData2 )
{
    char    buffer[128];
    int     i;

    switch( iType )
    {
        // nothing needed here unless PCAuthorize talks to us
    } // switch...

    return NULL;
} // DdeCallback...
```

```
// sends the credit card info to PCAuthorize
void
SendCreditInfo( void *inFD )
{
    HSZ    hService, hTopic, hItem;
    HCONV hConv;
    DWORD result = 0;
    HDDEDATA     responseH;
    char buffer[512];
    int    fd = (int)(inFD);

    // now get the data from the CGI/ISAPI client
    // and send it via DDE to PCAuthorize
    recv(fd, buffer, sizeof(buffer),0);

    // now create handles for our DDE service and topic
    hService = DdeCreateStringHandle( idInst, "PCAuthorize", 0 );
    hTopic = DdeCreateStringHandle( idInst,
        "AuthorizeTransaction", 0 );

    // connect to DDE process
    hConv = DdeConnect( idInst, hService, hTopic, NULL );

    // if it fails, load it
    if ( !hConv )
    {
        WinExec( "PCAuthorize", SW_SHOWMINNOACTIVE );
        hConv = DdeConnect( idInst, hService, hTopic, NULL );
    }

    // give a hoot, don't pollute
    DdeFreeStringHandle( idInst, hService );
    DdeFreeStringHandle( idInst, hTopic );

    if ( !hConv )
    {
        // can't display an error -- we're a server!
        // we have to return a meaningful result to
        // the caller
        gConnInfo.errors++;
        // send response to CGI/ISAPI client
        strcpy(buffer,"DDE failure");
        send( fd, buffer, strlen(buffer), 0 );
    }
    else
    {
        hItem = DdeCreateStringHandle( idInst, buffer, 0 );
```

```
        // send the DDE request
        responseH = DdeClientTransaction( NULL, 0, hConv, hItem,
            CF_TEXT, XTYP_REQUEST , 60000, &result );

        // check the result
        result = DdeGetLastError( idInst );
        if ( responseH && !result )
        {
            DdeGetData( responseH, (unsigned char *)buffer,
                sizeof(buffer)-1, 0 );

            // send response to CGI/ISAPI client
            send( fd, buffer, strlen(buffer), 0 );

            // keep running tabs of the transactions
            if ( strstr(buffer,"APPROVED") ||
                strstr(buffer, "Approved") )
                gConnInfo.successfulConns++;
            else
                gConnInfo.failedConns++;
        }
        else
            gConnInfo.errors++;

        // give a hoot, don't pollute
        DdeFreeStringHandle( idInst, hItem );
        DdeFreeDataHandle( responseH );
    }

    close( fd );
} // SendCreditInfo...

// set up listening on a socket
void
SetupListens()
{
    // network socket
    int     s;
    // TCP connection
    int     fd;
    // length
    int     len;
    // socket address
    struct sockaddr_in sin;

    // now set up Winsock
    WORD     version = MAKEWORD(1,1);
```

```
WSADATA    data;
(void)WSAStartup(version,&data);

// set up our struct for a listen
sin.sin_family - AF_INET;
sin.sin_addr.s_addr - INADDR_ANY;
sin.sin_port - htons(cCreditPort);

// create the actual socket
if ((s - socket(AF_INET, SOCK_STREAM, 0)) < 0)
{
    perror("socket");
    exit(1);
}


//    Bind address to local end of socket
if (bind(s, (struct sockaddr *) &sin, sizeof(sin)) < 0)
{
    perror("bind");
    exit(1);
}


//accept the connection from remote clients
listen(s, 5);
while(1)
{
    // accept is synchronous -  it returns
    // from execution when the TCP stack has
    // received a connection from a client
    if ((fd - accept(s, (struct sockaddr *)&sin, &len)) < 0)
    {
        perror("accept");
        exit(1);
    }

    // create a thread to handle everything
    _beginthread( SendCreditInfo, 0 ,(void *)fd );
}

// let Winsock clean up after itself
WSACleanup();
} // SetupListens...
```

We had to write a server to bridge with ICVerify and PCAuthorize, so the Windows server I wrote is the perfect place to add statistical information for your Web site's financial transactions. We can keep track of how many connections

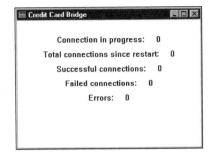

Figure 11.5
The Credit Card Bridge window.

are in progress, how many successful transactions there are, and so on. Figure 11.5 shows the window that just displays text showing this information.

You might want to add a vector to keep track of the average cost per transaction, how many sales there were in the last few hours, and so on. Use an STL vector to do this—much like how I keep track of the average time per transaction—and then use the **accumulate**() function to total your numbers.

Our Client

Before we process the order (after we have gathered the credit card information), we'll generate another dynamic page for the customer to review the order. This allows the customer one last chance to review the shopping cart, see the actual total, and decide to cancel—or even go back and shop some more and order later on. Here, we add shipping costs—and sales tax if the customer is blessed with being a California resident. Our credit card HTML form asks for the customer name exactly as it appears on the card; next we'll ask for the card number and the beginning and ending expiration dates, as shown in Figure 11.6.

Interfacing from CGI and ISAPI is easy. We need to open a socket to the server we've just written and pass the credit information over. We then wait until a response comes back, at which point we create a "thank you" page for our customer, and store the information with a credit card reference approval code in our datastore. I've written a new class, **CCreditCard**, that handles the transactions by calling the **DoCreditCard**() member function. This class is totally portable between CGI and ISAPI, and is shown in Listing 11.2.

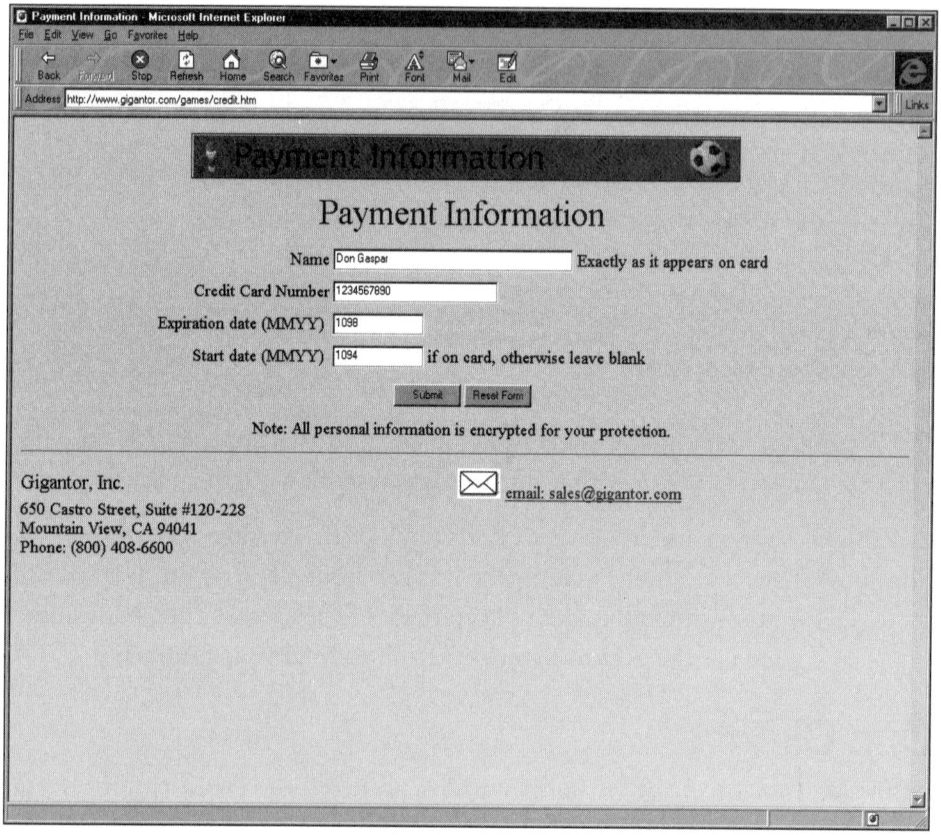

Figure 11.6
Credit card HTML form.

DoCreditCard() first uses the Luhn algorithm to validate the card number with the possible types of cards you accept. My site accepts Visa, MasterCard, American Express, Carte Blanche, and Diners Club, and these options are set in the **CCreditCard** constructor. I put this information inside the constructor so that the class won't have to change; even if you change what cards you accept, you only need to update your code fragment's use of the **CCreditCard** constructor, which is how you should design it. A client of this **CCreditCard** class needs to tell it what types of services to use.

CCreditCard will validate every current credit card that I could find information about; as new cards arrive, we'll update our support site with an updated **CCreditCard** class. The member functions that do the check-sum validation are named after the card like **CCreditCard::CheckAmex()** for Amercian Express, **CCreditCard::CheckVisa()** for Visa, and so on.

CCreditCard.cpp has some conditional compile directives depending on if you're using Windows or Unix for your code fragment. If you're using Unix, **#define UNIX** somewhere. I added the conditional compile directives so that we could use the same code with Winsock, or regular sockets under TCP. The code is nearly identical with a few exceptions: For Winsock, we have to initialize the TCP stack by calling **WSAStartup()**, and when we're done we call **WSACleanup()**—you don't call these under Unix. Next, Winsock uses **send()** and **recv()** for sending and receiving data, whereas Unix uses **read()** and **write()** with a file descriptor. If you try **read()** and **write()** with Winsock, you will get an invalid file descriptor error since **read()** and **write()** do not work with Winsock. **send()** and **recv()** take one additional argument than their **read()** and **write()** Unix counterparts, so be sure to review the source code for specific details.

If you're on a Macintosh, you should **#define UNIX** so that your TCP code is not using the Winsock routines (unless you're using the Netmanage Winsock Mac code fragment). Next, there is a library called GUSI (Grand Unified Socket Interface) that maps the MacTCP and/or Open Transport routines directly to Unix TCP socket calls. GUSI comes with CodeWarrior for the Mac from Metrowerks (**www.metrowerks.com**).

LISTING 11.2 CREDITCARD.CPP.

```
//
//     File: CreditCard.cpp
//     By:    Don Gaspar
//
//     This is the source code for the CCreditCard class
//     from Chapter 11 in the book,
//     Visual Developer Web Commerce Programming
//          in Visual C++.
//     The publisher is the Coriolis Group.
//
//     The author is Don Gaspar
//
//     You may reach the author at: don@gigantor.com
//

// headers we've written
#include "CFormParser.hpp"
#include "CreditCard.hpp"
#include "CookieMonster.hpp"
#include "ShoppingCart.hpp"
```

```
// general use
#include <sys/types.h>
#include <stdio.h>
#include <ctype.h>
#include <sql.h>

// for TCP/IP networking
#ifdef UNIX
#include <sys/socket.h>
#include <netinet/in.h>
#include <arpa/inet.h>
#include <netdb.h>
#elif WIN32
#include "stdafx.h"
#include <WinSock.h>
#include <io.h>
//////////////////////////////////////////////////////////////////
// The one and only CWinApp object
// NOTE: You may remove this object if you alter your project to no
// longer use MFC in a DLL.
CWinApp      theApp;
#endif

//   basic SQL queries, etc.
const char *cSQLAddCreditInfo = "INSERT INTO "
    "creditInfo(name, appCode, cookieID, cardNum,"
    "expDate, startDate, amount) VALUES( '%s', '%s',"
    "%s', '%s', '%s', '%s',%s)";

// now for the code

//
//    function:    CCreditCard::CCreditCard()
//    purpose:     Our base constructor.
//    returns:     nothing
//
CCreditCard::CCreditCard( CFormParser &inParser, bool inMC,
    bool inVisa, bool inAmex, bool inDC,
    bool inCB, bool inJCB, bool inDiscover )
{
    // get outta here if we're missing stuff we need
    THROWIF( inParser["name"].length() < 2 ||
        inParser["expDate"].length() < 2 ||
        inParser["cardNumber"].length() < 13 );
```

```
    // some simple member flags we're using
    m_acceptMasterCard = inMC;
    m_acceptVisa = inVisa;
    m_acceptAmex = inAmex;
    m_acceptDiners = inDC || inCB;
    m_acceptJCB = inJCB;
    m_acceptDiscover = inDiscover;

    // store information away
    m_cardNumber = inParser["cardNumber"];
    m_name = inParser["name"];
    m_expDate = inParser["expDate"];
    m_startDate = inParser["startDate"];
} // CCreditCard::CCreditCard...


//
//    function:   CCreditCard::~CCreditCard()
//    purpose:    Our base destructor. Not yet used.
//    returns:    nothing
//
CCreditCard::~CCreditCard()
{
} // CCreditCard::~CCreditCard...


//
//    function:   CCreditCard::StoreResultsInDB()
//    purpose:    Stores approval results in our db.
//    returns:    nothing
//
void
CCreditCard::StoreResultsInDB( const char *inBuffer )
{
    CCookieMonster    cookie;
    char              queryString[128];
    CFormParser       creditInfo(inBuffer);
    // ODBC Handles we need
    HSTMT    stmtH;
    HDBC     dbH;
    HENV     envH;

    try
    {
        // should never happen, but always be paranoid
        THROWIF( cookie["FoosballCookie"].length() < 1 );

        // make the query string
        sprintf( queryString, cSQLAddCreditInfo,
```

```
        m_name.c_str(),
        creditInfo["APPROVED"].c_str(),
        cookie["FoosballCookie"].c_str(),
        m_cardNumber.c_str(),
        m_expDate.c_str(),
        m_startDate.c_str(),
        creditInfo["AMOUNT"].c_str() );

    THROWIF( SQLAllocEnv( &envH ) != SQL_SUCCESS );
    THROWIF( SQLAllocConnect( envH, &dbH ) != SQL_SUCCESS );

    RETCODE result = SQLConnect( dbH,(unsigned char *)
        "Games",6,
        (unsigned char *)"sa",3,NULL,0 );
    THROWIF( result != SQL_SUCCESS &&
        result != SQL_SUCCESS_WITH_INFO);
    SQLAllocStmt( dbH, &stmtH );

    result = SQLPrepare( stmtH,
        (unsigned char *)queryString,
        strlen( queryString ) + 1 );
    THROWIF(result == SQL_ERROR);

    // execute the SQL statement we made
    result = SQLExecute( stmtH );
    THROWIF( result != SQL_SUCCESS &&
        result != SQL_SUCCESS_WITH_INFO);

    // commit the addition to the database
    SQLTransact( envH, dbH, SQL_COMMIT );

    // give a hoot, don't pollute
    if ( stmtH )
        SQLFreeStmt( stmtH, SQL_CLOSE );
    if ( dbH )
        SQLFreeConnect( dbH );
    if( envH )
        SQLFreeEnv( envH );
}

catch(...)
{
    SDWORD    err;
    char text[512], errText[512];
    SQLError(envH,dbH,stmtH,(unsigned char *)text,&err,
        (unsigned char *)errText,sizeof(errText),0);
```

```
            // show the error message
            cout << "<CENTER>" << errText << ": err = " <<
                text << "<BR></CENTER>";

            // give a hoot, don't pollute
            if ( stmtH )
                SQLFreeStmt( stmtH, SQL_CLOSE );
            if ( dbH )
                SQLFreeConnect( dbH );
            if( envH )
                SQLFreeEnv( envH );
    }
} // CCreditCard::StoreResultsInDB


//
//    function:    CCreditCard::DoCreditCard()
//    purpose:     Calls private member functions and processes
//                 any order associated with this customer.
//    returns:     nothing
//
void
CCreditCard::DoCreditCard()
{
    cout << "<CENTER>Checking card number...<BR>" << endl;
    if ( CheckCard() )
    {
        cout << "OK...<BR>Connecting to bank "
            "for approval...<BR>" << endl;
        if ( HandleCreditCard() )
            DisplayApproved();
        else
            DisplayRejected();
    }
    else
        DisplayBadCard();
    cout << "exiting DoCreditCard<BR>";
} // CCreditCard::DoCreditCard...


//
//    function:    CCreditCard::DisplayApproved()
//    purpose:     Outputs approved message
//    returns:     nothing
//
void
CCreditCard::DisplayApproved()
{
```

```
      cout << "<CENTER>Your order has been approved. Please expect"
          " shipment in 3-4 weeks. Thank you for your business"
              ".<BR><BR><BR>";
} // CCreditCard::DisplayApproved...

//
//    function:   CCreditCard::DisplayBadCard()
//    purpose:    Outputs bad card number message.
//    returns:    nothing
//
void
CCreditCard::DisplayBadCard()
{
    cout << "<CENTER>Sorry, but your card number was either entered"
          " incorrectly or is a type we do not accept. Please re-enter"
          " and try again.<BR><BR><BR>";
} // CCreditCard::DisplayBadCard...

//
//    function:   CCreditCard::DisplayRejected()
//    purpose:    Outputs a rejected card message.
//    returns:    nothing
//
void
CCreditCard::DisplayRejected()
{
    cout << "<CENTER>Sorry, but your order was declined."
              " Please call our"
              " toll-free number for further assistance or feel free"
              " to re-enter your credit information and "
              "try again.<BR><BR><BR>";
} // CCreditCard::DisplayRejected...

//
//    function:   CCreditCard::CheckCard()
//    purpose:    Checks the credit card length and digits
//    returns:    true if valid, false otherwise
//
bool
CCreditCard::CheckCard()
{
    bool    result = false;

    switch ( m_cardNumber.length() )
    {
```

```
        case 13:
            // must be a VISA
            if ( m_acceptVisa )
                result = CheckVisa();
            break;

        case 14:
            // Diners Club
            if ( m_acceptDiners )
                result = CheckDiners();
            break;

        case 15:
            // American Express, JCB
            if ( m_acceptJCB )
                result = CheckJCB();
            if ( !result && m_acceptAmex )
                result = CheckAmex();
            break;

        case 16:
            // MasterCard, Visa, Discover, JCB
            if ( m_acceptMasterCard )
                result = CheckMasterCard();
            if ( !result &&  m_acceptVisa )
                result = CheckVisa();
            if ( !result && m_acceptDiscover )
                result = CheckDiscover();
            else if ( !result && m_acceptJCB )
                result == CheckJCB();
            break;

        default:
            ;
    } // switch...

    return result;
} // CCreditCard::CheckCard...

//
//    function:    CCreditCard::CheckVisa()
//    purpose:     Checks the credit card as type Visa
//    returns:     true if valid, false otherwise
//
bool
```

```
CCreditCard::CheckVisa()
{
    bool     result = false;

    short number = m_cardNumber.c_str()[0] - '0';
    if ( number == 4 )
        result = DoCheckSum();

    // all we ever needed
    return result;
} // CCreditCard::CheckVisa...

//
//    function:   CCreditCard::CheckMasterCard()
//    purpose:    Checks the credit card as type MasterCard
//    returns:    true if valid, false otherwise
//
bool
CCreditCard::CheckMasterCard()
{
    bool     result = false;
    char     value[2];

    strncpy(value, m_cardNumber.c_str(),sizeof(value));
    short number = atoi( value );
    if ( number >=51 && number <=55 )
        result = DoCheckSum();

    // all we ever needed
    return result;
} // CCreditCard::CheckMasterCard...

//
//    function:   CCreditCard::Amex()
//    purpose:    Checks the credit card as type
//                       American Express.
//    returns:    true if valid, false otherwise
//
bool
CCreditCard::CheckAmex()
{
    bool     result = false;
    char     value[2];

    strncpy(value, m_cardNumber.c_str(),sizeof(value));
    short number = atoi( value );
```

```
    if ( number ==34 || number ==37 )
        result = DoCheckSum();

    // all we ever needed
    return result;
} // CCreditCard::CheckAmex...

//
//    function:    CCreditCard::CheckDiners()
//    purpose:     Checks the credit card as type Diners
//                 Club or Carte Blanche.
//    returns:     true if valid, false otherwise
//
bool
CCreditCard::CheckDiners()
{
    bool    result = false;
    char  value[2];

    strncpy(value, m_cardNumber.c_str(),sizeof(value));
    short number = atoi( value );
    if ( number ==36 || number ==38 )
        result = DoCheckSum();
    else
    {
        char    temp[3];
        strncpy( temp, m_cardNumber.c_str(),sizeof(temp) );
        number = atoi( temp );
        if ( number >=300 && number <= 305 )
            result = DoCheckSum();
    }

    // all we ever needed
    return result;
} // CCreditCard::CheckDiners...

//
//    function:    CCreditCard::CheckDiscover()
//    purpose:     Checks the credit card as type
//                 Discover.
//    returns:     true if valid, false otherwise
//
bool
CCreditCard::CheckDiscover()
{
    bool    result = false;
    char  value[4];
```

```
    strncpy(value, m_cardNumber.c_str(),sizeof(value));
    short number = atoi( value );
    if ( number == 6011 )
        result = DoCheckSum();

    // all we ever needed
    return result;
} // CCreditCard::CheckDiscover...

//
//    function:    CCreditCard::JCB()
//    purpose:    Checks the credit card as type
//                Japanese Bank Card.
//    returns:    true if  valid, false otherwise
//
bool
CCreditCard::CheckJCB()
{
    bool    result = false;
    char    value[4];

    strncpy(value, m_cardNumber.c_str(),sizeof(value));
    short number = atoi( value );
    if ( m_cardNumber.length() == 15 &&
        (number ==2131 || number ==1800) )
        result = DoCheckSum();
    else if ( m_cardNumber.length() == 16 )
    {
        char temp = m_cardNumber.c_str()[0];
        number = m_cardNumber.c_str()[0] - '0';
        if ( number == 3 )
            result = DoCheckSum();
    }

    // all we ever needed
    return result;
} // CCreditCard::CheckJCB...

//
//    function:    CCreditCard::DoCheckSum()
//    purpose:    Checks the credit card digits via the
//                Luhn Mod 10 Algorithm
//    reutrns:    true if digits are valid, false otherwise
//
bool
CCreditCard::DoCheckSum()
{
```

```
    // always be a pessimist with money involved
    bool    result = false;
    vector<short>    digitArray;
    short            dummy;

    for( short index = 0; index < m_cardNumber.length(); index ++ )
    {
        // convert to an integer
        dummy = m_cardNumber.c_str()[index] - '0';
        // array keeps track of everything
        digitArray.push_back( dummy );
    }


    // now total the reverse digits and double them -
    //    part of the Luhn algorithm
    vector<short>::reverse_iterator    iter;
    bool skip = true;
    short sum = 0;
    for ( iter = digitArray.rbegin(); iter != digitArray.rend();
        iter++ )
    {
        if ( skip )
            // total the digits
            sum += *iter;
        else
        {
            short value = *iter * 2;
            if ( value >= 10 )
            {
                sum += 1;
                value -= 10;
            }
            sum += value;
        }
        // toggle every number
        skip = !skip; }


    return ( sum %10 == 0 );
}  // CCreditCard::DoCheckSum...


//
//    function:   CCreditCard::HandleCreditCard()
//    purpose:    Validates the credit card with our
//                authentication dial-up server.
//    returns:    true if approved, false otherwise
//
bool
```

```
CCreditCard::HandleCreditCard()
{
    char    queryInfo[256];
    string  zipCode;
    float   amount;
    bool    result = false;

    // get some information from the shoppingcart object
    CFormParser         form;
    CShoppingCart       theCart(form);
    // get the zip code for address verification system checks
    theCart.GetZipCode( zipCode );

    // get the order total
    theCart.GetOrderTotal( amount );

    // some extra stuff needed for Winsock
#ifdef WIN32
    WORD    version = MAKEWORD(1,1);
    WSADATA     data;
    (void)WSAStartup(version,&data);
#endif

    // now put the string in a format that Gigantor uses,
    // and also our bridge application uses for interfacing
    // with ICVerify and PCAuthorize
    sprintf( queryInfo, "%s|%s|%.2f|%s|%s|%s|",
        m_cardNumber.c_str(),
        m_expDate.c_str(),
        amount,
        zipCode.c_str(),
        " ",
        "Foosball Supplies" );

    // now send it synchronously and wait for a reply!
    // socket address
    struct  sockaddr_in     sin;
    // host entry
    struct  hostent         *ph;
    // TCP socket
    int         s;
    // length
    int         len;
    // IP address
    long    address;
    // data buffer for TCP stream
    char    buf[BUFSIZ];
```

```
// this is your credit card server's address
char    *host = "206.184.228.202";

if (isdigit(host[0])) // dotted ip address?
{
    if (( address = inet_addr(host)) == -1)
    {
        fprintf(stderr, "CreditCard.exe: invalid credit "
            "card server %s\n", host);
        exit(1);
    }
    sin.sin_addr.s_addr = address;
    sin.sin_family = AF_INET;
}
else if ((ph = gethostbyname(host)) == NULL)
{
    switch (h_errno)
    {
        case HOST_NOT_FOUND:
            fprintf(stderr,
                "CreditCard.exe: no such host\n",host);
            exit(1);
        case TRY_AGAIN:
            fprintf(stderr,
            "CreditCard.exe: host %s, try again later\n", host);
            exit(1);
        case NO_RECOVERY:
            fprintf(stderr,
                "CreditCard.exe: host %s DNS Error\n", host);
            exit(1);
        case NO_ADDRESS:
            fprintf(stderr,
                "CreditCard.exe: No IP address for %s\n", host);
            exit(1);
        default:
            fprintf(stderr, "Unknown error : %d\n",h_errno);
            exit(1);
    } // switch...
}
else
{
    sin.sin_family = ph->h_addrtype;
    memcpy(ph->h_addr, (char *) &sin.sin_addr, ph->h_length);
}

// now actually connect
sin.sin_port = htons( eGigantorPort );
```

```
    //    open a socket
    if ((s = socket(AF_INET, SOCK_STREAM, 0)) == INVALID_SOCKET )
    {
        s = WSAGetLastError();
        if ( s==0 )
            ;
        perror("socket");
        exit(1);
    }

    cout << "Opening TCP/IP connection...<BR>" << endl;
    //    connect to the remote echo server
    if (connect(s, (struct sockaddr *) &sin, sizeof(sin)) < 0)
    {
        perror("connect");
        exit(1);
    }

    // now send the data for validation
    cout << "Submitting card information...<BR>" << endl;
#ifdef UNIX
    if (write(s, queryInfo, strlen(queryInfo)) < 0)
#elif WIN32
    if (send(s, queryInfo, strlen(queryInfo),0) < 0)
#endif
    {
        perror("write");
        exit(1);
    }

    cout << "OK...<BR>Waiting for response...</CENTER><BR>" << endl;
#ifdef UNIX
    if ((len = read(s, buf, BUFSIZ)) < 0)
#elif WIN32
    if ((len = recv(s, buf, BUFSIZ,0)) < 0)
#endif
    {
        perror("read");
        exit(1);
    }
    else
    {
        // was the transaction approved???
        if ( strstr( buf, "APPROVED" ) )
        {
            cout << "Within the DB...<BR>";
            cout << buf << "<BR>";
```

```
            StoreResultsInDB(buf);
            cout << "Done StoreResults stuff<BR>" << endl;
            result = true;
        }
    }

// extra code needed for Winsock
#ifdef WIN32
    WSACleanup();
#endif

    return result;
} // CCreditCard::HandleCreditCard...
```

DoCreditCard() calls various member functions, but you don't need to concern yourself with them unless you want to. This member function collects the information from the credit card form we showed in Figure 11.6 and processes the results via the various credit card servers we've mentioned in here.

Now to use the **CCreditCard** class, we need to process the credit card form that we should mention here briefly. The form requested the customer's name as it appears on the credit card, the card number, the expiration date, and the start date. While these fields normally are never used, if there is a dispute over a credit transaction, you will be required to show this information to the credit card company. Ask for it and store it in your database: you will only use it for rare dispute cases.

Using the **CCreditCard** class requires that we make a code fragment to handle the credit card form, and the source for this fragment is inside ProcessCredit-Card.cpp, shown in Listing 11.3. Using the class requires that we pass in our **CFormParser** instance as an argument to the **CCreditCard** constructor, then call the **DoCreditCard**() member function. Because of the **CCreditCard** class, our code fragment used only two lines of code to process the credit card transaction for us.

You will notice that **CCreditCard** uses **CShoppingCart** for getting order totals, and so on. I expanded the **CShoppingCart** class for dealing with this automatically. **CCreditCard** knows nothing about what the customer ordered, the sales tax, shipping costs, or anything other than validating the credit card. **CShoppingCart** knows all of this, so that's why I added the functionality for calculating shipping and other details in that class. The final version of **CShoppingCart** is discussed in more detail in Chapter 13.

LISTING 11.3   PROCESSCREDITCARD.CPP.

```
//
//      File: ProcessCreditCard.cpp
//      By:    Don Gaspar
//
//      This is the source for the Credit Card Handler,
//      an example from Chapter 11
//      in the book Visual Developer Web Commerce
//          Programming With Visual C++.
//      The publisher is the Coriolis Group.
//
//      The author is Don Gaspar
//
//      You may reach the author at: don@gigantor.com
//

// some standard headers we're going to need in here
#include <ostream.h>
#include <fstream.h>
#include <stdio.h>
#include <stdlib.h>
#include <sql.h>

// now headers we've written
#include "CFormParser.hpp"
#include "CookieMonster.hpp"
#include "CreditCard.hpp"

// our header and footer file names
const char *cHeaderName =
    "c:\\inetpub\\gigantor\\games\\head.htm";
const char *cFooterName =
    "c:\\inetpub\\gigantor\\games\\foot.htm";
const char *cErrorFile =
    "c:\\inetpub\\gigantor\\games\\sadbob.htm";
const char *cCreditForm =
    "f:\\gigantor\\games\\credit.htm";

//
//      Function: BeginHeader
//      Purpose: Outputs the appropriate header
//                  information to stdout for a
//                  Web browser to display.
//      Arguments: inTitle, the title of the dynamic
//                  page you are creating.
//
void
```

```
BeginHeader(const char* inTitle)
{
    cout << "Content-type:TEXT/HTML\n\n" <<
        "<HTML><HEAD><TITLE>\n" <<
        inTitle << "\n</TITLE></HEAD><BODY>\n";
} // BeginHeader...

//
//    Function: EndHeader
//    Purpose: Outputs the delimiter tags
//                corresponding to those set by
//                PrintHeader() for proper HTML display.
//    Arguments:    None
//
void
EndHeader()
{
    cout << "</BODY></HTML>\n";
} // EndHeader...

//
//    StreamFile
//    Input:      char* which is the name of the
//                file to use with path.
//    Purpose:    Opens the designated file and
//                streams it out through the CHttpServerContext
//                so the client's browser will get this
//                dynamic HTML page.
//
void
StreamFile( const char* inFile )
{
    try
    {
        ifstream    file( inFile );   // file stream

        if ( !file )                  // if we don't get the file, then
            throw(-1);                // throw an exception

        char buffer[80];              // just a line of characters

        // here we loop through the file line by
        //    line until we hit the end
        //    sending all the data to cout.
        while ( file.getline(buffer,sizeof(buffer)) )
            cout << buffer;
```

```
                file.close();
        }

        catch(...)
        {
            cout << "<center><b>Couldn't locate the "
                "header file.<br></center></b>";
        }
} // CGamesExtension::StreamFile...

//
//      function:       HandleForm
//      purpose:        Creates a CFormParser object and passes the
//                      data received from a POST
//                      in cin to CFormParser. Checks length, etc.
//                      and throws and exception
//                      upon detection of any error.
//      returns:        Nothing, exceptions are used for error handling.
//
void
HandleForm()
{
        char *buffer;

        try
        {
            char *streamSize = getenv("CONTENT_LENGTH");
            THROWIF( !streamSize );
            long dataSize = atol( streamSize );
            THROWIF( !dataSize );

            buffer = new char[dataSize];
            cin >> buffer;

            // get our form data and parse
            CFormParser     ourParser( buffer );

            // remember: pass in the cards you accept here
            // otherwise the defaults are always used. The
            // defaults are the cards my sites accept, not yours! :-)
            CCreditCard     custCreditCard( ourParser );

            // all we need to do for validation, etc.
            custCreditCard.DoCreditCard();
```

```
        delete [] buffer;
        cout << "delete<BR>";
    }

    catch(...)
    {
        cout << "<CENTER><H1>Please enter "
            "all information requested."
            "</CENTER></H1><BR><BR><BR>";
        delete [] buffer;
    }
} // HandleForm...

//
//    well, we gotta start somewhere
//
void
main()
{
    BeginHeader("Credit Validation");

    // go handle things for us
    StreamFile( cHeaderName );
    HandleForm();
    StreamFile( cFooterName );

    EndHeader();
} // main...
```

Storing Credit Tables

Now that we've collected the information from the client and have an approved transaction, we need to store this information in the datastore for reference. We may need this verification number should the merchandise or the transaction ever become disputed. There could even be a fraud case—it's hard to imagine all the possibilities, but store the information as a record of the transaction and add a date-time stamp too.

This is a simple process and can be done with either ODBC or **CRecordset**; all we want is the information stored inside our database correctly for future reference. We'll store the customer cookie, the order total, a timestamp, the credit card number and expiration date, and the authorization code. All of this is handled automatically by **CCreditCard** with its **StoreResultsInDB**() member function. Be sure to review the source code in Listing 11.2 for further reference.

CyberCash

CyberCash is another solution for credit card processing, but you won't have to buy a server! What, I don't have to buy a server? One less component always simplifies your design, so why didn't we do this earlier? Well, CyberCash does have a server and several other components, but it doesn't charge for the software. We'll explore here why CyberCash is unacceptable for high-performance realtime sites.

First off, CyberCash doesn't use a modem, and transmits credit card information over the Internet. Therefore, your server will receive the data over SSL; then CyberCash will use its encryption code (provided by RSA at **www.rsa.com**) and transmit the information to its server. Because it uses the Net, you would think this would be faster than a modem, right? It's not. It's at least twice as slow as the average performance I get with a modem-based credit card server.

CyberCash uses PERL, so you get the overhead of a PERL interpreter for each script that you now instantiate from your server. We discussed this extra overhead—and how much of a performance degradation you will get—back in Chapter 2. However, you might want to use a script to link CyberCash into your system for processing if you're not performing very many simultaneous transactions and your server can handle connections properly.

The transaction cost is also higher than what you can get when using a modem-based solution. The quotations I received for using CyberCash were 30 percent more expensive per transaction. For a large volume of transactions, you might find CyberCash costly.

Additionally, a CyberCash transaction is slow because it's going through central processing and validation services. I prefer to choose my own clearing house or bank for transactions, and you should too. This way, you can change your software and go to another bank and your business will still function. If you choose CyberCash, you will have to switch software if you want a different clearing house.

CyberCash is working on new payment methods besides just credit cards, and if you use its system you will be able to use these digital wallets. Take a look at the CyberCash site for more information (**www.cybercash.com**). This cool eCash solution will be taking off in the near future, so be sure to keep up with it. Credit cards are not necessarily forever, and CyberCash knows this.

Consequently, CyberCash gives you the benefit (or drawback) of not using a modem, but it is substantially slower than other approaches we've taken in this chapter. PERL adds overhead for your server, so the per-transaction cost (CPU) is much higher than modem-based solutions, and feedback is not as immediate as other low-cost solutions. I would expect that in the future, CyberCash will offer developer libraries that will eliminate the PERL requirement, and that the speed issue over the Net will also beat any modem-based solution. However, looking at this product today, the modem solutions we mentioned earlier win the performance contest. I also expect costs over the Net to go down per credit card transaction as CyberCash's volume increases. Evaluate your needs and visit the site to see if it's something you can use. The startup costs are minimal.

Emailing Status

When someone orders from your store and the order is approved (you've collected payment), you might want to be notified. It's much more convenient for your server to notify you than to constantly query your server to check for orders. When your store starts getting sufficient bandwidth, you will prefer to query your datastore daily rather than receiving email on completed transactions; but we have to start somewhere, so let's explore how.

Email is sent via SMTP (Simple Mail Transport Protocol), and is read via a different protocol, POP3. Why two different standards? I have no idea. All I can imagine is that they were developed independently and each gained a large following. Because we're going to send mail to ourselves, we're only concerned with SMTP.

In Appendix E, I have written an SMTP mailer class, and here I'll provide a code snippet to show how to use it. The source code is 100 percent compatible with CGI and ISAPI, and the class is very easy to use. Listing 11.4 shows how to send some email notifying us that an order has been placed on our server. Note how little code we need to use for this functionality.

LISTING 11.4   USING CPONYEXPRESS.

```
CPonyExpress    emailer("smtp.gigantor.com",
    "don@gigantor.com", "New Order" );
```

```
emailer.setsubject("new sale");
emailer.addmessage("sale information here");
emailer.send();
```

The constructor lets you specify your email server and options, such as the destination address of the person you're sending the email to (yourself, in this case). You could use this class to send a customer a response about his or her order when you ship it, and if you decided to not perform realtime transactions, you could verify or reject the order and notify the customer through this method.

The **send**() member fires the message off to the SMTP server you specified in your constructor, but you don't have to use this member, the destructor also sends the message. This way when your object leaves the scope of the current member function, it is sent automatically.

Summary

In this chapter, we discussed some credit card servers and how to interface with them. We also interfaced with some of them by writing a threaded TCP server that talked with the credit card servers. Additionally, we wrote our CGI/ISAPI code fragments to open a socket and pass a message to our server, which passed it to the credit card server using a different protocol. After the transaction was verified or rejected, we stored the result in our datastore and sent the user a proper message about his or her order. We then showed how to email a confirmation back to us.

We've covered everything you need to know about processing credit card transactions in realtime from your Web site. With all the information and code written thus far, you should be able to put up a high-performance realtime store that can handle large amounts of traffic browsing your pages.

This realtime processing is great for stores with merchandise in stock or easy-to-order items. But what about a store in which the merchandise changes every month, like a comic book store? You will need to know how much to order, and how far in advance. You can't really bill a client for a full order until you've shipped it in its entirety, so you will need to keep the information in your datastore, order your goods, and when they arrive, batch process the payments. We know how to do this in realtime, but realtime is not the appropriate method to use here. For this unique case, we need to process batches using a queue, which is covered in Chapter 12.

12

Queued Order Processing

I have traveled the length and breadth of this country and talked with the best people, and I can assure you that data processing is a fad that won't last out the year.

The editor managing business books for Prentice Hall, 1957

O rdering goods on the Internet is not only a tremendous opportunity for you; it is also the future way of conducting commerce globally. It will not be going away. In order to make sure that your business or your client's business stays competitive, you will need to develop a system that can handle not only realtime orders, but also batches of orders that are not—such as when you ship a back order. In some situations, you will need to queue orders up for later batch processing—like the old mainframe jobs of yesteryears. Hold on! We're not going to use mainframes or any programming techniques that belong in antique journals—we're going to use your Web server and add an application for batch processing.

When your store is unable to ship orders to customers immediately, you'll have to wait to bill them until you are ready to ship the order (barring prepaid orders). To handle such cases, you'll store the orders in a database table and mark them with a label that indicates the items within are "to be ordered."

The contents of the customer's order will be stored away and you will later fill these orders using the records from all of your customers' order tables. Billing the customer before you ship the merchandise requires you to use the credit card class **CCreditCard**. However, as we use this class for realtime scenarios, we need to find an alternative. In this chapter, we're going to discuss how to develop a program that would handle this batch processing or "order jobs," as well as cover the database tables necessary for such order processing. We use some new concepts from the ANSI STL, including an adapter called a queue.

Queues

A fundamental data structure that all software engineers use frequently is a queue. To review, a *queue* is a data structure that is designed so that the first element added to it is also the first element that will be removed. This is called *FIFO*, an acronym for First-In-First-Out. Elements (or data) are added to the queue usually via a function called **push()**, and then elements are removed at some specified time later with a **pop()**. Figure 12.1 shows the FIFO concept in action.

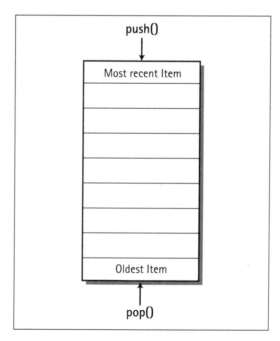

Figure 12.1
FIFO queue structure.

These **push**() and **pop**() functions provide all of the functionality we need for such a simple structure, and you can envision the implementation for a queue class if you were to write one. We would make a queue of some size, like an array, and we would add elements as pointers starting from the array[0] element until we reached array[n]. We would have a member variable that would be an index to keep track of where we were in this array while using the **push**() and **pop**() member functions to add and remove items. Simple enough, but there are some problems—what about the problem of using a fixed-size array when we don't know how many items are going to be added? It wouldn't be efficient for us to assume fixed sizes for our data, so a static array is a poor choice for a container within a queue. Enter STL.

Any STL container that supports the **push_back**() or **pop_front**() member functions can be "adapted" to work as a queue. Any container supporting **push_back**() and **pop_back**() can be "adapted" to work with a stack (a *stack* is the opposite of a queue, that is it's a Last-In-First-Out, or *LIFO*, architecture).

> *Note: Containers that can be used for a queue are the STL deque (pronounced deck—short for double-ended queue) and STL list. The list is a doubly linked list that STL has templatized. Of these two, the deque will provide us with superior performance, and lower overhead. When using an adapter, you will lose those iterators we've fallen in love with in earlier chapters—remember all the problems they solved for us? An adapter solves another set of problems, and accessing members is generally through **push()** and **pop()** members, not an iterator.*

Using the STL deque template gets around the need for using a static array, and we no longer need to rely on a fixed-size limit of data elements added to the queue. How do we apply this vector to the queue? With an STL adapter.

> *Note: Don't be afraid of using the deque container. We've covered a lot of ground in this book using the vector and map containers, and the deque is not going to be too overwhelming if you've used these other containers we introduced earlier. STL builds upon earlier concepts, and presents a commonality—where it makes sense—among its containers and iterators. If you use a deque directly, you still would have all the member functions available that the vector container we used previously had—plus you would have some new member functions for inserting members in the front rather than in the back (like the vector container did).*

STL provides adapters, which are templates that don't do anything by them-selves. However, when STL adapters are applied to a container class, they add some powerful capabilities. The two adapters available now are the stack and queue. Using this adapter, we can make a deque behave just like a stack or queue. We use the **push()** and **pop()** member functions and take advantage of the dynamic memory-resizing capabilities that we gain from STL. We also no longer have to store pointers in our queue. Rather, we can use anything that fits into an STL container—any C++ data structure or class that I can think of.

> *Note: A C++ structure and class are the same thing. Within a structure you can also add constructors and destructors, member functions, and so on.*

The adapters are normal templates, and need an STL container to give them any storage capability. Listing 12.1 shows the declaration and use of the queue adapter. It's powerful, flexible, and simple. Why did we use a deque rather than a vector for our data container? Our data was FIFO, and a deque offers con-stant time performance for insertions and removals at both ends of the container—beginning and end. A vector only offers constant performance with removals and insertions at the end—which would be perfect for a LIFO adapter. We're adding objects to the end of the container, and removing them off from the beginning using **pop()**, so the deque provides the best time performance. Does time really matter that much? Always. Time is particularly important when you are designing a server; the code must be efficient because several processes may be running concurrently, and good engineered code always includes time calculations and code profiling before you ship a finished product.

LISTING 12.1   SAMPLE USING THE STL QUEUE ADAPTER.

```
#include <deque.h>
#include <adapter.h>

void
main()
{
    queue< deque< int > >  ourQueue;
    ourQueue.push(12);
    ourQueue.push(37);
    ourQueue.push(24);
    ourQueue.push(44);
```

```
    // now move through the container - without an iterator
    while( !ourQueue.empty() )
        cout << ourQueue.pop() << endl;
} // main...

output is...
44
24
37
12
```

Now that we've briefly looked at the STL queue adapter and decided to use the deque container, we need to see how to apply this to a batch-processing application. One approach is to store a CGI/ISAPI code fragment on your server that you can instantiate remotely and that will display all orders from your "to be ordered" database table with check boxes. Another approach is to compare all merchandise that has arrived and process that against outstanding orders from your customer's "to be ordered" tables, and then process orders for all goods received.

This code fragment could then display the orders as they are processed via dynamically generated HTML, and total the orders using the **accumulate**() ANSI function as we did in earlier chapters. Why use a code fragment and not a Win32 application? For the following three reasons:

- HTML is portable, so we can process orders from any machine not dependent upon the OS.

- CGI/ISAPI are executed on the Web server, not a local machine.

- Quicker time to market. I'm a Win32 developer but can write a single fragment with HTML much faster than I can write a native Windows application.

You have no doubt considered using an iterator, and possibly a vector container. This solution will work, but I used the queue here for two reasons: Once an item is processed, it's removed from the queue via a call to **pop**()—and I could extend the queue while it's processing other items. Although both approaches will work, I preferred a queue here. Neither solution is more difficult than the other, but it came down to a conceptual-design decision: The queue followed a standard data structure that we normally use in such cases.

Batch Processing A Code Fragment

We'll write a code fragment that we'll call ShowOldOrders. This fragment will open an ODBC connection to our database, and process all orders that are stored within our "to be ordered" table. We've cleverly named this TBO and it is shown in Table 12.1 with another database table, InStock. When we fill a customer's order, we search for all items within the InStock table that match the TBO table's fields.

You will notice that Table 12.1 shows a TimeShipped field—this tells us when we processed the order and shipped it out to the customer. We are operating under the assumption that when you bill for the back-ordered items, you are planning on shipping them to your customer—doing otherwise is not advisable from a business perspective. There is no flag in the table to indicate whether or not the merchandise has shipped—such a flag would be redundant, as we'll keep the TimeShipped field empty until such a case happens. Table 12.2 shows a small database table that I've added to process new merchandise and its status as it arrives in our virtual store.

TABLE 12.1

TBO DATABASE TABLE.

Field	Data Type	Example
InventoryID	varchar	1234ABC
CookieID	integer	123445
Quantity	integer	12
TimeShipped	DateTime	August 31,1998:2:00am

TABLE 12.2

INSTOCK DATABASE TABLE.

Field	Data Type	Example
InventoryID	varchar	1234ABC
InStock	integer	12
DateArrived	DateTime	August 8,1997:4:31pm

The InStock table is relatively simple and parallels previous tables we've used earlier in this book. The InventoryID dentifies the merchandise, which we link to our inventory table (discussed in Chapter 9) as a key. The InStock field tells us how many of the items actually arrived at our warehouse. We will decrement this value by one for each TBO item that is filled. There will be cases in which we don't receive enough items to supply to all our customers. In these cases, our code needs to check all these values and count everything accurately. There's nothing more frustrating than receiving an incomplete order in the mail.

So, once we retrieve all matching items, we match this with the CreditInfo table and C++ structure that we used in the **CCreditCard** class in Chapter 11 so that we can accurately bill the client. When the merchandise and its payment are validated, we mark the order as filled, and your business will ship it to the customer. Hopefully the US Postal Service, UPS, or whoever ships it will get it to your customer.

The orders are processed identically to the code fragment in Chapter 11 that did realtime credit card transactions, except that here we place them in a queue and don't process the next transaction until the previous one is completed. Listing 12.2 shows the source code for ShowOldOrders.cpp.

LISTING 12.2   SHOWOLDORDERS.CPP.

```
//
//      File: ShowOldOrders.cpp
//      By:   Don Gaspar
//
//      This is the source for the batch order processor,
//      an example from Chapter 12
//      in the book, Visual Developer Web Commerce
//      Programming With Visual C++.
//      The publisher is the Coriolis Group.
//
//      The author is Don Gaspar
//
//      You may reach the author at: don@gigantor.com
//

// some standard headers we're going to need in here
#include <ostream.h>
#include <fstream.h>
#include <stdio.h>
```

```c
#include <stdlib.h>
#include <sql.h>

// now headers we've written
#include "CFormParser.hpp"
#include "CookieMonster.hpp"
#include "CreditCard.hpp"

// our header and footer file names
const char *cHeaderName =
    "c:\\inetpub\\gigantor\\games\\head.htm";
const char *cFooterName =
    "c:\\inetpub\\gigantor\\games\\foot.htm";
const char *cErrorFile =
    "c:\\inetpub\\gigantor\\games\\sadbob.htm";

// some SQL statements we'll need
const char *cSelectCustomerInfo =
    "SELECT ('name', 'expDate', 'cardNumber') FROM credit"
    " WHERE cookieID=%ld";
const char *cCheckInStock =
    "SELECT ('productID') FROM InStock WHERE"
    " inStock > 0 ";
const char *cUpdateInStock =
    "UPDATE InStock "
    "SET inStock = %ld "
    "WHERE productID=%s";
const char *cUpdateTBO =
    "UPDATE TBO "
    "SET timeShipped=%s "
    "WHERE cookieID=%ld";
const char *cSelectTBOInfo =
    "SELECT ('inventoryID','quantity','cookieID') FROM TBO"
    "WHERE productID=%s
const char *cUpdateWithTimeStamp =
    "UPDATE ('TimeStamp') FROM TBO "
    "SET timeStamp = %s "
    "WHERE cookieID=%ld AND productID=%s";

//
//    Function: BeginHeader
//    Purpose: Outputs the appropriate header information
//             to stdout for a
//             Web browser to display.
//    Arguments: inTitle, the title of the dynamic page
//               you are creating.
//
```

```cpp
void
BeginHeader(const char* inTitle)
{
    cout << "Content-type:TEXT/HTML\n\n" <<
        "<HTML><HEAD><TITLE>\n" <<
        inTitle << "\n</TITLE></HEAD><BODY>\n";
} // BeginHeader...

//
//    Function:  EndHeader
//    Purpose:   Outputs the delimiter tags corresponding to those set
//               by PrintHeader() for proper HTML display.
//    Arguments: None
//
void
EndHeader()
{
    cout << "</BODY></HTML>\n";
} // EndHeader...

//
//    StreamFile
//    Input:    char* which is the name of the file to use
//                  with path.
//    Purpose:  Opens the designated file and streams it out
//                  through the cout
//                  so the client's browser will get this dynamic
//                  HTML page.
//
void
StreamFile( const char* inFile )
{
    try
    {
        ifstream    file( inFile );   // file stream

        if ( !file )                  // if we don't get the file, then
            throw(-1);                // throw an exception

        char buffer[80];              // just a line of characters

        // here we loop through the file line by line until
        //    we hit the end
        //    sending all the data to cout.
        while ( file.getline(buffer,sizeof(buffer)) )
            cout << buffer;
```

```
        file.close();
    }

    catch(...)
    {
        cout << "<center><b>Couldn't locate the header file."
            "<br></center></b>";
    }
} // CGamesExtension::StreamFile...

//
//    function:    DoTimeStamp
//    purpose:     Adds some amount to the table since the item,
//                 was not approved
//    returns:     Nothing, exceptions are used for error handling.
//
void
UpdateInStock( ProductInfo *inProduct)
{
    // ODBC needed handles
    HENV    envH = NULL;
    HDBC    dbH = NULL;
    HSTMT   stmtH;

    try
    {
        THROWIF( SQLAllocEnv( &envH ) != SQL_SUCCESS );
        THROWIF( SQLAllocConnect( envH, &dbH ) != SQL_SUCCESS );

        RETCODE result = SQLConnect( dbH,(unsigned char *)"Games",6,
            (unsigned char *)"sa",3,NULL,0 );
        THROWIF( result != SQL_SUCCESS &&
            result != SQL_SUCCESS_WITH_INFO);
        SQLAllocStmt( dbH, &stmtH );

        // used for our SQL statements
        char    command[512];
        // check to see if they already exist in the database
        sprintf( command, cUpdateInStock,
            inProduct.qty,
            inProduct.inventoryID.c_str() );

        RETCODE result = SQLPrepare( m_stmtH,
            (unsigned char *)command, strlen( command ) + 1 );
        THROWIF(result == SQL_ERROR);
```

```
        // execute the SQL statement we made
        result = SQLExecute( m_stmtH );
        THROWIF( result != SQL_SUCCESS &&
            result != SQL_SUCCESS_WITH_INFO);

        // commit the addition to the database
        SQLTransact( m_envH, m_dbH, SQL_COMMIT );

        if ( stmtH )
            SQLFreeStmt( stmtH, SQL_CLOSE );
        if ( dbH )
            SQLFreeConnect( dbH );
        if( envH )
            SQLFreeEnv( envH );
    }

    catch(...)
    {
        SDWORD    err;
        char text[512], errText[512];
        SQLError(envH,dbH,stmtH,(unsigned char *)text,&err,
            (unsigned char *)errText,sizeof(errText),0);

        // show the error message
        cout << "<CENTER>" << errText << ": err = " <<
            text << "<BR></CENTER>";

        if ( stmtH )
            SQLFreeStmt( stmtH, SQL_CLOSE );
        if ( dbH )
            SQLFreeConnect( dbH );
        if( envH )
            SQLFreeEnv( envH );
    }
} // UpdateInstock...

//
//    function:    DoTimeStamp
//    purpose:     Called by an STL for_each()
//    returns:     Nothing, exceptions are used for error handling.
//
void
DoTimeStamp( ProductInfo &inProduct )
{
    char        buffer[64];
    time_t        now = time(NULL), later;
    tm            *timeInfo;
```

```
timeInfo = gmtime(&now);
strftime( buffer, sizeof(buffer), "%A, %d-%b-%Y %H:%M:%S GMT",
        gmtime(&now));

// ODBC needed handles
HENV    envH = NULL;
HDBC    dbH = NULL;
HSTMT   stmtH;

try
{
    THROWIF( SQLAllocEnv( &envH ) != SQL_SUCCESS );
    THROWIF( SQLAllocConnect( envH, &dbH ) != SQL_SUCCESS );

    RETCODE result = SQLConnect( dbH,(unsigned char *)"Games",6,
        (unsigned char *)"sa",3,NULL,0 );
    THROWIF( result != SQL_SUCCESS &&
        result != SQL_SUCCESS_WITH_INFO);
    SQLAllocStmt( dbH, &stmtH );

    // used for our SQL statements
    char    command[512];
    // check to see if they already exist in the database
    sprintf( command, cUpdateWithTimeStamp,
        buffer,
        inProduct.cookieID,
        inProduct.inventoryID.c_str() );

    RETCODE result = SQLPrepare( m_stmtH,
        (unsigned char *)command, strlen( command ) + 1 );
    THROWIF(result == SQL_ERROR);

    // execute the SQL statement we made
    result = SQLExecute( m_stmtH );
    THROWIF( result != SQL_SUCCESS &&
        result != SQL_SUCCESS_WITH_INFO);

    // commit the addition to the database
    SQLTransact( m_envH, m_dbH, SQL_COMMIT );

    if ( stmtH )
        SQLFreeStmt( stmtH, SQL_CLOSE );
    if ( dbH )
        SQLFreeConnect( dbH );
    if( envH )
        SQLFreeEnv( envH );
}
```

```
    catch(...)
    {
        SDWORD    err;
        char text[512], errText[512];
        SQLError(envH,dbH,stmtH,(unsigned char *)text,&err,
            (unsigned char *)errText,sizeof(errText),0);

        // show the error message
        cout << "<CENTER>" << errText << ": err = " <<
            text << "<BR></CENTER>";

        if ( stmtH )
            SQLFreeStmt( stmtH, SQL_CLOSE );
        if ( dbH )
            SQLFreeConnect( dbH );
        if( envH )
            SQLFreeEnv( envH );
    }
} // DoTimeStamp...


//
//    function:   BatchProcessOrders
//    purpose:    Batch process all orders stored in TBO tables
//                when the
//                merchandise arrives in the InStock DB table
//    returns:    Nothing, exceptions are used for error handling.
//
void
BatchProcessOrders()
{
    queue< deque< CustOrder > > tboQueue;
    CustOrder    item
    CustInfo     info;

    // load the queue
    MakeQueue( tboQueue );

    // now output

    while( !tboQueue.empty() )
    {
        try
        {
            item = tboQueue.pop();
            // get outta here on unfulfilled orders
            THROWIF( item.total <= 0.0 );
```

```
            // get the customer billing information
            // and set up in a CFormParser class
            // for CCreditCard to authenticate
            GetCustInfo( info, item.cookieID );

            CFormParser     form;
            form["cardNumber"] = info.cardNumber;
            form["name"] = info.name;
            form["expDate"] = info.expDate;
            form["startDate"] = info.startDate;

            // assumes exception on failure
            CCreditCard processIt( form );
            process.DoCreditCard();
            cout << "Customer " << info.name.c_str() <<
                ", card = " << info.cardNumber.c_str() <<
                ", for " << item.total <<
                " APPROVED<BR><BR>\n";
            // later in Appendix E we can email this to
            // the customer with CPonyExpress
            // update the db tables since this
            // merchandise shipped, so mark
            // the timestamp
            for_each( item.products.begin().
                item.products.end(),
                DoTimeStamp );
        }

    catch(...)
    {
        // we get an exception on authentication failure
        cout << "REJECTED Customer " << info.name.c_str() <<
            ", card = " << info.cardNumber.c_str() <<
            ", for " << item.total <<
            " REJECTED<BR><BR>\n";
        // later in Appendix E we can email this to
        // the customer with CPonyExpress
        // for now update the db tables since this
        // quantity of merchandise wasn't approved
        for_each( item.products.begin().
            item.products.end(),
            UpdateInStock );
    }
    } // while

} // BatchProcessOrders...
```

```
//
//    function:    HandleForm
//    purpose:     Creates a CFormParser object and passes the
//                     data received from a POST
//                     in cin to CFormParser. Checks length, etc.
//                     and throws and exception
//                     upon detection of any error.
//    returns:     Nothing, exceptions are used for error handling.
//
void
HandleForm()
{
    char *buffer;

    try
    {
        char *streamSize = getenv("CONTENT_LENGTH");
        THROWIF( !streamSize );
        long dataSize = atol( streamSize );
        THROWIF( !dataSize );

        buffer = new char[dataSize];
        cin >> buffer;

        // get our form data and parse
        CFormParser    ourParser( buffer );

        // go and process everything...
        DoBatchProcess();
        delete [] buffer;
        cout << "delete<BR>";
    }

    catch(...)
    {
        cout << "<CENTER><H1>Please enter all "
            " information requested."
            "</CENTER></H1><BR><BR><BR>";
        delete [] buffer;
    }
} // HandleForm...

//
//    well, we gotta start somewhere
//
void
main()
{
```

```
BeginHeader("Batch Credit Validation");

// go handle things for us
StreamFile( cHeaderName );
HandleForm();
StreamFile( cFooterName );

EndHeader();
} // main...
```

The only item of interest is that this code fragment is not threaded as we did in Chapter 11! Wait a minute, why wouldn't we want to thread it? Here, we want to process orders sequentially, and we display the results as they arrive from the code fragment. Adding threads does not simplify our task as there is only one point of execution of order processing—we're performing the transactions in bulk, not for various users concurrently connected to our Web server. The threaded model in Chapter 11 made sense for the earlier case, because we created and maintained a thread for each user who performed a transaction—this kept the transactions separate for each user, and simplified our design. Be sure to take a look at the use of the STL **for_each**() function and how it is used— here we call **for_each**() and pass a **begin**() and **end**() iterator, and a function pointer that is called for each item. The process is very simple, the effects very powerful. All we do is update the InStock quantities for a credit authorization failure, and on success we update the TimeStamp field of the TBO table.

If you are implementing a large commercial Web site, it will be hard to keep all merchandise in stock at all times—it can't be done. You will need to track items that are not in stock, or that cannot be shipped from the distributor immediately and batch process them later. Although this is not difficult, it is conceptually different than a realtime transaction and that's why we made the distinction in this chapter.

Summary

We covered STL adapters and queues, and applied them to batch processing orders that are designated as not being realtime. Although this worked logically, we could have accomplished the same task by using a vector container with an STL iterator. The choice is yours—it is a design decision.

We displayed the orders via the code fragment ShowOldOrders, and did so in dynamically generated HTML. We then selected which items we wanted to process and generated another form that sequentially displayed the transactions as they were processed, marking approvals and rejections. The batch was totaled at the end, so we know exactly how much money was transferred into our account.

Now that we've seen how to process transactions in realtime (in Chapter 11), and how to perform batch transactions, we need to implement a real Internet store. Chapter 13 explores how I implemented an online Foosball store that takes orders in realtime. We'll go over the entire HTML, and the final revision of the **CShoppingCart** class that we've used in earlier chapters.

13 THE FOOSBALL STORE

Great moments in science:
Einstein discovers that time is actually money.

Gary Larson, "The Far Side"

Throughout this book, we've been covering the Foosball store. Here, we'll complete the entire site, which we'll design to be operational 24×7. At the time the customer places his or her order, we'll collect payment for our merchandise in realtime and acknowledge the order. We will collect customer and credit card information ourselves via SSL so that we can be sure this information is secure.

The store we're covering here was actually implemented and you can visit it at **www.gigantor.com/games**. It's completely automated, so feel free to visit and order some items! We'll view the HTML, the database tables the information is stored in, and how they link together. We'll also show the final **CShoppingCart** class that includes calculating shipping costs and sales tax.

The Merchandise

Here, we need to discuss what merchandise the customer can purchase. We'll mainly sell Foosball tables, but we'll also sell accessories—such as those Bob's Big Boy guys that spin around on the tables, Foosballs, and other items. We'll also need to store

387

all the merchandise in our database. Figure 13.1 shows all the database tables and their relationship with each other.

When a customer first connects to our site, we'll display our main page, which shows what credit cards we accept, and describes our merchandise in general. On the bottom of the page, we put the Microsoft BackOffice logo to tell customers what software controls our site. Although this might seem like we're promoting Microsoft, it actually helps us. The customer probably hasn't heard of us before, but because he or she is most likely familiar with Microsoft, the Microsoft logo lends additional confidence to our site. Another logo we

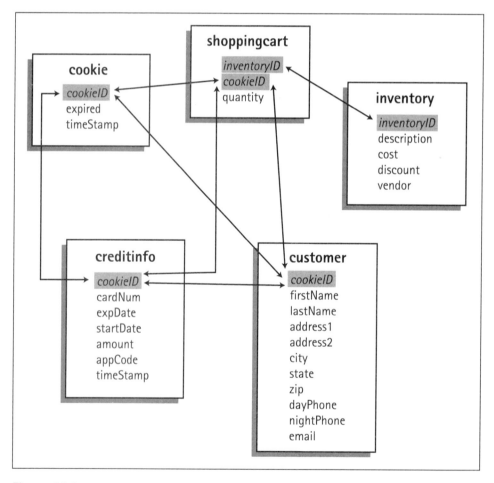

Figure 13.1
The Foosball store database tables.

insert is the Verisign secure certificate, which allows a customer to identify us through a third-party certificate authority. Figure 13.2 shows the main page of our online store.

Each item has a **inventoryID** in our database, and our HTML forms list this as the variable's NAME field. This might seem confusing to someone who didn't write the HTML, but the correlation to a field in our database is the perfect way to maintain this information. The first three pages of our Foosball site (Deluxe.htm, Economy.htm, and Arcade.htm) show the three kinds of Foosball tables for sale (see Figures 13.3, 13.4, and 13.5). The HTML source code for these pages is shown in Listings 13.1, 13.2, and 13.3.

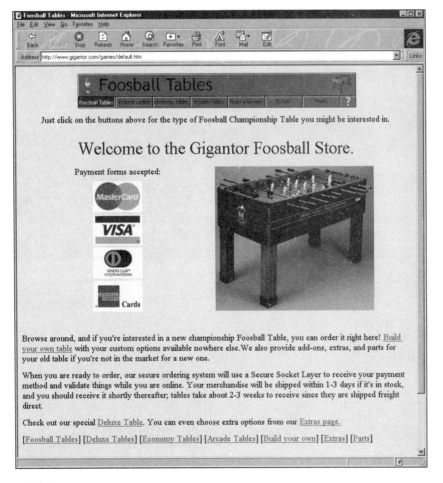

Figure 13.2
The Foosball store home page.

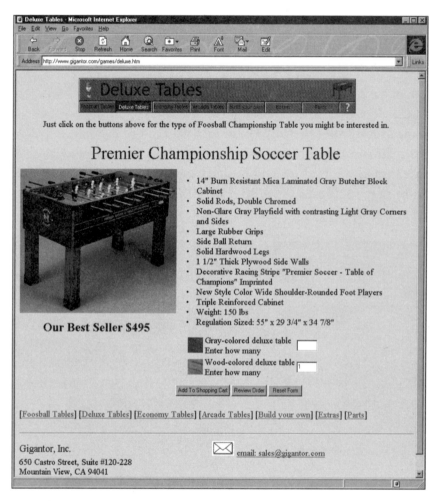

Figure 13.3
Deluxe Foosball tables.

LISTING 13.1   DELUXE.HTM.

```
<!DOCTYPE HTML PUBLIC "-//W3C//DTD HTML 3.2//EN">
<HTML>
<HEAD>
<TITLE>Deluxe Tables</TITLE>
<META NAME="Generator" " CONTENT="Built using
    BBEdit 4.02 on the Macintosh">
</HEAD>


<BODY BGCOLOR="#DDDDDD" LINK="#0000EE" VLINK="#EE0000"
    TEXT="#000000">
<FORM ACTION="/scripts/cgishoppingcart.exe" METHOD=POST>
```

```
<CENTER>
<TABLE BORDER=0 CELLSPACING=0 CELLPADDING=0>
<TR>
<TD COLSPAN=8>
<IMG HEIGHT=48 WIDTH=595 SRC="Header2.gif" BORDER=0
    ALT="Deluxe Tables">
</TD>
</TR>

<TR>
<TD WIDTH=80>
<A HREF="default.htm">
<IMG HEIGHT=24 WIDTH=80 SRC="OneOff.gif" BORDER=0
    ALT="Foosball Tables">
</A>
</TD>

<TD WIDTH=80>
<A HREF="deluxe.htm">
<IMG HEIGHT=24 WIDTH=80 SRC="TwoOn.gif" BORDER=0
    ALT="Deluxe Tables">
</A>
</TD>

<TD WIDTH=80>
<A HREF="economy.htm">
<IMG HEIGHT=24 WIDTH=80 SRC="ThreeOff.gif" BORDER=0
    ALT="Economy Tables">
</A>
</TD>

<TD WIDTH=80>
<A HREF="arcade.htm">
<IMG HEIGHT=24 WIDTH=80 SRC="FourOff.gif" BORDER=0
    ALT="Arcade Tables">
</A>
</TD>

<TD WIDTH=80>
<A HREF="build.htm">
<IMG HEIGHT=24 WIDTH=80 SRC="FiveOff.gif" BORDER=0
    ALT="Build your own">
</A>
</TD>

<TD WIDTH=80>
<A HREF="extras1.htm">
```

```
<IMG HEIGHT=24 WIDTH=80 SRC="SixOff.gif" BORDER=0
    ALT="Extras">
</A>
</TD>

<TD WIDTH=80>
<A HREF="parts.htm">
<IMG HEIGHT=24 WIDTH=80 SRC="SevenOff.gif" BORDER=0
    ALT="Parts">
</A>
</TD>

<TD WIDTH=35>
<A HREF="fooshelp.htm">
<IMG HEIGHT=24 WIDTH=35 SRC="HelpOff.gif" BORDER=0
    ALT="Help!">
</A>
</TD>
</TR>

</TABLE>
</CENTER>

<CENTER>
<P>Just click on the buttons above for the type of Foosball
Championship Table you might be interested in.
<br>
<br>
<br>

<FONT SIZE="+3">Premier Championship Soccer Table</FONT>
<br>
</CENTER>

<TABLE CELLPADDING=0 CELLSPACING=0 BORDER=0 WIDTH=100%>

   <TR>
    <TD HEIGHT=10></TD>
    </TR>

<TR VALIGN="top" ALIGN="left">
<TD>
<IMG HEIGHT=300 WIDTH=340 SRC="FB1.jpg" BORDER=0
    ALT="Deluxe Foosball Picture" >
<p>
```

```
<CENTER>
<B>
<FONT SIZE="+2">
Our Best Seller $495
</FONT>
</B>

</CENTER>
</TD>

<TD>

<UL TYPE="DISC">

<LI>
14&quot; Burn Resistant Mica Laminated Gray Butcher Block Cabinet
</LI>

<LI>
Solid Rods, Double Chromed
</LI>

<LI>
Non-Glare Gray Playfield with contrasting Light Gray
    Corners and Sides
</LI>

<LI>
Large Rubber Grips
</LI>

<LI>
Side Ball Return
</LI>

<LI>
Solid Hardwood Legs
</LI>

<LI>
1 1/2&quot; Thick Plywood Side Walls
</LI>

<LI>
Decorative Racing Stripe &quot;Premier Soccer - Table of
    Champions&quot; Imprinted
</LI>
```

```
<LI>
New Style Color Wide Shoulder-Rounded Foot Players
</LI>

<LI>
Triple Reinforced Cabinet
</LI>

<LI>
Weight: 150 lbs
</LI>

<LI>
Regulation Sized: 55&quot; x 29 3/4&quot; x 34 7/8&quot;
</LI>

</UL>
<P>

<TABLE>
<TR>
<TD WIDTH=20></TD>
<TD><IMG HEIGHT=32 WIDTH=32 SRC="swatchg.jpg" BORDER=0
    ALT="Gray-colored swatch"></TD>
<TD>Gray-colored deluxe table<br>Enter how many</TD>
<TD><INPUT TYPE="text" NAME="26-131" VALUE="" SIZE=5
    MAXLENGTH=1></TD>
</TR>

<TR>
<TD WIDTH=20></TD>
<TD><IMG HEIGHT=32 WIDTH=32 SRC="swatchw.jpg" BORDER=0
    ALT="Wood-colored swatch"></TD>
<TD>Wood-colored deluxe table<br>Enter how many</TD>
<TD><INPUT TYPE="text" NAME="26-130" VALUE="1" SIZE=5
    MAXLENGTH=1></TD>
</TR>
</TABLE>

<p>
<INPUT TYPE="submit" NAME="task" VALUE="Add To Shopping Cart">
<INPUT TYPE="submit" NAME="task" VALUE="Review Order" >
<INPUT TYPE="reset" NAME="" VALUE="Reset Form">
</TD>

</TR>
</TABLE>
```

```
<br>
<br>

[<A HREF="default.htm">Foosball Tables</A>]
[<A HREF="deluxe.htm">Deluxe Tables</A>]
[<A HREF="economy.htm">Economy Tables</A>]
[<A HREF="arcade.htm">Arcade Tables</A>]
[<A HREF="build.htm">Build your own</A>]
[<A HREF="extras1.htm">Extras</A>]
[<A HREF="parts.htm">Parts</A>]
<p>

<HR>

<TABLE CELLPADDING=0 CELLSPACING=0 BORDER=0 WIDTH=100%>

    <TR VALIGN="middle" ALIGN="left">
     <TD WIDTH=50%>
         <FONT SIZE="+1">Gigantor, Inc.</FONT>
     </TD>

     <TD WIDTH=50%><IMG HEIGHT=31 WIDTH=47 SRC="Envelope.gif"
         BORDER=0 ALT="Envelope Picture">
     <A HREF="mailto: sales@gigantor.com">email:
         sales@gigantor.com</A></TD>
    </TR>

     <TR>
     <TD>650 Castro Street, Suite #120-228</TD>
     </TR>

     <TR>
     <TD>Mountain View, CA 94041</TD>
     </TR>

     <TR>
     <TD>Phone: (800) 408-6600</TD>
     </TR>

</TABLE>

</FORM>
</BODY>
</HTML>
```

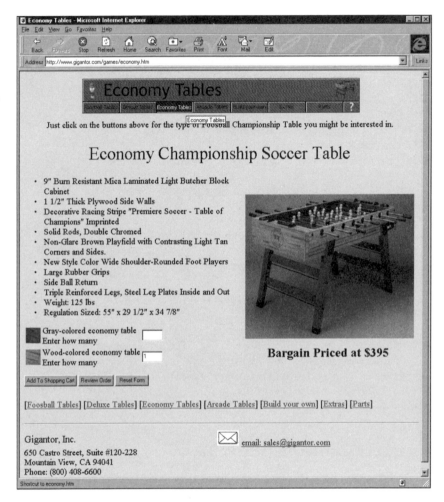

Figure 13.4
Economy Foosball tables.

LISTING 13.2   ECONOMY.HTM.

```
<!DOCTYPE HTML PUBLIC "-//W3C//DTD HTML 3.2//EN">

<HTML>
<HEAD>
<TITLE>Economy Tables</TITLE>
<META NAME="Generator" " CONTENT="Built using
    BBEdit 4.02 on the Macintosh">
</HEAD>
```

```
<BODY BGCOLOR="#DDDDDD" LINK="#0000EE" VLINK="#EE0000"
    TEXT="#000000">
<FORM ACTION="/scripts/cgishoppingcart.exe" METHOD=POST>

<CENTER>
<TABLE BORDER=0 CELLSPACING=0 CELLPADDING=0>
<TR>
<TD COLSPAN=8>
<IMG HEIGHT=48 WIDTH=595 SRC="Header3.gif" BORDER=0
    ALT="Economy Tables">
</TD>
</TR>

<TR>
<TD WIDTH=80>
<A HREF="default.htm">
<IMG HEIGHT=24 WIDTH=80 SRC="OneOff.gif" BORDER=0
    ALT="Foosball Tables">
</A>
</TD>

<TD WIDTH=80>
<A HREF="deluxe.htm">
<IMG HEIGHT=24 WIDTH=80 SRC="TwoOff.gif" BORDER=0
    ALT="Deluxe Tables">
</A>
</TD>

<TD WIDTH=80>
<A HREF="economy.htm">
<IMG HEIGHT=24 WIDTH=80 SRC="ThreeOn.gif" BORDER=0
    ALT="Economy Tables">
</A>
</TD>

<TD WIDTH=80>
<A HREF="arcade.htm">
<IMG HEIGHT=24 WIDTH=80 SRC="FourOff.gif" BORDER=0
    ALT="Arcade Tables">
</A>
</TD>

<TD WIDTH=80>
<A HREF="build.htm">
<IMG HEIGHT=24 WIDTH=80 SRC="FiveOff.gif" BORDER=0
    ALT="Build your own">
```

```
</A>
</TD>

<TD WIDTH=80>
<A HREF="extras1.htm">
<IMG HEIGHT=24 WIDTH=80 SRC="SixOff.gif" BORDER=0
    ALT="Extras">
</A>
</TD>

<TD WIDTH=80>
<A HREF="parts.htm">
<IMG HEIGHT=24 WIDTH=80 SRC="SevenOff.gif" BORDER=0
    ALT="Parts">
</A>
</TD>

<TD WIDTH=35>
<A HREF="fooshelp.htm">
<IMG HEIGHT=24 WIDTH=35 SRC="HelpOff.gif" BORDER=0
    ALT="Help!">
</A>
</TD>
</TR>
</TABLE>
</CENTER>

<CENTER>
<P>Just click on the buttons above for the type of Foosball
Championship Table you might be interested in.
<br>
<br>
<br>
<FONT SIZE="+3">Economy Championship Soccer Table</FONT>
<br>
</CENTER>

<TABLE CELLPADDING=0 CELLSPACING=0 BORDER=0 WIDTH=100%>

<TR>
<TD HEIGHT=10></TD>
</TR>

<TR>
<TD>

<UL TYPE="DISC">
```

```
<LI>
9&quot; Burn Resistant Mica Laminated Light Butcher Block Cabinet
</LI>

<LI>
1 1/2&quot; Thick Plywood Side Walls
</LI>

<LI>
Decorative Racing Stripe &quot;Premiere Soccer -
Table of Champions&quot; Imprinted
</LI>

<LI>
Solid Rods, Double Chromed
</LI>

<LI>
Non-Glare Brown Playfield with Contrasting Light Tan 
    Corners and Sides.
</LI>

<LI>
New Style Color Wide Shoulder-Rounded Foot Players
</LI>

<LI>
Large Rubber Grips
</LI>

<LI>
Side Ball Return
</LI>

<LI>
Triple Reinforced Legs, Steel Leg Plates Inside and Out
</LI>

<LI>
Weight: 125 lbs
</LI>

<LI>
Regulation Sized: 55&quot; x 29 1/2&quot; x 34 7/8&quot;
</LI>
```

```
</UL>

<TABLE>
<TR>
<TD><IMG HEIGHT=32 WIDTH=32 SRC="swatchg.jpg" BORDER=0
    ALT="Gray-colored swatch"></TD>
<TD>Gray-colored economy table<br>Enter how many</TD>
<TD><INPUT TYPE="text" NAME="26-129" VALUE="" SIZE=5
    MAXLENGTH=1></TD>
</TR>

<TR>
<TD><IMG HEIGHT=32 WIDTH=32 SRC="swatchw.jpg" BORDER=0
    ALT="Wood-colored swatch"></TD>
<TD>Wood-colored economy table<br>Enter how many</TD>
<TD><INPUT TYPE="text" NAME="26-128" VALUE="1" SIZE=5
    MAXLENGTH=1></TD>
</TR>
</TABLE>


<p>
<INPUT TYPE="submit" NAME="task" VALUE="Add To Shopping Cart" >
<INPUT TYPE="submit" NAME="task" VALUE="Review Order" >
<INPUT TYPE="reset" NAME="" VALUE="Reset Form">
</TD>

<TD>
<IMG HEIGHT=300 WIDTH=360 SRC="FB3.jpg" BORDER=0
    ALT="Economy Foosball Picture" >

<P>
<CENTER>
<B>
<FONT SIZE="+2">Bargain Priced at $395
</FONT>
</B>
</CENTER>
</TD>
</TR>
</TABLE>


<br>
<br>
```

```
[<A HREF="default.htm">Foosball Tables</A>]
[<A HREF="deluxe.htm">Deluxe Tables</A>]
[<A HREF="economy.htm">Economy Tables</A>]
[<A HREF="arcade.htm">Arcade Tables</A>]
[<A HREF="build.htm">Build your own</A>]
[<A HREF="extras1.htm">Extras</A>]
[<A HREF="parts.htm">Parts</A>]
<p>

<HR>

<TABLE CELLPADDING=0 CELLSPACING=0 BORDER=0 WIDTH=100%>

   <TR VALIGN="middle" ALIGN="left">
    <TD WIDTH=50%>
        <FONT SIZE="+1">Gigantor, Inc.</FONT>
    </TD>

    <TD WIDTH=50%><IMG HEIGHT=31 WIDTH=47 SRC="Envelope.gif"
        BORDER=0 ALT="Envelope Picture">
    <A HREF="mailto: sales@gigantor.com">email:
        sales@gigantor.com</A></TD>
   </TR>

   <TR>
   <TD>650 Castro Street, Suite #120-228</TD>
   </TR>

   <TR>
   <TD>Mountain View, CA 94041</TD>
   </TR>

   <TR>
   <TD>Phone: (800) 408-6600</TD>
   </TR>
</TABLE>

</FORM>
</BODY>
</HTML>
```

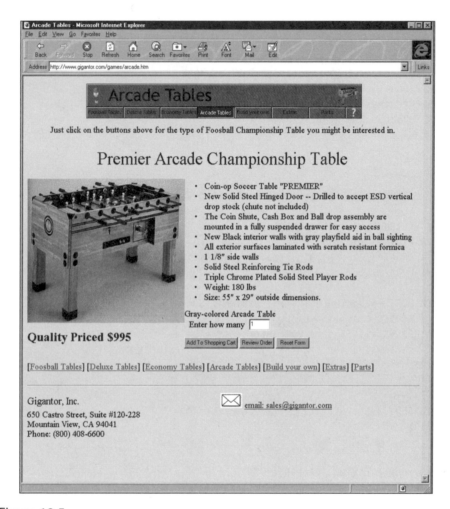

Figure 13.5
Arcade Foosball tables.

LISTING 13.3   ARCADE.HTM.

```
<!DOCTYPE HTML PUBLIC "-//W3C//DTD HTML 3.2//EN">

<HTML>
<HEAD>
<TITLE>Arcade Tables</TITLE>
<META NAME="Generator" " CONTENT="Built using
    BBEdit 4.02 on the Macintosh">
</HEAD>
```

```
<BODY BGCOLOR="#DDDDDD" LINK="#0000EE" VLINK="#EE0000"
    TEXT="#000000">
<FORM ACTION="/scripts/cgishoppingcart.exe" METHOD=POST>


<CENTER>
<TABLE BORDER=0 CELLSPACING=0 CELLPADDING=0>
<TR>
<TD COLSPAN=8>
<IMG HEIGHT=48 WIDTH=595 SRC="Header4.gif" BORDER=0
    ALT="Arcade Tables">
</TD>
</TR>

<TR>
<TD WIDTH=80>
<A HREF="default.htm">
<IMG HEIGHT=24 WIDTH=80 SRC="OneOff.gif" BORDER=0
    ALT="Foosball Tables">
</A>
</TD>

<TD WIDTH=80>
<A HREF="deluxe.htm">
<IMG HEIGHT=24 WIDTH=80 SRC="TwoOff.gif" BORDER=0
    ALT="Deluxe Tables">
</A>
</TD>

<TD WIDTH=80>
<A HREF="economy.htm">
<IMG HEIGHT=24 WIDTH=80 SRC="ThreeOff.gif" BORDER=0
    ALT="Economy Tables">
</A>
</TD>

<TD WIDTH=80>
<A HREF="arcade.htm">
<IMG HEIGHT=24 WIDTH=80 SRC="FourOn.gif" BORDER=0
    ALT="Arcade Tables">
</A>
</TD>

<TD WIDTH=80>
<A HREF="build.htm">
```

```
<IMG HEIGHT=24 WIDTH=80 SRC="FiveOff.gif" BORDER=0
    ALT="Build your own">
</A>
</TD>

<TD WIDTH=80>
<A HREF="extras1.htm">
<IMG HEIGHT=24 WIDTH=80 SRC="SixOff.gif" BORDER=0
    ALT="Extras">
</A>
</TD>

<TD WIDTH=80>
<A HREF="parts.htm">
<IMG HEIGHT=24 WIDTH=80 SRC="SevenOff.gif" BORDER=0
    ALT="Parts">
</A>
</TD>

<TD WIDTH=35>
<A HREF="fooshelp.htm">
<IMG HEIGHT=24 WIDTH=35 SRC="HelpOff.gif" BORDER=0
    ALT="Help!">
</A>
</TD>
</TR>
</TABLE>
</CENTER>

<CENTER>
<P>Just click on the buttons above for the type of Foosball
Championship Table you might be interested in.
<br>
<br>
<br>
<FONT SIZE="+3">Premier Arcade Championship Table</FONT>
<br>
</CENTER>

<TABLE CELLPADDING=0 CELLSPACING=0 BORDER=0>

<TR>
<TD HEIGHT=10></TD>
</TR>
```

```
<TR>
<TD>
<IMG HEIGHT=300 WIDTH=340 SRC="FB2.jpg" BORDER=0
    ALT="Premier Arcade Foosball Picture">
<P><B><FONT SIZE="+2">Quality Priced $995</FONT></B>
</TD>

<TD>
<UL TYPE="DISC">
<LI>
Coin-op Soccer Table &quot;PREMIER&quot;
</LI>

<LI>
New Solid Steel Hinged Door — Drilled to accept ESD
vertical drop stock (chute not included)
</LI>

<LI>
The Coin Shute, Cash Box and Ball drop assembly are
mounted in a fully suspended drawer for easy access
</LI>

<LI>
New Black interior walls with gray playfield aid in ball sighting
</LI>

<LI>
All exterior surfaces laminated with scratch resistant formica
</LI>

<LI>
1 1/8&quot; side walls
</LI>

<LI>
Solid Steel Reinforcing Tie Rods
</LI>

<LI>
Triple Chrome Plated Solid Steel Player Rods
</LI>

<LI>
Weight: 180 lbs
</LI>
```

```
<LI>
Size: 55&quot; x 29&quot; outside dimensions.
</LI>
</UL>
<p>
Gray-colored Arcade Table<br>
  Enter how many 
<INPUT TYPE="text" NAME="26-217" VALUE="1" SIZE=5
    MAXLENGTH=1 >
<p>

<INPUT TYPE="submit" NAME="task" VALUE="Add To Shopping Cart" >
<INPUT TYPE="submit" NAME="task" VALUE="Review Order" >
<INPUT TYPE="reset" NAME="" VALUE="Reset Form">

</TD>
</TR>
</TABLE>

<br>
<br>

[<A HREF="default.htm">Foosball Tables</A>]
[<A HREF="deluxe.htm">Deluxe Tables</A>]
[<A HREF="economy.htm">Economy Tables</A>]
[<A HREF="arcade.htm">Arcade Tables</A>]
[<A HREF="build.htm">Build your own</A>]
[<A HREF="extras1.htm">Extras</A>]
[<A HREF="parts.htm">Parts</A>]
<p>

<HR>

<TABLE CELLPADDING=0 CELLSPACING=0 BORDER=0 WIDTH=100%>

   <TR VALIGN="middle" ALIGN="left">
    <TD WIDTH=50%>
        <FONT SIZE="+1">Gigantor, Inc.</FONT>
    </TD>

    <TD WIDTH=50%><IMG HEIGHT=31 WIDTH=47
        SRC="Envelope.gif" BORDER=0 ALT="Envelope Picture">
    <A HREF="mailto: sales@gigantor.com">email:
        sales@gigantor.com</A></TD>
   </TR>
```

```
         <TR>
         <TD>650 Castro Street, Suite #120-228</TD>
         </TR>

         <TR>
         <TD>Mountain View, CA 94041</TD>
         </TR>

         <TR>
         <TD>Phone: (800) 408-6600</TD>
         </TR>
</TABLE>

</FORM>
</BODY>
</HTML>
```

As we already mentioned, we sell those ugly Bob's Big Boy guys that kick the balls around. Well, those plastic Foosball guys come in several colors, and the prices are all different. Figure 13.6 shows the Extras page where we sell this item in sets of 11. Other extras we're going to sell at this site include soccer balls, handles (grips), and beverage racks. We decided to implement a single page that contains multiple links to subpages, much like a stacked-pages concept. This allows a customer to connect to the Extras page, and then select any of the four available pages for items he or she wants. Figures 13.6, 13.7, 13.8, and 13.9 show all of these pages in detail.

These Extras pages all offer different items, and some require the customer to order certain quantities. The NAME of each variable is also the **inventoryID** from the database table. Listings 13.4, 13.5, 13.6, and 13.7 show the HTML for each page.

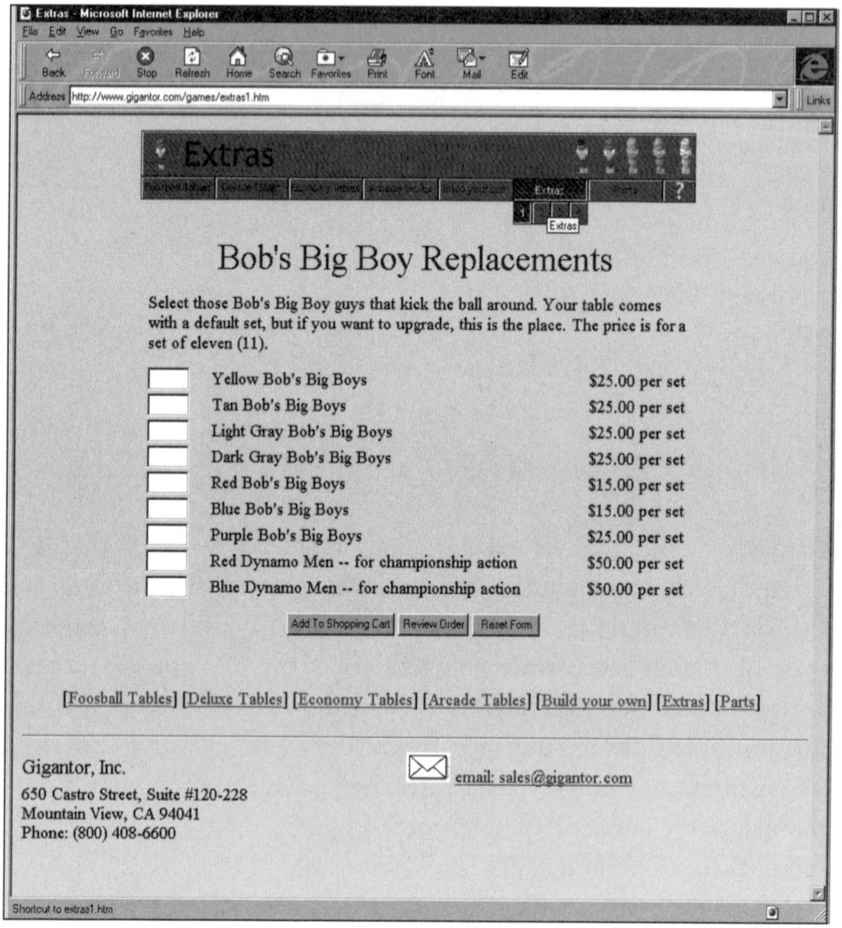

Figure 13.6
First Extras page.

LISTING 13.4   EXTRAS1.HTM.

```
<!DOCTYPE HTML PUBLIC "-//W3C//DTD HTML 3.2//EN">


<HTML>
<HEAD>
<TITLE>Extras</TITLE>
<META NAME="Generator" " CONTENT="Built using
    BBEdit 4.02 on the Macintosh">
</HEAD>


<BODY BGCOLOR="#DDDDDD" LINK="#0000EE" VLINK="#EE0000"
    TEXT="#000000">
<FORM ACTION="/scripts/cgishoppingcart.exe" METHOD=POST>
```

```
<CENTER>
<TABLE BORDER=0 CELLSPACING=0 CELLPADDING=0>
<TR>
<TD COLSPAN=8>
<IMG HEIGHT=48 WIDTH=595 SRC="Header6.gif" BORDER=0
    ALT="Extras">
</TD>
</TR>

<TR>
<TD WIDTH=80>
<A HREF="default.htm">
<IMG HEIGHT=24 WIDTH=80 SRC="OneOff.gif" BORDER=0
    ALT="Foosball Tables">
</A>
</TD>

<TD WIDTH=80>
<A HREF="deluxe.htm">
<IMG HEIGHT=24 WIDTH=80 SRC="TwoOff.gif" BORDER=0
    ALT="Deluxe Tables">
</A>
</TD>

<TD WIDTH=80>
<A HREF="economy.htm">
<IMG HEIGHT=24 WIDTH=80 SRC="ThreeOff.gif" BORDER=0
    ALT="Economy Tables">
</A>
</TD>

<TD WIDTH=80>
<A HREF="arcade.htm">
<IMG HEIGHT=24 WIDTH=80 SRC="FourOff.gif" BORDER=0
    ALT="Arcade Tables">
</A>
</TD>

<TD WIDTH=80>
<A HREF="build.htm">
<IMG HEIGHT=24 WIDTH=80 SRC="FiveOff.gif" BORDER=0
    ALT="Build your own">
</A>
</TD>

<TD WIDTH=80>
<A HREF="extras1.htm">
```

```
<IMG HEIGHT=24 WIDTH=80 SRC="SixOn.gif" BORDER=0
    ALT="Extras">
</A>
</TD>

<TD WIDTH=80>
<A HREF="parts.htm">
<IMG HEIGHT=24 WIDTH=80 SRC="SevenOff.gif" BORDER=0
    ALT="Parts">
</A>
</TD>

<TD WIDTH=35>
<A HREF="fooshelp.htm">
<IMG HEIGHT=24 WIDTH=35 SRC="HelpOff.gif" BORDER=0
    ALT="Help!">
</A>
</TD>
</TR>
</TABLE>
</CENTER>


<CENTER>
<TABLE BORDER=0 CELLSPACING=0 CELLPADDING=0>
<TR>
<TD WIDTH=400></TD>
<TD WIDTH=20>
<A HREF="Extras1.htm">
<IMG HEIGHT=24 WIDTH=20 SRC="Ext1On.gif" BORDER=0
    ALT="Extras page 1">
</A>
</TD>

<TD WIDTH=20>
<A HREF="Extras2.htm">
<IMG HEIGHT=24 WIDTH=20 SRC="Ext2Off.gif" BORDER=0
    ALT="Extras page 2">
</A>
</TD>

<TD WIDTH=20>
<A HREF="Extras3.htm">
<IMG HEIGHT=24 WIDTH=20 SRC="Ext3Off.gif" BORDER=0
    ALT="Extras page 3">
</A>
</TD>
```

```
<TD WIDTH=20>
<A HREF="Extras4.htm">
<IMG HEIGHT=24 WIDTH=20 SRC="Ext4Off.gif" BORDER=0
    ALT="Extras page 4">
</A>
</TD>

<TD WIDTH=115></TD>

</TR>
</TABLE>
</CENTER>

<CENTER>
<TABLE WIDTH=580>

<TR>
<TD COLSPAN=3 HEIGHT=10>
</TD>
</TR>

<TR>
<TD ALIGN=CENTER COLSPAN=3>
<FONT SIZE="+3">Bob's Big Boy Replacements</FONT>
</TD>
</TR>

<TR>
<TD COLSPAN=3 HEIGHT=10>
</TD>
</TR>


<TR>
<TD COLSPAN=3>
Select those Bob's Big Boy guys that kick the ball around.
Your table comes with a default set, but if you want to upgrade,
this is the place.  The price is for a set of eleven (11).
</TD>
</TR>

<TR>
<TD COLSPAN=3 HEIGHT=10>
</TD>
</TR>
```

```
<TR>
<TD WIDTH=40><INPUT TYPE="text" NAME="23-165" VALUE="" SIZE=5
    MAXLENGTH=2 ></TD>
<TD WIDTH=410>Yellow Bob's Big Boys</TD>
<TD ALIGN="right" WIDTH=130>$25.00 per set</TD>
</TR>

<TR>
<TD><INPUT TYPE="text" NAME="23-166" VALUE="" SIZE=5
    MAXLENGTH=2 ></TD>
<TD>Tan Bob's Big Boys</TD>
<TD ALIGN="right">$25.00 per set</TD>
</TR>

<TR>
<TD><INPUT TYPE="text" NAME="23-171" VALUE="" SIZE=5
    MAXLENGTH=2 ></TD>
<TD>Light Gray Bob's Big Boys</TD>
<TD ALIGN="right">$25.00 per set</TD>
</TR>

<TR>
<TD><INPUT TYPE="text" NAME="23-172" VALUE="" SIZE=5
    MAXLENGTH=2 ></TD>
<TD>Dark Gray Bob's Big Boys</TD>
<TD ALIGN="right">$25.00 per set</TD>
</TR>

<TR>
<TD><INPUT TYPE="text" NAME="23-113" VALUE="" SIZE=5
    MAXLENGTH=2 ></TD>
<TD>Red Bob's Big Boys</TD>
<TD ALIGN="right">$15.00 per set</TD>
</TR>

<TR>
<TD><INPUT TYPE="text" NAME="23-114" VALUE="" SIZE=5
    MAXLENGTH=2 ></TD>
<TD>Blue Bob's Big Boys</TD>
<TD ALIGN="right">$15.00 per set</TD>
</TR>

<TR>
<TD><INPUT TYPE="text" NAME="23-175" VALUE="" SIZE=5
    MAXLENGTH=2 ></TD>
<TD>Purple Bob's Big Boys</TD>
<TD ALIGN="right">$25.00 per set</TD>
</TR>
```

```
<TR>
<TD><INPUT TYPE="text" NAME="48-3511" VALUE="" SIZE=5
    MAXLENGTH=2 ></TD>
<TD>Red Dynamo Men — for championship action</TD>
<TD ALIGN="right">$50.00 per set</TD>
</TR>

<TR>
<TD><INPUT TYPE="text" NAME="48-3521" VALUE="" SIZE=5
    MAXLENGTH=2 ></TD>
<TD>Blue Dynamo Men — for championship action</TD>
<TD ALIGN="right">$50.00 per set</TD>
</TR>

<TR>
<TD HEIGHT=10></TD>
</TR>

</TABLE>

<INPUT TYPE="submit" NAME="task" VALUE="Add To Shopping Cart" >
<INPUT TYPE="submit" NAME="task" VALUE="Review Order" >
<INPUT TYPE="reset" NAME="" VALUE="Reset Form">
</CENTER>
<br>
<br>
<br>
<br>
<CENTER>
[<A HREF="default.htm">Foosball Tables</A>]
[<A HREF="deluxe.htm">Deluxe Tables</A>]
[<A HREF="economy.htm">Economy Tables</A>]
[<A HREF="arcade.htm">Arcade Tables</A>]
[<A HREF="build.htm">Build your own</A>]
[<A HREF="extras1.htm">Extras</A>]
[<A HREF="parts.htm">Parts</A>]
<p>
</CENTER>
<HR>

<TABLE CELLPADDING=0 CELLSPACING=0 BORDER=0 WIDTH=100%>

   <TR VALIGN="middle" ALIGN="left">
    <TD WIDTH=50%>
        <FONT SIZE="+1">Gigantor, Inc.</FONT>
    </TD>

    <TD WIDTH=50%><IMG HEIGHT=31 WIDTH=47 SRC="Envelope.gif"
        BORDER=0 ALT="Envelope Picture">
```

```
    <A HREF="mailto: sales@gigantor.com">email:
        sales@gigantor.com</A></TD>
    </TR>

    <TR>
    <TD>650 Castro Street, Suite #120-228</TD>
    </TR>

    <TR>
    <TD>Mountain View, CA 94041</TD>
    </TR>

    <TR>
    <TD>Phone: (800) 408-6600</TD>
    </TR>
</TABLE>

</FORM>
</BODY>

</HTML>
```

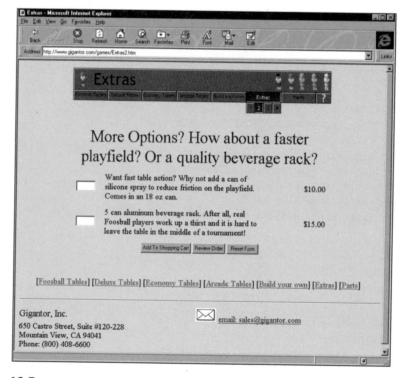

Figure 13.7
Second Extras page.

LISTING 13.5   EXTRAS2.HTM.

```
<!DOCTYPE HTML PUBLIC "-//W3C//DTD HTML 3.2//EN">

<HTML>
<HEAD>
<TITLE>Extras</TITLE>
<META NAME="Generator" " CONTENT="Built using
    BBEdit 4.02 on the Macintosh">
</HEAD>

<BODY BGCOLOR="#DDDDDD" LINK="#0000EE" VLINK="#EE0000"
    TEXT="#000000">
<FORM ACTION="/scripts/cgishoppingcart.exe" METHOD=POST>

<CENTER>
<TABLE BORDER=0 CELLSPACING=0 CELLPADDING=0>
<TR>
<TD COLSPAN=8>
<IMG HEIGHT=48 WIDTH=595 SRC="Header6.gif" BORDER=0 ALT="Extras">
</TD>
</TR>

<TR>
<TD WIDTH=80>
<A HREF="default.htm">
<IMG HEIGHT=24 WIDTH=80 SRC="OneOff.gif" BORDER=0
    ALT="Foosball Tables">
</A>
</TD>

<TD WIDTH=80>
<A HREF="deluxe.htm">
<IMG HEIGHT=24 WIDTH=80 SRC="TwoOff.gif" BORDER=0
    ALT="Deluxe Tables">
</A>
</TD>

<TD WIDTH=80>
<A HREF="economy.htm">
<IMG HEIGHT=24 WIDTH=80 SRC="ThreeOff.gif" BORDER=0
    ALT="Economy Tables">
</A>
</TD>

<TD WIDTH=80>
<A HREF="arcade.htm">
```

```
<IMG HEIGHT=24 WIDTH=80 SRC="FourOff.gif" BORDER=0
    ALT="Arcade Tables">
</A>
</TD>

<TD WIDTH=80>
<A HREF="build.htm">
<IMG HEIGHT=24 WIDTH=80 SRC="FiveOff.gif" BORDER=0
    ALT="Build your own">
</A>
</TD>

<TD WIDTH=80>
<A HREF="extras1.htm">
<IMG HEIGHT=24 WIDTH=80 SRC="SixOn.gif" BORDER=0
    ALT="Extras">
</A>
</TD>

<TD WIDTH=80>
<A HREF="parts.htm">
<IMG HEIGHT=24 WIDTH=80 SRC="SevenOff.gif" BORDER=0
    ALT="Parts">
</A>
</TD>

<TD WIDTH=35>
<A HREF="fooshelp.htm">
<IMG HEIGHT=24 WIDTH=35 SRC="HelpOff.gif" BORDER=0
    ALT="Help!">
</A>
</TD>
</TR>
</TABLE>
</CENTER>

<CENTER>
<TABLE BORDER=0 CELLSPACING=0 CELLPADDING=0>
<TR>
<TD WIDTH=400></TD>
<TD WIDTH=20>
<A HREF="Extras1.htm">
<IMG HEIGHT=24 WIDTH=20 SRC="Ext1Off.gif" BORDER=0
    ALT="Extras page 1">
</A>
</TD>
```

```
<TD WIDTH=20>
<A HREF="Extras2.htm">
<IMG HEIGHT=24 WIDTH=20 SRC="Ext20n.gif" BORDER=0
    ALT="Extras page 2">
</A>
</TD>

<TD WIDTH=20>
<A HREF="Extras3.htm">
<IMG HEIGHT=24 WIDTH=20 SRC="Ext30ff.gif" BORDER=0
    ALT="Extras page 3">
</A>
</TD>

<TD WIDTH=20>
<A HREF="Extras4.htm">
<IMG HEIGHT=24 WIDTH=20 SRC="Ext40ff.gif" BORDER=0
    ALT="Extras page 4">
</A>
</TD>

<TD WIDTH=115></TD>

</TR>
</TABLE>
</CENTER>

<CENTER>
<TABLE WIDTH=580>

<TR>
<TD COLSPAN=3 HEIGHT=30>
</TD>
</TR>

<TR>
<TD ALIGN=CENTER COLSPAN=3>
<FONT SIZE="+3">
More Options? How about a faster playfield? Or a quality
    beverage rack?
</FONT>
</TD>
</TR>

<TR>
<TD COLSPAN=3 HEIGHT=10>
</TD>
</TR>
```

```
<TR>
<TD ALIGN="top" WIDTH=40><INPUT TYPE="text" NAME="23-135"
    VALUE="" SIZE=5 MAXLENGTH=2 ></TD>
<TD WIDTH=410>Want fast table action? Why not add a can of silicone
spray to reduce friction on the playfield. Comes in an
    18 oz can.</TD>
<TD ALIGN="right" WIDTH=130>$10.00</TD>
</TR>

<TR>
<TD COLSPAN=3 HEIGHT=10>
</TD>
</TR>

<TR>
<TD ALIGN="top" WIDTH=40><INPUT TYPE="text" NAME="23-147"
    VALUE="" SIZE=5 MAXLENGTH=2 ></TD>
<TD WIDTH=410>5 can aluminum beverage rack.
    After all, real Foosball
    players work up a thirst and it is hard to leave the table
    in the middle of a
    tournament!</TD>
<TD ALIGN="right" WIDTH=130>$15.00</TD>
</TR>

<TR>
<TD COLSPAN=3 HEIGHT=10>
</TD>
</TR>

</TABLE>

<INPUT TYPE="submit" NAME="task" VALUE="Add To Shopping Cart" >
<INPUT TYPE="submit" NAME="task" VALUE="Review Order" >
<INPUT TYPE="reset" NAME="" VALUE="Reset Form">

</CENTER>
<br>
<br>
<br>
<br>
<CENTER>
[<A HREF="default.htm">Foosball Tables</A>]
[<A HREF="deluxe.htm">Deluxe Tables</A>]
[<A HREF="economy.htm">Economy Tables</A>]
```

```
[<A HREF="arcade.htm">Arcade Tables</A>]
[<A HREF="build.htm">Build your own</A>]
[<A HREF="extras1.htm">Extras</A>]
[<A HREF="parts.htm">Parts</A>]
<p>
</CENTER>
<HR>

<TABLE CELLPADDING=0 CELLSPACING=0 BORDER=0 WIDTH=100%>

   <TR VALIGN="middle" ALIGN="left">
    <TD WIDTH=50%>
        <FONT SIZE="+1">Gigantor, Inc.</FONT>
    </TD>

    <TD WIDTH=50%><IMG HEIGHT=31 WIDTH=47 SRC="Envelope.gif"
        BORDER=0 ALT="Envelope Picture">
    <A HREF="mailto: sales@gigantor.com">email:
        sales@gigantor.com</A></TD>
   </TR>

    <TR>
    <TD>650 Castro Street, Suite #120-228</TD>
    </TR>

    <TR>
    <TD>Mountain View, CA 94041</TD>
    </TR>

    <TR>
    <TD>Phone: (800) 408-6600</TD>
    </TR>
</TABLE>

  </FORM>
  </BODY>

</HTML>
```

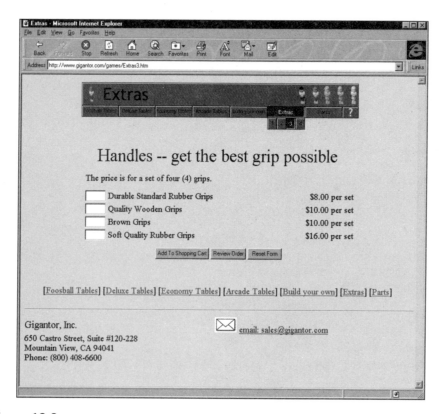

Figure 13.8
Third Extras page.

LISTING 13.6   EXTRAS3.HTM.

```
<!DOCTYPE HTML PUBLIC "-//W3C//DTD HTML 3.2//EN">

<HTML>
<HEAD>
<TITLE>Extras</TITLE>
<META NAME="Generator" " CONTENT="Built using
    BBEdit 4.02 on the Macintosh">
</HEAD>

<BODY BGCOLOR="#DDDDDD" LINK="#0000EE" VLINK="#EE0000"
    TEXT="#000000">
<FORM ACTION="/scripts/cgishoppingcart.exe" METHOD=POST>

<CENTER>
<TABLE BORDER=0 CELLSPACING=0 CELLPADDING=0>
<TR>
```

```
<TD COLSPAN=8>
<IMG HEIGHT=48 WIDTH=595 SRC="Header6.gif" BORDER=0
    ALT="Extras">
</TD>
</TR>

<TR>
<TD WIDTH=80>
<A HREF="default.htm">
<IMG HEIGHT=24 WIDTH=80 SRC="OneOff.gif" BORDER=0
    ALT="Foosball Tables">
</A>
</TD>

<TD WIDTH=80>
<A HREF="deluxe.htm">
<IMG HEIGHT=24 WIDTH=80 SRC="TwoOff.gif" BORDER=0
    ALT="Deluxe Tables">
</A>
</TD>

<TD WIDTH=80>
<A HREF="economy.htm">
<IMG HEIGHT=24 WIDTH=80 SRC="ThreeOff.gif" BORDER=0
    ALT="Economy Tables">
</A>
</TD>

<TD WIDTH=80>
<A HREF="arcade.htm">
<IMG HEIGHT=24 WIDTH=80 SRC="FourOff.gif" BORDER=0
    ALT="Arcade Tables">
</A>
</TD>

<TD WIDTH=80>
<A HREF="build.htm">
<IMG HEIGHT=24 WIDTH=80 SRC="FiveOff.gif" BORDER=0
    ALT="Build your own">
</A>
</TD>

<TD WIDTH=80>
<A HREF="extras1.htm">
<IMG HEIGHT=24 WIDTH=80 SRC="SixOn.gif" BORDER=0
    ALT="Extras">
```

```
</A>
</TD>

<TD WIDTH=80>
<A HREF="parts.htm">
<IMG HEIGHT=24 WIDTH=80 SRC="SevenOff.gif" BORDER=0
    ALT="Parts">
</A>
</TD>

<TD WIDTH=35>
<A HREF="fooshelp.htm">
<IMG HEIGHT=24 WIDTH=35 SRC="HelpOff.gif" BORDER=0
    ALT="Help!">
</A>
</TD>
</TR>
</TABLE>
</CENTER>

<CENTER>
<TABLE BORDER=0 CELLSPACING=0 CELLPADDING=0>
<TR>
<TD WIDTH=400></TD>
<TD WIDTH=20>
<A HREF="Extras1.htm">
<IMG HEIGHT=24 WIDTH=20 SRC="Ext1Off.gif" BORDER=0
    ALT="Extras page 1">
</A>
</TD>

<TD WIDTH=20>
<A HREF="Extras2.htm">
<IMG HEIGHT=24 WIDTH=20 SRC="Ext2Off.gif" BORDER=0
    ALT="Extras page 2">
</A>
</TD>

<TD WIDTH=20>
<A HREF="Extras3.htm">
<IMG HEIGHT=24 WIDTH=20 SRC="Ext3On.gif" BORDER=0
    ALT="Extras page 3">
</A>
</TD>

<TD WIDTH=20>
<A HREF="Extras4.htm">
```

```
<IMG HEIGHT=24 WIDTH=20 SRC="Ext4Off.gif" BORDER=0
    ALT="Extras page 4">
</A>
</TD>

<TD WIDTH=115></TD>

</TR>
</TABLE>
</CENTER>

<CENTER>
<TABLE WIDTH=580>

<TR>
<TD COLSPAN=3 HEIGHT=30>
</TD>
</TR>

<TR>
<TD ALIGN=CENTER COLSPAN=3>
<FONT SIZE="+3">
Handles — get the best grip possible
</FONT>
</TD>
</TR>

<TR>
<TD COLSPAN=3 HEIGHT=10>
</TD>
</TR>

<TR>
<TD COLSPAN=3>
The price is for a set of four (4) grips.
</TD>
</TR>

<TR>
<TD COLSPAN=3 HEIGHT=10>
</TD>
</TR>

<TR>
<TD WIDTH=40><INPUT TYPE="text" NAME="23-122" VALUE="" SIZE=5
    MAXLENGTH=2 ></TD>
```

```
<TD WIDTH=410>Durable Standard Rubber Grips</TD>
<TD WIDTH=130 ALIGN="right">$8.00 per set</TD>
</TR>

<TR>
<TD WIDTH=40><INPUT TYPE="text" NAME="23-123" VALUE="" SIZE=5
    MAXLENGTH=2 ></TD>
<TD WIDTH=410>Quality Wooden Grips</TD>
<TD WIDTH=130 ALIGN="right">$10.00 per set</TD>
</TR>

<TR>
<TD WIDTH=40><INPUT TYPE="text" NAME="23-167" VALUE="" SIZE=5
    MAXLENGTH=2 ></TD>
<TD WIDTH=410>Brown Grips</TD>
<TD WIDTH=130 ALIGN="right">$10.00 per set</TD>
</TR>

<TR>
<TD WIDTH=40><INPUT TYPE="text" NAME="23-176" VALUE="" SIZE=5
    MAXLENGTH=2 ></TD>
<TD WIDTH=410>Soft Quality Rubber Grips</TD>
<TD WIDTH=130 ALIGN="right">$16.00 per set</TD>
</TR>

<TR>
<TD COLSPAN=3 HEIGHT=10>
</TD>
</TR>

</TABLE>

<INPUT TYPE="submit" NAME="task" VALUE="Add To Shopping Cart" >
<INPUT TYPE="submit" NAME="task" VALUE="Review Order" >
<INPUT TYPE="reset" NAME="" VALUE="Reset Form">

</CENTER>
<br>
<br>
<br>
<br>
<CENTER>
[<A HREF="default.htm">Foosball Tables</A>]
[<A HREF="deluxe.htm">Deluxe Tables</A>]
[<A HREF="economy.htm">Economy Tables</A>]
[<A HREF="arcade.htm">Arcade Tables</A>]
```

```
[<A HREF="build.htm">Build your own</A>]
[<A HREF="extras1.htm">Extras</A>]
[<A HREF="parts.htm">Parts</A>]
<p>
</CENTER>
<HR>

<TABLE CELLPADDING=0 CELLSPACING=0 BORDER=0 WIDTH=100%>

   <TR VALIGN="middle" ALIGN="left">
    <TD WIDTH=50%>
        <FONT SIZE="+1">Gigantor, Inc.</FONT>
    </TD>

    <TD WIDTH=50%><IMG HEIGHT=31 WIDTH=47 SRC="Envelope.gif"
        BORDER=0 ALT="Envelope Picture">
    <A HREF="mailto: sales@gigantor.com">email:
        sales@gigantor.com</A></TD>
   </TR>

    <TR>
    <TD>650 Castro Street, Suite #120-228</TD>
    </TR>

    <TR>
    <TD>Mountain View, CA 94041</TD>
    </TR>

    <TR>
    <TD>Phone: (800) 408-6600</TD>
    </TR>
</TABLE>

  </FORM>
  </BODY>

</HTML>
```

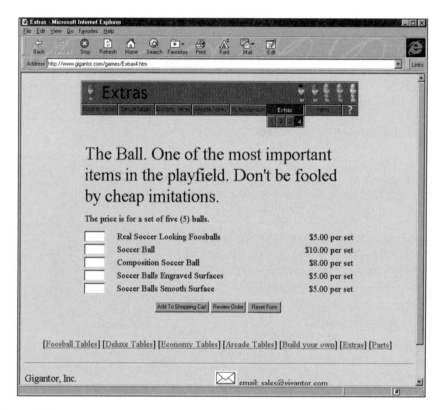

Figure 13.9
Fourth Extras page.

LISTING 13.7   EXTRAS4.HTM.

```
<!DOCTYPE HTML PUBLIC "-//W3C//DTD HTML 3.2//EN">

<HTML>
<HEAD>
<TITLE>Extras</TITLE>
<META NAME="Generator" " CONTENT="Built using
    BBEdit 4.02 on the Macintosh">
</HEAD>

<BODY BGCOLOR="#DDDDDD" LINK="#0000EE" VLINK="#EE0000"
    TEXT="#000000">
<FORM ACTION="/scripts/cgishoppingcart.exe" METHOD=POST>

<CENTER>
<TABLE BORDER=0 CELLSPACING=0 CELLPADDING=0>
<TR>
<TD COLSPAN=8>
```

```
<IMG HEIGHT=48 WIDTH=595 SRC="Header6.gif" BORDER=0
    ALT="Extras">
</TD>
</TR>

<TR>
<TD WIDTH=80>
<A HREF="default.htm">
<IMG HEIGHT=24 WIDTH=80 SRC="OneOff.gif" BORDER=0
    ALT="Foosball Tables">
</A>
</TD>

<TD WIDTH=80>
<A HREF="deluxe.htm">
<IMG HEIGHT=24 WIDTH=80 SRC="TwoOff.gif" BORDER=0
    ALT="Deluxe Tables">
</A>
</TD>

<TD WIDTH=80>
<A HREF="economy.htm">
<IMG HEIGHT=24 WIDTH=80 SRC="ThreeOff.gif" BORDER=0
    ALT="Economy Tables">
</A>
</TD>

<TD WIDTH=80>
<A HREF="arcade.htm">
<IMG HEIGHT=24 WIDTH=80 SRC="FourOff.gif" BORDER=0
    ALT="Arcade Tables">
</A>
</TD>

<TD WIDTH=80>
<A HREF="build.htm">
<IMG HEIGHT=24 WIDTH=80 SRC="FiveOff.gif" BORDER=0
    ALT="Build your own">
</A>
</TD>

<TD WIDTH=80>
<A HREF="extras1.htm">
<IMG HEIGHT=24 WIDTH=80 SRC="SixOn.gif" BORDER=0
    ALT="Extras">
</A>
</TD>
```

```
<TD WIDTH=80>
<A HREF="parts.htm">
<IMG HEIGHT=24 WIDTH=80 SRC="SevenOff.gif" BORDER=0
    ALT="Parts">
</A>
</TD>

<TD WIDTH=35>
<A HREF="fooshelp.htm">
<IMG HEIGHT=24 WIDTH=35 SRC="HelpOff.gif" BORDER=0
    ALT="Help!">
</A>
</TD>
</TR>
</TABLE>
</CENTER>

<CENTER>
<TABLE BORDER=0 CELLSPACING=0 CELLPADDING=0>
<TR>
<TD WIDTH=400></TD>
<TD WIDTH=20>
<A HREF="Extras1.htm">
<IMG HEIGHT=24 WIDTH=20 SRC="Ext10ff.gif" BORDER=0
    ALT="Extras page 1">
</A>
</TD>

<TD WIDTH=20>
<A HREF="Extras2.htm">
<IMG HEIGHT=24 WIDTH=20 SRC="Ext20ff.gif" BORDER=0
    ALT="Extras page 2">
</A>
</TD>

<TD WIDTH=20>
<A HREF="Extras3.htm">
<IMG HEIGHT=24 WIDTH=20 SRC="Ext30ff.gif" BORDER=0
    ALT="Extras page 3">
</A>
</TD>

<TD WIDTH=20>
<A HREF="Extras4.htm">
<IMG HEIGHT=24 WIDTH=20 SRC="Ext40n.gif" BORDER=0
    ALT="Extras page 4">
</A>
</TD>
```

```
<TD WIDTH=115></TD>

</TR>
</TABLE>
</CENTER>

<CENTER>
<TABLE WIDTH=580>

<TR>
<TD COLSPAN=3 HEIGHT=30>
</TD>
</TR>

<TR>
<TD COLSPAN=3>
<FONT SIZE="+3">
The Ball. One of the most important items in the playfield.
Don't be fooled by cheap imitations.
</FONT>
</TD>
</TR>

<TR>
<TD COLSPAN=3 HEIGHT=10>
</TD>
</TR>

<TR>
<TD COLSPAN=3>
The price is for a set of five (5) balls.
</TD>
</TR>

<TR>
<TD COLSPAN=3 HEIGHT=10>
</TD>
</TR>

<TR>
<TD WIDTH=40><INPUT TYPE="text" NAME="23-108" VALUE="" SIZE=5
    MAXLENGTH=2 ></TD>
<TD WIDTH=410>Real Soccer Looking Foosballs</TD>
<TD WIDTH=130 ALIGN="right">$5.00 per set</TD>
</TR>

<TR>
<TD WIDTH=40><INPUT TYPE="text" NAME="23-109" VALUE="" SIZE=5
    MAXLENGTH=2 ></TD>
```

```
<TD WIDTH=410>Soccer Ball</TD>
<TD WIDTH=130 ALIGN="right">$10.00 per set</TD>
</TR>

<TR>
<TD WIDTH=40><INPUT TYPE="text" NAME="23-110" VALUE="" SIZE=5
    MAXLENGTH=2 ></TD>
<TD WIDTH=410>Composition Soccer Ball</TD>
<TD WIDTH=130 ALIGN="right">$8.00 per set</TD>
</TR>

<TR>
<TD WIDTH=40><INPUT TYPE="text" NAME="23-111" VALUE="" SIZE=5
    MAXLENGTH=2 ></TD>
<TD WIDTH=410>Soccer Balls Engraved Surfaces</TD>
<TD WIDTH=130 ALIGN="right">$5.00 per set</TD>
</TR>

<TR>
<TD WIDTH=40><INPUT TYPE="text" NAME="23-112" VALUE="" SIZE=5
    MAXLENGTH=2 ></TD>
<TD WIDTH=410>Soccer Balls Smooth Surface</TD>
<TD WIDTH=130 ALIGN="right">$5.00 per set</TD>
</TR>

<TR>
<TD COLSPAN=3 HEIGHT=10>
</TD>
</TR>
</TABLE>

<INPUT TYPE="submit" NAME="task" VALUE="Add To Shopping Cart" >
<INPUT TYPE="submit" NAME="task" VALUE="Review Order" >
<INPUT TYPE="reset" NAME="" VALUE="Reset Form">
</CENTER>
<br>
<br>
<br>
<br>
<CENTER>
[<A HREF="default.htm">Foosball Tables</A>]
[<A HREF="deluxe.htm">Deluxe Tables</A>]
[<A HREF="economy.htm">Economy Tables</A>]
[<A HREF="arcade.htm">Arcade Tables</A>]
[<A HREF="build.htm">Build your own</A>]
[<A HREF="extras1.htm">Extras</A>]
[<A HREF="parts.htm">Parts</A>]
```

```
<p>
</CENTER>
<HR>

<TABLE CELLPADDING=0 CELLSPACING=0 BORDER=0 WIDTH=100%>

   <TR VALIGN="middle" ALIGN="left">
    <TD WIDTH=50%>
        <FONT SIZE="+1">Gigantor, Inc.</FONT>
    </TD>

    <TD WIDTH=50%><IMG HEIGHT=31 WIDTH=47 SRC="Envelope.gif"
        BORDER=0 ALT="Envelope Picture">
    <A HREF="mailto: sales@gigantor.com">email:
        sales@gigantor.com</A></TD>
   </TR>

    <TR>
    <TD>650 Castro Street, Suite #120-228</TD>
    </TR>

    <TR>
    <TD>Mountain View, CA 94041</TD>
    </TR>

    <TR>
    <TD>Phone: (800) 408-6600</TD>
    </TR>
</TABLE>

  </FORM>
  </BODY>

</HTML>
```

Custom Options

Some customers won't want to order the standard items on our pages. We'll provide a custom page where these customers can select all of their options and then get an immediate price quotation for their custom table. The customer may want the Deluxe Foosball Table and purple Bob's Big Boy soccer guys—whatever. All options are possible, so we need to write a code fragment that calculates prices for the customer and provides immediate feedback. Figure 13.10 shows the Custom Options page. You'll notice the Calculate Price button, which performs the submit action that retrieves the price for the custom table. Listing 13.8 shows the HTML for this form.

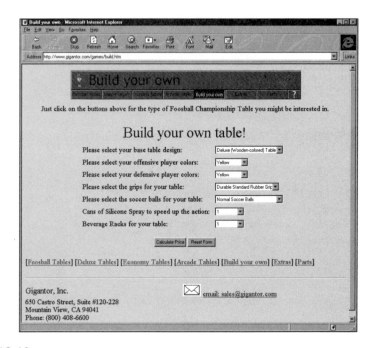

Figure 13.10
The Custom Options page.

Listing 13.8 Custom.htm.

```
<!DOCTYPE HTML PUBLIC "-//W3C//DTD HTML 3.2//EN">

<HTML>
<HEAD>
<TITLE>Build your own</TITLE>
<META NAME="Generator" " CONTENT="Built using
    BBEdit 4.02 on the Macintosh">
</HEAD>

<BODY BGCOLOR="#DDDDDD" LINK="#0000EE" VLINK="#EE0000"
    TEXT="#000000">
<FORM ACTION="/scripts/cgishoppingcart.exe" METHOD=POST>

<CENTER>
<TABLE BORDER=0 CELLSPACING=0 CELLPADDING=0>
<TR>
<TD COLSPAN=8>
<IMG HEIGHT=48 WIDTH=595 SRC="Header5.gif" BORDER=0
    ALT="Build your own">
</TD>
</TR>
```

```
<TR>
<TD WIDTH=80>
<A HREF="default.htm">
<IMG HEIGHT=24 WIDTH=80 SRC="OneOff.gif" BORDER=0
    ALT="Foosball Tables">
</A>
</TD>

<TD WIDTH=80>
<A HREF="deluxe.htm">
<IMG HEIGHT=24 WIDTH=80 SRC="TwoOff.gif" BORDER=0
    ALT="Deluxe Tables">
</A>
</TD>

<TD WIDTH=80>
<A HREF="economy.htm">
<IMG HEIGHT=24 WIDTH=80 SRC="ThreeOff.gif" BORDER=0
    ALT="Economy Tables">
</A>
</TD>

<TD WIDTH=80>
<A HREF="arcade.htm">
<IMG HEIGHT=24 WIDTH=80 SRC="FourOff.gif" BORDER=0
    ALT="Arcade Tables">
</A>
</TD>

<TD WIDTH=80>
<A HREF="build.htm">
<IMG HEIGHT=24 WIDTH=80 SRC="FiveOn.gif" BORDER=0
    ALT="Build your own">
</A>
</TD>

<TD WIDTH=80>
<A HREF="extras1.htm">
<IMG HEIGHT=24 WIDTH=80 SRC="SixOff.gif" BORDER=0
    ALT="Extras">
</A>
</TD>

<TD WIDTH=80>
<A HREF="parts.htm">
<IMG HEIGHT=24 WIDTH=80 SRC="SevenOff.gif" BORDER=0
    ALT="Parts">
```

```
</A>
</TD>

<TD WIDTH=35>
<A HREF="fooshelp.htm">
<IMG HEIGHT=24 WIDTH=35 SRC="HelpOff.gif" BORDER=0
    ALT="Help!">
</A>
</TD>
</TR>
</TABLE>
</CENTER>

<CENTER>
<P>Just click on the buttons above for the type of Foosball
Championship Table you might be interested in.
<br>
<br>
<br>
<FONT SIZE="+3">Build your own table!</FONT>
<br>
</CENTER>

<CENTER>
<TABLE CELLPADDING=0 CELLSPACING=0 BORDER=0 WIDTH=535>

<TR>
<TD HEIGHT=10></TD>
</TR>

<TR>
<TD><P>Please select your base table design:</TD>
<TD>
    <SELECT NAME="foosball">
    <OPTION VALUE="26-131">Deluxe (Gray) Table</OPTION>
    <OPTION VALUE="26-130" SELECTED>
        Deluxe (Wooden-colored) Table</OPTION>
    <OPTION VALUE="26-129">Economy (Gray) Table</OPTION>
    <OPTION VALUE="26-128">Economy (Wooden-colored) Table</OPTION>
    <OPTION VALUE="26-217">Arcade Premier Table</OPTION>
    </SELECT>
</TD>
</TR>

<TR>
<TD HEIGHT=10></TD>
</TR>
```

```
<TR>
<TD><P>Please select your offensive player colors:</TD>
<TD>
    <SELECT NAME="offense">
    <OPTION VALUE="48-3511">Red Dynamo</OPTION>
    <OPTION VALUE="48-3521">Blue Dynamo</OPTION>
    <OPTION VALUE="23-165" SELECTED WIDTH=15>Yellow</OPTION>
    <OPTION VALUE="23-166">Tan</OPTION>
    <OPTION VALUE="23-171">Light Gray</OPTION>
    <OPTION VALUE="23-172">Dark Gray</OPTION>
    <OPTION VALUE="23-175">Purple</OPTION>
    <OPTION VALUE="23-113">Red Regular</OPTION>
    <OPTION VALUE="23-114">Blue Regular</OPTION>
    </SELECT>
</TD>
</TR>

<TR>
<TD HEIGHT=10></TD>
</TR>

<TR>
<TD><P>Please select your defensive player colors:</TD>
<TD>
    <SELECT NAME="defense">
    <OPTION VALUE="48-3511">Red Dynamo</OPTION>
    <OPTION VALUE="48-3521">Blue Dynamo</OPTION>
    <OPTION VALUE="23-165" SELECTED WIDTH=15>Yellow</OPTION>
    <OPTION VALUE="23-166">Tan</OPTION>
    <OPTION VALUE="23-171">Light Gray</OPTION>
    <OPTION VALUE="23-172">Dark Gray</OPTION>
    <OPTION VALUE="23-175">Purple</OPTION>
    <OPTION VALUE="23-113">Red Regular</OPTION>
    <OPTION VALUE="23-114">Blue Regular</OPTION>
    </SELECT>
    </TD>
</TR>

<TR>
<TD HEIGHT=10></TD>
</TR>

<TR>
<TD><P>Please select the grips for your table:</TD>
<TD>
    <SELECT NAME="handles">
    <OPTION VALUE="23-122" SELECTED>Durable
        Standard Rubber Grips</OPTION>
```

```
    <OPTION VALUE="23-123">Quality Wooden Grips </OPTION>
    <OPTION VALUE="23-167">Brown Grips</OPTION>
    <OPTION VALUE="23-176">Soft Quality Rubber Grips </OPTION>
    </SELECT>
</TD>
</TR>

<TR>
<TD HEIGHT=10></TD>
</TR>

<TR>
<TD><P>Please select the soccer balls for your table:</TD>
<TD>
    <SELECT NAME="hits">
    <OPTION VALUE="23-108">Real Soccer Looking Foosballs</OPTION>
    <OPTION VALUE="23-109" SELECTED>Normal Soccer Balls</OPTION>
    <OPTION VALUE="23-110">Composition Soccer Ball</OPTION>
    <OPTION VALUE="23-111">Soccer Balls Engraved Surfaces</OPTION>
    <OPTION VALUE="23-112">Soccer Balls Smooth Surface</OPTION>
    </SELECT>
</TD>
</TR>

<TR>
<TD HEIGHT=10></TD>
</TR>

<TR>
<TD><P>Cans of Silicone Spray to speed up the action:</TD>
<TD>
    <SELECT NAME="23-135">
    <OPTION VALUE="one" SELECTED>1</OPTION>
    <OPTION VALUE="two">2</OPTION>
    <OPTION VALUE="three">3</OPTION>
    <OPTION VALUE="four">4</OPTION>
    <OPTION VALUE="five">5</OPTION>
    <OPTION VALUE="none">None</OPTION>
    </SELECT>
</TD>
</TR>

<TR>
<TD HEIGHT=10></TD>
</TR>

<TR>
<TD><P>Beverage Racks for your table:</TD>
```

```
<TD>
    <SELECT NAME="23-147">
    <OPTION VALUE="one" SELECTED>1</OPTION>
    <OPTION VALUE="two">2</OPTION>
    <OPTION VALUE="none">None</OPTION>
    </SELECT>
</TD>
</TR>

<TR>
<TD HEIGHT=10></TD>
</TR>

</TABLE>
<br>
<INPUT TYPE="submit" NAME="task" VALUE="Calculate Price" >
<INPUT TYPE="reset" NAME="" VALUE="Reset Form">
</CENTER>
</TR>

<br>
<br>

[<A HREF="default.htm">Foosball Tables</A>]
[<A HREF="deluxe.htm">Deluxe Tables</A>]
[<A HREF="economy.htm">Economy Tables</A>]
[<A HREF="arcade.htm">Arcade Tables</A>]
[<A HREF="build.htm">Build your own</A>]
[<A HREF="extras1.htm">Extras</A>]
[<A HREF="parts.htm">Parts</A>]
<p>

<HR>

<TABLE CELLPADDING=0 CELLSPACING=0 BORDER=0 WIDTH=100%>

    <TR VALIGN="middle" ALIGN="left">
    <TD WIDTH=50%>
        <FONT SIZE="+1">Gigantor, Inc.</FONT>
    </TD>

    <TD WIDTH=50%><IMG HEIGHT=31 WIDTH=47 SRC="Envelope.gif"
        BORDER=0 ALT="Envelope Picture">
    <A HREF="mailto: sales@gigantor.com">email:
        sales@gigantor.com</A></TD>
    </TR>
```

```
    <TR>
    <TD>650 Castro Street, Suite #120-228</TD>
    </TR>

    <TR>
    <TD>Mountain View, CA 94041</TD>
    </TR>

    <TR>
    <TD>Phone: (800) 408-6600</TD>
    </TR>
</TABLE>

</FORM>
</BODY>
</HTML>
```

After our code fragment processes the custom options, we'll generate a dynamic form that displays the results and shows all items that are needed to build the custom table. The price for these items is also shown, and is generated by calling a variation of the **CShoppingCart**'s class **RecalcOrder**() member. This new addition to the **CShoppingCart** class does not add the items to the customer's shopping cart unless he or she does so, or clicks on the Order Now button from the dynamic page we've created.

We now need to calculate shipping costs and sales tax for all orders. My business is in California, so if the order is shipped to a California resident, I need to charge 8.25 percent sales tax. I've accomplished the tax calculation by searching the customer table in our database and inspecting the state the customer listed—if it is "CA," then I add the tax. For shipping and handling, I add 15 percent, which is fairly standard for most businesses. For Foosball tables, I don't add shipping costs at all because these items are shipped from the factory directly to the customer and the freight company charges for the shipping costs. To calculate the shipping costs correctly, I wrote an STL comparator I called **isFoosballTable**() that I use with the STL **remove_if**() function. Here, I remove the item from the customer's order if it's a table, and use this vector to calculate the shipping costs that then exclude the Foosball tables from the calculation.

The **FromCalifornia**() member function tells me whether or not to add the tax multiplier, and if it is True we add it. The **GetOrderTotal**() member function gives me the total with tax and shipping. Listing 13.9 shows the source code for the final **CShoppingCart** class.

LISTING 13.9 SHOPPINGCART.CPP.

```cpp
//
//      File: CFormParser.hpp
//      By:    Don Gaspar
//
//      This is the source for translating and displaying
//      form variables from an example in Chapter 9,
//      expanded on in Chapters 11 and 13,
//      from the book Visual Developer Web Commerce
//      Programming With Visual C++.
//      The publisher is The Coriolis Group.
//
//      The author is Don Gaspar
//
//      You may reach the author at: don@gigantor.com
//

// standard headers we need all over
#include <stdio.h>
#include <stdlib.h>

// headers we've written and need
#include "CFormParser.hpp"
#include "ShoppingCart.hpp"
#include "CookieMonster.hpp"

// these are the various SQL queries we perform from
// this class, from this file only.
const char *cSQLInsertCmd = "INSERT INTO "
    "shoppingCart(cookieID,"
    " inventoryID, quantity) VALUES(%ld,'%s',%ld)";
const char *cSQLGetCartCmd = "SELECT quantity FROM "
    "shoppingCart WHERE cookieID=%ld AND inventoryID='%s'";
const char *cSQLUpdateCartCmd = "UPDATE shoppingCart"
    " SET quantity = %ld"
    " WHERE cookieID=%ld AND inventoryID='%s'";
const char *cSQLDeleteCartCmd = "DELETE FROM shoppingCart "
    " WHERE cookieID=%ld";
const char *cSQLDeleteCartItemCmd = "DELETE FROM shoppingCart "
    " WHERE cookieID=%ld AND inventoryID='%s'";
const char *cSQLDeleteCartQtyCmd = "DELETE FROM shoppingCart "
    " WHERE cookieID=%ld AND quantity < %ld";

const char *cSQLNewCookieCmd = "INSERT INTO "
    "cookie(expired) VALUES(0)";
const char *cSQLMaxCookieCmd = "SELECT MAX(cookieID) FROM cookie";
```

```c
const char *cSQLCheckCookieCmd = "SELECT cookieID FROM "
    "cookie WHERE cookieID=%ld";

const char *cSQLSelectCartCmd = "SELECT inventoryID, "
    "quantity FROM shoppingCart WHERE cookieID=%ld";

const char *cSQLSelectCatalogCmd = "SELECT * FROM inventory";

const char *cSQLGetZipCode = "SELECT zip "
    "FROM customer WHERE cookieID=%s";

const char *cSQLGetState = "SELECT state "
    "FROM customer WHERE cookieID=%s";


// code begins here

//
//    function:    CShoppingCart::CShoppingCart
//    purpose:     Constructor for the CShoppingCart class.
//                 Takes a CFormParser as input.
//                 Propagates exceptions out after
//                 displaying any appropriate errors.
//    returns:     Constructors can't return anything
//
CShoppingCart::CShoppingCart( CFormParser &inParser )
{
    try
    {
        m_parser = inParser;
        m_cookie = 0;
        m_envH = NULL;
        m_dbH = NULL;

        THROWIF( SQLAllocEnv( &m_envH ) != SQL_SUCCESS );
        THROWIF( SQLAllocConnect( m_envH, &m_dbH ) != SQL_SUCCESS );

        RETCODE result = SQLConnect( m_dbH,
            (unsigned char *)"Games",6,
            (unsigned char *)"sa",3,NULL,0 );
        THROWIF( result != SQL_SUCCESS &&
            result != SQL_SUCCESS_WITH_INFO);
        SQLAllocStmt( m_dbH, &m_stmtH );

        // make sure user has one, if not make a new one
        CheckCookie();
    }
```

```
    catch(...)
    {
        ShowSQLError();
        throw(-1);    // propagate to next catch...
    }
} // CShoppingCart::CShoppingCart...


//
//    function:    CShoppingCart::~CShoppingCart
//    purpose:     Destructor. Closes and frees any
//                 ODBC connections, etc. that we
//                 may have allocated
//    returns:     Constructors can't return anything
//
CShoppingCart::~CShoppingCart()
{
    // give a hoot, don't pollute
    if ( m_stmtH )
        SQLFreeStmt( m_stmtH, SQL_CLOSE );
    if ( m_dbH )
        SQLFreeConnect( m_dbH );
    if( m_envH )
        SQLFreeEnv( m_envH );
} // CShoppingCart::~CShoppingCart...


//
//    function:    CShoppingCart::ShowSQLError
//    purpose:     Sends the appropriate SQL error
//                 via cout.
//    returns:     Nothing
//
void
CShoppingCart::ShowSQLError()
{
    SDWORD    err;
    char text[512], errText[512];
    SQLError(m_envH,m_dbH,m_stmtH,(unsigned char *)text,&err,
        (unsigned char *)errText,sizeof(errText),0);

    // show the error message
    cout << "<CENTER>" << errText << ": err = " <<
        text << "<BR></CENTER>";
} // CShoppingCart::ShowSQLError...


//
//    function:    CShoppingCart::VerifyCookieInDB
//    purpose:     Verified m_cookie to make sure it's
//                 also in our database.
```

```
//     returns:    true if m_cookie is in the DB.
//
bool
CShoppingCart::VerifyCookieInDB()
{
    bool    memberResult = false;    //always the pessimist

    try
    {
        // if no exception is thrown, it's in the DB
        char command[256];
        sprintf( command, cSQLCheckCookieCmd, m_cookie );
        RETCODE result = SQLPrepare( m_stmtH,
            (unsigned char *)command,
            strlen( command ) + 1 );
        THROWIF( result == SQL_ERROR );

        result = SQLExecute( m_stmtH );
        THROWIF( result != SQL_SUCCESS &&
            result != SQL_SUCCESS_WITH_INFO);

        // now bind the columns and the data type
        SDWORD    dwTypeLen;
        long    cookieID;
        SQLBindCol( m_stmtH,1,SQL_C_LONG, &cookieID,
            sizeof(cookieID), &dwTypeLen );

        result = SQLFetch( m_stmtH );
        memberResult = ( result == SQL_SUCCESS ||
            result == SQL_SUCCESS_WITH_INFO )?
            true: false;
    }

    catch(...)
    {
        ShowSQLError();
        throw(-1);    // propagate to next catch...
    }

    return memberResult;
} // CShoppingCart::VerifyCookieInDB...


//
//    function:    CShoppingCart::MakeCookieInDB
//    purpose:    Makes a new cookie in the DB and
//                sets outCookieString to contain the same
//                value.
```

```
//    returns:    Nothing. Throws an exception on failure.
//
void
CShoppingCart::MakeCookieInDB( string &outCookieString )
{
    try
    {
        // now make our SQL insert command
        RETCODE result = SQLPrepare( m_stmtH,
            (unsigned char *)cSQLNewCookieCmd,
            strlen( cSQLNewCookieCmd ) + 1 );
        THROWIF( result == SQL_ERROR );

        result = SQLExecute( m_stmtH );
        THROWIF( result != SQL_SUCCESS &&
            result != SQL_SUCCESS_WITH_INFO);

        // need a new statement, use old handle
        SQLFreeStmt( m_stmtH, SQL_CLOSE );
        SQLAllocStmt( m_dbH, &m_stmtH );

        // now add our string
        result = SQLPrepare( m_stmtH,
            (unsigned char *)cSQLMaxCookieCmd,
            strlen( cSQLMaxCookieCmd ) + 1 );

        result = SQLExecute( m_stmtH );
        THROWIF( result != SQL_SUCCESS &&
            result != SQL_SUCCESS_WITH_INFO );

        // now bind the columns and the data type
        SDWORD    dwTypeLen;
        SQLBindCol( m_stmtH,1,SQL_C_SLONG,
            &m_cookie,sizeof(m_cookie), &dwTypeLen );

        result = SQLFetch( m_stmtH );
        THROWIF( result != SQL_SUCCESS &&
            result != SQL_SUCCESS_WITH_INFO );

        char    temp[32];
        sprintf(temp,"%ld",m_cookie);
        // copy the cookie to a string
        outCookieString = temp;
    }

    catch(...)
    {
```

```
        ShowSQLError();
        throw(-1);    // propagate to next catch...
    }
} // CShoppingCart::MakeCookieInDB...

//
//    function:    CShoppingCart::CheckCookie
//    purpose:     Makes sure the user has a cookie and
//                 that it's in the DB, and creates one
//                 if there's a problem, or it's missing.
//    returns:     Nothing.
//
void
CShoppingCart::CheckCookie()
{
    // used for fetching cookies
    CCookieMonster    cookie;
    // a general purpose string
    string    cookieStr;

    try
    {
        // did we get a cookie?
        cookieStr = cookie["FoosballCookie"];

        // extra level of paranoia in case it's bad
        if ( cookieStr.length() )
        {
            m_cookie = atol( cookieStr.c_str() );

            // always make sure we have a record in the
            // db that matches it.
            THROWIF( !VerifyCookieInDB() );
        }
        else
            throw(-1);
    }

    catch(...)
    {
        // let this member do the dirty work
        MakeCookieInDB( cookieStr );

        // make a format browsers understand
        cookie.MakeCookie("FoosballCookie",
            (char *)cookieStr.c_str(),
            "www.gigantor.com","",
            1,false, cookieStr);
```

```
            // send it to their browser
            // DO NOT forget the "\r\n" or
            // you will have debugging nightmares
            cout << cookieStr.c_str() << "\r\n";
    }
} // CShoppingCart::CheckCookie...


//
//      function:    CShoppingCart::AddItemToCart
//      purpose:     Adds the item inItem to the user's
//                   shopping cart in the DB.
//      returns:     Nothing. Throws an exception on failure.
//
void
CShoppingCart::AddItemToCart( CartItem &inItem )
{
    try
    {
        // used for our SQL statements
        char    command[512];
        // check to see if they already exist in the database
        sprintf( command, cSQLGetCartCmd, inItem.cookieID,
            inItem.inventoryID.c_str() );

        RETCODE result = SQLPrepare( m_stmtH,
            (unsigned char *)command, strlen( command ) + 1 );
        THROWIF(result == SQL_ERROR);

        // execute the SQL statement we made
        result = SQLExecute( m_stmtH );
        THROWIF( result != SQL_SUCCESS &&
            result != SQL_SUCCESS_WITH_INFO);

        SDWORD    dwTypeLen;
        long    quantity = 0;
        SQLBindCol( m_stmtH,1,SQL_C_LONG,
            &quantity,sizeof(quantity), &dwTypeLen );

        result = SQLFetch( m_stmtH );
        SQLFreeStmt( m_stmtH, SQL_CLOSE );
        SQLAllocStmt( m_dbH, &m_stmtH );

        // are they actually there????
        if ( result == SQL_SUCCESS ||
            result == SQL_SUCCESS_WITH_INFO )
            sprintf( command, cSQLUpdateCartCmd, inItem.quantity,
                inItem.cookieID, inItem.inventoryID.c_str() );
```

```
            else//not there, so add them
                // now add our string
                sprintf( command, cSQLInsertCmd, inItem.cookieID,
                    inItem.inventoryID.c_str(), inItem.quantity );

            // prepare our actual data now
            result = SQLPrepare( m_stmtH,
                (unsigned char *)command, strlen( command ) + 1 );
            THROWIF(result == SQL_ERROR);

            // execute the SQL statement we made
            result = SQLExecute( m_stmtH );
            THROWIF( result != SQL_SUCCESS &&
                result != SQL_SUCCESS_WITH_INFO);

            // commit the addition to the database
            SQLTransact( m_envH, m_dbH, SQL_COMMIT );
        }

    catch(...)
    {
        ShowSQLError();
        throw(-1);
    }
} // CShoppingCart::AddItemToCart...

//
//    function:      CShoppingCart::RemoveItemFromCart
//    purpose:       Removes the item inItem to the user's
//                   shopping cart in the DB.
//    returns:       Nothing. Throws an exception on failure.
//
void
CShoppingCart::RemoveItemFromCart( CartItem &inItem )
{
    try
    {
        // used for our SQL statements
        char    command[512];

        // check to see if they already exist in the database
        sprintf( command, cSQLGetCartCmd, inItem.cookieID,
            inItem.inventoryID.c_str() );
        RETCODE result = SQLPrepare( m_stmtH,
            (unsigned char *)command, strlen( command ) + 1 );
        THROWIF(result == SQL_ERROR);
        // execute the SQL statement we made
```

```
        result = SQLExecute( m_stmtH );
        THROWIF( result != SQL_SUCCESS &&
            result != SQL_SUCCESS_WITH_INFO);

        char inventoryInDB;
        SDWORD    dwTypeLen;
        long    cookieInDB;
        SQLBindCol( m_stmtH,1,SQL_C_LONG,
            &cookieInDB,sizeof(cookieInDB), &dwTypeLen );
        SQLBindCol( m_stmtH,2,SQL_C_CHAR,
            &inventoryInDB,sizeof(inventoryInDB), &dwTypeLen );

        result = SQLFetch( m_stmtH );
        SQLFreeStmt( m_stmtH, SQL_CLOSE );
        SQLAllocStmt( m_dbH, &m_stmtH );

        // are they actually there????
        if ( result == SQL_SUCCESS ||
            result == SQL_SUCCESS_WITH_INFO )
            sprintf( command, cSQLDeleteCartItemCmd,
                inItem.cookieID, inItem.inventoryID.c_str() );
        else//not there, so add them
            // now add our string
            sprintf( command, cSQLDeleteCartQtyCmd,
                inItem.cookieID, inItem.quantity );

        // prepare our actual data now
        result = SQLPrepare( m_stmtH,
            (unsigned char *)command, strlen( command ) + 1 );
        THROWIF(result == SQL_ERROR);

        // execute the SQL statement we made
        result = SQLExecute( m_stmtH );
        THROWIF( result != SQL_SUCCESS &&
            result != SQL_SUCCESS_WITH_INFO);

        // commit the addition to the database
        SQLTransact( m_envH, m_dbH, SQL_COMMIT );
    }

    catch(...)
    {
        ShowSQLError();
        throw(-1);
    }
} // CShoppingCart::RemoveItemFromCart...
```

```
//
//    function:    CShoppingCart::RecalcOrder
//    purpose:     Adds the items from the HTML form
//                 to the user's shopping cart table.
//                 Also removes the items if the quantity
//                 specified is zero or less. Calls
//                 ReviewOrder() to display results when
//                 finished.
//    returns:     Nothing.
//
void
CShoppingCart::RecalcOrder()
{
    CartItem     item;
    vector<InventoryItem>    catalog;

    // need a new statement, use old handle
    SQLFreeStmt( m_stmtH, SQL_CLOSE );
    SQLAllocStmt( m_dbH, &m_stmtH );

    map< string, string, less<string> >::iterator    iter;
    for ( iter = m_parser.begin();
        iter != m_parser.end();
        iter++ )
    {
        item.cookieID = m_cookie;
        item.inventoryID = (*iter).first;
        item.quantity = -1L;
        int strSize = (*iter).second.length();

        if ( strSize )
        {
            if ( !(strSize == 1 &&
                (*iter).second.c_str()[0] == ' ') )
                item.quantity = (long)atol(
                    (*iter).second.c_str () );
        }

        if ( item.quantity > 0 )
            AddItemToCart( item );
        else if ( item.quantity == 0 )
            RemoveItemFromCart( item );
    } // for...

    ReviewOrder();
} // CShoppingCart::RecalcOrder...
```

```
//
//    function:    CShoppingCart::ReviewOrder
//    purpose:     Gets the shopping cart contents and
//                 cross-references every item with our
//                 inventory DB table. Outputs all items
//                 as an HTML form the user can edit.
//    returns:     Nothing.
//
void
CShoppingCart::ReviewOrder()
{
    vector<CartItem>          cartContents;
    vector<InventoryItem>     catalog;
    vector<float>             orderCost;
    char      tempStr[256];

    GetCartContents( cartContents );
    GetCatalog( catalog );

    cout << "<H1><CENTER>Shopping Cart Contents</H1><BR>\n";
    cout << "Change any quantity of any items here<BR>\n" <<
        "and press <B>Recalculate Order</B> to see "
        "your new order.<BR>\n" <<
        "To remove an item set the quantity to "
        "<B>zero</B>.<BR>\n" <<
        "To order press <B>Order Now</B>.<BR><BR><BR>\n";

    cout << "<FORM ACTION=/scripts/cgishoppingcart.exe  "
        "METHOD=POST>\n";
    cout << "<TABLE>\n";

    if ( !cartContents.empty() && !catalog.empty() )
    {
        vector<CartItem>::iterator      iter;
        vector<InventoryItem>::iterator catIter;

        // display each item in the user's cart
        for( iter = cartContents.begin();
            iter != cartContents.end();
            iter++ )
        {
            cout << "<TR><TD><INPUT TYPE=text SIZE=5 "
                "MAXLENGTH=2 NAME=" <<
                iter->inventoryID.c_str() <<
                " VALUE = " <<
                iter->quantity << "></TD>\n";
```

```
            // another loop! ouch!
            for ( catIter = catalog.begin();
                catIter != catalog.end();
                catIter++ )
            {
                if ( !iter->inventoryID.compare(
                    catIter->inventoryID) )
                {
                    float lineTotal = catIter->cost *
                        iter->quantity;
                    sprintf(tempStr, "<TD>%s at %.2f each = "
                        "%.2f<BR></TD>\n",
                        catIter->description.c_str(),
                        catIter->cost,
                        lineTotal );
                    cout << tempStr;

                    // add the order up
                    orderCost.push_back( lineTotal );
                    break;
                }
            }
        } // for...
    }
    else
        cout << "<CENTER>Nothing found!</CENTER><BR><BR><BR>\n";

    sprintf(tempStr,"</TABLE><P>Your order subtotal "
        "(excluding tax if in California "
        "and excluding shipping) is <B>$%.2f</B><BR><BR><BR>",
            accumulate( orderCost.begin(), orderCost.end(),0.0 ) );
    cout << tempStr;

        // add buttons and end the form's scope
    cout<< "<CENTER><INPUT TYPE=submit NAME=task"
            "VALUE='Order Now'>" <<
        "<INPUT TYPE=submit NAME=task VALUE='Recalculate Order'>" <<
        "<INPUT TYPE=submit NAME=task "
            "VALUE='Cancel Order'></CENTER>" <<
        "</FORM><BR><BR><BR>\n";
} // CShoppingCart::ReviewOrder...

//
//    function:    CShoppingCart::CancelOrder
//    purpose:     Deletes all items in the user's
//                 shopping cart.
//    returns:     Nothing. Throws an exception on failure.
//
```

```cpp
void
CShoppingCart::CancelOrder()
{
    try
    {
        // need a new statement, use old handle
        SQLFreeStmt( m_stmtH, SQL_CLOSE );
        SQLAllocStmt( m_dbH, &m_stmtH );

        char    command[128];
        sprintf( command, cSQLDeleteCartCmd, m_cookie );
        // now make our SQL insert command
        RETCODE result = SQLPrepare( m_stmtH,
            (unsigned char *)command,
            strlen( command ) + 1 );
        THROWIF( result == SQL_ERROR );

        result = SQLExecute( m_stmtH );
        THROWIF( result != SQL_SUCCESS &&
            result != SQL_SUCCESS_WITH_INFO);

        // commit the addition to the database
        SQLTransact( m_envH, m_dbH, SQL_COMMIT );

        cout << "<H1><CENTER>Your shopping cart has "
            "been emptied.</H1><BR>\n";
        cout << "Thank you for visiting our site!<BR><BR><BR>";
    }

    catch(...)
    {
        ShowSQLError();
        throw(-1);    // propagate to next catch...
    }
} // CShoppingCart::CancelOrder...

//
//    function:    CShoppingCart::GetCatalog
//    purpose:     Gets all items we have in our product catalog
//                 and adds them to the vector<> outCatalog.
//    returns:     Nothing. Throws an exception on failure.
//
void
CShoppingCart::GetCatalog( vector<InventoryItem> &outCatalog )
{
    try
    {
```

```cpp
// need a new statement, use old handle
SQLFreeStmt( m_stmtH, SQL_CLOSE );
SQLAllocStmt( m_dbH, &m_stmtH );

// now add our string
RETCODE result = SQLPrepare( m_stmtH,
    (unsigned char *)cSQLSelectCatalogCmd,
    strlen( cSQLSelectCatalogCmd ) + 1 );
THROWIF( result == SQL_ERROR );

result = SQLExecute( m_stmtH );
THROWIF( result != SQL_SUCCESS &&
    result != SQL_SUCCESS_WITH_INFO);

// now bind the columns and the data type
SDWORD    dwTypeLen;
char id[32], description[128],vendor[32];
float cost, discount;
SQLBindCol( m_stmtH,1,SQL_C_CHAR, &id,sizeof(id),
    &dwTypeLen );
SQLBindCol( m_stmtH,2,SQL_C_CHAR, &description,
    sizeof(description), &dwTypeLen );
SQLBindCol( m_stmtH,3,SQL_C_FLOAT, &cost,sizeof(cost),
    &dwTypeLen );
SQLBindCol( m_stmtH,4,SQL_C_FLOAT,
    &discount,sizeof(discount), &dwTypeLen );
SQLBindCol( m_stmtH,5,SQL_C_CHAR, &vendor,sizeof(vendor),
    &dwTypeLen );

// fetch and add each item to the catalog vector...
InventoryItem    item;
do
{
    result = SQLFetch( m_stmtH );
    if ( result != SQL_SUCCESS &&
        result != SQL_SUCCESS_WITH_INFO )
        break;

    // copy info from the database
    item.inventoryID = id;
    item.description = description;
    item.cost = cost;
    item.discPercent = discount;
    item.vendor = vendor;

    // add the item to our vector
    outCatalog.push_back(item);
}
```

```
            while( true );
    }

    catch(...)
    {
        ShowSQLError();
        throw(-1);
    }
} // CShoppingCart::GetCatalog...

//
//    function:    CShoppingCart::GetCartContents
//    purpose:    Gets all items from the user's shopping cart
//                and adds them to the vector<> outCart.
//    returns:    Nothing. Throws an exception on failure.
//
void
CShoppingCart::GetCartContents( vector<CartItem> &outCart )
{
    try
    {
        // need a new statement, use old handle
        SQLFreeStmt( m_stmtH, SQL_CLOSE );
        SQLAllocStmt( m_dbH, &m_stmtH );

        // now add our string
        char command[128];
        sprintf( command, cSQLSelectCartCmd, m_cookie );
        RETCODE result = SQLPrepare( m_stmtH,
            (unsigned char *)command,
            strlen( command ) + 1 );
        THROWIF( result == SQL_ERROR );

        result = SQLExecute( m_stmtH );
        THROWIF( result != SQL_SUCCESS &&
            result != SQL_SUCCESS_WITH_INFO);

        // now bind the columns and the data type
        SDWORD    dwTypeLen;
        char id[32];
        long quantity;
        SQLBindCol( m_stmtH,1,SQL_C_CHAR, &id,sizeof(id),
            &dwTypeLen );
        SQLBindCol( m_stmtH,2,SQL_C_LONG,
            &quantity,sizeof(quantity), &dwTypeLen );

        // get each item from the virtual shopping cart
        CartItem    item;
```

```
        do
        {
            result = SQLFetch( m_stmtH );
            if ( result != SQL_SUCCESS &&
                result != SQL_SUCCESS_WITH_INFO )
                break;

            // copy info from the database
            item.cookieID = m_cookie;
            item.inventoryID = id;
            item.quantity = quantity;

            // add the item to our vector
            outCart.push_back(item);
        }
        while( true );
    }

    catch(...)
    {
        ShowSQLError();
        throw(-1);
    }
} // CShoppingCart::GetCartContents...


//
//    function:    isFoosballTable()
//    purpose:     STL comparator that we use to identify if the
//                    item is a Foosball table based on its price.
//    returns:     true if the price indicates a Foosball table
//
bool
isFoosballTable( float &inCost )
{
    bool result = false;

    if ( inCost == 395.00 || inCost == 495.00
        || inCost == 995.00 )
        result = true;

    return result;
} // isFoosballTable...

//
//    function:    CShoppingCart::DisplayStaticContents
//    purpose:     Displays the order for the user with the
//                    shipping costs, etc. for verification
//
```

```
//                    but is not editable. This is called only
//                    before validating the credit card.
//                    returns:    Nothing.
//
void
CShoppingCart::DisplayStaticOrder()
{
    vector<CartItem>         cartContents;
    vector<InventoryItem>    catalog;
    vector<float>            orderCost;
    char    tempStr[256];
    float    orderTotal, shipCost, salesTax = 0.0;

    GetCartContents( cartContents );
    GetCatalog( catalog );

    cout << "<H1><CENTER>Shopping Cart Contents</H1><BR>\n";
    cout << "Select <B>Continue</B> to proceed, or"
        " <B>Cancel Order</B> to stop.<BR><BR>\n";

    cout << "<FORM ACTION=/scripts/cgishoppingcart.exe  "
        "METHOD=POST>\n";
    cout << "<TABLE>\n";

    if ( !cartContents.empty() && !catalog.empty() )
    {
        vector<CartItem>::iterator     iter;
        vector<InventoryItem>::iterator catIter;

        // display each item in the user's cart
        for( iter = cartContents.begin();
            iter != cartContents.end();
            iter++ )
        {
            cout << "<TR><TD>" << iter->quantity;

            // another loop! ouch!
            for ( catIter = catalog.begin();
                catIter != catalog.end();
                catIter++ )
            {
                if ( !iter->inventoryID.compare(
                    catIter->inventoryID) )
                {
                    float lineTotal = catIter->cost *
                        iter->quantity;
                    sprintf(tempStr, "<TD>%s at %.2f each = "
                        "%.2f<BR></TD>\n",
```

```
                                catIter->description.c_str(),
                                catIter->cost,
                                lineTotal );
                        cout << tempStr;

                        // add the order up
                        orderCost.push_back( lineTotal );
                        break;
                    }
                }
            } // for...
        }
        else
            cout << "<CENTER>Nothing found!</CENTER><BR><BR><BR>\n";

        orderTotal = accumulate( orderCost.begin(),
            orderCost.end(),0.0 );
        sprintf(tempStr,"</TABLE><P>Your order subtotal is "
                "<B>$%.2f</B><BR>",
                orderTotal);
        cout << tempStr;

        // sales tax
        if ( FromCalifornia() )
        {
            salesTax = orderTotal * cTaxRate;
            sprintf(tempStr,"Sales Tax is <B>$%.2f</B><BR>",
                salesTax );
            cout << tempStr;
        }

        // shipping and handling
        remove_if( orderCost.begin(), orderCost.end(),
            isFoosballTable );
        shipCost =  orderTotal * cBaseShippingRate;

        sprintf(tempStr,"Shipping and handling "
            "(excludes table shipping costs) are <B>$%.2f</B><BR>",
                shipCost );
        cout << tempStr;

        // the order total
        sprintf(tempStr,"<H2>Your order total is <B>$%.2f</B><BR>",
                shipCost + orderTotal + salesTax );
        cout << tempStr << "</H2>";

            // add buttons and end the form's scope
        cout<< "<CENTER><INPUT TYPE=submit NAME=task "
```

```
                "VALUE='Continue'>" <<
                "<INPUT TYPE=submit NAME=task "
                "VALUE='Cancel Order'></CENTER>" <<
                "</FORM><BR><BR><BR>\n";

} // CShoppingCart::DisplayStaticContents...

//
//    function:    CShoppingCart::HandleCart
//    purpose:     Based on the "task" variable specified on
//                 an HTML form, takes the appropriate shopping
//                 cart action.
//    returns:     Nothing.
//
void
CShoppingCart::HandleCart()
{
    if ( !m_parser["task"].compare("Continue") )
        DisplayStaticOrder();
    else if ( !m_parser["task"].compare("Recalculate Order") ||
        !m_parser["task"].compare("Add To Shopping Cart"))
        RecalcOrder();
    else if ( !m_parser["task"].compare("Review Order") )
        ReviewOrder();
    else if ( !m_parser["task"].compare("Cancel Order") )
        CancelOrder();
    else
        cout << "<H1><CENTER>Unknown task directive...<H1>"
            "</H1></CENTER><BR><BR><BR>\n";
} // CShoppingCart::HandleCart...

//
//    function:    CShoppingCart::GetZipCode()
//    purpose:     Retrieves the user's zip code from our db.
//    returns:     nothing
//
void
CShoppingCart::GetZipCode( string &inZipCode )
{
    CCookieMonster    cookie;
    char              queryString[128];

    try
    {
        // should never happen, but always be paranoid
        THROWIF( cookie["FoosballCookie"].length() < 1 );
```

```
        // make the query string
        sprintf( queryString, cSQLGetZipCode,
            cookie["FoosballCookie"].c_str() );

        // need a new statement, use old handle
        SQLFreeStmt( m_stmtH, SQL_CLOSE );
        SQLAllocStmt( m_dbH, &m_stmtH );

        RETCODE result = SQLPrepare( m_stmtH,
            (unsigned char *)queryString,
            strlen( queryString ) + 1 );
        THROWIF(result == SQL_ERROR);

        // execute the SQL statement we made
        result = SQLExecute( m_stmtH );
        THROWIF( result != SQL_SUCCESS &&
            result != SQL_SUCCESS_WITH_INFO);

        SDWORD    dwTypeLen;
        char    temp[32];
        SQLBindCol( m_stmtH,1,SQL_C_CHAR,
            temp,sizeof(temp),
            &dwTypeLen );
        result = SQLFetch( m_stmtH );

        // did we actually get the zip code?
        if ( result == SQL_SUCCESS ||
            result == SQL_SUCCESS_WITH_INFO )
            inZipCode = temp;
        else
            inZipCode = " ";
    }

    catch(...)
    {
        SDWORD    err;
        char text[512], errText[512];
        SQLError(m_envH,m_dbH,m_stmtH,(unsigned char *)text,&err,
            (unsigned char *)errText,sizeof(errText),0);

        // show the error message
        cout << "<CENTER>" << errText << ": err = " <<
            text << "<BR></CENTER>";
        throw(-1);
    }
} // CShoppingCart::GetZipCode...
```

```
//
//      function:      CShoppingCart::GetOrderTotal()
//      purpose:       Retrieves the user's order total from the db.
//      returns:       nothing
//
void
CShoppingCart::GetOrderTotal( float &inAmount )
{
    vector<CartItem>         cartContents;
    vector<InventoryItem>     catalog;
    vector<float>             orderCost;
    CFormParser                notUsedHere;
    CShoppingCart              theCart(notUsedHere);

    // get their items and get the catalog we use to sell our goods
    theCart.GetCatalog( catalog );
    theCart.GetCartContents( cartContents );

    // now we need to retrieve the order total so
    // we charge the right amount
    if ( !cartContents.empty() && !catalog.empty() )
    {
        vector<CartItem>::iterator     iter;
        vector<InventoryItem>::iterator catIter;

        // display each item in the user's cart
        for( iter = cartContents.begin();
            iter != cartContents.end();
            iter++ )
        {
            // another loop! ouch!
            for ( catIter = catalog.begin();
                catIter != catalog.end();
                catIter++ )
            {
                if ( !iter->inventoryID.compare(
                    catIter->inventoryID) )
                {
                    orderCost.push_back( catIter->cost *
                        iter->quantity );
                    break;
                }
            }
        } // for...
    }

    // total the order - use STL accumulate function
    inAmount = accumulate( orderCost.begin(), orderCost.end(), 0.0 );
```

```
    // now to calculate the sales tax!
    float salesTax = 0.0;
    if ( FromCalifornia() )
        salesTax = inAmount * cTaxRate;
    inAmount += salesTax;

// Now to add shipping - here I charge 15 percent, which is about my cost
// If we offered overnight and other options, we would need to check
// for that here. Also, shipping for tables is charged by the freight
// company, so we don't charge for that item here.
    remove_if( orderCost.begin(), orderCost.end(), isFoosballTable );
    inAmount += accumulate( orderCost.begin(),
        orderCost.end(),0.0 ) * cBaseShippingRate;
} // CShoppingCart::GetOrderTotal...

//
//     function:    CShoppingCart::FromCalifornia()
//     purpose:     Sees if the customer is from CA.
//     returns:     true if customer is from California -
//                      we get this from the db.
//
bool
CShoppingCart::FromCalifornia()
{
    bool     fromCA = false;
    CCookieMonster     cookie;
    char             queryString[128];

    try
    {
        // should never happen, but always be paranoid
        THROWIF( cookie["FoosballCookie"].length() < 1 );

        // make the query string
        sprintf( queryString, cSQLGetState,
            cookie["FoosballCookie"].c_str() );

        // need a new statement, use old handle
        SQLFreeStmt( m_stmtH, SQL_CLOSE );
        SQLAllocStmt( m_dbH, &m_stmtH );

        RETCODE result = SQLPrepare( m_stmtH,
            (unsigned char *)queryString,
            strlen( queryString ) + 1 );
        THROWIF(result == SQL_ERROR);

        // execute the SQL statement we made
        result = SQLExecute( m_stmtH );
```

```
        THROWIF( result != SQL_SUCCESS &&
            result != SQL_SUCCESS_WITH_INFO);

        SDWORD    dwTypeLen;
        char    state[4];
        SQLBindCol( m_stmtH,1,SQL_C_CHAR,
            state,sizeof(state),
            &dwTypeLen );
        result = SQLFetch( m_stmtH );

        // did we actually get the state?
        // throw an exception if not, because we're
        // missing it, or our DB is corrupt
        THROWIF( !(result == SQL_SUCCESS ||
            result == SQL_SUCCESS_WITH_INFO) );

        // see if they're from beautiful California
        if ( _stricmp( state, "CA") == 0 )
            fromCA = true;

    }

    catch(...)
    {
        SDWORD    err;
        char text[512], errText[512];
        SQLError(m_envH,m_dbH,m_stmtH,(unsigned char *)text,&err,
            (unsigned char *)errText,sizeof(errText),0);

        // show the error message
        cout << "<CENTER>" << errText << ": err = " <<
            text << "<BR></CENTER>";
        throw(-1);
    }

    return fromCA;
} // CShoppingCart::FromCalifornia...
```

> *Note:* *For your stores, I recommend that you subclass the **CShoppingCart** class and add any specific items that are unique for your business. This enables you to maintain the flexibility and power of the base class, and benefit from possibly reusing existing code among several projects (storefronts).*

The dynamic form uses our existing class **CShoppingCart**, so no new code is used there. The **CalculatePrice()** member iterates through the items much like

RecalcOrder() does, and creates a dynamic HTML form, as shown in Figure 13.11. This is where the customer can order the merchandise, make some changes, and recalculate the new costs—or cancel altogether.

That's the completed source code. To implement this site, we've used the **CFormParser** class for handling form data and variable items. We use the **CCookieMonster** class for maintaining state information between the client's browser and our Web server and datastore. Next, we'll use the **CShoppingCart** class to store merchandise in a virtual shopping cart for the customer within our datastore, and use the same class for retrieving the merchandise as well as calculating shipping and handling, tax, and the order total. The last class we used was the **CCreditCard** class we developed in Chapter 11—this class validated the card number, and then interfaced with the bank via three different low-cost credit card

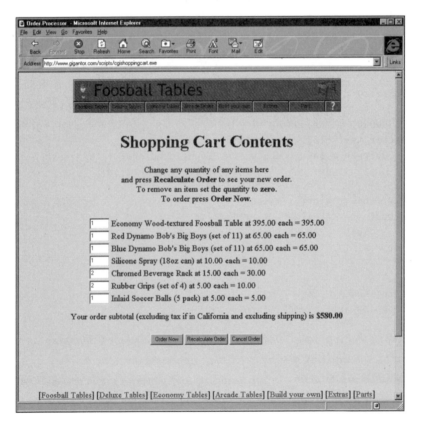

Figure 13.11
Results of CShoppingCart::CalculatePrice().

servers that are available for you to use now. For one of these credit card servers, we wrote a DDE/TCP/IP bridge program that simplified our tasks considerably.

Summary

We provided all of the source code, HTML, and C++ for the Foosball store, a real 24×7 business that's on the Net. The store contains a variety of merchandise and we provided custom options, as well as calculated shipping costs, prices and so on. We even collect payment in realtime. We've covered everything that you need to do to put your business online and collect payment, including some new C++ classes to simplify all the common tasks that nearly every business on the Net will need to perform. These techniques are excellent for regular tangible merchandise, but for items such as software, can you think of another distribution method? How about giving it away?

We can distribute our software in much the same way you sell merchandise from your Web site. You could then distribute your software over the Net, perhaps disabling some key feature like printing or saving files unless the customer has paid you for the product. We can do this with security, much like SSL and Web servers. Am I crazy? Well, read Chapter 14 and let me know if I should be committed.

14
SOFTWARE
DISTRIBUTION IDEAS

There are always possibilities.

Mr. Spock, Star Trek: The Return

An excellent approach to distributing your software all over the global market is to just give it away. Wait a minute—give it away? If we give it away, where do commerce and profit fit in? You can disable a few key items of your software—such as printing or saving to disk, or you can even restrict how many times a user can launch your program. You can add a dialog box or a window in your program so that the customer can fill out an online registration form and submit it to your company to unlock the disabled features. This ensures that key features remain disabled until payment is received.

What about hackers? Well, you're always going to get a few no matter what you do, or how cleverly you design your code. The trick here is to make it difficult—or nearly impossible—for someone to enable the functionality you disabled. In all businesses, there is some theft by a small minority; what we need to do is make this percentage very low or nonexistent. In this chapter, we'll cover some techniques to encrypt data and generate new keys to decipher registration information from your

465

software, which will make it extremely uninteresting for hackers to attack. In Chapter 15, we'll cover an encryption algorithm called Blowfish, which still hasn't been broken by hackers, or the NSA.

How does all of this fit in with our Web server and commerce on the Internet? Actually, we won't be using our Web server here, but rather the commerce servers we mentioned and used in Chapter 11. Our program will open a direct socket and submit certain information that can be processed in realtime. We can encrypt the data and guarantee its safety over the Internet via Blowfish, or even another algorithm, if you prefer.

Have you used some popular shareware programs before? They usually ask you to pay the author a specified sum. The problem with these programs is that the form of payment usually includes mailing a check, faxing credit card information, and so on—and the unlocking is not done in realtime. In earlier chapters, we mentioned that if customers don't get immediate feedback, most will do business with another site. The same is true with a software program—if the software is not unlocked in realtime but payment is collected immediately, the customer may go elsewhere, or get frustrated and not pay at all. I have to confess—not out of being diabolical or cheap—to not paying for some programs I use due to the difficulty and time involved in paying the author. We're all so busy these days—printing out a hard copy, faxing it, mailing a check, and then receiving an unlocking code via email or pony express is just a pain! Why not just click on an order button, fill out a form, and have everything handled electronically, immediately, and with nothing further required?

Internet distribution for shareware is great, but I think that it's an equally excellent technique for selling commercial software packages. Even if your product is on the shelves of major software retailers, opening Internet distribution may attract other customers and increase market share for your products. Many times, we are looking to perform a key task on our computers only to find we don't have a certain program on our local machines. At times like that, I would pay nearly anything to immediately get a program that fits my needs—and if software were distributed with an unlocking mechanism in place, it would be possible. If I can't get the program immediately, on the other hand, I usually figure out a workaround within a day or so and then have no need to buy the program I was looking for in the first place—meaning someone lost a sale.

You can use the same mechanism for unlocking software over the Internet for registering commercial packages you get from the store. I recently purchased Claris Works, and filled out the online registration form—I thought this would be electronic and fast, and would help Claris notify me of special offers and advertisements. When I finished filling out the form, it asked me to print it out and fax it to them, or place it in the pony express mail. As you might guess, I threw the form out and didn't register. Don't make this mistake with your products—unlock them or register them in realtime over the Internet. Only offer printouts and faxes as options, not as the main approach of sending you this information.

In this chapter, we're going to explore the possibilities of distributing and unlocking your own software programs over the Internet. Later in Chapter 15, we'll develop an MFC dll for your Win32 programs to use that covers all the development techniques we mention here.

Distribution Costs

If you want a software product to appear on the shelf of a major store, you will have to work out a deal with a large distributor such as Ingram Micro D. You will have to pay the stores that display your merchandise for shelf space in order to get the most attention from potential customers. But wait! This is outrageously expensive. Most small companies or even independent developers cannot afford to do this—even if they offer great products. As a result, some fine products never see the light of day. If we get lucky, some of them get distributed as shareware.

In our discussion of distributing a commercial product in the retail channel, we left out advertising costs, which could run $10,000 a month for a small advertising campaign. For small shops, it makes retail distribution an even more unrealistic alternative. Enter the Internet.

Use your Web page to describe your products, and when users click on it, direct them to an address book and get some customer information. Then let them download your programs (with some functions disabled). You can advertise your Web page for free with all the major search engines (Yahoo!, Excite, and so on), and any generic search that covers a term you specify will create a link to your page. The cost can't be beat, and the free advertising does generate a substantial number of hits to your site. If you want more hits and more potential customers, try advertising on Hotbot or AltaVista as well—you can literally generate millions of hits for a fraction of what it costs to advertise in commercial software magazines.

Another option is to publish your FTP site, but I do not recommend this. For one, you won't be able to collect data about customers (so that you can ask them questions later, or use it for product pricing and analysis). Another reason is that you cannot advertise your product with any cool Java or HTML advertisements, feature information, and so on. Your Web site can be linked to a private FTP server that users can access only when they fill out an information form. An advantage is that people without Web browsers can still access your software.

What is the real cost here? Well, you already have a Web server, which can be your software distribution node to the Internet. If you're selling merchandise, you will have something like the Gigantor Commerce Server. Using these existing software packages, you will be able to collect payment for software in realtime without having to pay for anything other than your basic Web commerce setup. The real cost is only your time and depends upon the features you would like to use in your software unlocking.

Overhead

We've mentioned the costs of setting the system up to collect payments, but haven't enumerated all of the tasks you must accomplish to perform this. You will need a Web page where you can advertise your products, and provide links so that your customers can download them. This might take you a single day to complete.

One option is handling registration for copies of your software distributed via the normal retail channel. You could create a simple TCP/IP server to do this and to store each registration record inside the same database that your commerce server uses. It might take a few days to get such a sophisticated server to perform these tasks, and maybe another week depending on your feature requirements.

You can place your commerce server (or your registration server if you write one) at a known IP address, and your software will be able to contact this for payment collection and verification. You can even place your commerce server on the same machine as your Web server, provided your Web site isn't already overloaded with business.

Concepts

The concepts are basic: Give your product away and disable a key feature until the customer pays you. You will store some information in a file (or the Registry in Windows) that will tell you whether or not the customer has paid for your product. This requires your program to inspect this state (payment or not) when the program starts up each and every time—this is fast, so don't worry, it won't affect performance. This distribution allows a few variations; depending on your product, you might want to try something different. Figure 14.1 shows an example interface that we'll explore in more detail in Chapter 15.

You might also consider giving away a fully functional version of your product. You could enable all features so the customer can test everything out for a specified time period, like 30 days or so. Then, until the customer has paid you, you can remind him or her how many days are left every time he or she launches your program. You could also provide a button to allow the customer to pay for and register the product now. This immediacy is great.

What about for a full-blown, colossus product that is commercial quality? Some of these products can be $500 or more, so is this a good distribution vehicle for them? You bet. You might also rent your program. You could very easily enable

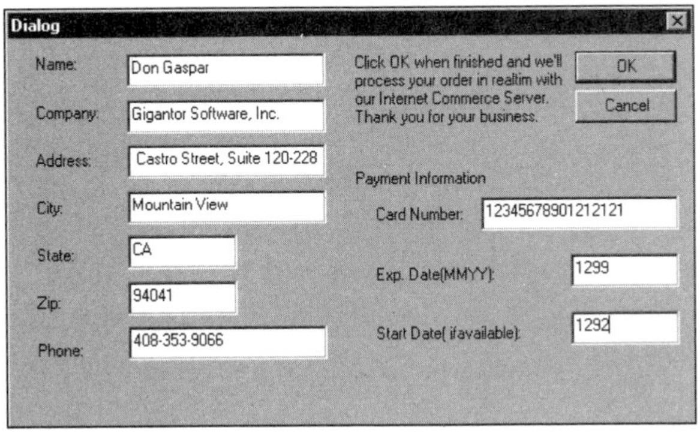

Figure 14.1
Typical online registration dialog box.

your program in some specified time intervals that the customer chooses—maybe charge a monthly fee, and reduce the rate for more and more months that the customer purchases. Perhaps charge $20 or so and give the customer an unimpeded evaluation period of 30 days—some products that normally cost $500 on the shelf are well worth a $20 evaluation period. The possibilities are limited by your imagination and customer demand.

Because you are in contact with a server for unlocking the distributed software, you could write another server that could be an advertising server, or an upgrade-information server. These servers would then notify a customer of an upgrade, or maybe a similar product when it becomes available. Although this is a great distribution model, you do not want to advertise items unless the customer has the option of turning the advertisements off—or even better yet, don't do this unless the customer selects a menu item inquiring about your products or upgrade information. Regardless of your feature set, it's still simple to implement. We're already using TCP/IP for commerce transactions, so now we'll use it for upgrades and so on.

If a user wants an upgrade option or a new product, your advertisement screen should display a link to a transfer program that will download the upgrade file automatically. A great way of doing this in Windows is by using the **WinExec()** launch a Web browser, and pointing the customer to your upgrade or new product page by passing the browser your URL. You could also build the transfer mechanism into your software if you feel adventurous.

What about manuals and disks? You can distribute the manuals as HTML pages and provide links to your own online support site. This eliminates both hardcopy manuals and shipping costs, as you are distributing everything electronically. As a result, it costs less for a developer to release a product, which allows the developer to pass the savings on to the customer. Any reduced cost is a bargain for a customer, considering the high prices of most software packages.

If you do plan to offer upgrades, remember that many customers still use slow modems to connect to the Internet. Therefore, make your upgrade programs small, and only upgrade the changes that have occurred in your product—this saves lots of time when a customer is copying to a local disk from the Internet, and will most likely bring in repeat business for you from the same customer. Always simplify for your customers.

Online Software Stores

We've seen stores and malls online, but how about a repository of software that we can try before we buy? I would much prefer to test something out and make sure it does what I need before someone I don't know gets my credit card number. The 1997 Internet stores offer shrink-wrap products, but you still have to pay before testing. This will change.

We'll soon see online stores that contain an entire spectrum of software products that you will be able to browse. Then, instead of paying for a product up front, you will get to test it out for a month or so to see if it is exactly what you want. With increased competition on the software front, you can expect clever distribution channels like this to appear in 1998 and beyond.

There's no reason that a software store cannot be on the Internet exclusively. Its inventory can be online and updated in realtime. Its costs for conducting business could be reduced substantially with the electronic distribution model.

Some sites distribute massive volumes of shareware applications—the biggest is **www.shareware.com**. If shareware authors had a mechanism to collect payments for them, and the servers were low-cost, viable solutions, this alternative would become very attractive. Commercial outfits would also join this distribution approach when they saw the potential profit.

Commercial Solutions

Some businesses provide software distribution SDKs (Software Development Kits) and charge you a fee (typically 20 to 25 percent) per transaction for using their system. This raises several issues: Can you trust these other companies to collect your payments and then pay you, and is the percentage they charge too high? Let's inspect the pros and cons of using a third party.

A third party will already have written an SDK, and has probably addressed lots of issues that developers brought up in various feedback sessions. Investigate what is being offered, and see if it can meet your requirements. A common problem that I have seen with one of these companies is that it contained horrible, bug-laden, and unstable code—using its SDK would then make your product unstable, and not many people would purchase it. Test out the third party's software before you use it—don't assume that because the company has been in business a while that its software is good. Inspect its encryption algo-rithm and its key size—it's probably a public-domain algorithm that you can find on the Internet yourself. If your requirements are not very sophisticated, then write your own.

What about paying someone 20 to 25 percent for every transaction that you perform? I personally think that's way too high, and will force you to pass on this extra cost to your customer. If you use an inexpensive commerce solution, you can bypass paying someone large a percentage, so you will keep 100 per-cent of the profits to yourself—hopefully you could lower your prices, pass the savings on, and attract more customers.

Can you trust someone you don't personally know with your business transac-tions? I would suggest rolling out your own unlocking software and linking it to a commerce server over the Internet. It's far from rocket science. In Chapter 15, we'll write a basic Win32 dll unlocking mechanism that is royalty free with your unlimited distribution.

Summary

In this chapter, I illustrated the advantages to giving your software away over the Internet. We briefly discussed the logic of unlocking mechanisms, feature disabling, time locking, and renting of software. In Chapter 15, we'll develop an MFC DLL and discuss the concepts of the locking/unlocking mechanism, encryption, and payment collection using the commerce servers from previous chapters. You will be able to use this code for your own distribution of software products.

If you're working in another environment, or using something like Java, the code in Chapter 15 should easily port. If you do port the code, please let me know so we can publish it on our site for others to take advantage of. Also, check our support site (**www.gigantor.com/coriolis**) for the latest code—if we receive several requests for something that we've left out, I'll implement it and post it on the support site for you to use. On to Chapter 15, so I can continue to argue my sanity and present some actual code to perform unlocking mecha-nisms and payment collection in realtime.

15

INTERNET SOFTWARE DISTRIBUTION

Everything that can be invented has been invented.

Charles H. Duell, Commissioner, U.S. Office of Patents, 1899

O ur requirements are not very sophisticated: to ship a software product over the Internet, and to get paid for it if and when a customer chooses to purchase the program. As we discussed in Chapter 14, we will disable some of the product's functionality until the customer pays us for it. Before we do this, let's detail all the requirements for our unlocking module:

- We need to be able to unlock a module or an entire product over the Internet.

- The unlocking can be for a specified time interval, which will enable us to allow fully functional and demonstrable software for any time we specify. This option also lets us rent or lease software for certain time intervals.

- We need to prevent our application from being duplicated once someone has paid for it. This is key. We must add a mechanism that prevents someone from paying for a single copy, and from it propagating hundreds of copies like a virus.

- Our mechanism has to be difficult and troublesome for hackers to break. We need to prevent the obvious detection of our pattern of encryption, and also prevent key detection. If the pattern is recognized, then our algorithm is deciphered. Our design must require that a hacker be unable to learn both the algorithm and the key individually. Both are required to break the encryption.

- We need to perform the unlocking in realtime over the Internet. We can permit the customer to fax an order or even email it to us, but these must be options, not requirements. Our server must then be available 24×7, and possibly will redirect to another sever for load balancing, and so on.

- We need to log all customer information inside our central datastore. This allows us to store the payment information for our software, much like we did for regular Internet purchases of other merchandise.

- Our software must be distributed over the Internet from a Web site.

With these requirements in mind, we can now design the software for a formidable software distribution system over the Internet. Your Web server—which is now commerce enabled—is a repository for various software programs that you have written. Customers will download a version of your program, and use it free for a time interval that you specify. In this chapter, we'll specify 30 days and require payment after that.

We won't cover leasing or renting of software in this chapter—this should be obvious for you to implement (with very few modifications) after you complete this chapter. Let's go ahead and design the software, implement it, and deploy it within our product over the Internet.

Design

For starters, we will add what is called a *serialization code* that encrypts certain information our customer provides us when he or she first launches our program and tries to use it. The interface here should be a dialog box if you are in Win32, and in HTML if you are distributing a server product that has no application interface. Figure 15.1 shows an example of encrypted customer information. This information is generally the customer's name, and possibly the company name. This will allow us to track who is using this product if it's redistributed.

Figure 15.1
Unlocking approach.

When this information is sent to the server, we'll unlock the software for 30 days. We do this by providing an *authentication code*, which the server uses to encrypt the unlocking information that is returned to the customer's product. We'll cover this information in detail shortly, but for now we're working on the mechanism. This authentication code is the same as the serialization code, but it is generated by the server and contains additional fields of data—such as how long to enable the product, and what features to enable—all encrypted. The serialization and authentication codes are encrypted with the same algorithm, but we use different keys to do so.

Additionally, we need to unlock the software permanently (unless we're only charging for a time-based subscription) when the customer decides to pay us for our product. However, just like when we were selling regular merchandise from our Web site, we need to encrypt this information to guarantee the integrity and privacy of our customer's data. We can't use SSL from our own software (unless the interface is in HTML, much like Netscape's servers), so what do we do? We write our own. We will use the same encryption code that we use for the serialization and authentication codes, and we'll use a unique key here as well.

There are several well-known encryption algorithms that hackers or the NSA have not broken. The integrity of these algorithms is sound, and the source code is freely available—well, freely available in most countries in addition to North America. To find the actual source for many of these programs, I had to connect to Web sites in the Czech Republic, France, and Germany. An excellent book that I highly recommend if you are interested in cryptography is *Applied Cryptography* by Bruce Schneier, published by Wiley & Sons.

Finally, we'll write a class similar to our **CCreditCard** class from Chapter 11 that will take the user information and unlock their software in realtime.

U.S. Export Regulations

America is the land of the free. The First Amendment guarantees your right to free speech and expression. However, the U.S.government will not allow you to export any software that contains an encryption key that exceeds five characters—that's a whole 40 bits. Apparently, the First Amendment is being interpreted as not applying to software.

Apparently Uncle Sam and the NSA are concerned that drug smugglers and anti-American government forces might use information in your product, so they insist on small key sizes so that the federal government can decipher your information that happens to be encrypted.

In July 1997, the first encryption trial took on the government and won; the government's export restrictions on such software were shut down—the court ruled that the State Department had no rights to suppress the First Amendment. However, the Clinton Administration moved the authority of enforcing encryption software to the Commerce Department, and now you must get an export license from both the State and Commerce departments until another trial occurs and our rights are upheld.

> *Note: Until the constitutionality of these restrictions is overturned by the court, you must restrict your keys to 40 bits as well as get a license for export from the State and Commerce departments—this usually takes about seven days for keys of this size.*

I confronted such a problem when I was working on a project for Norwegian telephone company and writing the software in North America. The 40-bit key restriction prevented my team from using large keys to encrypt the data. This restriction transferred the encryption portion of the project away from my company to a company in Europe that had no such restrictions. The other company used the same encryption algorithm that we did, but added a one-line change for a larger key and received a substantial payment. In this case, the restriction that the United States imposed took away my business and gave it to a company abroad.

Another problem that we have discovered is that it is difficult to find any encryption software on Web sites based in North America. Encryption algorithms developed in North America are available more readily in Europe, and even Eastern Europe where freedoms were considered rare. Two sites that I found in North America that contain links to other pages for this was **www.counterpane.com/blowfish.html** and **www.sni.net**, and it contained many implementations of various algorithms in C and even some in Java.

Carefully choose the size of your encryption key to meet government regulations, and choose a good secure algorithm. A great choice is to require that any would-be hacker have both the encryption key and the algorithm to decipher the information—this makes your protection difficult to break.

Encryption

Our book is about Internet commerce, not encryption—there are several well-written books on encryption and various algorithms (As I mentioned earlier, *Applied Cryptography* is one). For our commerce information to remain secure and meet all of the requirements we specified earlier, we decided to use an algorithm by Bruce Schneier called Blowfish. Blowfish originally appeared in an article in *Dr. Dobb's Journal* and met the following design criteria:

- Fast encryption/decryption at 26 bytes per clock cycle

- Needs little memory

- Encryption key is of variable length, to a maximum of 448 bits

Blowfish's variable-length key hides the data fairly well through a multiple pass procedure. For us to use it, we'll call the **encrypt()** or **decrypt()** routines, passing our data to encrypt/decrypt with a key used to encrypt/decrypt the data. Using these is very simple, and as Blowfish is optimized for 32-bit microprocessors, our software will encrypt/decrypt data we specify at phenomenal speeds. Although Blowfish can handle 448-bit keys, we'll restrict ours to the U.S.-regulated 40 bits.

Now let's go through the steps of encrypting and decrypting the information that will activate the program for the customer. Choose what information you want to encrypt, and store it locally. This information could be a customer's name or phone number. Local storage of this information prevents someone

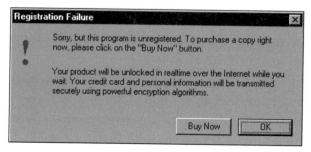

Figure 15.2
Alert for a customer who moves your software.

from copying the software to other machines and using it—if the customer did this, your software should display an alert similar to that shown in Figure 15.2. In our example, we have chosen the customer name and company name as the unique encrypted information. After encrypting these names, we use the serialization key, which generates what is called the *serialization code*. With this serialization code, if we know the key and the algorithm—which we obviously do—we can later decrypt the customer's name and company name, or whatever information we decided to make a part of this code. This is key here—this information can be sent to us to retrieve an authentication code to activate the customer's software. When we receive this information, we can use the serialization key and our algorithm to decipher the user name. We can then store this in our datastore as a trial-copy user, and create an authentication code using this information, the time of the trial period, and what features to enable. The customer's software will receive the authentication code back electronically, validates the user and the duration of usage, and enables the proper features. The codes also appear undecipherable to the customer, but are required to use the product.

Let's consider an instance where a customer doesn't unlock the software automatically over the Internet, but instead decides to call or fax you the information to perform the same action. If a customer calls you with the unique information, or faxes it to you, you should be able to obtain the customer information with a program that uses the serialization key and Blowfish algorithm to decrypt it, and then generate and provide the authentication code immediately after receiving payment—of course we prefer to automate this process entirely with our server and use the Internet, but there are some people who are still not comfortable with electronic commerce.

The Windows Registry

For Win32 applications, store this information in the Windows Registry. For Macintosh products, just create an invisible file in the Preferences Folder within the System Folder. If the software is copied to another machine, the new customer will have to provide the required information to try the product out for the test period.

Create two keys: one for the serialization encryption key, and one for the authentication key. Keep both keys under 40 bits. I made the keys a 40-bit character array (5 characters). Another key that we will use is for encrypting the customer information when it's sent to our server, not just to the local file system (or Registry); we'll call this third key the *data transmission key*.

> *Note: As this book is subject to export requirements, we've left out the encryption source code and have referred you to other sites for obtaining that information.*

The information that we require is the customer's name and his or her company information, which module ID to unlock (which we hide in our structure), and the period the software should be unlocked for. We can encapsulate this inside a class as follows:

```
struct UserInformation
{
    char    customerName[32];
    char    company[32];
    // modules to unlock. Minus 1 means enable everything
    uint    moduleID;
    // time in days
    int     unlockPeriod;
}
```

When the customer first launches the application, we display the dialog box shown in Figure 15.3. We get this customer information, and call **encrypt()** with the serialization key and store the information locally. The information is then sent to our server where we decipher, store in our local database for tracking purposes, and then use the authentication key to generate an authentication code—this code is returned to the customer program, which contains the entire structure **UserInformation** shown earlier.

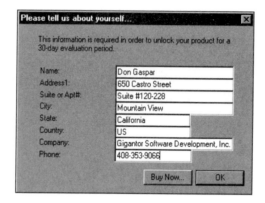

Figure 15.3
Customer information dialog box.

The program then takes the authentication code and deciphers it, compares the user name and company fields—if they match, the customer can continue with the moduleID module for the number of days specified by the unlockPeriod. We can now validate the customerName and company fields from both the serialization code and authentication codes—if they don't match, one code is wrong and we should disable use of the program.

What about when the customer is ready to pay for our program? When this is the case, a payment dialog box, as shown in Figure 15.4, appears. Here, the customer enters information to purchase the product, and we authenticate using an authentication server; we'll discuss this in the next section. We generate a new authentication code that lists the unlock period as -1, which means the specified module is unlocked forever. Voilà—instant distribution.

Payment Collection

The first section of code gathers the customer name and company name, and places it within a **UserInformation** structure. We then use the serialization key to create the serialization code. This information is then transmitted to a server we've written, which takes this information, stores it within our database, and generates an authentication key that is transmitted back. The customer then has free reign of our product for 30 days.

The code for the customer credit information gathering interface in Win32 is shown in Listing 15.1. You will notice a few noteworthy functions. The code

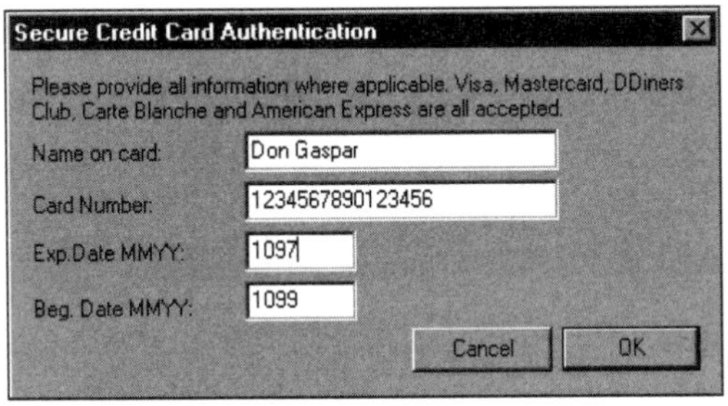

Figure 15.4
Payment dialog box.

here is simple and I refer you to our Web site or the CD-ROM enclosed with this book for complete details.

We did need to develop a credit card verification class, which I made in an MFC DLL. We gather the user information, and then process the credit card in realtime. The information is identical to what we used in Chapter 11, except that we can encrypt it. How will our commerce server validate this? We'll make our Credit Card Bridge listen on two sockets: one for unencrypted information, like our Web server (remember the information from the browser to the Web server is encrypted, but our commerce server is on the same machine and gets this unencrypted from CGI or ISAPI code fragments), the other for identical information but encrypted. I've left the encryption code out but mocked it up so that you can paste in the key and algorithm that you choose.

The MFC DLL provides various dialog subclasses, one is **CCreditVerify**, which resembles our **CCreditCard** class from Chapter 11. This class will take the information after calling its **DoModal**() member and process the transaction: you then unlock the program after receiving an approval.

LISTING 15.1   VERIFYCARD.CPP.

```
// CreditVerify.cpp : implementation file
//

#include "stdafx.h"
#include "stdafx.h"
#include "CreditVerify.h"

#ifdef _DEBUG
#define new DEBUG_NEW
```

```
#undef THIS_FILE
static char THIS_FILE[] - __FILE__;
#endif


//////////////////////////////////////////////////////////////////////
//
// CCreditVerify dialog


CCreditVerify::CCreditVerify(CWnd* pParent /*=NULL*/)
  : CDialog(CCreditVerify::IDD, pParent)
{
  //{{AFX_DATA_INIT(CCreditVerify)
    // NOTE: the ClassWizard will add member initialization here
  //}}AFX_DATA_INIT
}


void CCreditVerify::DoDataExchange(CDataExchange* pDX)
{
  CDialog::DoDataExchange(pDX);
  //{{AFX_DATA_MAP(CCreditVerify)
    // NOTE: the ClassWizard will add DDX and DDV calls here
  //}}AFX_DATA_MAP
}


BEGIN_MESSAGE_MAP(CCreditVerify, CDialog)
  //{{AFX_MSG_MAP(CCreditVerify)
  //}}AFX_MSG_MAP
END_MESSAGE_MAP()


int CCreditVerify::DoModal()
{
  // TODO: Add your specialized code here and/or call the base class

  return CDialog::DoModal();
}

BOOL CCreditVerify::OnInitDialog()
{
  CDialog::OnInitDialog();

  // TODO: Add extra initialization here
```

```
  return TRUE;  // return TRUE unless you set the focus to a control
                // EXCEPTION: OCX Property Pages should return FALSE
}

void CCreditVerify::OnCancel()
{
  // TODO: Add extra cleanup here
  // you might want to keep track how many times this
  // is cancelled or attempted and store in the registry.

  CDialog::OnCancel();
}

void CCreditVerify::OnOK()
{
  // go process the order now
  if ( ProcessCreditCard() )
    CDialog::OnOK();
}

BOOL CCreditVerify::Create(LPCTSTR lpszClassName, LPCTSTR lpszWindowName,
DWORD dwStyle, const RECT& rect, CWnd* pParentWnd, UINT nID,
CCreateContext* pContext)
{
  // TODO: Add your specialized code here and/or call the base class
  // we might want to get the user's name that we've stored away
  // previously in the registry.
  return CDialog::Create(IDD, pParentWnd);
}

bool CCreditVerify::ProcessCreditCard()
{
  bool result = false;

  // get the credit card and other information
  CString  name, cardNum, expDate, begDate;
  GetDlgItemText(IDC_CARDNAME, name);
  GetDlgItemText(IDC_CARDNUMBER, cardNum);
  GetDlgItemText(IDC_EXDATE, expDate);
  GetDlgItemText(IDC_STARTDATE, begDate);

  if ( !name.GetLength() || !cardNum.GetLength() ||
    !expDate.GetLength() )
    {
    MessageBox( NULL, "Please provide all information requested",
      "Missing Information", MB_OK);
```

```
    }
    else
    {
      // process just like we did for CGI/ISAPI with
      // CCreditCard-like member functions!
      DoCreditCard();
      result = true;
    }

    return result;
  }

//
//    function:    CCreditVerify::DoCreditCard()
//    purpose:     Calls private member functions and processes
//    any order associated with this customer.
//    returns:     nothing
//
void
CCreditVerify::DoCreditCard()
{
  if ( CheckCard() )
  {
    if ( HandleCreditCard() )
      DisplayApproved();
    else
      DisplayRejected();
  }
  else
    DisplayBadCard();
} // CCreditVerify::DoCreditCard...

//
//    function:    CCreditVerify::DisplayApproved()
//    purpose:     Outputs approved message
//    returns:     nothing
//
void
CCreditVerify::DisplayApproved()
{
  MessageBox( NULL, "Your order has been approved and your software
unlocked."
    "Thank you for your order","Order Approval", MB_OK);
} // CCreditVerify::DisplayApproved...
```

```
//
//    function:   CCreditVerify::DisplayBadCard()
//    purpose:    Outputs bad card number message.
//    returns:    nothing
//
void
CCreditVerify::DisplayBadCard()
{
  MessageBox( NULL, "Your card number or expiration date was entered
incorrectly."
    "Please re-enter and try again.","Bad Card", MB_OK);
} // CCreditVerify::DispalyBadCard...


//
//    function:   CCreditVerify::DisplayRejected()
//    purpose:    Outputs a rejected card message.
//    returns:    nothing
//
void
CCreditVerify::DisplayRejected()
{
  MessageBox( NULL, "Your order has NOT been approved. Please call our."
    "support staff at 408-353-9066 for further assistance.","Order
    Decline", MB_OK);
} // CCreditVerify::DispalyRejected...


//
//    function:   CCreditVerify::CheckCard()
//    purpose:    Checks the credit card length and digits
//    returns:    true if valid, false otherwise
//
bool
CCreditVerify::CheckCard()
{
  bool    result = false;

  switch ( m_cardNumber.length() )
  {
    case 13:
      // must be a VISA
      if ( m_acceptVisa )
        result = CheckVisa();
      break;

    case 14:
      // Diner's Club
```

```
        if ( m_acceptDiners )
          result = CheckDiners();
        break;

    case 15:
      // American Express, JCB
      if ( m_acceptJCB )
        result = CheckJCB();
      if ( !result && m_acceptAmex )
        result = CheckAmex();
      break;

    case 16:
      // MasterCard, Visa, Discover, JCB
      if ( m_acceptMasterCard )
        result = CheckMasterCard();
      if ( !result &&  m_acceptVisa )
        result = CheckVisa();
      if ( !result && m_acceptDiscover )
        result = CheckDiscover();
      else if ( !result && m_acceptJCB )
        result == CheckJCB();
      break;

    default:
        ;
  } // switch...

  return result;
} // CCreditVerify::CheckCard...

//
//    function:   CCreditCard::CheckVisa()
//    purpose:    Checks the credit card as type Visa
//    returns:    true if valid, false otherwise
//
bool
CCreditVerify::CheckVisa()
{
  bool  result = false;

  short number = m_cardNumber.c_str()[0] - '0';
  if ( number == 4 )
    result = DoCheckSum();
```

```
    // all we ever needed
    return result;
} // CCreditVerify::CheckVisa...


//
//    function:   CCreditVerify::CheckMasterCard()
//    purpose:    Checks the credit card as type MasterCard
//    returns:    true if valid, false otherwise
//
bool
CCreditVerify::CheckMasterCard()
{
  bool  result = false;
    char  value[2];

    strncpy(value, m_cardNumber.c_str(),sizeof(value));
    short number = atoi( value );
    if ( number >=51 && number <=55 )
    result = DoCheckSum();

    // all we ever needed
    return result;
} // CCreditVerify::CheckMasterCard...


//
//    function:   CCreditVerify::Amex()
//    purpose:    Checks the credit card as type
//    American Express.
//    returns:    true if valid, false otherwise
//
bool
CCreditVerify::CheckAmex()
{
  bool  result = false;
    char  value[2];

    strncpy(value, m_cardNumber.c_str(),sizeof(value));
    short number = atoi( value );
    if ( number ==34 || number ==37 )
    result = DoCheckSum();

    // all we ever needed
    return result;
} // CCreditVerify::CheckAmex...
```

```
//
//    function:   CCreditVerify::CheckDiners()
//    purpose:    Checks the credit card as type Diner's
//    Club or Carte Blanche.
//    returns:    true if valid, false otherwise
//
bool
CCreditVerify::CheckDiners()
{
  bool  result = false;
    char  value[2];

    strncpy(value, m_cardNumber.c_str(),sizeof(value));
    short number = atoi( value );
    if ( number ==36 || number ==38 )
    result = DoCheckSum();
  else
  {
    char  temp[3];
    strncpy( temp, m_cardNumber.c_str(),sizeof(temp) );
    number = atoi( temp );
    if ( number >=300 && number <= 305 )
      result = DoCheckSum();
  }

    // all we ever needed
    return result;
} // CCreditCard::CheckDiners...

//
//    function:   CCreditVerify::CheckDiscover()
//    purpose:    Checks the credit card as type
//    Discover.
//    returns:    true if valid, false otherwise
//
bool
CCreditVerify::CheckDiscover()
{
  bool  result = false;
    char  value[4];

    strncpy(value, m_cardNumber.c_str(),sizeof(value));
    short number = atoi( value );
    if ( number == 6011 )
    result = DoCheckSum();
```

```
    // all we ever needed
    return result;
} // CCreditVerify::CheckDiscover...


//
//    function:    CCreditVerify::JCB()
//    purpose:     Checks the credit card as type
//    Japanese Bank Card.
//    returns:     true if  valid, false otherwise
//
bool
CCreditVerify::CheckJCB()
{
  bool  result = false;
    char  value[4];

    strncpy(value, m_cardNumber.c_str(),sizeof(value));
    short number = atoi( value );
    if ( m_cardNumber.length() == 15 &&
    (number ==2131 || number ==1800) )
    result = DoCheckSum();
  else if ( m_cardNumber.length() == 16 )
  {
    char temp = m_cardNumber.c_str()[0];
    number = m_cardNumber.c_str()[0] - '0';
    if ( number == 3 )
      result = DoCheckSum();
  }

    // all we ever needed
    return result;
} // CCreditVerify::CheckJCB...


//
//    function:    CCreditVerify::DoCheckSum()
//    purpose:     Checks the credit card digits via the
//                 Luhn Mod 10 Algorithm
//    returns:     true if digits are valid, false otherwise
//
bool
CCreditVerify::DoCheckSum()
{
    // always be a pessimist with money involved
    bool    result = false;
    vector<short>    digitArray;
    short            dummy;
```

```cpp
    for( short index = 0; index < m_cardNumber.length(); index ++ )
    {
        // convert to an integer
        dummy = m_cardNumber.c_str()[index] - '0';
        // array keeps track of everything
        digitArray.push_back( dummy );
    }


    // now total the reverse digits and double them -
    //     part of the Luhn algorithm
    vector<short>::reverse_iterator    iter;
    bool skip = true;
    short sum = 0;
    for ( iter = digitArray.rbegin(); iter != digitArray.rend(); iter++ )
    {
        if ( skip )
            // total the digits
            sum += *iter;
        else
        {
            short value = *iter * 2;
            if ( value >= 10 )
            {
                sum += 1;
                value -= 10;
            }
            sum += value;
        }
        skip = !skip;                            // toggle every number
    }

    return ( sum %10 == 0 );
}  // CCreditVerify::DoCheckSum...

//
//    function:    CCreditVerify::HandleCreditCard()
//    purpose:     Validates the credit card with our
//    authentication dial-up server.
//    returns:     true if approved, false otherwise
//
bool
CCreditVerify::HandleCreditCard()
{
  char  queryInfo[256];
  string  zipCode;
```

```
float   amount;
bool   result = false;

// get the zip code for address verification system checks
GetZipCode( zipCode );

// get the order total
GetOrderTotal( amount );

// some extra stuff needed for WINSOCK
WORD   version = MAKEWORD(1,1);
WSADATA data;
(void)WSAStartup(version,&data);

// now put the string in a format that Gigantor uses,
// and also our bridge application uses for interfacing
// with ICVerify and PCAuthorize
sprintf( queryInfo, "%s|%s|%.2f|%s|%s|%s|",
  m_cardNumber.c_str(),
  m_expDate.c_str(),
  m_amount,
  m_zipCode.c_str(),
  " ",
  "Your software product description goes here" );

// now send it synchronously and wait for a reply!
// socket address
struct  sockaddr_in  sin;
// host entry
struct   hostent   *ph;
// TCP socket
int     s;
// length
int     len;
// IP address
long address;
// data buffer for TCP stream
char buf[BUFSIZ];
// this is your credit card server's address
char  *host = "your IP address goes here";

if (isdigit(host[0])) // dotted ip address?
{
  if (( address = inet_addr(host)) == -1)
  {
```

```
      MessageBox(NULL, "Couldn't find the credit card server."
        "Please call 408-353-9066 for assistance.", "Lost Server", MB_OK);
      throw(-1);
    }
    sin.sin_addr.s_addr = address;
    sin.sin_family = AF_INET;
  }
  else if ((ph = gethostbyname(host)) == NULL)
  {
    switch (h_errno)
    {
      case HOST_NOT_FOUND:
        MessageBox(NULL,"Can't find host.","Lost host", MB_OK);
        throw(1);
      case TRY_AGAIN:
        MessageBox(NULL, "An error occurred. Please try again.",
          "Host error", MB_OK);
        throw(1);
      case NO_RECOVERY:
        MessageBox(NULL, "A DNS error occurred. Please retry later.",
          "DNS Error", MB_OK);
        throw(1);
      case NO_ADDRESS:
        MessageBox(NULL, "NO IP Address was specified.
          Please call support at 408-353-9066",
          "Bad IP Address", MB_OK);
        throw(1);
      default:
        MessageBox(NULL, "An unknown internal error occurred.
          Please call support at 408-353-9066",
          "Unknown Error", MB_OK);
        throw(1);
    } // switch...
  }
  else
  {
    sin.sin_family = ph->h_addrtype;
    memcpy(ph->h_addr, (char *) &sin.sin_addr, ph->h_length);
  }

  // now actually connect
  sin.sin_port = htons( eGigantorPort );


  //  open a socket
  if ((s = socket(AF_INET, SOCK_STREAM, 0)) == INVALID_SOCKET )
  {
```

```
    s = WSAGetLastError();
    /*if ( s==0 )
        ;
    perror("socket");*/
    throw(1);
}

// connect to the remote echo server
if (connect(s, (struct sockaddr *) &sin, sizeof(sin)) < 0)
{
    MessageBox(NULL,"An error occurred connecting to the
        credit card validation server"
        ".Please retry later.", "Connect Error", MB_OK);
    throw(1);
}

// now send the data for validation
// ENCRYPT DATA HERE — USE SOMETHING LIKE BLOWFISH WITH YOUR KEY
// encrypt( queryInfo, strlen(queryInfo), myEncryptionKey)
if (send(s, queryInfo, strlen(queryInfo),0) < 0)
{
    MessageBox(NULL,"An error occurred sending data to the credit card
validation server"
        ".Please retry later.", "Connect Error", MB_OK);
    throw(1);
}

if ((len = recv(s, buf, BUFSIZ,0)) < 0)
{
    MessageBox(NULL,"An error occurred reading data from the credit card
        validation server"
        ".Please retry later.", "Connect Error", MB_OK);
    throw(1);
}
else
{
    // DECRYPT DATA HERE — USE SOMETHING LIKE BLOWFISH WITH YOUR KEY
    // decrypt( buf, BUFSIZ, myServerEncryptionKey)
    // was the transaction approved???
    if ( strstr( buf, "APPROVED" ) )
        StoreApprovalCode();
}

// extra code needed for WINSOCK
WSACleanup();
```

```
    return result;
} // CCreditVerify::HandleCreditCard...

void
CCreditVerify::SetCardTypes( bool inMC,
  bool inVisa, bool inAmex, bool inDC,
  bool inCB, bool inJCB, bool inDiscover )
{
  // some simple member flags we're using
  m_acceptMasterCard = inMC;
  m_acceptVisa = inVisa;
  m_acceptAmex = inAmex;
  m_acceptDiners = inDC || inCB;
  m_acceptJCB = inJCB;
  m_acceptDiscover = inDiscover;
} // CCreditVerify::SetCardTypes...

void
CCreditVerify::SetAmountToCharge( float &inAmount )
{
  m_amount = inAmount;
} // CCreditVerify::SetAmountToCharge...

void
CCreditVerify::SetZipCode( string &inZipCode )
{
  m_ZipCode = inZipCode;
} // CCreditCard::SetZipCode...
```

There are a few supporting C functions that we use to help facilitate the verifying process. The **MakeSerialCode**() and **GetAuthCode**() makes sure that the customer can use our software unimpeded for 30 days. Check the CD-ROM enclosed with this book or our Web site (**www.gigantor.com/coriolis**) for a listing.

Every time the customer launches your program, you should call **CanProceed**() to make sure the customer has authorization to use your product. If not, you should display an error dialog box that explains what the customer must do to proceed. You should also display this dialog box if the serialization and authentication codes don't match—this could happen if the program was copied to another machine, or someone was hacking around with it trying to get a free copy. Provide a Buy Now button that the user can select and instantiate a **CCreditVerify** modal dialog to handle collection of payment for you.

Another part of this product is the authentication server, which listens over a known TCP/IP socket. This threaded server receives this information and creates the authentication code that our customer program receives. For credit card authentication, our software authentication server talks to the Credit Card Bridge (introduced in Chapter 11), or the Gigantor Commerce Server directly. To modify the sources from earlier chapters to accommodate this, you will merely use the same encryption key your DLL used, and call the **encrypt**() or **decrypt**() functions.

You can easily modify the authentication server to be a registration server for software that you have distributed over commercial channels—channels in which the product has already been paid for. To register your shrink-wrap software, you would just send the required information to the authentication server separated by tabs "\t"—the server breaks up the values using **strtok**() and stores them in the datastore using ODBC.

Summary

This entire book has concentrated on processing payments and collecting them in realtime. In this chapter, we did the same thing but from a software program rather than from a Web page. This software is then given a serialization code that is based upon unique information provided by the customer. Given this information, we then contact an authentication server to create an authentication code that is sent back to the customer's software. This unlocks the software for a free 30-day trial, and both codes are used to secure the authenticity of this copy of the software for a single customer to use.

When the customer wants to pay for our product, we store this information via the authentication server, and also send payment information that we have encrypted via Blowfish. This information is then transmitted to a commerce server (or the Credit Card Bridge) for credit authentication. Then, another authentication code is sent to the customer's software and designates the software as available for unimpeded use for an unlimited time period (unless you design it otherwise, like when you rent or lease software).

This mechanism allows you to sell your programs over the Internet, and keep your software store open 24×7. Using the same server we covered in Chapter 11, it allows you to be paid immediately, and it does a few more things, such as making this a registration server. So not only can you sell hard goods over the Internet and collect payments in realtime, but you can now distribute software globally, and also collect realtime payments for your products.

Using the procedure we've outlined in this chapter and Chapter 14 you can distribute your products to a larger audience and at a lower cost than doing so over the conventional store counter. Your potential market share becomes quite substantial, while your costs are low; you should pass on the savings to your customers. Eventually, we might see Web sites dedicated to such distribution, and the current shareware sites (**www.shareware.com**) will be such sites when shareware developers start using this mechanism or a similar one. This is also a great distribution mechanism for regular shrink-wrapped software as the market is potentially much larger.

This book has taught you how to enable your Web sites for commerce, and sell your programs that are distributed with a built-in unlocking mechanism. The commercial enabling of your products and services can be 24×7, and the setup cost makes it a very attractive business model. When are you going to sell your software this way? Applying realtime commerce solutions for your business will enable you to thrive in a economically evolving world. A global market awaits your Web site and your software—all you need do is take advantage of the technology that's already here.

MORE HTML

In Chapter 2 and beyond, we discussed using HTML for a variety of situations and went through the process of implementing literally dozens of forms and pages. Here, we'll cover just HTML by itself and some of the basic tags as a reference. I highly recommend Ian Graham's book, *The HTML Source Book Version 3.0*, published by Wiley and Sons. This is an excellent HTML reference book as well as a solid tutorial. It covers many HTML topics in depth, and although it doesn't cover CGI too deeply, we covered that thoroughly throughout this book beginning in Chapter 3.

All HTML pages start with a beginning tag (<HTML>) that denotes where any HTTP header that is being sent over ends and where the actual pages begin. Your entire page will lie between an <HTML> tag and an </HTML> delimiter. Almost all HTML tags have the concept of a beginning tag, and a delimiter, which always starts with </. The body of your HTML program will be embedded within a <BODY> tag and a </BODY> delimiter.

The tags affect the text that lies between them. For example, to make some text bold, we use the Bold tag (<B>) and do something like:

```
<B>Now all this text is bold, whereas,</B> this text is now
normal.
```

To make the text underlined, we would use the following tags:

```
<U>This text is underlined,</U>whereas this text is not.
```

You can mix HTML tags; their effect on an item will occur until the delimiter tag is encountered. Here's an example of mixing and matching text styling options:

```
<U><B>This is underlined, bold text</B>, whereas this text is only
underlined, and </U>this text is normal.
```

Tables

HTML does not offer pixel or equivalent granularity of item placement within a browser's window, so to align items, forms, and so on, you will need to use tables. You can place all of your items within the body of a table, and specify options for placement within. For example, to center a table within a browser window, you could do:

```
<CENTER>
<TABLE COLS=3 ROWS=2 WIDTH="80%">
<TR>
<TD>Here's the first item</TD>
<TD>Next item</TD>
<TD><B>And a bold text item</B></TD>
</TR>
<TR>
<TD><U>Underlined items</U></TD>
<TD><INPUT ITEM="text" NAME="variableName"
    VALUE="something">Input Here:</TD>
<TD><B><U>Bold underlined</U></B>
</TABLE>
</CENTER>
```

I'll explain the above code briefly—here, we declare an HTML table that is three columns by two rows, whereas the width is 80 percent of the browser's window. The COLS, ROWS, and WIDTH fields within the **<TABLE>** tag are attributes that affect the table itself. Each row of the table begins with a **<TR>** tag, for Table-Row, which identifies where a row begins; the **</TR>** identifies the end. Each item of the row begins with a **<TD>** tag, which is a Table-Data tag, and of course the delimiter is the **</TD>** tag. Within the table we added some text with adornments (like bold or underlined) and even added a form item for input text. Any of these items is allowed within the confines of a table. There are even alignment options for **<TR>** and **<TD>** tags that allow positioning within the row or column within a table. There are many other options for tables and the row and data items, such as drawing a border around it (with the TABLE BORDER attribute). Be sure to get a decent book on HTML for lots of detail.

So, why discuss tables in so much detail? Remember that with HTML, we can't specify the position of items within the HTML page; therefore, we need tables. Learn them well. The best way is to write your own, and view them in your browser while you make various changes to them.

Forms

Forms are the single most important topic within HTML for us. We processed information that was provided from our clients by using information passed from the client's browser, which came from an HTML form. Although the data is passed over with separators, and there's even some translation of the data, our **CFormParser** class handles all of this for us. Therefore, we can use the [] **operator** to access variables, or even the **begin**() or **end**() iterators to move through every variable. If none of this sounds familiar to you, be sure to review Chapter 3 in detail.

An HTML form begins with a **<FORM>** tag, and one of the attributes that you need is the ACTION attribute, which tells the Web server what process to instantiate. So something like

```
<FORM ACTION="/scripts/login.exe" METHOD="POST">
```

tells the Web browser that when the client submits this form, the Web server should instantiate the login.exe process. It also tells the browser that we're using the **POST** method, rather than **GET**. For more on **POST** and **GET**, please review Chapters 2 and 3.

Every **<INPUT>** tag that lies in between the **<FORM>** tag and the **</FORM>** delimiter will be part of the data submitted to a Web server upon a SUBMIT action. These items are part of HTML forms, and include common interface elements such as drop-down list boxes, checkboxes, radio buttons, and buttons. The **<INPUT>** tag has no delimiter because the form item solely exists within the <>s.

The NAME attribute within an **<INPUT>** tag is the variable name that the browser will process and send to the Web server. The VALUE is what the variable will be equal to. Briefly, let's create a form that contains most of these user interface elements:

```
<CENTER>
<FORM ACTION="/scripts/runscript.exe" METHOD="POST">
Your first name: <INPUT TYPE="text" NAME="firstName"
    VALUE="" SIZE=12 MAXLENGTH = 16>
Your last name: <INPUT TYPE="text" NAME="lastName"
    VALUE="" SIZE=12 MAXLENGTH = 16>
<INPUT TYPE="radio" NAME="group1" VALUE="firstItem">
<INPUT TYPE="radio" NAME="group1" VALUE="secondItem">
<INPUT TYPE="radio" NAME="group1" VALUE="thirdItem">
<INPUT TYPE="submit" NAME="task" VALUE="Send it">
<INPUT TYPE="reset">
</FORM>
</CENTER>
```

Here, we created a simple form that is centered within the browser window. The form contains two editable text fields for the client to enter his or her first or last name. There are also three radio buttons with different values depending upon which is selected. Next, we have a Submit button that causes the browser to send us the contents of this form when the user selects that button. The other button is Reset, which makes the form and all of its associated items reset to their default values—the values they had when the form was first loaded.

Radio buttons return only one variable, and that's for the group they belong to—for example, in our last code snippet, we have one group called "group1." The VALUE of the selected item will be returned to the Web server with "group1" as the variable name. Checkboxes (see Chapter 2) return only a value when they are selected.

Don't always rely on the form remaining static—that is, with only a fixed number of items on the form—when dealing with orders. Orders are variable, so use **CFormParser**'s **begin()** and **end()** iterators to process each item.

Frames

Our book never touched the subject of frames, but these can be important design elements within a Web site. Essentially, a *frame* is more than one Web page shown in a single view within a browser window. Each frame is like a pane, or subpane within a window. To tell the browser what frames to put into its window and where, you will need to place them relative to each other.

The **<FRAMESET>** tag identifies where a frame begins. An HTML file that uses **<FRAMESET>** must not embed this within the **<BODY>** or **</BODY>** tags or the display will not work correctly with most browsers. Within the **<FRAMESET>** tag and its delimiter, you can identify what belongs within it. You can specify a CGI/ISAPI code fragment to instantiate and generate content, or you can even directly provide HTML files that are broken into multiple views.

A great application for forms is a logical breakdown of components within your window. For example, controls that are common to all of your Web pages on your site could be one frame, whereas the dynamic content could be another.

There is a **<NOFRAMES>** tag, which also has a delimiter. This tag is useful when embedded within the **<FRAMESET>** tag and delimiter and will display whatever HTML is within it if the browser viewing your site does not support frames. It is typical in this case to tell the client to use Netscape or Microsoft's Internet Explorer, and to provide links to their sites to retrieve them.

Be sure to look at our support site (**www.gigantor.com/coriolis**) for more information. Also get a good reference book on HTML. Another site worth visiting for more HTML details is **www.w3.org**, which is a site dedicated solely to the HTML language and standard. This site contains introductions and tutorials, and will keep you up to date on all the latest HTML tags.

TCP/IP Clients
and Servers

We covered how to set up basic servers and clients throughout this book, but we only discussed how to do this specifically for our needs. Let's look at using TCP/IP for socket-level communications from both clients and servers in more general usage. As we need something to **listen**() for connections, we'll begin by listing a server that does this and echoes whatever it receives back—an echo server.

The server here will receive text input and then just send it back to the client (we will write this part shortly). What do we need for this simple task? We must set up a socket that listens on a known port, which can have a range of an unsigned short integer (to about 65K, approximately).

Doing this requires us to bind the socket so that the TCP/IP driver will listen for us. Then we make a call to **accept**(), which is synchronous. When we return from it, we've got a live connection. We should either call this routine from a thread, or when we return from it, call another **accept**() from a newly created thread. If we're in Unix and can afford to create a new process, we could immediately call **fork**() afterwards. Throughout this book, I've covered Windows with Unix occasionally, so here we'll change our tune and show the example from Unix. To make this example work with Windows, be sure to:

- Include the wsock32.lib with your project at link time

- Include calls to **WSAStartup**() before using any TCP/IP calls

- Use **WSACleanup**() when you're finished

Also note that Windows does not provide a **fork**() call, so at that point you will want to create a thread that calls **accept**().

LISTING B.1 SERVER.C.

```c
// simple server listening on a TCP/IP socket.
// by Don Gaspar
//
#include <sys/types.h>
#include <sys/socket.h>
#include <netinet/in.h>
#include <arpa/inet.h>
#include <netdb.h>
#include <errno.h>
#include <stdio.h>
#include <ctype.h>

#define TESTPORT    1070
extern errno;

main (argc, argv)
int     argc;
char    *argv[];
{
    int     s;          /*    network socket            */
    int     fd;         /*    TCP connection            */
    int     len;        /*    length                    */
    struct servent *ps; /*    server entry              */
    struct sockaddr_in sin;  /*    socket address        */
    char    buf[BUFSIZ];

    /*
     *    Get port number of TCP echo service
     */

    sin.sin_family = AF_INET;
    sin.sin_addr.s_addr = INADDR_ANY;
/*    sin.sin_port = ps->s_port;*/
```

```
sin.sin_port = htons(TESTPORT);

/*
 *    Create the socket
 */

if ((s = socket(AF_INET, SOCK_STREAM, 0)) < 0)
{
    perror("socket");
    exit(1);
}

/*
 *    Bind address to local end of socket
 */

if (bind(s, (struct sockaddr *) &sin, sizeof(sin)) < 0)
{
    perror("bind");
    exit(1);
}

/*
 *    accept the connection from remote clients
 */

listen(s, 5);
while(1)
{
    if ((fd = accept(s, (struct sockaddr *)&sin, &len)) < 0)
    {
        perror("accept");
        exit(1);
    }
    /*
     * Create child process to perform the work. Server
     * then waits for additional connections.
     */
    if ( fork() == 0)
    {
        while((len = read(fd, buf, BUFSIZ)) > 0)
        if ( write(fd, buf, len) < 0 )
        {
            perror("write");
            exit(1);
        }
```

```
            exit(0);
        }
        close(fd);
    }
}
```

The other difference between Windows and Unix is that Unix's **read**() and **write**() calls use file descriptors that will break on Windows. Use **send**() and **recv**() to take care of that problem.

We've provided an echo server that receives text and sends back the same text until the connection is broken. How would we send the text to this server? Simple. Write a client that takes text we type on the command line and sends it over the same socket (1070 here). Listing B.2 shows such a client.

LISTING B.2   CLIENT.C.

```c
// sample Unix TCP/IP Client
// by Don Gaspar
//
#include <sys/types.h>
#include <stdio.h>
#include <sys/socket.h>
#include <netinet/in.h>
#include <arpa/inet.h>
#include <netdb.h>
#include <ctype.h>

#define    TESTPORT    1070
extern int h_error;

main(argc, argv)
int     argc;
char    *argv[];
{
    struct    sockaddr_in    sin;    /*    socket address         */
    struct    servent        *ps;    /*    server entry        */
    struct    hostent        *ph;    /*    host entry         */
    int       s;    /*    TCP socket         */
    int       len;    /*    length             */
    long      address;/*    IP address         */
    char      buf[BUFSIZ];        /*    data buffer        */
    char      *host;            /*    remote host        */

    /*
     * check for single command line argument
     */
```

```c
if ( argc != 2 )
{
    fprintf(stderr, "Usage: %s destination\n", argv[0]);
    exit(1);
}
/*
 *     find Internet address of host
 */
host = argv[1];
if (isdigit(host[0])) /* dotted ip address? */
{
    if (( address = inet_addr(host)) == -1)
    {
        fprintf(stderr, "%s: invalid host name %s\n", argv[0],
            host);
        exit(1);
    }
    sin.sin_addr.s_addr = address;
    sin.sin_family = AF_INET;
}
else if ((ph = gethostbyname(host)) == NULL)
{
    switch (h_errno)
    {
        case HOST_NOT_FOUND:
            fprintf(stderr,"%s: no such host\n",argv[0], host);
            exit(1);
        case TRY_AGAIN:
            fprintf(stderr, "%s: host %s, try again later\n",
                argv[0], host);
            exit(1);
        case NO_RECOVERY:
            fprintf(stderr, "%s: host %s DNS Error\n",
                argv[0], host);
            exit(1);
        case NO_ADDRESS:
            fprintf(stderr, "%s: No IP address for %s\n",
                argv[0], host);
            exit(1);
        default:
            fprintf(stderr, "Unknown error : %d\n",h_errno);
            exit(1);
    }
}
else
{
```

```
        sin.sin_family = ph->h_addrtype;
        bcopy(ph->h_addr, (char *) &sin.sin_addr,
            ph->h_length);
    }
    /*
     * get the port number of the echo server
     */
/*   if ((ps = getservbyname("echo", "tcp")) == NULL)
    {
        fprintf(stderr, "%s: unknown service echo \n",
            argv[0]);
        exit(1);
    }
    sin.sin_port = ps->s_port;*/

    sin.sin_port = htons(TESTPORT);
    /*
     *    open a socket
     */
    if ((s = socket(AF_INET, SOCK_STREAM, 0)) < 0)
    {
        perror("socket");
        exit(1);
    }
    /*
     *    connect to the remote echo server
     */
    if (connect(s, (struct sockaddr *) &sin, sizeof(sin)) < 0)
    {
        perror("connect");
        exit(1);
    }
    /*
     *    until end of file, copy data from standard input to echo
     *    server and echo copy echo server's response to stdout
     */
    while(fgets(buf, BUFSIZ, stdin) != NULL )
    {
        if (write(s, buf, strlen(buf)) < 0)
        {
            perror("write");
            exit(1);
        }
        if ((len = read(s, buf, BUFSIZ)) < 0)
        {
            perror("read");
            exit(1);
```

```
        }
        if (write(fileno(stdout), buf, len) < 0)
        {
            perror("write");
            exit(1);
        }
    }
}
```

The client needs no threads or **fork**() calls because it is only handling one request at a time—that's the text you type in—and it gets echoed back by the server.

Play with the server and client provided here to get more familiar with TCP/IP, and be sure to add new code that you come up with. This will enhance your networking coding ability. The best way to swim is to jump in the water and give it a try—use the source code here as your lake.

C

THREADS

We covered threads in slight detail in Chapter 11 when we used the Credit Card Bridge to interface with various credit card authentication servers from TCP/IP in our CGI/ISAPI code fragments. We briefly mentioned Posix non-kernel threads and kernel threads, and we even mentioned the Mac's cooperative non-preemptive threads. Here, we're going to briefly describe in more detail what happens when a thread is created and executed—we're going to assume you're on a threaded OS like NT, Win95, Unixware, or Sun's Solaris.

When you create a thread, you will specify a function pointer that tells the thread manager (OS) where to create a new point of execution. Note that I said "point" and not "process." A *process* is a separate application that contains its own process space with the OS. A *point of execution* is a place where the OS will maintain context.

The OS will call this function when told (depending on your **beginthread**() call or equivalent) and give it a time slice that is OS dependent. The stack and heap are maintained, and your thread on some OSs can even specify its own stack. A certain number of instructions are executed, and then the OS will context switch to another point of execution. The OS will do this until all designated points of execution (some are processes) get a time slice, and then come back full circle. This cyclical approach is commonly called *round robin*, and dates back to early CPU time-slicing programs.

The OS must preserve where the program counter is (that is, the instruction it's pointing to within your point of execution) and its stack (the local variables it contains), and so on. This overhead is very small for an OS and the context switching is very efficient.

Note that while a process is always a point of execution, a point of execution is not a process. A process can contain several threads, and thus several points of execution. This lets the OS switch between each of them, providing sufficient time for each task to pay its dues. Why use threads?

Threads are efficient. It's very cost effective in terms of CPU cycles to let the CPU manage time slices between your tasks and all the other processes and tasks running on it. It's also easier to code with, once you understand re-entrancy (this is defined in the following section). In a program without threads, the extra work you will implement to provide time slices can be overwhelming. Take the following case in point:

An engineer that worked for me many years ago implemented a POP3/SMTP mailing component that wasn't threaded. This engineer had to write a flotilla of state flags to remember the member function that was being processed and where he was in his code. Then, he would switch to another member function within the same class. A time-slicing class gave this class CPU time every time through the event loop, and the state flags would determine what actions to take. The state flags took days to write, and the periodical time-slicing class was provided by a framework we were using. Moving this to threads simplified the design.

We stripped out all the state flags, the setting and resetting, and the checking of values everywhere and anywhere. We then removed the periodical time class that was providing CPU cycles—although this was a fine class, we didn't need it here. The next task was to block a few critical areas that required a few lines of code. The component worked more efficiently than before, and performed better (there was less code, as the state flags were gone) because the OS scheduled time slices based on its loads. The code was also easier to maintain because it was substantially smaller.

Re-entrancy

Re-entrancy is where your code is entered through multiple points of execution. Remember that your process can have several such points and entering through another point can wreak havoc on your program. Debugging such instances in your code can be a nightmare because the information in your debugger will not make any sense at first. There are a few items that can prevent this.

If you modify a global variable, a static variable, or a static member variable from a thread, always block where the modification takes place. This prevents two points of execution from changing the same variable. If two or more points of execution were changing the same variable, and then checking for certain values, you could get caught in a situation called *deadlock*. The symptom is that your program will be frozen and unresponsive. In Windows, use the **CSingleLock** class to help out. In Unix, use whatever block/lock routines are available.

There are cases where you want to wait for several items to happen before unlocking a critical section, or maybe you want to time out and exit at a certain point. Use a mutex (a mutually exclusive thread) in these cases. All kernel-threaded OSs support these.

As always, design and take advantage of the features your OS offers. Use threads rather than timed-state machines with flags—they're more efficient and even easier to use than archaic state machines.

HTML Editors D

Dozens of new applications out there allow you to create Web pages graphically and then deploy them. These are great time savers, and are well worth their purchase price. You can use them to generate full-blown, powerful Web sites. Although they do generate sites well, they don't produce great HTML—which is still acceptable if you use them for a large site. Here, I'll cover a few of the more popular systems that I have direct experience using, as well as briefly mention their main functions.

NetObjects Fusion

This is an awesome product produced by some excellent programmers. It manages a complete Web site for you and will display it as a hierarchical tree with each node representing a page, as shown in Figure D.1. Double-clicking on a node will bring up a graphical page editor where you can add, remove, and place various elements just like you do in some of the most popular drawing programs, except here it does so with HTML.

You can use templates to create a basic site as well as build sophisticated and robust sites within hours. You can create forms, and even write the interface requirements so that you can make them work with your CGI/ISAPI code fragments. Another cool feature that it offers is remote site import—that is, you can give it a URL for a remote site, and it will download the site to your hard drive and make it a Fusion file so that you can edit it. You

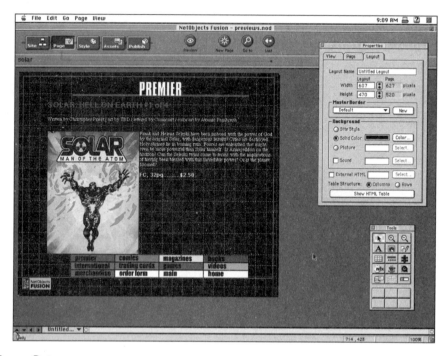

Figure D.1
Fusion in action.

can even FTP your sites. I worked on Fusion in 96 and 97 as a consultant, and can vouch for this product personally. Try an evaluation copy out for 30 days at **www.netobjects.com**. It's an addictive product, much like caffeine.

Microsoft FrontPage

This is another awesome product. I wasn't very impressed with FrontPage 97, but FrontPage 98 is really something. The feature set now offers nearly everything Fusion does, including templates, CGI/ISAPI links, and even site import. An additional feature of FrontPage 98 is integration with the various Microsoft Office products—exchanging data and so on. Figure D.2 shows a FrontPage design session.

FrontPage 98 is great. The only complaint I have is that you cannot place various design elements on a page like you can in Fusion. Fusion generates HTML tables to approximate their relative positions, and the free-form movement is great. FrontPage 98 is an excellent product, and I urge you to try it out. Microsoft

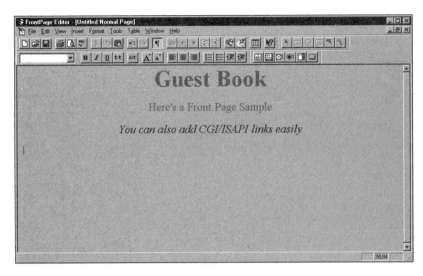

Figure D.2
FrontPage in action.

has tons of information on it, and you can get a beta copy from **www.microsoft. com/frontpage**. Warning: Using FrontPage 98 can also be addicting.

Others

There are several other page-editing programs out there; however, I have not found any with features sets that rival Fusion and FrontPage. Site development, deployment, and management—an overwhelming task for huge sites when you write HTML by hand—are the important issues to consider. Fusion and FrontPage are the only products that cut the muster for that. If your needs are not as demanding, then take a look at Adobe's PageMill (**www.adobe.com**) or Claris' home page (**www.claris.com**). An HTML editor can save you quite a bit of time.

CPONYEXPRESS E

I wrote **CPonyExpress** as a simple mailing class for use in your programs. It notices you about orders that a customer places with your site, or informs (via email) your customer that their order is in the mail. There are many different tasks you can perform with this class.

The **CPonyExpress** class requires knowledge of your SMTP server, the server in which your mail clients sends email to others. It requires a few bits of other information, but you can customize if for your own use and deploy it in your own programs with only a few minutes of customization work. Listing E.1 shows the header file and Listing E.2 shows the full source code. The code is also available on the CD-ROM enclosed with this book.

LISTING E.1 PONYEXPRESS.HPP.

```
//
//      File: PonyExpress.hpp
//      By:    Don Gaspar
//
//      This is the source for the CPonyExpress class
//      from Chapter 11 and Appendix E
//      in the book, Visual Developer Web Commerce
//      Programming with Visual C++.
//      The publisher  is the Coriolis Group.
//
//
//      You may reach the author at: don@gigantor.com
//
```

```
// headers we need that others have written
#include <bstring.h>

// cool exception macros that help simplify tasks around here
#define THROWIFNULL(value)     \
    if ( value == NULL ) throw(-1)

#define THROWIF(condition)     \
    if (condition) throw(-1)

//how about the SMTP error messages?

//System status, or system help reply
const int cSMTP_SYS_STAT = 211;
//Help message
const int cSMTP_HELP_MSG = 214;
//<domain> Service ready
const int cSMTP_DOMAIN_RDY = 220;
//<domain> Service closing transmit channel
const int cSMTP_DOMAIN_CLS = 221;
//Requested mail action okay, completed
const int cSMTP_ACTION_OK = 250;
//User not local; will forward to <path>
const int cSMTP_USR_NLOCAL = 251;
//Start mail input; end with <CRLF>.<CRLF>
const int cSMTP_START_INP = 354;
//<domain> Service not available
const int cSMTP_SRVC_NA = 421;
//Requested mail action not taken
const int cSMTP_ACTION_NA = 450;
//Requested action aborted
const int cSMTP_ACTION_ABRT = 451;
//insufficient system storage
const int cSMTP_ACTION_MEM = 452;
//Syntax error, command unrecognized
const int cSMTP_SYNTAX = 500;
//Syntax error in parameters or arguments
const int cSMTP_PARAMS = 501;
//Command not implemented
const int cSMTP_CMD_NA = 502;
//Bad sequence of commands
const int cSMTP_BAD_CMD_SEQ = 503;
//Command parameter not implemented
const int cSMTP_BAD_PARAM = 504;
//mailbox unavailable
const int cSMTP_MBOX_NA = 550;
```

```
//User not local; please try <forward-path>
const int cSMTP_USR_TRY = 551;
//exceeded storage allocation
const int cSMTP_MEM_OVRFLW = 552;
//mailbox name not allowed
const int cSMTP_MBOX_NAME = 553;
//Transaction failed
const int cSMTP_TRAN_FAILED = 554;

// other needed items
const int cSMTPMailPort = 25;

// now our class declaration!!!
class CPonyExpress
{
public:
    CPonyExpress(char *inMailHost = NULL,
        char *inReceiver = NULL, char *inSubject = NULL,
        char *inMessage = NULL, char *inSender = NULL);
    ~CPonyExpress();

    // main message - send mail out
    void    send();

    // member variable setters
    void    setmessage( char *inMessage )
        { m_Message = inMessage; }

    void    setsubject( char *inSubject )
        { m_Subject = inSubject; }

    void    setreceiver( char *inReceiver )
        {   m_Receiver = inReceiver; }

    void    setsender( char *inSender )
        { m_Sender = inSender; }

    void    setmailhost( char *inMailHost )
        { m_Host = inMailHost; }

  private:
     // member variable accessors!
     string& getmessage()
         { return m_Message; }

     string&   getsubject()
         { return m_Subject; }
```

```cpp
        string& getreceiver()
            { return m_Receiver; }

        string& getsender()
            { return m_Sender; }

        string& getmailhost()
            { return m_Host; }

        // sending and receiving
        void    sendstring(int inSock, char *inBuffer);

        int        sendandwait(int inSock, char *inBuffer, int inSize);

        // member variables
        string    m_Message;
        string    m_Subject;
        string    m_Receiver;
        string    m_Sender;
        string    m_Host;
};
```

LISTING E.2   PONYEXPRESS.CPP.

```cpp
//
//    File: PonyExpress.cpp
//    By:   Don Gaspar
//
//    This is the source for the CPonyExpress class
//    from Chapter 11 and Appendix E
//    in the book,  Visual Developer Web Commerce
//    Programming with Visual C++.
//    The publisher is the Coriolis Group.
//
//
//    You may reach the author at: don@gigantor.com
//


// general use
#include <sys/types.h>
#include <stdio.h>
#include <ctype.h>

// for TCP/IP networking
#ifdef UNIX
#include <sys/socket.h>
#include <netinet/in.h>
```

```
#include <arpa/inet.h>
#include <netdb.h>
#elif WIN32
#include <WinSock.h>
#include <io.h>
#endif

// headers we've written and need
#include "PonyExpress.hpp"

// start the code somewhere

//
//    function:    CPonyExpress::CPonyExpress
//    purpose:     Constructs CPonyExpress object; copies any
//                 input vars passed.
//    returns:     Constructors can't return anything
//
CPonyExpress::CPonyExpress(char *inMailHost,
        char *inReceiver, char *inSubject,
        char *inMessage, char *inSender)
{
    // copy any args passed to constructor
    if ( inMailHost )
        m_Host = inMailHost;
    if ( inReceiver )
        m_Receiver = inReceiver;
    if ( inSubject )
        m_Subject = inSubject;
    if ( inMessage )
        m_Message = inMessage;
    if ( inSender )
        m_Sender = inSender;
} // CPonyExpress::CPonyExpress...

//
//    function:    CFormParser::CFormParser
//    purpose:     Don't do anything here yet, but later?
//    returns:     Destructors can't return anything
//
CPonyExpress::~CPonyExpress()
{

} // CPonyExpress::~CPonyExpress...

//
//    function:    CPonyExpress::send
```

```
//      purpose:    Sends the mail message that has been
//                  configured.
//      returns:    Nothing.
//
void
CPonyExpress::send()
{
#ifdef WIN32
    // special initialization for WinSock
    WORD    version = MAKEWORD(1,1);
    WSADATA    data;
    (void)WSAStartup(version,&data);
#endif

    // now send it synchronously and wait for a reply!
    // socket address
    struct    sockaddr_in    sin;
    // host entry
    struct    hostent    *ph;
    // TCP socket
    int    s;
    // IP address
    long    address;
    // data buffer for TCP stream
    char    buf[BUFSIZ];


    if (isdigit(getmailhost()[0])) // dotted ip address?
    {
        if (( address = inet_addr(getmailhost().c_str())) == -1)
        {
            fprintf(stderr, "CPonyExpress: invalid SMTP "
                "server %s\n", getmailhost().c_str());
            exit(1);
        }
        sin.sin_addr.s_addr = address;
        sin.sin_family = AF_INET;
    }
    else if ((ph = gethostbyname(getmailhost().c_str())) == NULL)
    {
        switch (h_errno)
        {
            case HOST_NOT_FOUND:
                fprintf(stderr,"CPonyExpress: no such host\n",
                    getmailhost().c_str());
                exit(1);
```

```
            case TRY_AGAIN:
                fprintf(stderr, "CPonyExpress: host %s, "
                    "try again later\n",
                    getmailhost().c_str());
                exit(1);
            case NO_RECOVERY:
                fprintf(stderr, "CPonyExpress: host %s "
                    "DNS Error\n",
                    getmailhost().c_str());
                exit(1);
            case NO_ADDRESS:
                fprintf(stderr, "CPonyExpress: No IP "
                    "address for %s\n",
                    getmailhost().c_str());
                exit(1);
            default:
                fprintf(stderr, "Unknown error : %d\n",h_errno);
                exit(1);
        } // switch...
    }
    else
    {
        sin.sin_family = ph->h_addrtype;
        memcpy(ph->h_addr, (char *) &sin.sin_addr, ph->h_length);
    }

    // now actually connect
    sin.sin_port = htons( cSMTPMailPort );


    //   open a socket
    if ((s = socket(AF_INET, SOCK_STREAM, 0)) == INVALID_SOCKET )
    {
#ifdef WIN32
        s = WSAGetLastError();
        if ( s==0 )
            ;// need to perform some action here - you define -DG
#endif
        perror("socket");
        exit(1);
    }

    //   connect to the remote echo server
    if (connect(s, (struct sockaddr *) &sin, sizeof(sin)) < 0)
    {
        perror("connect");
        exit(1);
    }
```

```
// now send the data for validation
sprintf(buf,"helo %s\r\n", getmailhost().c_str());

// did the server acknowledge us?
if ( sendandwait(s,buf,BUFSIZ) == cSMTP_ACTION_OK )
{
    char *domainName = strchr(
        getmailhost().c_str(),'.');
    domainName++;
    sprintf(buf,"mail from:<%s@%s>",
        getsender().c_str(),
        domainName);
    if ( sendandwait(s,buf,BUFSIZ) == (cSMTP_ACTION_OK ||
        cSMTP_USR_NLOCAL) )
    {
        strcpy(buf,"data\r\n");
        if ( sendandwait(s,buf,BUFSIZ) == cSMTP_START_INP )
        {
            // set the subject and date field items
            sprintf(buf,"X-Sender: %s\r\n",
                getsender().c_str());
            sendstring(s, buf);
            sendstring(s,"Mime-Version: 1.0\r\n");
            sendstring(s,"Content-Type: text/plain; "
                "charset=\"us-ascii\"\r\n");
            // sender and receiver
            sprintf(buf,"To: %s\r\n",getreceiver().c_str());
            sendstring(s,buf);
            sprintf(buf,"From: %s\r\n",getsender().c_str());
            sendstring(s,buf);
            // subject, mailer
            sprintf(buf,"Subject: %s\r\n",getsubject().c_str());
            sendstring(s,buf);
            sendstring(s,"C-Mailer: <smsmtp>\r\n\r\n");
            // now the message
            sprintf(buf,"%s\r\n.\r\n",getmessage().c_str());
            if ( sendandwait(s, buf, BUFSIZ) ==
                cSMTP_ACTION_OK )
            {
                // looks like the mail was sent to the
                // SMTP server fine!
                strcpy(buf,"quit\r\n");
                sendandwait(s, buf, BUFSIZ);
            }

        }
    }
}
```

```
// extra code needed for WINSOCK
#ifdef WIN32
    WSACleanup();
#endif

} // CPonyExpress::send...

//
//    function:    CPonyExpress::sendandwait
//    purpose:     Sends the buffer inBuffer via the socket inSock
//                 and works with Unix and Windows source bases.
//                 Returns response as an integer.
//    returns:     int from recv() or read().
//
int
CPonyExpress::sendandwait(int inSock, char *inBuffer, int inSize)
{
    int len;    // receive byte count
#ifdef UNIX
    if (write(inSock, inBuffer, strlen(inBuffer)) < 0)
#elif WIN32
    if (::send(inSock, inBuffer, strlen(inBuffer),0) < 0)
#endif
    {
        perror("write");
        exit(1);
    }

#ifdef UNIX
    len = read(inSock, inBuffer, inSize);
#elif WIN32
    len = recv(inSock, inBuffer, inSize,0);
#endif

    return atol(inBuffer);
} // CPonyExpress::sendandwait...

//
//    function:    CPonyExpress::sendandwait
//    purpose:     Sends the buffer inBuffer via the socket inSock
//                 and works with Unix and Windows source bases.
//    returns:     Nothing.
//
void
CPonyExpress::sendstring(int inSock, char *inBuffer)
{
#ifdef UNIX
```

```
    if (write(inSock, inBuffer, strlen(inBuffer)) < 0)
#elif WIN32
    if (::send(inSock, inBuffer, strlen(inBuffer),0) < 0)
#endif
    {
        perror("write");
        exit(1);
    }
} // CPonyExpress::sendstring...
```

CREDIT CARD PROCESSING COMPANIES

I can't count how many companies are processing credit cards at any given time. Always do a search on the Internet using Yahoo, HotBot, or Excite to find the latest players. When you do find them, make sure that you can answer the following questions satisfactorily:

- What cards can I process with your system?

- What percentage do you charge per transaction?

- What protocol does your network use?

- When do you credit my account with processed transactions?

Also, if you are satisfied with your bank, see what it offers and its prices—many banks like Bank of America and Wells Fargo support Internet transaction businesses. I compared my bank's charges with those of a credit card clearing house. The clearing house beat my bank by 50 percent! I guess the bank wasn't exactly set up to handle Internet credit card transactions. Your bank's charges might be more reasonable.

Below, I've provided a list of a few companies that both process credit cards and work with some of the various software commerce servers I mentioned in this book. I do not have any opinions or information on any of these companies other than they advertise that they provide this service. Our support site, **www.gigantor.com/coriolis**, will always show any updates, so please be sure to check there also.

www.firstdata.com (these guys also provide X.25 and direct TCP/IP connections)

www.cardservice.com

www.bofa.com

www.wellsfargo.com

www.fusa.com

npsglobal.com

www.foomp.com

www.anacom.com

www.ecsonline.com

www.jetstreamatm.com

www.unifiedmerchants.com

CREDIT CARD SOFTWARE SERVERS

Evaluate your needs in terms of what type of connection to the commerce server you need, and what kind of performance you expect. For some of these, you can use the Credit Card Bridge we developed in Chapter 11 to facilitate a TCP/IP bridge. Here is a list and a succinct description of a few Internet commerce servers available now. These products are evolving all the time, so be sure to check their sites for their latest feature sets.

Be sure to check for product support plans, a developer program (make sure they really have one), and CGI/ISAPI code fragments (whatever ones you need) in C or C++.

PCAuthorize, MacAuthorize
www.tellan.com
This server provides a DDE or an AppleEvent interface to its product, so you will need to use the Credit Card Bridge to make it work over TCP/IP. It supports all major banking protocols.

ICVerify
www.icverify.com
This product uses a file communication method—information is written out to a file, and a program scans the directory periodically to inspect the file and then processes the information inside. You can use the bridge from Chapter 11, or you can

write a CGI/ISAPI code fragment to do this. It supports all major banking protocols. One downside is that ICVerify requires your merchant account number to unlock its software, and you have to do this over the phone. I'm reluctant to give that number out, as someone could access your account and the transactions that happen with it. ICVerify has a killer developer program.

CyberCash
www.cybercash.com
This solution represents a collection of software and PERL scripts. It is difficult to configure and only works through its network. A nice benefit, though, is that you get the software, support, and transaction clearing from one place.

Gigantor Commerce Server
www.gigantor.com
This server has a threaded TCP/IP interface for transactions and comes with CGI and ISAPI samples, so you don't need a bridge. While it supports dial-up and X.25, it supports only a few major banking protocols.

DIGITAL CERTIFICATES

In Chapter 10, we discussed secure transactions via SSL (Secure Socket Layer) and mentioned that you needed to generate a key-value pair using your server. This key-value pair is stored in a file that you send to a digital certificate provider, and it verifies who you are and creates another key that your server will use for encryption with Web browsers when a client is connected to it with https (Secure HTTP). For more details about this, please visit **www.verisign.com**.

To make sure that the Web server you are using is supported, first make sure your server supports SSL, then check on **digitalid.verisign.com/server_ids.html** before proceeding. You will be able to fill everything out—including payment information—online. Verisign takes about 24 hours to get back to you with your SSL key, and its support staff is excellent and knowledgeable. It currently supports over 50 different Web servers.

WebStar And The Mac

WebStar is an easy server to configure and get up and running—usually within minutes of downloading it. You can get a demo copy from StarNine at **www.starnine.com**. The Macintosh never was and never will be a character-based interface, so you cannot use **stdio**. Normally, when a programmer uses **stdio**, the development environment he is using will create a simple Mac Window Manager window and output the text there using the Text Manager from the Toolbox. There's nothing wrong with this—the Mac was designed this way—and this only turns into a problem if you're using CGI and a Mac Web server.

WebStar has a protocol called *WSAPI (WebStar API)*, which uses a structure to pass information from the server to your code fragment, and from the code fragment to the server (to the client's browser). To send information back, you'll use routines like **WSAPI_SendHTTPData()**. Be sure to review its manual for more information on specific calls—you can get it with a demo copy from **www.starnine.com**.

I wrote a simple WSAPI code fragment for anyone who wants to authenticate credit cards using WebStar. The fragment talks to the Gigantor Commerce Server and the Credit Card Bridge from Chapter 11, so be sure to have those running if you're using this. I didn't use the **CCreditCard** class as this was written in straight ANSI C, but you could easily modify it to be included. Listing I.1 shows the source code. Note that the WSAPI code fragments are real PowerPC code fragments, much like DLLs are in the Windows world. The source code is based on a template that StarNine provided, and I added all the credit card processing code, and a utility **SaveToFile**() that stores the transaction to disk and not a database, as the Mac had no secure link to my NT SQL Server.

There is a way of doing CGI with WebStar, which involves AppleEvents and a third-party CGI library. However, I do not recommend AppleEvents for credit card transactions, as there is no guarantee that the event will ever make it to the server. While it's highly unlikely that it won't, it is still possible, and therefore brings an element of unreliability to your server. WSAPI appears to be robust, and somewhat resembles other module extension formats for other Web servers.

LISTING I.1   GIGANTOR-PLUGIN.C.

```
//
//      Realtime credit processing module using W*API
//          By Don Gaspar
//          For use with the Gigantor Commerce Server
//          Install the executable module in your Plug-ins
//          Folder for WebStar
//
//      For Visual Developer Web Commerce Programming With
//          Visual C++
//      By Don Gaspar
//      Published by The Coriolis Group
//

#include <stdio.h>
#include <string.h>
#include <stdlib.h>
#include <ctype.h>
#include <time.h>
// some STL stuff
#include <vector.h>
#include <string>
// headers we've provided and written
#include "CTCPConnection.h"
#include "gigantor_plugin.h"
```

```
#include "WSAPI.h"

#define MyPlugInAction      "Credit"
//up to 31 char action name for W* suffix
//mapping transfer type. Must be unique.

#define MyPlugInName      "Gigantor_Credit_Card_Plugin"
//up to 31 char unique ID for your plug-in
//must conform to same rules as Action paths

#define kMySuffix     ".gig"
//URLs with this suffix will map to our action

#define MyVersionNumber "1.0"
//version of this plug-in
#define MyAdminURLPath     "/pi_admin.demo"
//path portion ONLY of a URL to invoke your plug-in's
//administration functions if necessary. This should
//always be "/pi_admin" followed by your suffix.
//Defining an admin URL is optional.


/***************************** Globals *******************/
/*
You may define your own global variables here,
but they are global across all
threads of execution, so you'll
need to use semaphores to control
concurrent access.
*/

char *header = "HTTPS/1.0 200 OK\r\nMIME-Version: 1.0\r\nServer: "
    "WebSTAR\r\nContent-type: text/html\r\n\r\n";
int counter = 0;
char *roles [] = {"CGI","PreProcessor","PostProcessor","Logging",
    "Security","Error","NoAccess","Index"};

short myResRef = 0;
//the resource file ref for the code fragment's resources
unsigned long serverUniqueID = 0;
char hostname [256];

// Local routine prototypes
static WSAPI_ErrorCode
    CreateAndSendHTTPResponse (WSAPI_CommandPBPtr pb);
static WSAPI_ErrorCode
    MyInit (WSAPI_CommandPBPtr pb);
```

```c
static WSAPI_ErrorCode
    MyShutdown (WSAPI_CommandPBPtr pb);
static char *
    MyGetParameterValue (WSAPI_CommandPBPtr pb,
        OSType which, char *buffer, unsigned long *dsize);


/***************************** Functions *********************/
/*
WSAPI_Dispatch:
This is the only subroutine you are REQUIRED
to implement. It is called from the main
routine in the WSAPI_Lib and you are passed
a pointer to a CommandPB structure as defined
in WSAPI.h
*/


WSAPI_ErrorCode WSAPI_Dispatch (WSAPI_CommandPBPtr commandPtr)
{
WSAPI_ErrorCode err = WSAPI_I_NoErr;
char s[80];
    //check that the API versions match
    if (commandPtr->api_version < WSAPI_VERSION) {
        //this *may* be a problem.
        //You'll have to decide in the future
        return WSAPI_E_MessageNotHandled;
    }
    else {
        switch (commandPtr->command) {
            case WSAPI_Register:
                //return plug-in name and abilities,
                //register actions and suffixes.

                //your code must make at least one of
                //the following WSAPI_RegisterAction calls or
                //there's no way for Web Star to pass CGI requests
                //to your plug-in

                if (err = WSAPI_RegisterAction (commandPtr,
                    MyPlugInAction, MyPlugInName))
                    //this was a bad thing. Do something smart
                    //instead of just printing a message.
                    WSAPI_DisplayMessage (commandPtr, "PLUGIN:
                        Couldn't register the action.");

                if (err = WSAPI_RegisterSuffix (commandPtr,
                    MyPlugInAction, kMySuffix, '*   ', '*   ', "text/
                    html"))
```

```
        WSAPI_DisplayMessage (commandPtr,
            "PLUGIN: Couldn't register the suffix.");

    //finally, fill in info about the plug-in itself
    strcpy (commandPtr->param.init.pluginName,
        MyPlugInName);
    strcpy (commandPtr->param.init.version,
        MyVersionNumber);
    strcpy (commandPtr->param.init.adminURL,
        MyAdminURLPath);
    break;

case WSAPI_Init:
    //set up global data, resources, etc.
    err = MyInit (commandPtr);
    break;

case WSAPI_Shutdown:
    //deallocate memory, close files, etc.
    err = MyShutdown (commandPtr);
    break;

case WSAPI_Idle:
    //do any global processing on a regular basis here,
    // outside the context of a
    // specific connection with an HTTP client.
    WSAPI_DisplayMessage (commandPtr,
        "PLUGIN: It's alive!!!");
    //commandPtr->param.idle.ticksToSleep = 300;
    //sleep for 5 more seconds
    break;

case WSAPI_Run:
    //main processing entry point.
    //Do your CGI-like processing here.
        // if we're running as a post processor
    //(or security or logging role), there's no client
    //   to talk to, so let's just put a message on the
     //WebStar screen to prove we got called
    if (commandPtr->param.run.role ==
        WSAPI_PostProcessor_Role ||
            commandPtr->param.run.role ==
            WSAPI_Security_Role ||
            commandPtr->param.run.role ==
            WSAPI_Logging_Role ) {
```

```
                              sprintf (s, "demo-plugin called with role: %s",
                                  roles [commandPtr->param.run.role]);
                              WSAPI_DisplayMessage (commandPtr, s);
                          }
                          else
                          { //build some sort of response for the client
                              err = CreateAndSendHTTPResponse (commandPtr);
                          }
                          break;

                  case WSAPI_Emergency:
                      //bad things are going on inside WebStar.
                      //Free up memory, disk space, etc.
                      break;

                  case WSAPI_ServerStateChanged:
                      //one or more of the server's settings have changed.
                      // Take appropriate action if you
                      //depend on specific settings values.
                      //     WSAPI_DisplayMessage (commandPtr,
                      //"PLUGIN: Server reports some settings have changed.");
                      break;

                  case WSAPI_AccessControl:
                  //The server should never send these messages, since we aren't
                  case WSAPI_Filter:
                   // asking for them. If we do get them, it's an error for now.
                  default:
                  //     sprintf (s,
                  //     "PLUGIN: received bad message, %d",
                  //      commandPtr->command);
                  //     WSAPI_DisplayMessage (commandPtr, s);
                          return WSAPI_E_MessageNotHandled;
              }
          }

      return err;
  }



/**********************************************/
// Perform plug-in specific initializations

static WSAPI_ErrorCode MyInit (WSAPI_CommandPBPtr pb)
{
```

```
short oldres;
Handle h;
WSAPI_DescPtr d1;
char s[256];
WSAPI_ErrorCode err;
unsigned long dsize;

    //set this global counter
    counter = 0;

    dsize = sizeof (hostname)-1;
    MyGetParameterValue (pb, piServerName, hostname, &dsize);

    myResRef = pb->param.init.resRef;
    //save the resource reference number for future use

    return WSAPI_I_NoErr;
}


/*********************************************/
// Perform plug-in specific shutdown

static WSAPI_ErrorCode MyShutdown (WSAPI_CommandPBPtr pb)
{
    return WSAPI_I_NoErr;
}


/*********************************************/
// ## Retrieve the string data for a specific parameter
// Warning! This routine is for demo purposes only
// and will crash if you extract data
//  from a descriptor that is larger than the buffer you
//  pass in. If you care, you should
//  fix this!!!

static char *MyGetParameterValue (WSAPI_CommandPBPtr pb,
    OSType which, char *buffer, unsigned long *dsize)
{
WSAPI_DescPtr d;
OSType dtype;
WSAPI_ErrorCode err;
char s[32];
    buffer [0] = '\0';

    //get the actual parameter data
    err = WSAPI_GetParameter (pb,
        static_cast<WSAPI_ParamKeywords>(which), &d);
```

```
        if (err == WSAPI_I_NoErr) {
            //pull the data out of the descriptor
            // and copy it to the buffer var
            err = WSAPI_GetDescriptor (pb, d, &dtype, buffer, dsize);
            if (err != WSAPI_I_NoErr)
                WSAPI_DisplayMessage (pb,
                    "PLUGIN: Error getting data from descriptor");
            else {
                //if this is character data, make sure a
                // null is on the end of the buffer.
                if (dtype == typeChar)
                    buffer [*dsize] = '\0';
            }
            //dispose of the descriptor
            err = WSAPI_DisposeDescriptor (pb, &d);
            if (err != WSAPI_I_NoErr) {
                sprintf (s, "Dispose error %d", err);
                WSAPI_DisplayMessage (pb, s);
            }

            return buffer;
        }
        else {
            WSAPI_DisplayMessage (pb,
                "PLUGIN: Error getting parameter");
            return NULL;
        }

}


/*********************************************/
// Build an HTTP response and send it back


static WSAPI_ErrorCode
    CreateAndSendHTTPResponse (WSAPI_CommandPBPtr pb)
{
char *buffer;
char s[1024], data [1024];
unsigned long dsize;
time_t now;
unsigned long connectionID = 0;
long tlong = 0;
short tshort = 0;
WSAPI_ErrorCode err = WSAPI_I_NoErr;
```

```
    //allocate some memory for our output
    buffer = static_cast<char *>(WSAPI_AllocateMemory (pb, 8192));
    if (!buffer)
        return WSAPI_E_InsufficientMemory;

    //stuff the header in there
    strcpy (buffer, header);
#ifndef TESTING
    strcat( buffer, "<BODY BGCOLOR=\"#FFFFFF\">");
</CENTER>");
    strcat( buffer, "<BR><HR>");
#else
    //strcat (buffer, "<META HTTP-EQUIV=\"Refresh\" CONTENT=5>");
    strcat (buffer, "<h2>Gigantor Debug Plug-In</h2>");

    //add the current date and time
    now = time (NULL);
    sprintf (s, "%s<br>This plug-in has run %ld "
        "times since start-up.<p>", ctime (&now), ++counter);
    strcat (buffer, s);

    //figure out what our role is
    sprintf (s, "Running as: %s<br>", roles [pb->param.run.role]);
    strcat (buffer, s);

    //add all the various parameters we're interested in.

    //path args
    dsize = sizeof (data)-1;
    sprintf (s, "<b>Path Args:</b> %s<br>",
        MyGetParameterValue (pb, piPathArgKeyword, data, &dsize));
    strcat (buffer, s);

    //Just to make things interesting, let's not return
    // anything if we're running as a
    //preprocessor and the path args contain something.
    // This allows us to test preprocessor behavior
    //when the preprocessor wants WebStar to handle the URL.
    if (strlen(data) && pb->param.run.role ==
        WSAPI_PreProcessor_Role) {
        //deallocate the memory we were using
        WSAPI_FreeMemory (pb, buffer);
        WSAPI_DisplayMessage (pb,
            "Gigantor Plugin: Preprocessor is letting "
            "WebSTAR handle the URL.");
        return WSAPI_I_NoErr;
    }
```

```
      //if we're here, let's continue building the reply

      //search args
      dsize = sizeof (data)-1;
      sprintf (s, "<b>Search Args:</b> %s<br>",
         MyGetParameterValue (pb, piSearchArgKeyword, data, &dsize));
      strcat (buffer, s);

      //action
      dsize = sizeof (data)-1;
      sprintf (s, "<b>Action:</b> %s<br>",
         MyGetParameterValue (pb, piActionKeyword,
         data, &dsize));
      strcat (buffer, s);

      //dump_buf_size
      dsize = sizeof (tlong);
      MyGetParameterValue (pb, piDumpBufSize, (char *) &tlong, &dsize);
      //this is a gross hack to use this routine for
      //non-string data,
      sprintf (s, "<b>piDumpBufSize:</b> %ld<br>", tlong);
      // but as long as the type of data and buffer match,
      //it's probably OK.
      strcat (buffer, s);

      //MaxUsers
      dsize = sizeof (tshort);
      MyGetParameterValue (pb, piMaxUsers, (char *) &tshort, &dsize);
      sprintf (s, "<b>piMaxUsers:</b> %d<br>", tshort);
      strcat (buffer, s);

      //Current User Level
      dsize = sizeof (tshort);
      MyGetParameterValue (pb, piCurrentUserLevel,
         (char *) &tshort, &dsize);
      sprintf (s, "<b>piCurrentUserLevel:</b> %d<br>", tshort);
      strcat (buffer, s);

      //the complete request
      sprintf (s, "<b>piFullRequestKeyword:</b><br><pre>");
      strcat (buffer, s);
      dsize = 4096;
      MyGetParameterValue (pb, piFullRequestKeyword,
         &buffer[strlen(buffer)], &dsize);

      sprintf (s, "<p><b>piPostKeyword:</b><br><pre>");
      strcat (buffer, s);
#endif
```

```
// piMethodKeyword == POST, GET, etc.

    //send the buffer before it gets too full
    err = WSAPI_SendHTTPData (pb, buffer, strlen (buffer));

    //add a few more things for testing purposes
    dsize = 4096;
    MyGetParameterValue (pb, piPostKeyword, buffer, &dsize);
    strcat (buffer, "</pre>");

    // here we get all of the strings in the form of var=value
    // start with a buffer
    char varBuffer[1024];
    memset(varBuffer,0x00,1024);

    UserInformation    user;
    memset(&user, 0x00, sizeof(UserInformation));
    char *temp = strchr( buffer, '=' );
    if ( temp )
    // break up like var=value1, var2=value2, etc.
    {
        char    dummy[32];
        CopyUntil(user.name,++temp,'&');
        temp = strchr( temp, '=');
        CopyUntil(user.address1, ++temp, '&');
        temp = strchr( temp, '=');
        CopyUntil(user.address2, ++temp, '&');
        temp = strchr( temp, '=');
        CopyUntil(user.city, ++temp, '&');
        temp = strchr( temp, '=');
        CopyUntil(user.state, ++temp, '&');
        temp = strchr( temp, '=');
        CopyUntil(user.zip, ++temp, '&');
        temp = strchr( temp, '=');
        CopyUntil(user.country, ++temp, '&');
        temp = strchr( temp, '=');
        CopyUntil(user.email, ++temp, '&');
        temp = strchr( temp, '=');
        CopyUntil(user.cardType, ++temp, '&');

        /// get the credit card information
        temp = strchr( temp, '=');
        CopyUntil(dummy, ++temp, '&');
        strcpy( user.creditCard, dummy);
        temp = strchr( temp, '=');
        CopyUntil(dummy, ++temp, '&');
        strcat(user.creditCard,dummy);
```

```
        temp = strchr( temp, '=');
        CopyUntil(dummy, ++temp, '&');
        strcat(user.creditCard,dummy);
        temp = strchr( temp, '=');
        CopyUntil(dummy, ++temp, '&');
        strcat(user.creditCard,dummy);

        // get the credit card expiration date
        temp = strchr( temp, '=');
        CopyUntil(dummy, ++temp, '&');
        strcpy( user.expDate, dummy);
        temp = strchr( temp, '=');
        CopyUntil(dummy, ++temp, '&');
        strcat(user.expDate,dummy);

        temp = strchr( temp, '=');
        CopyUntil(user.cardHoldersName, ++temp, '\r');
    }

    if ( CheckCreditCard( user.cardType, user.creditCard ) )
    {
        char    creditCardString[512];
        memset(creditCardString,0x00,sizeof(creditCardString));
        sprintf(creditCardString,"%s|%s|%f|%s|%s|", user.creditCard,
            user.expDate,12.00 ,user.zip,user.address1);

        CTCPConnection    socket("0.0.0.0", 1080);
        socket.OpenConnection();
        socket.WriteString( creditCardString );
        unsigned short sizeo = sizeof(creditCardString);
        socket.Read(creditCardString,&sizeo);
        socket.CloseConnection();
        if ( strstr( creditCardString, "APPROVED") )
        {
            strcat( varBuffer, "<P><CENTER><B>Thank you</B> for "
                "your order. Your order will be shipped within the"
                " next 24 hours.</CENTER>");
            SaveToFile( "APPROVED", user, creditCardString );
        }
        else
        {
            strcat( varBuffer, "<P><CENTER>Sorry, your credit card"
                " was not accepted. Please "
                "<A HREF=\"https://www.gigantor.com/credit.html\">"
                " click here </A>");
```

```
                strcat( varBuffer, " to re-enter your information."
                    "</CENTER>" );
            }
        }
        else
        {
            strcat( varBuffer, "<P><CENTER>Sorry, your credit card was"
                " not accepted. Please "
               "<A HREF=\"https://www.gigantor.com/credit.htm\"> "
               "click here </A>");
            strcat( varBuffer, " to re-enter your information."
                "</CENTER>" );
        }


    //send the buffer
    err = WSAPI_SendHTTPData (pb, varBuffer, strlen (varBuffer));


    //free the memory
    WSAPI_FreeMemory (pb, buffer);

    return err;
}

//
//    function:    CopyUntil()
//    purpose:     Copies from inBuffer to outstring until delim
//                       character is reached.
//                 Used for getting name/value pairs from HTML forms.
//
//    returns:     Nothing.
//
void
CopyUntil( char *outString, char *inBuffer, char delim )
{
    char*    temp = outString;
    *temp = '\0';                       // clear this thing out first
    while ( *inBuffer )
    {
        if ( (char)(*inBuffer) == (char)delim )
            break;
        *outString++ = *inBuffer++;
    }
    while( (temp = strchr(temp,'+')))
        *temp++ = (char)' ';
    *outString++ = (char)'\0';
} // CopyUntil...
```

```
//
//    function:    appendBuffer()
//    purpose:     Appends inString and inString2 to outBuffer.
//                        Just a routine for convenience.
//    returns:     Nothing.
//

void
AppendBuffer( char *inString, char *inString2, char *outBuffer )
{
    char    s[256];
    sprintf( s, "%s = %s<br>",inString, inString2 );
    strcat(outBuffer,s);
} // AppendBuffer...


//
//    function:    CheckCreditCard()
//    purpose:     checks the card type and number, first
//                 validating the card type by its prefix
//                 and the number of digits, then the checksum
//                 by cal DoCheckSum()
//    returns      true on approval, false on failure
//
bool
CheckCreditCard( const char *inCardType, const char *inCardNumber )
{
    bool    result = false;
    // Note: Versions only takes MasterCard and VISA for now...
    if ( strcmp(inCardType, "MasterCard") == 0 )
    // is it a MasterCard???
    {
        if ( strlen( inCardNumber ) == 16 )
        {
            short number;
            char  value[2];
            strncpy(value, inCardNumber,sizeof(value));
            number = atoi( value );
            if ( number >=51 && number <=55 )
                result = DoCheckSum( inCardNumber );
        }
    }
    else if ( strcmp( inCardType, "VISA") == 0 )
    // how about a Visa?
    {
        short len = strlen( inCardNumber );
        // simplist check is size
        if ( len == 13 || len == 16 )
        {
```

```
            short number = inCardNumber[0] - '0';
            if ( number == 4 )
                result = DoCheckSum( inCardNumber);
        }
    }

    return result;    // all we ever needed
} // CheckCreditCard...

//
//    function:    DoCheckSum()
//    purpose:     Checks the credit card digits via the
//                     Luhn Mod 10 Algorithm
//    reutrns:     true if digits are valid, false otherwise
//
bool
DoCheckSum( const char *inCardNumber )
{
    bool    result = false;
   // always be a pessimist with money involved
    vector<short>    digitArray;
    short            dummy;

    for( short index = 0; index < strlen(inCardNumber); index ++ )
    {
        dummy = inCardNumber[index] - '0';
        // convert to an integer
        digitArray.push_back( dummy );
        // array keeps track of everything;
    }

    // now total the reverse digits and double them -
    // part of the Luhn algorithm
    vector<short>::reverse_iterator    iter;
    bool skip = true;
    short sum = 0;
    for ( iter = digitArray.rbegin(); iter !=
        digitArray.rend(); iter++ )
    {
        if ( skip )
            sum += *iter;
          // total the digits
        else
        {
            short value = *iter * 2;
            if ( value >= 10 )
            {
```

```
                        sum += 1;
                        value -= 10;
                    }
                    sum += value;
                }
                skip = !skip;
                // toggle every number
            }

        return ( sum %10 == 0 );
    } // DocheckSum...


    //
    //    function:    SaveToFile()
    //    purpose:     Saves user and approval information to
    //                     disk for later access.
    //    returns:     Nothing...
    //
    void
    SaveToFile( const char *inFileName, UserInformation &user,
        const char *approvalString )
    {
        FILE *file = fopen( inFileName, "wa" );
        // open file for appending
        if ( inFileName )
        {
            fwrite( user.name, strlen(user.name),1, file );
            fwrite( "|", 1, 1, file );
            fwrite( user.address1, strlen(user.address1),1, file );
            fwrite( "|", 1, 1, file );
            fwrite( user.address2, strlen(user.address2),1, file );
            fwrite( "|", 1, 1, file );
            fwrite( user.city, strlen(user.city),1, file );
            fwrite( "|", 1, 1, file );
            fwrite( user.state, strlen(user.state),1, file );
            fwrite( "|", 1, 1, file );
            fwrite( user.zip, strlen(user.zip),1, file );
            fwrite( "|", 1, 1, file );
            fwrite( user.country, strlen(user.country),1, file );
            fwrite( "|", 1, 1, file );
            fwrite( user.email, strlen(user.email),1, file );
            fwrite( "|", 1, 1, file );
            fwrite( user.cardType, strlen(user.cardType),1, file );
            fwrite( "|", 1, 1, file );
            fwrite( user.creditCard, strlen(user.creditCard),1, file );
            fwrite( "|", 1, 1, file );
            fwrite( user.expDate, strlen(user.expDate),1, file );
```

```
            fwrite( "|", 1, 1, file );
            fwrite( user.cardHoldersName,
               strlen(user.cardHoldersName),1, file );
            fwrite( "|", 1, 1, file );
            fwrite( approvalString, strlen(approvalString),1, file );
            fwrite( "|", 1, 1, file );
            fclose( file );
        }
} // SaveToFile...
```

INDEX

[] operator, 78-79, 499
<< operator, 122

A

accept(), 332, 503
accumulate(), 343
ACTION attribute, 25
ActiveX, 111
Adapter, 371-372
AddCustomerToDB(), 317-319
AddHeader(), 120, 258
AddItemToDB(), 278
AddNew(), 201, 205, 212, 239
Advertising, 467-468
Advertising server, 470
ALL_HTTP, 65
AltaVista, 468
Amazon.com, 9-11
American Express, 15, 320
ANSI string class, 35-36
AppleEvents, 536
Applied Cryptography, 475, 477
Associative container, 76, 265
ATM cards, 15
atof(), 36
atoi(), 36

AUTH_TYPE, 65
   Authentication code, 475
Authentication server, 495

B

Back orders, processing of, 369-385
Batch processing, 369-385
begin(), 499
BeginHeader(), 59
Bierce, Ambrose, 325
binary[n], 156
bit, 156
Block/lock routines, 513
Blowfish, 477
<BODY> tag...<BODY>
   delimiter, 497
bridge.cpp, 334-342

C

C++ class design, 266
C.O.D. orders, 15
C/C++, conversions to, 160
C/C++ structure, 34-36, 372
CalculatePrice(), 461
CallFunction(), 117, 120-121
CanAppend(), 200

CanBookmark(), 200
Cancel(), 202
CancelOrder(), 280
CancelUpdate(), 201
CanProceed(), 494
CanRestart(), 200
CanScroll(), 200
CanTransact(), 200
CanUpdate(), 200
Carte Blanche, 15, 320
Catch(), 63, 84
CCookieMonster, 245, 255
CCoolHttpServer, 123-128, 238
CCreditCard, 343-359
CCreditVerify, 481
CDatabase class, 213
Certification companies, 310, 533
cFormParser class, 74-84
CFormParser.cpp, 80-83, 247-254,
    439-461
CGI, 55-109
    advantages, 109
    cFormParser class, 74-84
    complex forms parsing, 88-106
    examples, 88-106
    extending the server, 57-60
    flow of control, 108
    guest book, 95-106
    Hello World, 57-59, 89-95
    intercepting/processing
        variables, 73-84
    ISAPI, contrasted, 112, 114,
        151-152
    overhead, 107-108
    POST/GET, 71-73
    process space (heaps), 109

    processing HTML controls, 84-88
    protected memory, 109
    server variables, 64-71
    STL, 74-77
    streaming files, 60-63
    uses, 56
    what is it, 56
CGuestset, 230
char[n], 156
Check boxes, 38
Check(), 202
CheckCookie(), 273
CheckRowsetError(), 203
CHtmlStream class, 114, 122, 152
CHttpServer class, 119-121
CHttpServer(), 120
CHttpServerContext class, 121-122
CISAPIGuestBookExtension, 240
Claris' home page, 517
Claris Works, 467
Classes, 255
Close(), 200, 212
Code evolution vs. code
    remodeling, 263-264
Code fragments, 56
Comic book
    C++ structure, 160
    order table, 162
    SQL table, 159
Commerce servers, 326-330
Commercial solutions, 471-472
Common gateway interface.
    See CGI.
Compare(), 98, 292
Configurable merchandise, 21-23
ConstructStream(), 120

Containers, 74-76, 267-268
CONTENT_LENGTH, 66, 70
CONTENT_TYPE, 66
Cookie cache, 241, 264
Cookies, 241-262
    CCookieMonster, 245
    deletion, 241-242
    foosball store, 244-246
    making, 255-258
    netiquette, 242
    retrieving, 246-254
    search engine pages, 243
    sending, 258
    separator character, 254-255
    stale, 258-261
    storing information, 242
CPonyExpress, 365, 519-528
CRecordset, 199-212
Credit Card Bridge, 334
Credit Card Bridge window, 343
Credit card HTML form, 320, 344
Credit card number
    validation, 319-323
Credit card processing, 325-367
    bridge.cpp, 334-342
    CCreditCard class, 343-359
    credit card servers, 326-330
    CreditCard.cpp, 345-359
    CyberCash, 364-365
    emailing confirmation, 365-366
    ProcessCreditCard.cpp, 359-363
    software distribution, 480-495
    storing results in database, 363
    threaded TCP server, 330-343
Credit card processing
    companies, 529-530
Credit card servers, 326-330

Credit card software servers, 531-532
Credit cards, 14-15
CreditCard.cpp, 345-359
Critical section, 239-240
Cryptography, 475
CShoppingCart, 273, 308, 438
CShoppingCartSet class, 204
CSingleLock, 239, 513
CString class, 36
Customer information dialog
    box, 480
Customer information HTML
    form, 317
Customizing a product, 21-23
Cyber-pay systems, 15-16
CyberCash, 364-365, 532
CyberCoin, 15
CyberWallets, 15

D

Dangling pointers, 151
Data transmission key, 479
Database, 155
Datastores, 153-176. See also ODBC.
    defined, 155
    design first, 174
    disk drive, 168
    dynamic order forms, 162-166
    foosball datastore, 168-172
    generating dynamic HTML
        forms, 166
    guest book, 166-167
    inventory storage, 157-160
    key, 157-158
    MS SQL Server, 173-174
    ODBC control panel, 175
    orders, 160-162

sharing tables, 175
tables, 155-157
datetime, 156
DDE/TCP/IP bridge program, 462
Deadlock, 513
Deallocate storage, 190
Debit cards, 15
Debugging, 138
decrypt(), 477, 495
Default(), 121-123, 130
DEFAULT_PARSE_COMMAND, 133
#define Unix, 345
Delete(), 201
Dell Computer site, 22, 24
Deque container, 371-373
Design first, 174, 263-264
Developer Studio, project
    settings, 189
Dialog boxes
    customer information, 480
    online registration, 469
    payment, 481
Digital certificates, 16, 309-310, 533
Diner's Club, 15, 320
Discover, 15, 320
DoBulkFieldExchange(), 203
DoCreditCard(), 343-344, 359
DoDatabaseStuff(), 189, 193-198
DoFieldExchange(), 203
DoModal(), 481
double, 156
Drop-down list, 32
Duell, Charles H., 473
Dynamic order forms, 162-166
DynamicForm.cpp, 60-63

E

ECB structure, 112-113
Echo server, 503-506
Edit(), 201
encrypt(), 477, 495
Encryption, 331, 475-480
end(), 499
EndContent(), 119-120
EndHeader(), 59
Environment variables
    CGI, 64-71
    ISAPI, 129-131
Error handling, 83-84
Examples. See Foosball store, Guest
    book, Hello world.
Exception handling, 83-84
Excite search, 243, 245
Export regulations, 476-477
Extension control block
    (ECB), 112-113

F

FIFO queue structure, 370
Float, 156
FlushResultSet(), 202
Foosball store. See also
    Online foosball store.
    cookies, 244-245
    datastore, 168-172
    dynamically generated table, 64
    merchandise-ordering page, 14
    overview, 12-13
    shopping cart, 246, 269-271,
        283-289
fork(), 330-331, 503
Form elements, 36-38

Form fields, 21
<FORM> tag...</FORM> delimiter,
    25, 51, 499
FormHandler.cpp, 84-88
Forms. *See* HTML forms.
40-bit key restriction, 476
for_each(), 84, 163, 384
Fragmented application heap, 151
Frames, 500-501
<FRAMESET> tag, 501
FrontPage, 516-517
Function pointers, 113
Fusion, 515-516

G

GATEWAY_INTERFACE, 66
Generating dynamic HTML
    forms, 166
GET, 71-73
GetAuthCode(), 494
GetBookmark(), 201
GetCart(), 281
GetCatalog(), 281
getdate(), 271
GetDefaultConnect(), 203, 206
GetDefaultSQL(), 203, 206
getenv(), 63-64, 130
GetExtensionVersion(), 120
GetFieldValue(), 202
GetODBCFieldCount(), 200
GetODBCFieldInfo(), 202
GetRecordCount(), 200
GetRowsetSize(), 202
GetRowsFetched(), 202
GetRowStatus(), 202
GetServerVariable(), 121, 130

GetSQL(), 200
GetStatus(), 200
GetTableName(), 200
GetTitle(), 120
GetVariable(), 79
Gigantor Commerce Server,
    329-330, 532
Glass, Graham, 268
Graham, Ian, 497
Guest book
    CGI, 218-229
    database table, 218-219
    datastores, 166-167
    GuestBook.HTM, 49-51,
        216-218
    HTML, 39-42
    ISAPI, 219-240
    ISAPIGuestBook.cpp, 140-146
    NewGuestook.cpp, 96-106
GuestInfo structure, 99
GUSI, 345

H

HandleCart(), 289, 292, 308, 312
HandleForm(), 92
Heaps, 151
Hello world
    coolHelloISAPIWorld.HTM,
        123-129
    HelloISAPIWorld.cpp, 117-119
    HelloISAPIWorldExtension.h,
        116
    HelloWorld.cp, 57-59
    HelloWorld.HTM, 59
    newHelloISAPIWorld.cpp,
        134-137

NewHelloWorld.cpp, 92-95
NewHelloWorld.HTM, 90-92
Hidden variables, 51
Hotbot, 468
HSE_REQ_SEND_URL, 316
HSE_REQ_SEND_URL_RE-
    DIRECT_RESP, 316
HTML, 57
HTML content type, 59
HTML editors, 24, 515-517
HTML forms, 19-53, 499-500
    C/C++ structures, 34-36
    calls, 51-52
    editors, 24
    examples, 38-48
    feedback, 52-53
    form elements, 36-38
    how server handles data, 33-48
    how server sees things, 48-53
    source code, 23-33
    starting/delimitin tags, 25
    variable names, 31-32
    variables, 34
HTML source code, 23-33
HTML Source Code Version 3.0,
    The, 497
<HTML> tag...<HTML>
    delimiter, 497
HTML tags, 497-498
HTML variables, 34
HTTP, 57
HTTP_ACCEPT, 65
HTTP_CONTENT_LENGTH, 65
HTTP_CONTENT_TYPE, 65
HTTP_COOKIE, 65
HTTP cookies. *See* Cookies.
HttpExtensionProc(), 120

HTTP_REFERER, 65, 70
HTTP response codes, 311
HTTP_USER_AGENT, 65

I

ICVerify, 326-327, 531
ifstream, 99
IIS, 310
Illustrations. *See* Foosball store,
    Guest book, Hello world.
Image, 156
InitInstance(), 120
<INPUT> tag, 499-500
INSERT, 181
InsertCartItem(), 206-212
int, 156
Internet commerce, 8
Internet server application program-
    ming interface. *See* ISAPI.
Internet software distribution.
    See Software distribution.
Inventory storage, 157-160
inventoryID, 389, 407
ISAPI, 111-152
    ActiveX, contrasted, 111
    cCoolHttpServer class, 123-128
    CGI, contrasted, 112, 114,
        151-152
    cHttpServer class, 119-121
    cHttpServerContext class,
        121-122
    crashing the Web server, 150
    debugging, 138
    defined, 112-114
    disadvantages, 150-152
    examples, 138-150
    guest book, 139-146

memory leaks, 151-152
order taking, 146-150
parsemaps, 131-137
reentrancy, 152
server variables, 129-131
weakness, 166
ISAPI filter, 116
ISAPIOrder.cpp, 147-150
ISAPIGuestBook.cpp, 140-146
ISAPITRACE(), 138
IsBOF(), 200
IsDeleted(), 201
IsEOF(), 201
IsFieldDirty(), 202
IsFieldNull(), 202
IsFieldNullable(), 202
IsOpen(), 200
Iterators, 76, 266-268
ITS_EMPTY, 163

J

Japan, 15
Japanese Bank Card, 15
Java, 179-180
JavaScript, 49, 321
JCB, 320
JDBC, 179-180

K

Kernel-level threads, 332
Key, 157-158
Key-value pair, 533

L

Larson, Gary, 387
LIFO architecture, 371

Lines of code, 88
listen(), 330-331, 503
Lock(), 239
LOGON_USER, 66
LPCTSTR data type, 134
Luhn algorithm, 319-323
Lycos search, 243-244

M

m_pECB, 121
m_pStream, 121
MacAuthorize, 328, 531
Macintosh, 173
MakeCookie(), 256-258
MakeCookieInDB(), 273
MakeSerialCode(), 494
Map container, 76-77
MasterCard, 15, 320
Memory leaks, 151
MFC DLL, 481
Microsoft FrontPage, 516-517
Microsoft Wallet, 16
Money, 156
Move(), 201
MoveFirst(), 201, 212, 239
MoveLast(), 201
MoveNext(), 201, 212
MovePrev(), 201
MS SQL Server, 173-174
Multiple submit buttons, 96-97
Mutex, 513

N

Netiquette, 242
NetObjects Fusion, 515-516
Netscape Enterprise Server 3.0, 310

New(), 151
NewGuestBook.cpp, 96-106
NewHelloIsapiWorld.cpp, 134-137
NewHelloWorld.cpp, 92-95
NewHelloWorld.HTM, 90-92
<NOFRAMES> tag, 501
NOMINMAX, 139
Non-ODBC database, 179
Numeric, 156

O

Object, 153
ODBC, 176-214
    basic steps, 182-183
    CDatabase class, 213
    CRecordset, 199-212
    functions, 183
    retrieving records, 192-199
    table insertions, 182-191
ODBC control panel, 175
ofstream, 99
ON_PARSE_COMMAND, 133
ON_PARSE_COMMAND_PARAMS, 133
Online foosball store, 387-463. See also Foosball store.
    arcade tables (arcade.htm), 402-407
    CalculatePrice(), 461-462
    classes used, 462
    Custom Options page (custom.htm), 431-438
    database tables, 388
    deluxe tables (deluxe.htm), 390-395
    economy tables (economy.htm), 396-401

Extras pages (extras.htm), 407-431
    home page, 389
    inventoryID, 389, 407
    logos, 388-389
    processing (shipping costs/taxes/credit cards), 438-461
Online registration dialog box, 469
Online software stores, 471
OnParseError(), 120, 138-139
OnSetOptions(), 203
Open database connectivity. See ODBC.
Open(), 200, 212
<OPTION> tag...</OPTION> delimiter, 31
Order taking, 146-150
Orders, 160-166
OutputMap(), 78, 84

P

PageMill, 517
Parsemap argument types, 132
Parsemaps, 131-137
PATH_INFO, 66
PATH_TRANSLATED, 66
Payment, 14-16, 374, 480-495. See also Credit card processing.
Payment dialog box, 481
PCAuthorize, 328, 531
PERL, 19-20
Pig-code, 71
Pizza order form, 45-48
Point of execution, 511
pop(), 370-372
POP3, 365
pop_back(), 371
pop_front(), 371

Posix threads, 332
POST, 71-73
Preferences Folder (Mac), 479
Process, 511
ProcessCreditCard.cpp, 359-363
Protected memory, 109
pThreads, 332
ptr_fun(), 163
Publishing your FTP site, 468
push(), 370-372

Q

QUERY_STRING, 66
Queued order processing, 369-385
Queues, 370-373

R

Radio buttons, 37, 500
Re-entrancy, 152, 513
ReadClient(), 114, 122
Real, 156
Real Internet store. *See* Online
    foosball store.
Realtime, 325-326
RecalcOrder(), 278
Record field exchange (RFX), 203
Redirection, 310-319
RefreshRowset(), 202
Registration server, 495
REMOTE_ADDR, 66
REMOTE_HOST, 66
REMOTE_USER, 66
Requery(), 202
REQUEST_METHOD, 66
Reset, 52
RetrieveCartContents(), 206-212
Retrieving records, 192-199

ReviewOrder(), 281
RFX, 203
Round robin, 511

S

SaveToFile(), 536
Schneier, Bruce, 477
Scripting languages, 49, 321
SCRIPT_NAME, 66
SCSI drives, 168, 177
Search engine pages, 243
Secure ordering, 16, 309-324
    credit card number validation,
        319-323
    getting SSL on your server,
        309-310
    Luhn algorithm, 319-323
    redirection, 310-319
Secure socket layer (SSL), 309-310
SELECT, 182, 192
select(), 332
<SELECT> tag...</SELECT>, 31
SELECTED attribute, 32
Serialization code, 474, 478
SERVER_NAME, 66
SERVER_PORT, 66
SERVER_PORT_SECURE, 66
SERVER_PROTOCOL, 67
SERVER_SOFTWARE, 67
Server variables
    CGI, 64-71
    ISAPI, 129-131
ServerSupportFunction(), 114, 122,
    315-316
ServerVars.cpp, 68-70
SET, 329-330
SetAbsolutePosition(), 201

SetBookMark(), 201
SetFieldDirty(), 202
SetFieldNull(), 202
SetLockingMode(), 202
SetRowsetCursorPosition(), 202
SetRowsetSize(), 203
Shareware programs, 466, 471, 496
Shopping cart, 263-308
    adding items to cart, 278-280
    conceptual overview, 264-268
    cookies, 273-278
    database tables, 270-273
    examples, 269-271
    handling the cart, 283-292
    removing items from
        cart, 280-281
    reviewing orders, 281-283
    source listing, 292-308
    task variable, 283, 288
    time requirements, 268
ShoppingCartSet.cpp, 204-205
ShowOldOrders.cpp, 375-384
Shrink-wrapped products, 471, 496
SignGuestBook(), 140, 146
Small base classes, 255
smalldatetime, 156
smallint, 156
smallmoney, 156
SMTP, 365
SMTP mailer class, 365, 519-528
Software distribution, 465-496
    advertising, 467-468
    commercial solutions, 471-472
    copying software to other
        machines, 477-478
    distribution costs, 467-468
    encryption, 475-480

feature disabling, 469
manuals, 470
online software stores, 471
overhead, 468
payment collection, 480-485
renting of software, 469-470
unlocking mechanism,
    469, 473-477
upgrades, 470
sort(), 106, 167
Southwest Airlines, 9-12
sprintf(), 228
SQL, 154, 181-182
SQL 92, 154
SQL data types, 156
SQL Server, 173-174
SQLAllocConnect(), 183
SQLAllocEnv(), 183
SQLAllocStmt(), 183, 189
SQLBindCol(), 183, 192-193, 198
SQLConnect(), 183, 189
SQLExecute(), 183, 189, 228
SQLFetch(), 183, 192, 198, 228
SQLFreeConnect(), 183
SQLFreeEnv(), 183
SQLFreeStmt(), 183
SQLPrepare(), 189
SqlTypes.h, 189-190
SSL, 309-310
Stack, 371
Stale cookies, 258-261
Standard template library
    (STL), 74-77, 163
StarNine, 535
StartContent(), 119-120, 122
State machines, 513
Stdout, 59-60, 63

STL, 74-77, 163
STL adapter, 371-372
STL containers, 74-76, 267-268
STL deque, 371-373
STL functions, 76, 167
STL iterators, 76, 266-268
STL list, 371
STL Primer, The, 268
STL queue adapter, 371-373
StoreResultsInDB(), 363
Stream iterators, 76
StreamFile(), 60-63
Streaming files, 60-63
strftime(), 258
String class, 35-36
Stroustrup, Bjarne, 76
strtok(), 495
Subclasses, 255
Submit, 33, 52, 59, 97
Support site, 472
Survey page HTML sources, 42-45

T

Table insertions, 182-191
<TABLE> tag... <TABLE>
    delimiter, 499
Tables, 155-157, 498-499.
    See also Datastores.
Task variable, 283, 289
TCP/IP clients/servers, 503-509
Text, 156
Text input items, 38
Thread safety, 114
Threads, 112-114, 331-332,
    511-513
300 codes, 311
Timed-state machines, 513

timestamp, 156
tinyint, 156
TRACE(), 138
24×7 store, 6-7
200-OK, 311

U

Ultra-wide SCSI, 168, 177
Unicode project, 122
unique(), 106, 167
U.S. export regulations, 476-477
Unlock(), 239
Unlocking mechanism,
    469, 473-477
Up-front analysis and
    design, 263-264
UPDATE, 182
Update(), 201, 205, 212, 239
Upgrade-information server, 470
URL, 67
User-level threads, 332
UserInformation, 479
USING_CGI, 189

V

VALUE attribute, 31
varbinary[n], 156
varchar[n], 156
Variable names, 31-32
VBScript, 49, 321
VBScript and ActiveX Wizardry, 49
Vector, 266
VerifyCard.cpp, 481-494
VerifyCookieInDB(), 273
Verisign, 16, 310, 533
Virtual mall, 3

Virtual shopping cart, 13, 264.
See also Shopping cart.
Virtual stores, 1-17
   examples, 9-13
   payment, 14-16
   physical stores, contrasted, 7-8
   prices, 7-8
   secure ordering, 16
   shopping carts, 13-14
   start-up costs, 3-6
   taxes, 3, 8
   24×7 store, 6-7
Visa, 15, 320

W
WebStar, 535-551
Windows Registry, 479
WinExec(), 470
WriteClient(), 114, 121-122
WriteFormItem(), 63
WriteTitle(), 120
WSACleanup(), 345
WSAPI, 535
WSAStartup(), 345

Guerilla Web Strategies

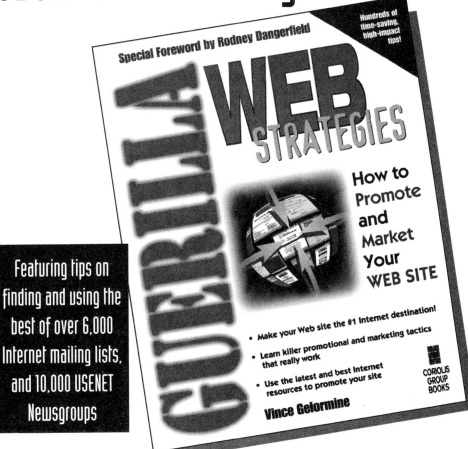

Featuring tips on finding and using the best of over 6,000 Internet mailing lists, and 10,000 USENET Newsgroups

Only $24.99

Call 800-410-0192

Fax 602-483-0193

Outside U.S. 602-483-0192

Get inside information on how to use marketing, advertising, and promotion to make your site one of the most popular on the Web. This is the only book available that provides in-depth, step-by-step instructions on generating traffic to your Web site. From determining if your site has the essential ingredients of success, to selling your products or services in Cybermalls, this title by Web promotion wizard Vince Gelormine has it all.

 CORIOLIS GROUP BOOKS

http://www.coriolis.com